DIVINE LOLA

DIVINE LOLA

A TRUE STORY *of* SCANDAL *and* CELEBRITY

CRISTINA MORATÓ
TRANSLATED BY ANDREA ROSENBERG

AMAZON **CROSSING**

To Pilar Latorre for her friendship, support, and affection

My Lolitta, the world despises and persecutes you; but how-ever much your enemies strive to tear us apart, my heart will cling all the more fondly to yours. The more they hate you, the more beloved you are, and the more surely you obtain what they wish to snatch from you; I shall never be riven from you.

> Letter from King Ludwig I of Bavaria to Lola Montez
> (Munich, July 6, 1847)

She has the evil eye and is sure to bring bad luck to anyone who closely links his destiny with hers.

> Alexandre Dumas (Paris, 1846)

If all that is said of me were true—nay, if half of it were true—I ought to be buried alive.

> Lola Montez, letter published in the *New York Herald*
> (January 15, 1852)

Contents

CHAPTER 1

Wild Beauty

It had been thirteen years since he'd said goodbye to her for the last time, but upon learning of her death, he found himself deeply moved. In all that time, King Ludwig I of Bavaria had been unable to forget his beloved Lola Montez, the beautiful Spanish dancer who'd burst into his life like a whirlwind one sunny fall morning. How could he fail to remember October 8, 1846, when he'd first seen her decked out in a black velvet dress that accentuated her splendid figure and the delicate pallor of her skin? He'd fallen in love instantly, captivated by her beauty, fire, and breathtaking personality.

Over the next few months, he had devoted himself obsessively, indifferent to her past and the notorious reputation that preceded her. In the conservative Bavarian court, rumors flew that the king had lost his head over a scandal-tainted woman who was trying to meddle in state affairs. Ignoring the critics, Ludwig granted her the title of countess, offered her a generous pension, and bought her a palatial mansion that he visited daily. Now, in his old age, a smile played on his lips as he recalled that happy period during which he'd felt so profoundly rejuvenated. He still trembled when he remembered the afternoons they'd spent reading *Don Quixote* in front of the fireplace, whiling away the hours dreaming about a life together far from the dull Munich court. It is true that he had a weakness for beautiful women and had been an incorrigible ladies' man, but Lola was different from the others—she was his great love. Though he'd lost his throne and his subjects' respect because of her, he bore her no ill will. He'd kept tabs on his lover's adventures through the years, after she had been forced to flee Bavaria and then had swiftly become an international celebrity. His ambassador to Paris sent newspaper clippings about her scandals, her love affairs, and the success she was enjoying as an actress and dancer on tours of Australia and the United States.

Without a doubt, Lola Montez had been an unconventional woman. She could be kind, generous, considerate, and even meek, but she was also reckless, volatile, and wild. She rode a horse like an Amazon, smoked cigarettes, was handy with a revolver, and wielded her riding whip against any man who dared to contradict her. In a time when women dedicated themselves to housework, she had traveled the world and had trodden the boards of the most important stages, from London to Sydney, even though her talent as a dancer left much to be desired. The king had kept hundreds of letters that she'd written to him over the course of their stormy relationship, as well as the poems she'd inspired as his muse and lover. He also kept, almost as a holy relic, Lola's foot sculpted in marble, which he used to kiss every night before bed. Today, upon receiving the letter from New York, he was overwhelmed once more by nostalgia:

> Sire,
> In early childhood, [I was] school companion in Scotland with a young girl who I little thought would ever have requested me on her death bed to write to your Majesty . . . She often spoke to me of your Majesty, and of your kindness and benevolence, which

she deeply felt—And wished me to tell you she had
changed her life and companions.

And now I redeem the promise I made to the late Mme.
Lola Montez, known to me as Eliza Gilbert, and to add that
she wished me to let you know she retained a sincere regard for
your great kindness to the end of her life.

She died a true penitent, relying on her Savior for pardon
and acceptance, triumphing only in His merit . . .

I have the Honor to be your Majesty's Obedt. & Humble Sert.

Maria E. Buchanan

Ludwig grew pensive for a moment, his eyes misting over. "My dear
Lolita, did you ever love me?"

No one could have imagined that the little girl who'd just been born
that cold, windy day in February 1821 in the town of Grange, Ireland,
would become one of the most famous women of her era. She was a
healthy, cheerful girl with lovely features much like her mother's. From
her father, Edward Gilbert, an ensign in the British army, she'd inherited her bravery and her thirst for adventure. The handsome officer had
arrived in County Cork with the Twenty-Fifth Regiment of Foot to
put down the Irish rebellion against King George III of England. Tall,
manly, and vigorous, he had thick blond sideburns and a slim mustache.
Among all the Irish girls, one in particular caught his eye. Her name
was Eliza Oliver. At fourteen—eight years younger than he—she was
working as a milliner's apprentice, even though she came from a good
family. She was beautiful, with deep black eyes, pale skin, and long,
curly hair. What Eliza saw in the dapper soldier, with his jollity and his
splendid red uniform, was an escape from a humdrum life.

The Olivers were a powerful, landowning Protestant family
in County Cork. Young Eliza was proud of her roots, even though

everybody knew she was illegitimate. Her father, Charles Silver Oliver, was a member of Parliament and an influential figure in his community. Before finally marrying at the age of forty, he'd sired four children with his lover, Mary Green. The couple lived in Castle Oliver, an ancient, stately mansion in the south of County Limerick. There Eliza came into the world in 1805, the same year her father took a proper lady to be his wife. Though that union produced seven legitimate heirs, Mr. Oliver did not abandon his bastards. Eliza, Mary, and their brothers, John and Thomas, all bore their father's last name, and the patriarch made sure they were taken care of. After their mother's death, the boys started working as apprentice shopkeepers and the two sisters with Mrs. Hall, a milliner who taught them the craft. When the distinguished Mr. Oliver died unexpectedly in 1817, he left them the considerable sum of five hundred pounds each, which they would receive when they turned twenty-one.

In the spring of 1820, Ensign Edward Gilbert and his beautiful fiancée made plans to wed. Theirs was a hasty engagement, as the groom-to-be's regiment would be leaving Cork to impose peace in a northern area that was being menaced by rebels. With his departure looming, the couple married on April 29 in Christ Church, in the presence of some of the most prominent members of the local Protestant elite.

For Eliza, an itinerant new life began. Discovering she was pregnant at fifteen meant she could no longer follow Edward along the rough, dusty roads of the Irish countryside. In midwinter the couple settled down in a gray stone cottage by the sea, lashed by wind and rain, in the town of Grange, County Sligo. In this remote corner of northern Ireland, Eliza's only daughter, Elizabeth Rosanna Gilbert—who became better known as Lola Montez—came into the world.

After his daughter's birth, Edward looked for a better-paid position that would offer greater opportunities for advancement. A year later he traded his post in County Sligo for one in India. During this period, trade with India was monopolized by the East India Company, which had been established in 1600 by a group of merchants and operated in the government's name in places under British control. Eliza was thrilled to leave cold, gloomy Ireland for such a remote and exotic locale. She imagined India as a sort of paradise where she'd be able to live like a real memsahib, a British officer's wife, ensconced in a colonial mansion with magnificent staircases and surrounded by a cloud of servants. She dreamed of attending parties and meeting a maharajah, one of those Indian princes who wore gold-embroidered garments and silk turbans like something out of an orientalist tale.

Though Edward knew the voyage would be risky for his young daughter, he was unwilling to be separated from her. At that time, very few British officers lived in India with their wives, since the journey was considered to be too hard on a woman's "fragile" nature. His family and friends tried to persuade him to leave Lola in their care, but it was no use. He was undeterred by arguments about India's unwholesome climate and the tropical diseases that ravaged European colonists. Officers' salaries were high there, and the low cost of living would allow him to indulge in a level of luxury that was out of reach in his own country. Eliza, with her adventurous spirit, was unconcerned about dangers and discomforts. The Gilberts packed their bags, said goodbye to their loved ones, and traveled to London, where they bought passage on a majestic East India Company steamer.

On the morning of March 14, 1823, Edward and his family set sail into the unknown. They couldn't afford a first-class cabin as they would have liked, but the couple and other officers on board took part in boisterous evenings in the main salon and gathered on the upper deck to enjoy the stunning sunsets over the Arabian Sea. At the time, prior to the construction of the Suez Canal, the journey to India took four long months, with only a stopover or two to restock water and provisions. Lola was just two years old, but she eagerly absorbed the new world of odors, colors, and sounds. She probably got seasick, as most did on the uncomfortable, tedious voyage, since powerful storms were commonplace after rounding the Cape of Good Hope. When the ship finally docked at Diamond Harbour, the worst was yet to come. As soon as he set foot on solid ground, Ensign Gilbert was informed that his unit had already left for the garrison of Dinapore, near the Nepalese border, and he was to catch up with them as soon as possible. Irritated, he relayed the news to his wife.

"I'm sorry, my dear, but we must leave immediately. My regiment is already on the road, and if I delay my arrival, I won't be able to justify it to my superiors."

"But we're exhausted," she protested, on the verge of tears. "We need to recover our strength."

"I know, Eliza, I know it's been a hard voyage, but I must follow orders. Soon we'll arrive at our destination and you can rest. Please trust in me."

And so they began traveling once more.

Edward didn't want to worry his wife, but the journey would be a difficult one. His unit was near Patna, some four hundred miles upriver on the Ganges, which they would have to travel on small, triangular-sailed boats, at the mercy of the wind. It was summer, monsoon season, and the frequent torrential rains wouldn't end until late September. The suffocating heat and the stench of the pestilent wetlands would accompany them throughout the entire journey.

The Gilberts joined the last regiment companies leaving Calcutta, the capital of British India. The fleet was able to navigate an average of only ten miles a day through the treacherous currents and sandbanks. Despite the insects, the meager food, and the vessels' slow progress, it was a fascinating spectacle. At some spots, the Ganges measured nearly three miles across, and lush vegetation grew along its fertile banks. The tropical forests full of shrieking gray monkeys gave way to wide grass-lands, steaming villages, and ancient fortress ruins. On occasion, they came upon small herds of water buffalo that ventured to the river at dusk. The natives who worked the rice paddies on either side of the majestic river sold them food only reluctantly.

Little Lola's first impressions of India during that journey through the marshy delta would be etched in her memory forever. Snuggled beside her mother, she surveyed the bright sky and the greenery exploding before her astonished eyes. Ensign Gilbert had come prepared to combat boredom; in one of his heavy trunks, he had brought a ten-volume *New British Theatre*, three volumes of work by his favorite poet, Alexander Pope, and a book on French grammar. Early in the trip, he whiled away the hours by pulling out his brushes and painting scenes of daily life on the Ganges. In the evenings, to Lola's delight, he would entertain the passengers with his silver-trimmed boxwood flute.

After countless days of travel, they reached Dinapore, a steep, desolate jungle outpost. They spotted the officers' bungalows, half hidden in lush vegetation, high on a promontory. From the small dock, a red dirt road led to the infantrymen's barracks. Unfortunately, Edward Gilbert was unable to enjoy his garrison mates' warm welcome or the music that the military band played in his honor. By the time they reached the river market at Patna, he'd begun vomiting and suffering from diarrhea, the first symptoms of cholera. When the military doctor confirmed how terribly ill he was, Eliza felt as if the earth were caving in. She was alone in a strange place with a tiny daughter who might very well meet the same fate as her father. Despite the risk of contagion, she remained staunchly beside the bed where her gaunt, haggard husband lay, nearly unrecognizable.

One day, feeling that his end was near, Edward took her hand and said weakly, "Eliza, you must be brave, for yourself and for our daughter. When I go, find a good husband. You cannot remain here on your own, promise me that."

"There, there, rest now," she murmured, daubing his temples with a damp cloth. "Don't say anything more. I'm sure you will recover and—"

"No, my love, I'm sorry. We had so many dreams . . ."

Those were his last words. Edward closed his eyes and his name joined the long list of his countrymen who had seen their hopes cut short in that remote outpost. After a solemn ceremony, he was buried next to the simple church. The many tombstones recalled the stories of the brave officers, missionaries, and soldiers of the empire who had met their deaths there. But what struck Eliza most were the tiny graves containing children who had never seen their parents' homeland. Dinapore was considered "the white man's tomb," ravaged by frequent epidemics of cholera, malaria, and yellow fever. Most of the brave women who had followed their husbands paid with their lives.

At eighteen, Eliza was a widow, alone with a daughter in an unfamiliar country. In the asphyxiating, hermetic society of the British colonies, there was no place for a woman like her unless she remarried. She wanted to flee that jungle full of mosquitoes, filth, and endless rain, but there was no regular passenger service along the river. A month after her husband's death, the regiment auctioned off all his personal effects, including his prized flute. They gave the sum collected plus the wages still owed to the deceased officer, a total of sixty pounds, to Eliza. With that money and a paltry widow's pension, she could survive in India for several months, though it wasn't enough to pay for passage back to England. Despite these misfortunes, the grief-stricken Mrs. Gilbert refused to give up. She needed to find a husband at once, and there would be no lack of suitors.

In November, Eliza and her daughter left Dinapore for Calcutta. After visiting Edward's grave one last time, they boarded an old riverboat along with a dozen other passengers. One was twenty-four-year-old Scottish lieutenant Patrick Craigie, a member of the Nineteenth Regiment of Native Infantry of the British East India Company and her dead husband's comrade in arms. He'd just been ordered back to Calcutta after making a name for himself as the Company's political agent at the court in Jaipur. Patrick got along well with his fellow officers, and his superiors held him in high regard. During the trip, to cheer

Divine Lola

9

up the beautiful widow, he told her amazing stories from his five years in India. In Jaipur he had seen the country at its most romantic, and he described in detail a world of tiger hunting, jewel-bedecked maharajahs, elephants draped in gold, and sumptuous galas in mansions nestled at the foot of the Himalayas. This was nothing like Eliza's experience in Dinapore, of which she remembered only the sticky damp, the mosquitoes, the generously sized rats, the roads that turned into expanses of mud, and the soporific five o'clock teas with snooty ladies who eyed her pityingly. Nor could she forget her shocking visit to the nearby village of thatch-roofed mud huts, where the overpowering smell of smoked fish mingled with the stench of stagnant water and wood fires. In such filthy, stinking towns, naked children splashed in wastewater a stone's throw from the clean bungalows where the whites resided. Eliza opened her heart to the young officer.

"Since I first arrived in this country, all I have experienced is pain and suffering," she confessed sadly. "All my dreams have disappeared."

"That's to be expected—you've just lost your husband, you're all on your own with a child to take care of . . . But I assure you that Calcutta will be very different. You'll have a new lease on life."

"I hope so. I've felt so abandoned. All I want is to forget the past and start a new life."

After Edward's death, Eliza had quickly lost interest in her child, leaving her in the care of native servants. Suddenly it occurred to her that being on the arm of a gallant, well-respected officer like Lieutenant Craigie would give her access to the closed circle of Calcutta's British high society. He was a tall, sturdy man, his face tanned by the sun, who wore thick brown sideburns and a white pith helmet. The romance between the Scottish officer and the widow Gilbert blossomed on that voyage through the mangrove swamps of the Ganges delta before the prying gazes of the other passengers. Despite a deep mutual attraction, Eliza had to respect the mourning period. She could not risk sullying her reputation.

In 1823 Calcutta was a bustling, cosmopolitan city that offered the creature comforts a colonist required to feel at home. Built around the imposing Fort William, which had been erected to house British troops, the city had paved streets, a hospital, a prison, a mosque, splendid government buildings, marble palaces, tidy gardens, several cricket fields, and a horse track. Eliza took up lodgings in the tranquil residential area along the banks of the Hooghly River, a golden ghetto where members of the British military and their families lived in isolation from the natives. Having been raised in the tedium of the Irish countryside, Eliza found her new surroundings immensely exciting. She was young and naive, but she didn't take long to learn the basic rules for being a respected memsahib: not being too familiar with her native servants, maintaining strict norms of cleanliness and obedience in her home, and never going without a corset, despite the heat and humidity. Captivated by the tales of some of the English ladies, she dreamed of attending dazzling balls and dancing to the music of grand orchestras, banqueting at luxurious oriental feasts, and rolling alongside the Ganges at dusk in an elegant carriage. Above all, she was eager for her name to be included on the very exclusive guest list of India's new governor-general, Lord Amherst.

Lola barely saw her mother, who was enjoying a vibrant social life. Like most British children in India, Lola was raised by a native nanny, an ayah, who sang beautiful lullabies, made up games, and humored her every whim. The ayah, Denali, was a kind, affectionate young woman from Punjab. She taught Lola a few words of Bengali and opened the door to an entirely new world of sensations. "Whenever Mother went out to dinner or to some gala or reception and did not return until dawn, I would stay with my dear ayah, and that was always a party. I would sit on her lap and she would tell me magical tales until I fell asleep in her arms. She was a great comfort for me, and I never forgot her," Lola would recall years later.

Calcutta's lush green foliage, the blinding sun, the violent storms, the brightly colored birds, the delicious fruit, the music, the ritual dances—everything—sparked Lola's curiosity. The penetrating aromas of spices, incense, and earth would remain with her forever. The slender Indian women wrapped in saris, with their arms covered in silver bangles, looked like princesses from a fairy tale.

From time to time, with Denali, she would go to the "black city," a tangle of narrow, dusty streets where the Europeans never ventured. There, the natives lived in a tumult that Lola found invigorating. She wasn't afraid of anything—not the snake charmers or the fakirs or the thick-bearded holy men who smeared their naked bodies with ash. But her biggest adventure happened on the day she accompanied her ayah to the temple dedicated to Kali, the patron goddess of Calcutta. Inside, barely lit by the dim light of the oil lamps, a striking statue of the goddess sat atop the altar, all in black marble except for the eyes and tongue, which were painted gold and blood red. At one time, Kali's devout worshipers had made human sacrifices to her, but now they offered only the blood of chickens and black goats. Legends of the powerful goddesses Kali and Durga, protectors of the truth and destroyers of evil, kindled the little girl's imagination and transported her to a magical world.

Twice a week she would bathe at twilight in the Hooghly River, even though her mother had forbidden it out of fear she might be bitten by a snake. As Lola grew older, she became more and more beautiful—and more and more reckless. She almost always went barefoot, she climbed trees, she chewed betel nuts until her mouth was stained bright red, and she played with the native children on streets littered with cow patties. She never forgot those sweltering afternoons when it was too hot to go outside and she would lie under a gauzy mosquito net, drifting off to the rhythmic whisper of the punkah, a cloth ceiling fan that a native boy would move by pulling on a rope in exchange for a few pence a day.

Less than a year after Edward's death, his widow agreed to marry Lieutenant Patrick Craigie. The officer had been posted to Dhaka, in central Bangladesh, where the pair were married on August 16, 1824, in a small civil ceremony. The city was a wealthy, bustling trading center for British India on the banks of the Buriganga River. Though it offered more comforts than Dinapore, summers were unbearably hot. And since it was at sea level, enormous monsoon floods would wipe out entire villages. After the wedding, Eliza and her daughter moved into a pretty bungalow near the military headquarters. Europeans considered Dhaka less civilized than vibrant Calcutta, but the house was large, with a lovely garden, and they had a dozen servants. In the center of the city were several well-stocked shops, a public park, a bank, a steepled church, a small school, and a club where officers gathered to have a whiskey and read weeks-old issues of the *Times*. Lola now had a stepfather, whom she always remembered fondly. Though he referred to her as "Mrs. Craigie's daughter," he was affectionate and invested in her well-being. Unfortunately, his military obligations forced him to spend long periods away from home.

When Lola turned five, her stepfather made a decision that brought her happy, lazy days in India to an end. Convinced that the child needed more discipline, one afternoon he suggested to his wife that they send her to Scotland to live with his elderly father. The conventional wisdom was that English children raised in India would become wayward sheep, and Lola was showing no signs of being an exception.

"It will be good for her," he said firmly. "India isn't her home and the education is inadequate."

"I suppose you're right," Eliza admitted, "but I'm worried about how she'll take it. She seems so happy here."

"She's too young to understand that we're doing it for her own good," Lieutenant Craigie said. "She'll be in the care of my family in Montrose. It's a quiet town where everybody knows one another."

Upon learning that she would be sent back to the British Isles in less than a month, Lola shut herself in her room and wept. She never forgave her mother, convinced that Eliza wanted to rid herself of her daughter's burdensome presence once and for all. In the winter of 1826, Patrick Craigie was named deputy assistant adjutant-general of the regiment in Meerut, northeast of Delhi. At the same time, his former commander, Lieutenant Colonel William Innes, decided to retire to England with his family. It was a happy coincidence, and the Inneses agreed to escort Lola to London; from there, the girl would continue on to Montrose.

It was the last Christmas she spent with her family in India, and Lola remembered it as the saddest she had ever experienced. As December drew to a close, she said goodbye and boarded the *Malcolm*, carrying her little suitcase. From the deck, hidden among the throng of passengers waving their handkerchiefs in the air, she watched the gangway be pulled back and the huge sails unfurl. She felt expelled from paradise, headed for an unfamiliar place where she didn't know a soul. She was leaving behind a childhood full of magical memories and her loving Denali, whom she would always carry in her heart.

Lieutenant Colonel Innes and his wife didn't have an easy time wrangling the willful, disobedient girl for the more than four endless months. It was a particularly difficult and hazardous journey from the moment they weighed anchor. The *Malcolm* stopped for provisions in Madras and then crossed the Indian Ocean, rocked by violent storms. Water and food were rationed, and the torrential downpours made life on board even more trying. By the time the ship passed the Cape of Good Hope, two soldiers returning home on leave had died, and a third died a month before they reached their destination. Luckily, they were able to restock their provisions at the port of Saint Helena, and the rest of the voyage was somewhat calmer.

Though Mrs. Innes was kind and patient with her, Lola was miserable. She spent most of the journey huddled behind the curtain that covered her bunk, refusing to talk to anybody. As the ship approached England's shores, she was gripped by a powerful sense of anguish and unease. On May 19, 1827, the *Malcolm* berthed in Blackwall, east of the Tower of London, and the luggage was unloaded in an intense downpour. On the docks, Lola said a chilly goodbye to the Inneses and left with one of her stepfather's relatives who had come to take her to Scotland.

After vibrant Calcutta, Montrose seemed as cold, damp, and gray as a cemetery. It was located between Dundee and Aberdeen on the banks of an estuary that formed an inlet and protected it from the North Sea's powerful storms. Wealthy merchants had built a few luxurious mansions on its main street, but the rest of the buildings were drab and charmless. Her step-grandfather, also named Patrick Craigie, had been provost of the town for a quarter century and was now enjoying his retirement. He and his wife, Mary, had nine children, the youngest just seven years older than Lola.

In a sleepy town like Montrose, a little girl arriving from the East Indies caused a sensation. Her unusual manner of dressing, her comportment, and the familiar way she addressed strangers provoked all sorts of commentary.

Contrary to her expectations, Lola's step-grandparents were kind to her. But the household's old governess tried unsuccessfully to reform the mutinous child. Lola relished being the center of attention and let her imagination run wild. She loved to recount how a rich maharajah in Jaipur had tried to pay her father a fortune in gold to allow her to marry the maharajah's son. The people of Montrose remembered her as a mischievous, lively girl who amused herself during Sunday mass by sticking flowers in the wigs of elderly gentlemen sitting in the next pew. Lola spent the next four years in the green, misty landscapes of the Scottish countryside. She learned to ride horses and galloped through the broad fields near her step-grandfather's farm every day. Though she wrote her stepfather several letters begging him to let her return to India, he ignored her pleas.

When Lola turned ten, her stepfather's older sister, Catherine Rae, and her husband, William, moved to Durham, England, where they opened a girls' boarding school in Monkwearmouth. Lola's step-grandfather decided that the girl should go with them.

"Sweetheart," he said tenderly, "you're nearly a woman now. You can't stay here. You know that we love you and you're part of this family, but at boarding school you'll learn good manners and be with other girls your age."

"Grandfather, I've been moving around my entire life," Lola said, downcast. "I've never had female friends, and all I want is to go back to India to be with my parents. I miss them so much."

"But that's not an option now. Your parents want what's best for you, and you have to be strong. It's already been decided, darling, don't make things more difficult."

Even at that young age, Lola was already well acquainted with loneliness and alienation. She'd been forced to abandon her native Ireland, her first home in Dinapore, and the house in Calcutta where she'd been happy; she'd watched her father die, been separated from her beloved Denali, and now was going to be deprived of her step-grandparents' love. But all she could do was pack her bags again.

Lola was at the boarding school in Monkwearmouth only a year, but her presence didn't go unnoticed. Her drawing teacher, Mr. Grant, remembered her as rebellious, eccentric, and very stubborn:

> Eliza Gilbert . . . was at that time a very elegant and beautiful child . . . [her charm] only lessened by . . . indomitable self-will . . . Her complexion was orientally dark, but transparently clear; her eyes were of deep blue, and, as I distinctly remember, of excessive beauty . . . [A]ltogether, it was impossible to look at

her for many minutes without feeling convinced that she was made up of very wayward and troublesome elements.

In late 1830 Lola's stepfather had been promoted to captain, which enabled him to enroll the girl in a more prestigious school recommended by his division mate, Major-General Sir Jasper Nicolls. The distinguished officer was planning to return to England on a two-year leave, and Craigie asked him to look after Lola until classes started. In mid-September 1832, Lola and Mrs. Rae made a long trip by horse-drawn carriage from Durham to Reading, west of London. The general, a rigid man who was used to giving orders and seeing them carried out, lived there with his wife and their eight daughters. From the start, he was convinced that the wild child would never come to anything good. Lola stayed with the Nicollses for a few weeks and enjoyed a level of comfort and luxury she'd never experienced before. Then she was sent to Bath, where she would continue her studies.

Her new boarding school was a prestigious and very expensive institution located on Camden Place (now Camden Crescent), a large, half-moon-shaped terrace of Georgian-style residences that included some of the city's most coveted mansions. The elegant academy occupied a two-story building with a neoclassical stone facade decorated with slender Corinthian columns. All the students—fifteen girls between the ages of ten and eighteen—came from wealthy families with good reputations. The rigorous curriculum included the customary feminine disciplines, such as dancing, needlepoint, drawing, singing, and piano, but they also learned French and Latin. The girls were allowed to speak English only on Sundays, and anyone who broke this rule had to pay a fine from her pocket money. Although Bath was an elegant resort city popular in British high society for its thermal waters, Lola was not able to enjoy its lively atmosphere. The rules at the Aldridge Academy were very harsh, and students were allowed to go out only very rarely and under strict supervision.

Still, Lola looked back on her years in Bath as a happy time during which she shared secrets and pranks with her first female friends. The education she received was fairly comprehensive for a girl of that era. Aldridge's young women were trained not only to be good wives and diligent housekeepers but also to cultivate their minds and spirits. Lola lived there for five years. She would never again spend so long in one place.

Though Sir Jasper Nicolls admired Captain Craigie and considered him one of his finest officers, he didn't care much for his wife. After eighteen months with Lola in his care, Eliza hadn't displayed the slightest interest in her daughter's education. The officer wrote in his diary on February 14, 1834:

At last we have heard from Mrs. Craigie, who was I supposed constrained to answer our numerous letters tho' she heard from us 6 times before this effect was produced—I felt great surprise—not a little vexed—and in some degree repented of having so easily undertaken an unpleasant and apparently thankless task. I likened her to a tortoise who buries her eggs lightly in the sand, and leaves them to sun, and to chance.

In the autumn of 1836, when Lola was almost sixteen, Eliza wrote a brief letter announcing that she was coming to Bath so they could return to India together. Her mother's impending arrival filled Lola with dread. She barely remembered Eliza's face and had conflicting emotions about her absent mother.

Mrs. Craigie left Calcutta for England on the steamship *Orient*. She hadn't seen her daughter in more than ten years. By now she was the wife of a very important man in the East India Company, a captain respected and admired by his superiors, who would soon be promoted to major. Unlike during her first voyage to India as a young romantic, Eliza was traveling as a grande dame, with copious luggage and a

first-class cabin. Her husband had given her a substantial sum in case
of unexpected obstacles.

Aboard the *Orient*, Eliza met Thomas James, a lieutenant working
for the East India Company who was returning to his native Ireland
on sick leave. Twenty-nine years old—two years her junior—he was
a slim man with blue eyes and brown hair. Romantic dalliances were
very common on these protracted voyages, and the handsome officer
soon began wooing her. Thomas was a member of the Protestant landed
gentry in County Wexford, but he did not enjoy a noble title or great
wealth. During the five-month journey, Eliza flirted with him openly
despite the other passengers' stern looks. One day she told him the
reason for her trip.

"My daughter is at boarding school in Bath, and I am headed there
to fetch her. I will be staying until her classes end. Maybe you could
visit us there—I am sure that the city's thermal waters would be most
beneficial, and we could have a lovely time."

"I can't make you any promises, my dear, however much I would
love to see you again and meet your daughter."

The morning that Eliza strode through the foyer at the Aldridge
Academy, she felt her heart pounding. For days she had been imagining
how the reunion would go. She'd last seen Lola when the little girl was
just five years old, and now she'd become a woman. The encounter was
a disastrous one. The girl eagerly embraced her mother, who gave her
a chilly kiss on the forehead. Lola was almost as tall as she, and more
beautiful than she'd expected.

"My dear child!" Eliza exclaimed, looking her up and down. "You
are so profoundly changed that I scarcely recognize you. That hairstyle
is most unbecoming."

"Welcome, Mother," Lola replied.

"Come along, grab your suitcase and say goodbye to your friends.
We must do some catching up—it's been such a long time, hasn't it?
You have so many things to tell me."

Lola had no idea how to react. Despite all the time that had passed, the elegant, handsome woman was utterly unchanged and seemed incapable of expressing any emotion. After a brief conversation with Lola's teachers, the two women left the school. Mrs. Craigie had rented some well-appointed rooms for them in Camden Place so she could spend time alone with her daughter while Lola was finishing her school year.

Eliza tried to be friendly, and in the afternoons the two would go shopping in the city's famous clothing stores. Lola was surprised by her mother's sudden generosity; no expense was spared in buying her dresses, corsets, silk stockings, shawls, boots, and even a flattering riding outfit that Lola loved. They also strolled together through the botanical gardens on the banks of the River Avon and visited the Roman baths. For a moment tensions seemed to wane between the two, and Lola was grateful for her mother's attentions and the gifts she showered on her. But Eliza found her daughter's radiant beauty irritating; it reminded her of herself in her youth. At thirty-two she was still a beautiful woman, but India's climate had taken its toll. She could not deny that her little girl had become a stunning woman who inspired admiration wherever she went. She was slender, with a slight, well-proportioned build, and she had magnificent blue eyes framed by long, thick eyelashes and voluptuous red lips. But her most striking feature was her long, curly black hair. She could have passed for Romany or Andalusian. Eliza would have liked to have had a demurer daughter, but Lola had been a troublemaker since early childhood. One day, after a heated argument, Eliza asked her to sit down next to her.

"I know you hate me because you have felt abandoned, but I did it all for you. Now I want you to listen to me—I have something very important to tell you."

"I don't hate you, Mother," the young woman stammered, "but many years have passed and you never even answered my letters. How could I not feel abandoned? I was only a girl when you sent me away."

"Forget about the past now and listen: you are of marrying age, you are beautiful and well educated . . . and there is an important man in India who would like to meet you. He has seen your portrait and fallen in love. It is a good match, believe me."

Suddenly everything became clear to Lola. Eliza had come from so far away only because she had arranged for her to marry a rich, distinguished gentleman. The prospect was the adjutant-general of Bengal, Sir James Lumley, an elderly widower. The general, who had two bachelor sons near Lola's age, was Captain Patrick Craigie's commanding officer. Upon hearing her mother's proposal, Lola lashed out. She couldn't believe Eliza would try to marry her off to a man fifty years her senior whom she'd never met and did not love. Now she understood why her mother had given her all those beautiful gowns.

After that, the relationship between the two became unsustainable. Lola tried to spend as little time as possible with her mother, a sophisticated, superficial, irresponsible woman for whom she felt no affection.

That's how matters stood when Lieutenant James unexpectedly arrived to visit Mrs. Craigie that hot summer of 1837. Lola, who'd had little contact with the opposite sex, thought him old—though he was only thirty—but also pleasant, courteous, and very protective of her mother. She was most struck by his handsome smile and "gleaming white teeth," a rarity at the time. From the start, Thomas was drawn to the innocent freshness of the schoolgirl, whose grace and charm eclipsed her mother's. Gradually he worked to gain Lola's trust and would walk with her from her rooms on Camden Place to the Aldridge Academy. In her stepfather's absence and without anyone to whom she could pour out her heart, Lola befriended the stranger, and he became her confidant. One day, in distress, she described her mother's plan to marry her off to an elderly stranger. Thomas, who had lost all interest in Eliza and was smitten instead with her daughter, began to reflect on his future. He would soon need to return to Calcutta to rejoin his regiment, and doing so with a beautiful young wife on his arm suited him very well. Out of the blue, he made an unexpected proposition.

"My dear, I will not allow your mother to ruin your life. If you marry the man she has chosen, you will be very unhappy."

"In just a few weeks I will be forced to leave with her," Lola said resignedly. "I have no choice."

"Yes, you do. Let's go away together without letting anyone know. We can get married in Ireland."

"But we hardly know each other, and what's more, my mother would never agree to it."

"Do not be afraid of your mother," Thomas said, taking her hands in his. "I know her well, and she does not want a scandal. She will acquiesce in the end."

Lola had not expected such a proposition from Thomas, whom she had come to see as a sort of father figure. He seemed sincere in his sentiment and willing to help her change her fate. She was not in love with him, but this exciting adventure was a perfect plan to annoy her mother. Eliza, who was so certain and firm in her convictions, still treated Lola like a little girl, completely disregarding her opinions and emotions.

Before leaving, the young woman wrote her mother a brief note, which she left on her bedside table:

Mother, I know you will never forgive me, but I cannot remain by your side. I am leaving with Thomas, who loves me and will look after me. I can't bear the way you treat me or your vile plotting. I refuse to throw my life away. I am still very young and must think of my own happiness.

Your daughter

As she stealthily packed her bags the next day, Lola was oblivious to the damage the elopement would cause to her reputation. She was a sixteen-year-old romantic who, until recently, had been sheltered in a boarding school. After night had fallen, Lieutenant James's carriage pulled up in front of Mrs. Craigie's residence at the appointed time. Lola crept out to meet him, carrying a suitcase with her few belongings, and they headed down the steep road to Bristol.

"Don't look back, you have me now. Soon I will be your husband," Thomas murmured as he held her in his arms. "I love and desire you so much, sweetheart."

Lola allowed herself to be carried away by passion, but she was distraught deep inside, imagining her mother's reaction. There was no turning back now. She would soon discover that she'd made a mistake she would regret for the rest of her life.

CHAPTER 2

A Broken Marriage

One hot July day, Lola and Lieutenant Thomas James were wed in the little stone church of Rathbeggan, on the outskirts of Dublin. The bridegroom's older brother, the Reverend John James, officiated the ceremony, which was attended by only the vicar's wife and nephew and a few onlookers. The young woman, expecting a festive wedding with music and a flower-bedecked altar, was disappointed. She missed her stepfather, and for a moment she thought how unhappy he would be to hear of her escape and her hasty marriage.

News of Lola's scandalous elopement soon reached Sir Jasper Nicolls's ears in England. He wrote in his diary, "I am not a bad prophet as to the figure which young people will make in life. I always predicted the 'vanity and lies' of EG would bring her to shame—She has started very badly, if not worse, for, leaving school in June, she married a Company Officer without a penny . . . Her mother, I fear, cannot be blameless."

In fact, when Eliza read the note her daughter had left, she flew into a rage. She left Bath at once and took an apartment in London to reflect on events. On such a delicate matter, she asked the advice of Sir Jasper's wife.

"How could she do this to me!" Eliza cried, trying to hold back tears. "Ungrateful child!"

"My dear," Lady Nicolls said in an effort to console her, "your daughter is very impulsive, but she will soon regret what she has done and write to you."

"What am I going to do? At all costs, I must keep my husband, Captain Craigie, from being harmed by the scandal. He has only ever wanted what is best for my daughter."

"Take a deep breath. You'll see, you will hear from her soon and she'll beg you for forgiveness. She's not a bad girl at heart."

Sir Jasper, too, advised Eliza to focus on her health, since she had a long trip back to Calcutta. He expressed dismay at the unpleasant situation and the hurt the news would cause his good friend, Captain Craigie. Though he'd always criticized Eliza harshly for her neglect, he felt somewhat sorry for her now.

"The ungrateful brat has thrown her life away with the first man she met and deeply upset her mother," he thought as they parted.

After the ceremony, the couple spent their honeymoon in Dublin, where they rented a room downtown. A few days later, the newly-weds pulled up in a carriage in front of her husband's family home in Wexford, Ballycrystal, an ancient, rambling stone house on a gentle slope of Mount Leinster, surrounded by fields and small farms. Lola's father-in-law, a widower also named Thomas James, was a powerful landholder and member of the local Protestant elite. The news of Lola's presence swept through the nearby villages, and several family members arrived to meet the bride. The young woman soon discovered that she had traded a return to India for the tedious Irish countryside her mother had fled. It rained nonstop, and the only creature comforts the old house offered were two enormous fireplaces in the drawing room that were always lit. She was suffocated by the routine, an endless succession of hunts, lavish family feasts, and tea with elderly women from the area. Though she rode from time to time and would gallop through the fields until she was exhausted, Lola was not happy. Her marriage was loveless, she had hardly any privacy, and the town offered few amusements. Shut away in that cold, damp house, she felt herself dying.

"I can't bear to live like this, Thomas," Lola finally declared. "It's always the same: hunt, eat, hunt, eat. And those ridiculous tea parties, always at the same time, in the same room, surrounded by gloomy faces, drive me to distraction."

"I'm sorry you're not comfortable here," her husband replied, irritated by her attitude. "My family has welcomed you with open arms. You shouldn't say such things."

"But I scarcely exist to them. They look askance at me as if I were a stranger—not a friendly word, not a smile . . . I want to leave here as soon as possible."

"Don't be ridiculous, you have nowhere to go. This is my house, and we are staying here whether you like it or not." He stalked out, slamming the door behind him.

Thomas had become sullen and gruff; he argued with his wife often and sometimes even hit her when he was drunk. The age difference caused problems from the start. Lola was an obstinate, impulsive teenager, and he was unwilling to humor her whims. He longed for his old life as an officer and escaped into alcohol to drown his sorrows. He'd first arrived in India when he was very young and had soon been sent with his company to a remote post that had no telegraphs or roads. Those had been difficult years of deprivation, with death ever lurking nearby. Several of his comrades had died of terrible illnesses, and he missed his loyal sepoys, the Indian soldiers recruited to join the ranks of the British army.

In those dark days, Lola couldn't help thinking about her mother. At a distance, she felt some regret about the hurt she'd caused her. In late November, Eliza had returned to Calcutta, alone and humiliated.

Months later, the Jameses went back to Dublin and rented a modest house on Westmoreland Street, in the city center. At long last they were

alone and Lola had her own space. The change of scenery improved
their relationship for a time. At night they would go out to dinner,
attend the theater, and host friends in their home. Lola had changed a
lot. She was coquettish; she liked dressing up and knew how to make
the most of her figure. Her exotic beauty drew men's eyes, and she loved
being the center of attention. One night they attended a fancy ball in
Dublin Castle, and the dapper Lord Normanby, viceroy of Ireland,
immediately started flirting with her. When the couple returned home,
Thomas flew into a jealous rage.

"You've made me look like a fool in front of everyone," he berated
her, pouring himself a drink. "You seem to have forgotten you are my
wife and must behave decently."

"I've done nothing wrong," Lola retorted. "He was the host, so I
could hardly refuse to dance with him. He struck me as a polite and
gallant man, unlike yourself, since you're always grumping about and
taking it out on me."

"It was clearly a mistake to marry you," Thomas said, considering
the argument over.

Lola pretended not to have heard this comment. When he insulted
her or got angry, she preferred to ignore him. She had married impul-
sively when she was still just a girl, convinced that this handsome older
man was a Prince Charming who would take care of her for the rest
of her days. Now, pretending was no longer possible: her marriage had
been a mistake, one that couldn't be set right.

One spring day, Lieutenant Thomas James received a letter informing him that he needed to return to his post in India. It had been nearly
two years since he'd left, and if he didn't go back, he would be jeopardiz-
ing his military career.

Lola was delighted to hear of their imminent departure. Now more
than ever, she longed to leave Ireland. She could not bear the hermetic,
provincial world she'd been living in since their wedding.

"I am so happy, Thomas," she sighed in relief. "I am counting the days till we set sail."

"Don't get your hopes up," Thomas said. "The life I can offer you in India is not what you are imagining. We will live without luxuries in some remote location far from Calcutta."

"I don't care," she responded joyfully. "I'm certain my stepfather will help us. I wrote him a letter months ago telling him I'd married a brave lieutenant with the Company; I'm sure he will be happy to see me."

On September 18, 1838, Lola and her husband left the port of Liverpool aboard the *Bland*, a steamer bound for Calcutta. The young woman had brought several trunks and a couple of hatboxes. One popular travel account of the era, by Miss Emma Roberts, listed the belongings that a lady would find essential on a trip to India. The author, a veteran globe-trotter and successful writer, advised bringing seventy-two shirts, seventy handkerchiefs, thirty pairs of panties, fifteen slips, sixty pairs of stockings, forty-five pairs of gloves, at least twenty different dresses, twenty shawls, two parasols, three hats, fifteen dressing gowns, cookies and jam, and a dozen boxes of laxative pills. She also recommended bringing six French corsets, which were of a higher quality and more suitable for the tropical climate. There was an explanation for this seemingly exaggerated quantity of clothing: there were few opportunities to do laundry on board a ship, as fresh water was scarce. Lola did not have such an extensive wardrobe, but in Bath her mother had bought her a complete trousseau to dazzle old General Lumley, Lola's supposed betrothed.

The voyage lasted four months, with a single stopover on the island of Santiago, in Cape Verde. Lola found it interminable, and her relationship with her husband deteriorated further. "The sea makes women sick and men extraordinarily unpleasant," she later recalled. "In the marital cabin you are constantly bumping into one another. You can't turn around without unwillingly embracing one another." They

quarreled constantly, and though they shared a cabin, they led separate
lives during the day.

Thomas avoided Lola, unable to endure her demands and childish
tantrums. He enjoyed getting together with other officers returning
from leave, playing cards, drinking dark beer, and taking long naps on
the upper deck. Lola amused herself by chatting with other passengers,
listening to their fabulous tales about the eccentricities of maharajahs,
and attending the balls held every evening. The trip provided plenty of
time to reflect on her circumstances. She had felt compelled to run away
with Thomas, but now she feared her mother's reaction. Eliza would
never forgive that affront, and Lola was certain she would be punished
for it. As they approached the mouth of the Ganges, the warm, damp
air transported her back into the past. Her heart leaped with nervous
excitement.

After more than eleven years in Great Britain, memories of her
childhood in Calcutta had grown hazy. But she had not forgotten the
sweet lullabies that Denali used to sing to her as she fell asleep and
how carefully she used to braid Lola's long hair with aromatic oils every
morning. Would she see Denali again? Would she recognize her? Surely
not. As the wife of a Company officer, she could no longer enjoy the
native woman's friendship and would not have the same freedom as
before. It was unthinkable for a white woman to wander through the
bazaars or enter the black city where the natives lived. The English
considered themselves a superior race and lived segregated from the
local population.

Instead, Lola would have to get used to the tiresome company of
haughty British ladies who spent their days calling on one another,
reading European fashion magazines, and gossiping. She would come to
detest bland English food—turkey loaf, five o'clock tea, and the dreary
formal dinners. She would learn to run a household, hire servants, and,
above all, keep up appearances in a society where scandals were the

order of the day. And she would not have an easy time, since, unlike her mother, she had never worried about what others thought of her.

In late January 1839, the *Bland* docked in Diamond Harbour at the mouth of the Hooghly River. The wharf where Lola had said a tearful goodbye to her stepfather twelve years earlier was now buzzing with energy. The arrival of any ship was an event and drew a crowd. Caught off guard by the commotion and suffocated by the heat and dust, the young woman made her way through a swirl of people of every race and religion. There were women in brightly colored saris, Englishmen in immaculate white linen suits, ragged "untouchables," and proud Punjabi men with their scarlet turbans and long beards. Sweaty porters, dressed only in loincloths, carried the passengers' heavy trunks and suitcases, shouting, "Memsahib! Luggage! Luggage!" The strong smells, the sweat clinging to her skin, and that blinding light evoked nearly forgotten memories.

"Nobody has come to meet us," Lola noted with disappointment as she scanned the crowd. "I'm afraid my mother wants nothing to do with me."

"Sooner or later she will have to see us. It's just a matter of time," Thomas replied, taking his wife's arm and leading her down the gangway.

When Lieutenant James met with his superior officers, they ordered him to immediately join his regiment in Karnal, north of Delhi and more than a thousand miles away. Lola was crushed. She had hoped to take up residence for a while in Calcutta's tranquil European neighborhood, in a pretty house with wide verandas and river views; to attend banquets and balls till dawn; and to enjoy the city's beautiful public buildings, squares, and gardens. But it was not to be. Soon Lola would board a ship once more and head upriver, traveling the same fateful route she had as a little girl. She began to fear that she, like her father, might end her days in a place like Dinapore. She had dreamed of this return for so long, but now she felt lost, forced to follow a man she did not love. Lola feared she could do nothing to change her fate. "It is my punishment," she told herself. "I am doomed to suffer just like my mother, to never find happiness, to be an aimless wanderer."

After a few days visiting old friends and making preparations in Calcutta, the Jameses left at dawn in a fleet of boats loaded with food and munitions. They were accompanied by several officers from their garrison, along with the officers' families, who were returning from a few days' leave in the city. Of that difficult journey, Lola remembered only the sweat that soaked her garments and constant squabbles with her husband. Thomas had started writing down everything she did wrong in a little notebook and then scolding her in public about her failings.

At the mercy of the winds, they sailed very slowly during the daylight hours. Their course took them toward Patna, and when they reached Dinapore, tears welled up in Lola's eyes. There, the grave of her father, whom she barely remembered, was in the small English cemetery. As the rainy season approached, the heat became stifling and the mosquitoes ravenous. Only the magical sight of the holy city of Benares, with its stone steps descending to the banks of the sacred river, pulled her out of her stupor. Men, women, the elderly, and the ailing—they were all performing their morning prayers and ablutions. It was a vivid, deeply spiritual picture. Farther along, the Ganges was unnavigable and the roads were not fit for horses; the passengers had to continue in sedan chairs carried on the shoulders of four native men.

For the next few days, Lola enjoyed a bit of privacy behind the curtain of her litter, letting herself drift off on the porters' monotone, rhythmic chanting. Several ox-drawn carts accompanied them over the rocky trails, transporting furniture and trunks. The landscape was green and leafy. They crossed rushing rivers, fields of sugarcane, and deserted villages. At night they would sleep in military tents around bonfires lit to scare off the tigers prowling nearby. The damp, the jungle sounds, and the monkeys' shrill cries kept the travelers awake.

Night was falling when they arrived in Karnal, a small, remote garrison at the foot of the Himalayas. The military post spread across a dusty plain, surrounded by a cluster of mud huts, street stalls, and a lively bazaar full of vendors. Vast swamps added a bit of green to the landscape but were infested with mosquitoes carrying the malaria that wreaked havoc among the soldiers. Lola's new home was a simple, rustic bungalow with white-painted wooden walls and a pleasant garden. For the moment, the army's meager pay wasn't enough for anything nicer.

"This is so dreary!" Lola exclaimed, looking around the interior of the house. "I imagined something a little more comfortable. I do hope we won't be here long."

"Stop complaining," Thomas scolded. "It's a palace compared to the miserable barracks my men live in. I warned you that life here wasn't going to be easy."

Lola hired several servants and decorated the rooms with the few pieces of furniture they'd brought from Calcutta. Though she would have few opportunities to wear the dresses her mother had bought, she wanted to stand out for her beauty and elegance. It would not be difficult. Karnal was home to only a few dozen British officers, and their wives were twice her age. The older ladies formed a closed, tight-knit community and made no effort to integrate into Indian society or learn any Hindi. They felt superior and looked down on the Indians, whom they considered to be ignorant, filthy, and savage. Life here was shaped by social conventions, and European women had almost no freedom. Lola could not go out on her own to walk, visit the market, or ride horses. Her only roles were housewife and caretaker to her husband. It was just the sort of life she'd so despised in Ireland, but for the moment she didn't have a choice.

When the monsoons came, her house was constantly flooding, insects abounded, and the strong winds kicked up clouds of dust. Sometimes the rain fell without stopping for seven days and seven nights, like a biblical plague. A few weeks after the couple's arrival,

Lola fell ill. She had a high fever, chills, and terrible headaches that kept her incapacitated in bed. The military doctor diagnosed malaria and treated her with large doses of quinine that left her very weak. Though Lola recovered, the disease would have lasting side effects that would haunt her for the rest of her life. Around that time, she received a letter from her mother in Calcutta. Eliza reported that she would be spending the hot season in Simla and invited her daughter to join her. Lola immediately went to her husband with the news.

"Thomas, I've heard from my mother. She's invited us to her summer residence in Simla. What do you think?"

"It will do you good, help restore your strength. It's a cool climate, and it's time you saw your parents. I will request some leave and go with you."

"Yes, I need to get out of this place, but I'm nervous about seeing my mother," Lola said anxiously. "I'm sure she still hates me."

Though she was unhappy with her husband, they made an effort to keep up appearances. "Days become centuries when you're trapped in an unhappy marriage," Lola confessed to a friend in a letter. At least they were no longer fighting: Thomas spent a lot of time out of the house with his regiment and drinking with his men. And plans for the upcoming trip to Simla revived Lola's spirits; she started packing her trunks, carefully selecting her wardrobe. Her marriage may have been a mistake, but she had no intention of letting her mother see that.

What Lola did not know was that people in Simla were awaiting her arrival with great anticipation. The gossipy British ladies of Calcutta had heard that the stepdaughter of the honorable officer Patrick Craigie was a real beauty. By now they'd all heard how the schoolgirl had been seduced by a poor officer without title or fortune and how they'd run away in the night. They felt sorry for Mrs. Craigie and understood her displeasure at her beloved daughter's deeply improper behavior. The grande dame of Simla high society, Emily Eden—sister of Bengal's governor-general, Lord Auckland—was eager to meet the beautiful, rebellious young woman. She offered her friend Eliza the sage advice that she make peace with her daughter and put the past behind them for a few days.

After the difficult months in Karnal, the city of Simla, perched some seven thousand feet above sea level, seemed magical to Lola. The clear air, dense evergreen forests, and tall mountains made her forget all the trials she'd faced since arriving in India. For five months this remote bastion of civilization became the summer capital for Britons fleeing the scorching heat of the lowlands. It was a lovely, tranquil spot boasting a wide avenue lined with elegant shops, tearooms, a post office, and, right in the center, an Anglican cathedral. As soon as the first terrible heat waves hit, the viceroy, extravagant maharajahs, foreign ambassadors, high-level administration officials, military officers, and a long list of high-society Englishwomen would arrive with their legions of servants and mountains of trunks. At the time, Simla was practically inaccessible by carriage, with the last stretch of the trip involving a steep, winding road over dizzying precipices and passes. The hard ascent could be made only on foot, on horseback, or in a sedan chair. An army of porters followed with the travelers' heavy trunks and boxes of sundries on their shoulders.

In a gesture of welcome, Eliza sent an elegant palanquin with uniformed porters in orange-and-brown livery to transport Lola to the door of her hilltop residence. Alongside them, Lieutenant James, dressed in a gleaming red velvet jacket and tight riding pants, accompanied her on a splendid horse. A large group of onlookers gathered along the Mall, the main avenue, to witness the couple's arrival. Eliza knew that all eyes were on her, and though she was still angry with her daughter, she was determined to play the part of the attentive mother. Lola, for her part, had no desire to disappoint in her first introduction into high society and was very polite and friendly with everybody. The only thing she could not help doing was lying about her age; out of vanity, she subtracted a year.

The newly promoted Major Craigie's summer residence was a spectacular two-story colonial mansion with balustrades and columns, perched atop a rocky promontory and surrounded by verdant hills. The large windows looked out on a garden that was his wife's pride and joy, with carefully tended roses, parterres of lilies and tulips, an artificial lake, and a thick carpet of lawn. Inside the house, servants swirled through the richly decorated rooms, which had huge crystal chandeliers hanging from the ceilings and were lit by candles at night. Though Lola was very nervous and tired, the reunion with her stepfather was an emotional one. When he saw Lola, he hugged her tight and kissed her cheeks as he had when she was a little girl.

"What a long time it's been, my dear! And what a beauty you've become! Let me take a look at you!" he exclaimed, making her twirl in front of him.

"Father, this is my husband, Lieutenant James, whom I've talked so much about in my letters."

"Welcome, it's a pleasure to meet you at last. There will be time to talk later. Right now, the two of you should get some rest and regain your strength. The maid will show you to your room. I want you both to feel right at home."

Emily Eden organized a magnificent dinner at Lord Auckland's Simla residence and invited the young Jameses. This woman, who was linked to England's most prominent families, had abandoned her London mansion to follow her brother to India when he was named governor-general. Since Lord Auckland was a bachelor, she had taken on the tedious role of first lady. Frail and sickly as Emily looked, the diminutive, pale woman with lively black eyes was a real tornado. She liked unpretentious Lola immediately and saw her as Irish through and through: passionate, temperamental, and rebellious. Thomas passed her test too: she found him to be charming and intelligent. Emily, an astute and perceptive observer, wrote about Lola in a letter home to her family:

Tuesday, Sept. 10 [1839]
We had a dinner yesterday. Mrs. J is undoubtedly very
pretty, and such a merry unaffected girl. She is only
seventeen now, and does not look so old, and when
one thinks that she is married to a junior lieutenant in
the Indian army, fifteen years older than herself, and
that they have 160 rupees a month, and are to pass
their whole lives in India, I do not wonder at Mrs. C's
resentment at her having run away from school.

Lola, who was by then known to all as Mrs. James, made a good
impression in Simla. Her exotic features, natural grace, and kindness
shone at all the parties and balls she attended on her husband's arm.
The young woman had never seen such splendid and elegant feasts as
those held in imperial India. The men wore tuxedos and the women
donned valuable jewels and fancy gowns made of fine silk. There were
always fresh rose centerpieces, silverware, fine china, and Bohemian
crystal glasses on white linen tablecloths embroidered with gold thread.
Behind every diner stood a servant in a white muslin tunic with a red
waist sash and a matching turban. Emily Eden was the perfect hostess,
expert at lavishing her guests with delights. She planned the menus and
taught her cook to prepare delicious desserts such as strawberry sorbet,
her favorite. After dinner, the men gathered on the cool veranda to
smoke and chat while the women enjoyed an evening of music in an
adjoining drawing room. Though no one engaged in talk of politics at
these dinners, worry about the possibility of war with Afghanistan was
palpable. The threat of a Russian invasion of India through central Asia
consumed Lord Auckland's thoughts.

Oblivious to the rumors of impending conflict, Eliza organized a
costume ball in Lola's honor that was the event of the season. Dinner
was to be served in a large white tent set up in the center of the lawn.
Numerous uniformed servants hastened to decorate the tables with

beautiful centerpieces of fresh-cut flowers and silver candelabra. Eliza wanted to show Lola everything she had achieved: access to a world of power, luxury, and privilege that her daughter would never have because she hadn't married well. Eliza, the illegitimate daughter, the humble milliner's apprentice from Cork, had become the respected wife of one of Bengal's most important men. She had a position, jewels, opulent residences, and a loving husband who showered her with attention.

When Lola arrived at the gala dressed as a Romany woman in a tight red dress with a plunging neckline and full skirts, an admiring murmur ran through the room. She wore her long curly hair pulled back in a bun with a tortoiseshell comb. She was stunning and very alluring. Her shoulders were draped in a beautiful manila shawl, and striking beaded necklaces hung around her neck.

Upon seeing her, Eliza rushed over and said in a low voice, "I hope you behave decently and don't make a fool of me in front of all my friends."

"Mother, I've come to have a good time like everybody else, and I don't intend to sit around the whole night. I want to dance, and it's such a wonderful evening."

"You can't help it; you always have to be the center of attention. You were born to get on my nerves," her mother muttered as she walked away.

After the lively dinner, a few Indian musicians in large turbans started playing a vibrant melody, with drums and castanets marking the rhythm. The torchlit garden looked like the perfect backdrop for *The Thousand and One Nights*.

Lola kicked off her shoes and went over to the musicians, letting herself be carried away by the magic of the moment. Swaying seductively to the hypnotic rhythm, she was soon surrounded by a group of young officers clapping and urging her to keep dancing. From the other end of the garden, Eliza watched in wordless embarrassment. Beside her,

Mr. Craigie was spellbound: "What a delightful girl. She dances so well, and she's so beautiful." Once more, Eliza's daughter had outshined her.

Simla in summer was a succession of dances, receptions, horse races, tennis tournaments, charitable auctions, and costume parties. It was the perfect place for love affairs, since many women went there without their husbands and many officers without their wives, if they had one at all. Emily Eden had noticed how much Lola loved male attention and warned her one day about the risk she was running.

"My dear, I must warn you that, in Simla, looking at a man a second longer than is called for indicates interest, and dancing with him more than once is as good as declaring your commitment. Do not forget that."

"I appreciate your concern, but I'm young and I want to enjoy myself. Life in Karnal is agonizingly boring, and I'm fed up with it."

"I understand completely. When I first arrived in Calcutta, my world crumbled around me. I thought it was an awful place with a horrible climate and little to recommend it. And my fellow Englishwomen seemed to me shallow and unpleasant, utterly lacking in manners and class and interested only in gossip. But you are different."

"I wish I could stay with you," Lola sighed sorrowfully. "Maybe we will see each other again."

"We shall, my dear. I plan to visit you soon."

The delightful days in Simla came to an end, and Lola had to return to Karnal with her husband. It was a sad farewell; for the first time in a long while, Lola had been happy. She admired Lady Eden and eagerly awaited her visit. Her mind lingered on the incredible vistas of snowy peaks, the carefree picnics on the riverbank, the polo matches, and the sumptuous feasts in opulent residences with food that rivaled that of the finest restaurants in Paris.

Six weeks later, Lord Auckland and his entourage left Simla at dawn. Emily Eden had grown accustomed to the nomadic tent life that she'd so hated at first and to every sort of transport imaginable, from horseback to elephant or camel, to palanquins, to hammocks, to sedan chairs. She had become an expert traveler and was unfazed by mosquitoes, sweltering heat, and the wild animals that prowled nearby at night. She had been away from Calcutta for more than a year and worried that she might still have many long months of involuntary exile ahead of her. Her brother had decided to organize a major expedition to explore some of India's border provinces outside British control and to persuade the princes there to collaborate with the British troops to intervene in Afghanistan. Lord Auckland was traveling with an impressive convoy of more than twelve thousand people, a small, mobile city that had to be dismantled each morning to continue on its way.

In Karnal they were given a splendid welcome and honored with a military parade. Despite the draining trip, Lady Eden was in a cheerful, energetic mood. She immediately summoned Mrs. James and greeted her with great affection. Lola seemed somewhat subdued, with a more serious expression and her face tanned by the sun.

"What a delight to see you again!" Lola exclaimed, hugging her tightly. "I've been waiting for this moment for weeks—you can't imagine how I've longed for it to come. You must tell me all your news."

"That I will, my dear. We will be here for five days, and I want you to have a wonderful time. Plus, I have a surprise for you."

"What kind of surprise?"

"Go ahead and open it," Lady Eden said, handing her a box tied with an exquisite ribbon.

Lola opened the box to find, wrapped in tissue paper, a lovely pink muslin dress with lace. The unexpected gift brought back memories of her happy days in Simla—dancing until dawn, the delicious candlelit dinner at Lord Auckland's residence, the red rhododendrons blooming in her stepfather's garden. Lola's eyes grew damp, but Emily was not about to allow the young woman to be sad and invited her to visit her lodgings. Although, with her usual wit, she'd dubbed it "Misery Hall," Lady Eden's private tent made a huge impression on Lola. It was spacious and decorated with plush Persian carpets and heavy Victorian furniture.

"How beautiful! I've always dreamed of having an elegant dressing table like yours, and a large canopy bed with a mosquito net. You even have your own dressing room!" Lola exclaimed, admiring every detail.

"That's not all, my dear. Come with me," Lady Eden said, taking her hand. "I'll show you the tent where we hold balls and receptions."

Emily organized a number of social events in Karnal, including a fancy banquet for the men, pony races, and a grand ball that Lola attended clad in the alluring dress her friend had given her. She once more enjoyed being the center of attention, and she was unquestionably the youngest and most arresting woman with the regiment.

The day before her departure on November 17, Lady Eden invited Lola to spend the day with her. They took a long walk outside the camp, drank tea with a few ladies they'd met in Simla, and the younger woman amused herself playing with her hostess's mischievous spaniel. As night fell, seeing that her friend was distressed by their parting, Lady Eden offered Lola a ride on her elephant so she could explore the land between them and the garrison. She felt sorry for Lola; her beauty and freshness would soon wither in that backwater. In her diary, predicting the events to come, Emily wrote:

> [The day] ended in her going back to Karnal on my elephant, with E. N. by her side and Mr. James sitting behind, and she had never been on an elephant before, and thought it delightful. She is very pretty, and a good little thing, apparently, but they are very poor, and she is very young and lively, and if she falls into bad hands she would soon laugh herself into foolish scrapes. At present the husband and wife are very fond of each other, but a girl who marries at fifteen hardly knows what she likes.

The next morning, very early, Lola rushed to the camp to say her last goodbyes to her friend. Though she wasn't an early riser, Emily was already at the head of the impressive caravan, mounted on her elephant. When she saw Lola, she waved and exclaimed, "I must go, darling, but I don't want to see you looking sad, so promise me you'll take care of yourself."

"Will we see each other again?" Lola asked, dodging through the clouds of dust kicked up by the animals.

"Of course we will, my dear child. I hope to return to Calcutta in a few months. You know where to find me. Be patient, we'll see each other soon."

Emily's departure was painful for Lola. Not only had a kind, loving woman left, a woman she would have liked to be her own mother, but all her dreams and prospects disappeared along with her. Still, she refused to be brought low by yearning or by the deadly tedium. Every day, as Lady Eden had suggested, she did herself up in front of the mirror as if she lived in Calcutta. She would order her maid to comb and plait her long, curly hair, put on one of her filmy muslin dresses, and select her finest jewelry in preparation to call on another wife and have tea. The inactivity was killing her, but she couldn't let herself get sucked under by such a depressing place. Lola had figured out that, to maintain her sanity at these latitudes, it was essential to get together with the women in town, even if she didn't like them or have anything to talk about.

She had already lost all hope of a better life when the news arrived that her husband's battalion would be sent to an even more remote post, close to the Nepalese border. Major Craigie had made sure that Thomas James, whom he considered to be part of the family, was chosen to lead the recruitment center at Bareilly, almost two hundred miles southeast of Karnal. In Bareilly, officers took care of enlisting and training the natives who were part of the East India Company's troops. Lieutenant James would perform administrative duties and would be the only English officer in charge of the sepoys. Lola was relieved at the idea of leaving Karnal and embarking on a new adventure. She'd heard that the landscapes were incredible. Her head full of dreams, she started packing her belongings and choosing the furniture that would travel with them by oxcart.

In late February 1840, after an exhausting journey on horseback along rough dirt roads, Lieutenant James's caravan reached its destination. Bareilly was even smaller and more desolate than Karnal, located on the banks of the mighty Ramganga River. It was one of the most sparsely populated camps in India. Although the land was not plagued with mosquitoes, living conditions were very challenging. The officers' quarters were run down and nearly swallowed by the dense vegetation. A cluster of huts, some street stalls, and the old barracks were visible in the distance. Thanks to Bareilly's higher altitude, the heat was less suffocating than in Karnal, but the humidity was even worse because it was so close to the tropical rain forest. There was little to do in town. After they'd completed their maneuvers and exercises, the soldiers and officers would drink beer in the canteen, do some target shooting, or go hunting. The surrounding area was full of tigers, water buffalo, antelopes, birds, and wild boar. Lola complained that she was lonelier and more isolated than ever; apart from her neighbor, the widow Mrs. Palmer, she was the only European woman around. Monotony and boredom took hold of her life once more. Her first glimpse of the sepoy soldiers, with their shabby red jackets and threadbare blue breeches, horrified her.

"It's awful! I never have anybody to talk to! It's like being dead. How could you do this to me? Do you care so little for my well-being?" Lola protested, near collapse.

"I don't choose where I'm posted," Thomas pointed out. "The climate is healthier here and I'm making better wages, but you think only about yourself."

"I can't live here," she whispered to herself. "I won't be able to bear it. But where can I go?"

Disappointed, she looked around. The crystalline lakes and green fields of tea plants carpeting the hills could not mask the harshness and poverty that were also present. In these isolated villages, she'd heard, men murdered their wives with impunity, women sold their daughters for a handful of rice, and widows burned themselves on their husbands' funeral pyres. One night in Simla, Lady Eden had told her that people in northern India would tie a criminal to an elephant's hind legs and have them dragged through the streets as punishment. If they didn't die during the process, the townspeople would finish them off by propping their head on a stone and letting the elephant crush them with its weight. Pondering these atrocities kept Lola up at night, and she often had terrible nightmares.

In Bareilly the couple had few opportunities to get away from each other, and life together became unbearable. As in most regiments, alcohol and opium helped the soldiers of Bareilly endure the harsh climate and painful isolation. Thomas started drinking heavily and grew more aggressive. One day when he came home drunk and in a foul mood, they had a heated argument and he struck her. It wasn't the first time, but Lola couldn't take it anymore. After months of insults and threats, she suddenly saw everything clearly. That same day she left the house with nothing but the clothes on her back and sought the protection of her neighbor, Mrs. Palmer. This elderly widow of an East India Company military veteran was her only friend and was well aware of tensions between the couple.

"Poor child!" she exclaimed upon seeing Lola. "This was bound to end badly. If you have your husband brought up before a military tribunal, it will cause a scandal and will mar the reputation of your stepfather, Major Craigie. You must keep up appearances."

"I've already thought about this. All I want is to leave this place as soon as possible. Please let me stay with you for a few days until I go."

"You may stay with me if that's what you want. We will write to your mother; she'll understand, and she'll take you in when you go back to Calcutta."

"Thank you, Mrs. Palmer, I don't know what I would have done without your help," Lola stammered, nervous about how her husband would react when he found that she wasn't home.

But Thomas didn't bother her again, and Lola left a few days later. She found the journey aboard a dilapidated boat much more pleasant than previous ones. Thanks to the river's swift current and the powerful wind, she reached the bustling port in only two weeks. Once more she was in Calcutta, the city of a thousand palaces bathed by the sacred waters of the Ganges, but now her situation was very different. She was no longer arriving proudly on her husband's arm; she was alone and determined to divorce a man she wanted to blot from her life. The worst part was being forced to ask her mother for help and admitting that her marriage had been a mistake. Mrs. Craigie didn't feel the slightest bit sorry for her daughter and refused to be outshined by her again. Unfortunately, Emily Eden was still traveling in Agra with her brother and would not be back in the capital city for more than a year. In that difficult moment, Lola could have used the older woman's wise advice and understanding.

Lola's first days in Calcutta were quite pleasurable, compared to the spartan life she'd led in Bareilly. Her mother put her up in a lovely, light-filled room that had a large canopy bed and looked out on a sweet-smelling English garden. It was decorated with teak furniture, mirrors with frames inlaid with mother-of-pearl, and elegant Persian carpets. But Eliza did not want to show off her daughter to her social circle. Rumors were already spreading like wildfire.

Desperate to avoid a new scandal, Eliza kept her daughter away from all social activities. A disgraced woman was automatically excluded from high-society parties and events. While her parents went to the theater and the horse track, Lola remained shut up at home. Though she was not yet twenty, she already had a past that her mother would go to any lengths to conceal.

Mrs. Craigie told her friends at the Bengal Club, who gathered every Tuesday, that Lola was recovering from a severe back injury. Her daughter, a fearless horsewoman, had supposedly suffered a fall in Meerut when her steed had stumbled. The doctors were hoping she would get better, but she might have to return to England.

One day she burst into Lola's bedroom and demanded that the young woman listen closely.

"If you'd listened to me, you wouldn't be in this situation. The only reason you married that man was to hurt me, and you brought your punishment on yourself."

"Mother," Lola replied, trying to control her irritation, "I know you're enjoying this, but I intend to set myself up in my own home in Calcutta as soon as possible. My stepfather will help me."

"No, my dear, I've already spoken to him on the subject and we are in complete agreement. You have only two options." A faint smile appeared on her face. "Either you go back to your husband or you return to England. Think about it carefully, and give me an answer as soon as possible."

Lola felt like a prisoner, on the verge of despair. Yet again, her chilly, pragmatic mother was getting rid of her to save herself a headache. Her stepfather had indeed been willing to buy her a house so she could live independently and receive her friends there, but his wife had convinced him that he would be exposing himself to serious risk. Eliza knew her daughter well. Lola might take a lover, or several, and end up pregnant. Major Patrick Craigie's reputation was at stake, and a scandal of that magnitude could jeopardize his brilliant career.

Lola didn't have to ponder her choice for long. Reluctantly, she agreed to return to England. The prospect of spending her twenties buried alive in a remote military outpost, beside a man whom she did not love, was intolerable.

At the beginning of August, Lieutenant James requested a three-month leave to travel to Calcutta and bring Lola her belongings. Despite his differences with his wife, he was willing to help with her voyage. It had been decided that the young woman would live in Scotland with Major Craigie's family. Her stepfather wrote to his sister, Catherine Rae, and his friends in London to ask them to take her in until she could find a steamer heading to Scotland. There, Lola would stay in the house owned by his brother, Thomas Craigie, in Leith, outside Edinburgh. Family members and friends were informed that Mrs. James was returning home because she had not recovered fully from her riding injury and the Indian climate was not good for her.

Major Craigie was still very fond of Lola and continued to treat her like his own daughter. Although he was convinced that the decision was for the best, he felt in his heart that he was losing her for good. The night before Lola's departure, he invited her to sit with him for a while after dinner.

"I know you're angry with me," he said sadly, "but you can't stay here, and you know it. Your mother is very nervous and unhappy, and you have to start a new life far away from this country."

"Nobody's asked me my opinion, Father. I know you love me, but I'm not a little girl anymore and my life is here, in Calcutta, with you."

"No, India isn't right for you," he said. "In Scotland you can live with my brother and his family. Listen to me—you know I've always looked out for you and wanted the best for you."

Eliza purchased a ticket for her daughter on the steamship *Larkins*, and the day before it weighed anchor, Lieutenant James boarded to inspect his wife's cabin. By chance, an American couple of his acquaintance, Henry Sturgis and his wife, Mary, of Boston, would also be traveling on the ship, and he begged them to look after Lola during the voyage.

On October 3, 1840, she said goodbye to her mother with a kiss on the cheek. Impassive, Eliza wished her a safe journey and told her to write. Lola's stepfather and Lieutenant James rode with her in the carriage to the docks, which swarmed with vendors, passengers, and onlookers. Before they parted, the major gave her an envelope with a check for a thousand pounds.

"This is for you, daughter," he said, his voice choked. "If you manage it well, it will be enough to live on for some time. Don't waste your life."

"Thank you, Father, I will miss you so much. I hope we'll see each other again soon, and that you'll write to me often. Do you promise?" she said as she hugged him.

"Of course, it's a temporary separation. You know you're my dearest treasure. But let's not be sad. Go on, you must board now. Go ahead, sweetheart." And he kissed her forehead.

Thomas helped Lola with her luggage and accompanied her part of the way down the Ganges before saying goodbye and boarding a boat that would take him to shore. Leaning on the railing of the upper deck, she watched sadly as the delicate silhouettes of Calcutta's palaces and temples disappeared into the early morning haze. She spent a long time lost in thought, trying to store away in her memory all the aromas, colors, and sensations that she was leaving behind. She had been terribly unhappy with her husband, and now she felt stronger and more sure of herself than ever. She'd always been convinced she deserved something better. "I remember it was the saddest, most heart-wrenching goodbye of my life. It broke my heart to leave my father, and I was afraid I might never see him again. That day I realized I was all alone in the world, but I refused to surrender."

CHAPTER 3

The Beautiful Spaniard

The *Larkins*, with its two tall smokestacks, sailed through storms and rough waves across the Indian Ocean. In mid-October, the temperature was still pleasant, and Lola amused herself on deck watching the albatrosses gliding overhead. As a girl, she'd been prone to seasickness and always sought her mother for comfort, but now she loved feeling the wind gusting against her face. She had several months of sailing ahead of her, but on this voyage she had no intention of remaining shut up in her cabin. She felt free of all ties and ready to forget the past.

Ten days after leaving the port of Calcutta, the *Larkins* made a brief stopover in Madras, and one of the passengers who boarded the ship caught Lola's eye. A handsome officer with elegant manners and an alluring smile, Lieutenant George Lennox was a member of the Fourth Madras Cavalry and aide-de-camp to Bombay's governor-general. He had spent three years in India and was on his way home for the first time. He was twenty years old and the nephew of the Duke of Richmond, one of the wealthiest and most influential members of the British aristocracy. A lover of worldly pleasures and beautiful women, he noticed Lola straightaway. The attraction was mutual, and they could be seen at all hours holding hands and sharing confidences. As the weeks passed, the young couple's romance scandalized the other passengers. Ingram, the captain of the *Larkins*, a strict man with a rigid sense of morality, saw that Lola, to his dismay, was behaving in an unseemly and reckless manner. Despite the disapproving looks she received, she continued to visit her lover's cabin alone and even stayed with him overnight. When told that her conduct was unbecoming to a lady, she replied that Lieutenant Lennox's cabin was larger and better lit than her own, considering the matter closed. Mary Sturgis, the American matron who'd been charged by Lieutenant James with looking after his wife, tried to make her see reason.

"Mrs. James, you are making a spectacle of yourself in front of all the passengers. What are they going to think of you?" she said, her expression stern.

"I'm not a little girl," Lola shot back, "and I would ask you to stay out of my affairs from now on."

"But you have a husband who worries about you. How can you be so irresponsible?" Mrs. Sturgis reproached her.

"Excuse me, madam, but my husband is dead to me, and I have no need of a governess."

Lola persisted in her brazen conduct until Captain Ingram lost his patience at last. Never in all his years of service had he seen such shameless behavior from a married woman. One bright Sunday morning, when the passengers and crew were gathered on deck to attend mass, Lola and her lover retired discreetly to her cabin as the hymns rang out. The captain and his wife had ordered their maid, Caroline, to keep an eye on Mrs. James's cabin, since the rolling of the ship occasionally made its door swing open. Their snooping was rewarded, and the maidservant was able to see the couple kissing on the lips and, at one point, George fastening his lover's corset. After these events, the nature of the relationship was undeniable, and the Ingrams shunned the pair. Lola was excluded from the Christmas and New Year's celebrations at the captain's table. Unfazed by the punishment, however, she continued to be just as provocative as ever.

After Lola's departure, Major Craigie had written to his family to arrange the details of her journey to Leith. In the letter, he insisted that she "should not be delivered for any time in London but that she should proceed at once to Scotland," perhaps fearing the temptations that lurked if she remained alone in the metropolis. Sarah Watson, a widowed sister of Lieutenant James who lived outside London, came to an agreement with Catherine Rae, the major's sister. Mrs. Rae traveled from Edinburgh and remained with Mrs. Watson to await Lola's arrival and accompany her to Scotland. But during the crossing, the young woman had changed her mind, having no intention of being shut away in the Scottish countryside. She wasn't a helpless child anymore, and the money from her stepfather would allow her to live comfortably in London. This shift in plans was cemented when, two weeks before the *Larkins* reached the coast of England, Lieutenant Lennox made Lola an appealing proposition.

"Darling," he began, "I won't let you go away to Scotland. I have excellent contacts in London and money to fulfill your every whim. We'll have a grand time together."

"I wasn't planning to go to Leith," she confessed, "but I don't want to depend on anybody either. I will rent my own apartment and—"

"That's ridiculous," George interrupted. "I'll look for a pretty house in Mayfair for you. You will have your own horse-drawn carriage and beautiful gowns, and I'll introduce you to influential friends. What do you say?"

Lola pondered for a moment. She had no home, no husband, and no income, and without a protector's support, she had no prospects. With appropriate recommendations, she might find a job as a governess or lady's maid. But the idea was hardly appealing, since a young woman who wanted to work in London for a good family would be offered "a comfortable home" but no salary. Meanwhile, she liked George and

only wanted to enjoy his company to the fullest. The young man was
an extremely eligible bachelor, a somewhat eccentric and dandyish bon
vivant who moved freely among the most distinguished members of
high society. The idea of living together in London, meeting important
people, and attending parties and plays was alluring.

When the *Larkins* docked in Portsmouth on February 20, 1841,
Lola proudly descended the gangway on her lover's arm, under the
disapproving stare of Captain Ingram. By the time the couple made
it through customs with their luggage, it was too late to continue on
to London, so they found lodging at a hotel near the boardwalk. To
keep up appearances, Lennox reserved a suite of two bedrooms with a
small shared sitting room. But once they were in the English capital,
they dropped such formalities. When they checked in at the Imperial
Hotel, near Covent Garden, they requested a room with a double bed,
had their dinner sent up, and spent the night together.

The next morning George collected his luggage, paid the hotel bill,
and hired a carriage to visit his family. His parents were eagerly waiting
for him at their home in Bognor, West Sussex, a fashionable seaside city
where he spent a few days with them. In the meantime, Lola rented an
apartment at 7 Great Ryder Street. Though she hadn't been in touch
with the family members who had traveled to meet her, they managed
to track her down. When she returned home one evening, she found
her sister-in-law, Sarah Watson, waiting in the parlor. The lady was no
prude and was aware of Lola's relationship with Lennox. Lola knew her
sister-in-law from her stay in Ballycrystal; the two women got on well,
but Lola was not going to let anybody lecture her.

"I'm not angry. I only want to warn you that you're putting your
future in jeopardy. You need to listen to reason," Sarah begged her.

"I want to live my own life. You don't know how awful things were
in India and how your brother treated me. Please go away. I don't need
your help."

"All right, I'll go, but you will end up regretting this. You're still a married woman, don't forget," her sister-in-law said.

Sarah Watson refused to give up. A few days later, she returned to Lola's apartment, this time with Catherine Rae in tow. Upon seeing her stepfather's older sister again, Lola softened. Mrs. Rae had been like a mother to her when she'd been sent to boarding school at just ten years old. But Mrs. Rae couldn't persuade her either. Lola was experiencing independence for the first time in her life, she was in love, and she adored the city. The two women left defeated, bemoaning Lola's obstinacy and obliviousness to consequences. After this visit, Sarah wrote her brother, Lieutenant James, a sorrowful letter in which she recounted the sad events and described the dissolute life his wife was leading in London.

George Lennox visited his lover every day, paid her rent, and stayed with her from nine o'clock in the morning until very late at night. Lola had become a familiar figure in London society; she was regularly seen in trendy spots and enjoyed riding through Hyde Park in an elegant phaeton drawn by a pair of gray ponies. She'd decided that she was going to divorce Lieutenant James and become Mrs. Lennox. She told her landlady that she was very much in love and would soon be engaged.

But those happy days came to an end. George soon tired of her and went back to his parents. By late July, the romance was over and Lola was forced to move out of her pretty house in Mayfair and into a smaller, shabbier place. It was a hard blow for the young woman, who once more had to swallow her pride and admit that she'd made a mistake. She moved several more times and, a few months later, was living in a modest little house in Islington, in outer London. Her stepfather's money was gone, and she had to face the unvarnished truth.

Lola didn't hear from her lover again, but she did not resent him. Thanks to his contacts, she had met important people who would open the doors of theaters for her. She later read in the papers that George Lennox had returned to India to rejoin his regiment in Madras and had died only a year later, having succumbed to fever during a military expedition near Hyderabad. He was twenty-three years old and the first of several of her lovers to lose his life in the full flush of youth.

After two months Lola packed her bags and climbed into a carriage that would take her to Edinburgh to live with Catherine Rae. With hardly any money, she led an anonymous, respectable life through the long, cold winter months in Scotland. But in March 1842, a stranger appeared at Mrs. Rae's home asking for Lola. Without a word, he handed her a summons: Lola was being charged with adultery and would have to appear before the ecclesiastical court in London to defend herself. Lieutenant James had petitioned for divorce and planned to publicly accuse his wife of adultery, the only valid reason for dissolving a marriage. With that, the possibility of finding decent work vanished, and she couldn't keep living with Mrs. Rae.

Returning to London, Lola was able to survive thanks to some influential men of good social standing who helped with her expenses in exchange for her companionship. In such an expensive city, she needed a protector to pay her bills in order to continue living the extravagant lifestyle to which she'd grown accustomed.

Then, for the first time, she thought of becoming an actress and conquering the stage. As a child she'd been drawn to dance and theater. She recalled one full-moon night in Calcutta when Denali had taken her to a temple on the outskirts of the city and she'd met some young devadasis who'd been training in religious and sacred dances since they were little girls. Lola had been fascinated by the exotic dancers, with their elaborate headdresses of gold and jewels and swaths of rich silk. They were barefoot, with their arms full of bangles, and their light garments barely covered them. Their sensual, mesmerizing movements by torchlight were etched in her memory.

A friend of Lennox told her about the famed actress Fanny Kelly and offered to introduce Lola so she could ask her advice. After a long, brilliant career at the Drury Lane Theatre, Fanny now gave classes to aspiring actresses. For Lola it was a dream to meet this grande dame. Fanny was born for the boards and, thanks to her enormous dramatic talent, had been able to play all of Shakespeare's heroines. Now retired, she had used her savings to set up a theater academy "exclusively for young ladies" behind her home in Soho. In puritanical 1842 England, where Victorian brides were instructed that their duty on their wedding night was to "lie still and think of the empire," actresses were considered fallen women. Fanny wanted to change this mindset and lay the groundwork for women to earn a decent salary so they could live without having to rely on the assistance of protectors who paid their bills in exchange for sexual favors.

One afternoon Lola visited the actress at 73 Dean Street, where she lived surrounded by cats and memories. A house girl opened the door and invited Lola into a large parlor with heavy velvet drapes, oriental-style furniture, Chinese lacquered screens, and plush rugs. On the walls, which were covered with exquisite brocades, hung two huge cornucopia mirrors and several portraits of the actress as a young woman. Fanny greeted Lola wrapped in a striking silk robe.

"Good afternoon, my dear, sit down next to me," she said, gesturing to a settee by the fireplace. "So you want to be an actress. Do you have any experience?"

"No, Mrs. Kelly, I have no experience, but I would like to take classes at your school, to learn from someone like you. I am ambitious and I need to earn a living."

"That's all well and good, but being a fine actress requires talent. I make no promises, but I'm willing to give you some classes."

"So you agree?"

"Yes, we'll start tomorrow. But don't thank me. This is a challenging craft that demands a great deal of sacrifice. Not everyone is cut out for it. Don't think that it's going to be easy."

For the next few weeks, Lola eagerly attended Fanny's studio, ready to give it her all. Fanny was a demanding teacher who overlooked no faults, but she could also be kind and caring with her students. The winter was damp and gray, and the young woman spent her afternoons at home, studying classic texts, memorizing dialogue, and trying to get inside her characters' heads.

"Focus now, girl, strip your soul bare. Your gestures and voice must convey feelings and emotions. You are Desdemona now, and you are trapped by Othello's paranoia, his twisted jealousy."

"I'm never going to get it. You're wasting your time with me."

"You're right, maybe you weren't meant to be an actress. But look at you—you're beautiful, you have a well-proportioned figure, long, shapely legs . . . You should try dance."

"I'm twenty-one. That's far too old to start ballet." Lola collapsed onto the sofa, dejected.

"No, my dear, I'm talking about Spanish dance. It's all the rage right now, and you look like you could be Andalusian yourself. And it's a less rigorous discipline than ballet," the teacher said encouragingly.

Fanny had been frank with her student. Lola moved awkwardly onstage, she had a hard time memorizing lines, and her diction was poor. But the possibility of becoming a Spanish dancer appealed to the young woman from the start. She was proud, bold, and sensual, qualities that worked well in this kind of dance, the origins of which were lost in the remote past. At the time, southern Spain had seized the English public's imagination. Romantic-era travelogues had sparked interest in a land of bandits, Gypsies, bullfighters, and fiery brunettes. The great ballerinas of the age were successfully introducing boleros, cachuchas, and fandangos into their repertoires.

Fanny Kelly introduced Lola to a dance teacher who had drunk from the fountains of flamenco and bolero. For four months she learned the basic steps and movements, to stomp and play the castanets. With her hair pulled back in a graceful bun, clad in a flamenco dress and mantilla, she would lose herself in the rhythm of the guitar. The rehearsals were exhausting and demanded a good deal of discipline. She had to maintain the proper pose: head raised, back arched, and arms curved upward. Since her teacher spoke to her in Spanish, Lola learned a few words and even developed the habit of rolling and smoking cigarettes. When her classes came to an end, she paid her landlady the rent she owed and abruptly left London. She told her friends she was going to Spain to perfect her technique. But that was a lie.

Lola was in crisis. She felt betrayed and used by men; she needed time to think about her future. She had taken an important step in studying flamenco, but there was a lot of competition and she wasn't as skilled as other performers. If she wanted to make a living on the stage, she would have to offer the audience something different, become a mysterious figure who could captivate the press. More than once, Fanny had told her that she looked Spanish.

At this crossroads, she decided to call herself Lola Montez. She would not only change her name but also invent a past of opulence and poverty in Spain. She would be a beautiful, proud Andalusian woman, born in Seville into the bosom of a family that, despite its ancient pedigree, had been forced into exile and destitution by the First Carlist War.

"Elizabeth Gilbert James has died for good," she thought. "I'll never depend on anybody again. I have suffered a great deal, but all my travails will have been worth it because I'm going to go further than anyone could imagine." With a smile on her lips, she left London and headed into the unknown.

For nearly a year, nobody heard from her, and in mid-April 1843, she reappeared as Lola Montez, ready to launch her artistic career. She was seen at the port of Southampton and then boarded a London-bound train. On that short journey, she met a new protector, the man who would help her debut as an artist. James Howard Harris, Earl of Malmesbury, was a distinguished aristocrat and conservative politician of thirty-six. He was married and immensely wealthy. Lola sat down next to him and, in short order, had told him her sad life story. Visibly distressed, she informed him that she was the widow of Don Diego de

León, who had been executed for his involvement in an unsuccessful coup against Queen Isabella II and the regent, Maria Christina. When the plot was discovered, her husband had refused to run and had faced a firing squad at dawn.

"So you see, sir," Lola sighed, dabbing her tears with a handkerchief, "I am a young widow who's been forced to abandon my homeland, Spain, to make my way in the world, having lost everything."

"My dear Lola, your story is very moving. Your husband was a hero, a very brave man. I will try to help you however I can; you can count on me."

"You are a true gentleman, sir. I will always be grateful to you," Lola said, pleased with her new conquest.

The Earl of Malmesbury was the first of many prominent men whom Lola duped over the course of her life. He not only organized a benefit show in his Stratford Place mansion, at which the young woman danced a bolero and sold Andalusian mantillas and lace fans to the guests, but also introduced her to Benjamin Lumley, the powerful administrator of Her Majesty's Theatre in London. The earl was an eminent patron of the institution, which had revolutionized English theater by introducing the Italian operas of Verdi and Donizetti. Lumley unhesitatingly met with the unknown artist in his office on Haymarket. Accustomed as he was to the whims and demands of the great stars of classical ballet, such as the vain and insufferable Marie Taglioni, he was charmed by Lola's natural manner and youth.

In his two years running the theater, Lumley had garnered a reputation as a shrewd businessman. Handsome and well dressed, with a neat beard and penetrating black eyes, he enjoyed rubbing elbows with the aristocracy. He realized immediately that Lola was not a typical dancer, that her exotic beauty, passion, and provocative sensuality formed a potent combination that could work in his favor. Impressed by the beautiful Spaniard's charms, he scheduled her debut for June 3 of that year in a staging of *Il barbiere di Siviglia*. Lola would dance "El Oleano" between the two acts of Rossini's famous opera. The dance was a cachu-cha, an Andalusian variant of the bolero accompanied by guitar and castanets, into which Lola had incorporated the "Spider Dance" that would make her famous around the world. In this lively, spicy number, Lola pretended to search her clothing for a spider that was trying to bite her, her movements growing increasingly more frenzied; the dance reached its climax when she managed to crush the spider with her foot. Since the performance was being held in honor of Queen Victoria's uncle, the elderly King Ernst August of Hanover, Lola hoped that the evening would give her career a substantial boost. The monarch would be sitting in the principal box, and the event would be attended by the crème de la crème of English society.

To ensure the success of Lola Montez's debut, Mr. Lumley invited one of his good friends, the *Morning Post*'s culture critic, to a rehearsal. After watching the performance, the journalist was allowed into the young artist's dressing room to spend some time with her one on one. Aware of how important the meeting could be to her future, Lola employed all her charms and seductive wiles. The critic could see immediately that she wasn't a great dancer, but there was something compelling about her; she had a surprising, exotic beauty, an odd foreign accent, and a remarkable figure. Most striking, though, were her wit, intelligence, and brilliant conversation. He was used to dealing with actresses and dancers who attempted to seem erudite to gain his approval, so her genuine eloquence came as a surprise. Once she'd told him several tales of her life in Spain and smoked a cigarette, which was somewhat scandalous at that time, the critic promised to do everything in his power to help her. Before leaving, however, he felt obligated to warn her about a rival in the dance world.

"I imagine, Lola, that you will have seen Marie Taglioni perform in *La sylphide*," he said, pausing to gauge her reaction. "She has revolution-ized the scene with her dancing en pointe, and her grace, poetry, and ethereal effortlessness have made her an object of worship."

"I have heard of her," she responded scornfully, "but my dancing is different. Taglioni is from Sweden, and when she performs a dance from my country, she doesn't do it with the same passion. Flamenco is an art; you carry it in your blood."

"No doubt, but comparisons will be inevitable. What's more, she has a coterie of devoted followers. On one occasion a group of admirers managed to steal one of her slippers and worshipfully ate it as part of a lavish banquet—I swear that is not a joke. I wish you the best of luck." And he said goodbye, convinced that this fiery young woman would give the world plenty to talk about.

On the morning of her debut, Lola read with satisfaction the lengthy article that her new admirer had published in the main pages of the *Morning Post*:

> Donna Lolah Montes, who makes her debut to-night upon this stage, will for the first time introduce the Spanish dance to the English public . . . The French danseuse executes her pas with the feet, the legs, and the hips alone. The Spaniard dances with the body, the lips, the eyes, the head, the neck, and with the heart. Her dance is the history of a passion . . . In person she is truly the Spanish woman—in style, she is emphatically the Spanish dancer—and we feel sure that none who can relish natural beauty and instinctive art, will fail to appreciate that which . . . all praise. El Olano is, like the Cachuca—not the Cachuca of Duvernay, Elssler, or Cerito—an intensely national dance, and will be as new to the generality of English eyes as we believe it to be beautiful. The variety of passion which it embodies—the languor, the abandon, the love, the pride, the scorn—one of the steps which is called death to the tarantula and is a favourite pas of the country, is the

very poetry of avenging contempt—cannot be sur-
passed. The head lifted and thrown back, the flashing
eye, the fierce and protruded foot which crushed the
insect, make a subject for the painter which would
scarcely be easy to forget.

Lola couldn't complain. With that kind of publicity, the performance quickly sold out, and her debut promised to be a smashing
success. On the warm night of June 3, as the lobby of Her Majesty's
Theatre gradually filled with London's most prominent people—
bankers, diplomats, ministers, and aristocrats—Lola was trying to calm
her nerves by smoking one cigarette after another in her dressing room.
On this elegant stage, which had made its own debut in 1705 and where
the world's most famous operas had been performed and internationally
renowned artists had played, Lola was preparing to conquer the English
with her passionate dancing. She was fully aware of her limitations and
knew that the public would be severe in its demands. She could not
compete with the great stars of the moment, such as Austrian Fanny
Elssler, the queen of romantic ballet, and Taglioni, who danced the
cachucha with immense speed and technical precision, two qualities
that Lola lacked.

To calm herself, she mused as she dressed that her rivals lacked
the fire she could bring to her dancing. She had chosen a white satin
bodice that accentuated her bust and a full skirt made of maroon velvet
that revealed flashes of her shapely legs clad in flesh-colored stockings.
As the first act of *Il barbiere di Siviglia* ended, she braced herself to go
onstage. The dimly lit stage set mimicked a Mozarabic hall of columns
in Granada's Alhambra. With the first strummed notes of the guitar,
Lola appeared in the center of the stage, wrapped in a black lace mantilla. At a signal from the director, she tossed the mantilla into the air
and began to dance, her arms curving gracefully above her head to the
rhythm of the castanets as she jumped and swayed. She did not execute

the steps flawlessly, but she infused her dancing with an extraordinary grace and mischievousness as she pretended to search for the spider hiding somewhere on her body.

At the end of her act, the audience sat in stunned silence. Her steps and movements were unlike any known style of dance. But many of the spectators were admirers of Lola, and they stood and began to applaud. Their enthusiasm was catching. As Lola bowed, a shower of bouquets covered the stage floor. When the curtain came down and the applause continued, Lola knew she had the audience in the palm of her hand. Lumley rushed to congratulate her, delighted to imagine the profits to come thanks to this Spanish beauty who'd just startled a sophisticated and demanding audience with her unusual dancing.

Indeed, London's major newspapers trumpeted Lola's success across the city. Admirers swarmed her dressing room to congratulate her and give her flowers. The next day, the press rained down praise on the young artist, predicting that a bright future lay in store for her. As expected, the *Morning Post*'s critic was the most enthusiastic:

> Her wonderfully supple form assumed attitudes that were not dreamt of—the line of beauty still being preserved, in spite of the boldness of her movements. At one moment she bent down to the ground, moving her arms as if she were gathering roses in a parterre—and at the next moment starting to her feet, and raising her arms playfully in the air, as if she were showering the flowers on a lover's head. At one moment, her dancing represented seduction and entreaty—and next, she suddenly stamped her feet on the ground, placing her hand on her hip with a look of pride and defiance.

Lola felt as if she were in a waking dream. The *Morning Herald* noted that "the young lady came, saw, and conquered," and the influential *Times* expressed gratitude for having finally seen "a Spanish dance by a Spaniard, executed after the Spanish fashion." The *Era* also devoted an entire column to her, and its critic concluded, "The only fault found with the donna's dance was that it was far too short." Of all the commentaries, Lola's favorite was offered by the critic at the *Evening Chronicle*, who highlighted the originality of her art as well as the ardor and irresistible passion that marked her dancing.

She had seamlessly adopted her new identity. She was an impostor, but in her physical appearance she was the spitting image of the archetypal Andalusian woman: dark, fiery, and free spirited. Her unusual accent and ardent spirit lent her story credibility. Elizabeth Gilbert James no longer existed—she was in the past, or so Lola believed. The dancer charmed the critics with her beauty and seductive arts. She told each one a different version of her life in Spain and her family's origins.

But her moment of glory was to be fleeting. Unknown to her, a group of men met with Lumley after her performance to inform him that his new star was an adulteress and a fraud. Someone in the audience had recognized the beautiful Mrs. James, the Irish-born wife of an officer of the East India Company. The impresario was less concerned about her infamous reputation than he was about the fact that she wasn't Spanish. If this came to light, it could mean the end of his career. Embarrassed, Lumley assured the men that he would take the appropriate measures. The next day, he summoned Lola to his office.

"I am sorry to say that serious accusations have been leveled against you. It seems that you are not Spanish, but Irish. You have lied not just to me but to all of London, which has treated you like a great star."

"Sir," the dancer replied calmly, "I am sure this is all a misunderstanding. Some spiteful rival has made up this story to sink my career."

"You cannot deny the facts," Lumley retorted, growing more agitated. "Several gentlemen insist that you are Mrs. James, former wife of a Company officer, and that your husband petitioned for divorce because of adultery. It is shameful!"

"I am quite offended by these accusations. Of course I am Spanish—just look at me," Lola declared, getting to her feet. "How humiliating that men would cast doubt on a poor woman who only wishes to earn a dignified living. I will take this matter to my lawyer."

"Mrs. Montez, as long as I am the director of this theater, you will not tread these boards again," Lumley declared, and sent her away.

Over the next few days, Lola strove to remain calm, but she was in a tight spot. Her dream of success as a dancer in London had evaporated. Lumley's accusations were true. On December 15, 1842, her husband had obtained his divorce. Though she had not appeared at the public trial, several witnesses had testified to her inappropriate conduct aboard the *Larkins*, including the maid who had spied on her and Anne Ingram, the pious captain's wife. Lola was now a divorced woman, but neither spouse could legally remarry as long as the other was alive. Now that she'd been found out, Lola realized that her past might not be so easy to leave behind.

When the news of her false identity appeared in the papers, a barrage of attacks began, spearheaded by the *Age*, a weekly. Lola flew into a rage when she read in its pages that

> [t]he 'Senorita' . . . whom he seeks to palm off on the credulity of Opera subscribers, is a personage who has received [*sic*] for some time past in the nomenclature of Mrs. James, and who, though a remarkably pretty woman, knows more of many other things than she knows of dancing and more of the locality of Clarges-street [a fashionable area of London] . . . than she does of the Teatro Real, Seville.

Determined to salvage her honor, she sent several letters to the editors of the major newspapers, expressing outrage. In one written to the *Morning Post* on June 12, 1843, she vehemently denied all accusations:

Sir:

I am a native of Seville; and in the year 1833, when ten years old, was sent to a Catholic lady at Bath, where I remained seven months, and was then taken back to my parents in Spain. From that period, until the 14th of April last, when I landed in England, *I have never set foot in this country, and I never saw London before in my life.* The imperfect English I speak I learned at Bath, and from an Irish nurse, who has been many years in my family. The misfortunes caused by the political events of my country, obliged me to seek a livelihood elsewhere, and I hoped that my native dances might be appreciated here, especially those that are new to the English . . .

Believe me to be your humble and obedient servant,
    Lola Montez

But the conflict didn't end there. She also turned up unannounced at the *Age*'s editorial offices, where she waited for four hours, smoking cigarettes endlessly and demanding to speak with somebody in charge. This incident only made her situation worse, since the weekly threatened to publish a list of names of the prominent figures associated with her, and Lola became afraid of causing an even bigger scandal that would close all doors to her for good. With public opinion arrayed firmly against her, she had no choice but to leave London. She had made her debut and triumphed in England's most prestigious theater, but now she was a marked woman.

After weeks during which she had time to ponder her future, a fortuitous new encounter helped her regain her happiness and pay her

debts. An old acquaintance, Lord Arbuthnot, who had also been a passenger on the *Larkins*, introduced her to a Prince Heinrich of the small
German territories of Reuss-Lobenstein and Reuss-Ebersdorf. Heinrich
was a bachelor of almost fifty, not particularly attractive, and very rich.
He was related to Queen Victoria and had come to London on a state
visit. When Lola met him, she spoke with him animatedly in French,
and the prince fell under the beautiful Spaniard's spell. Before they
parted, he whispered in her ear, "Madame Montez, if you ever visit
Germany, get in touch with me."

In late July 1843, Lola left London, telling her friends that she
was embarking on a European tour and should arrive in Russia by
autumn, where she planned to perform at the Imperial Theatres in Saint
Petersburg. In fact, she had no contracts or scheduled performances.
Fleeing from scandal, she boarded a ship that took her to the small city
of Hamburg, where she remained only briefly. Compared to London,
the German city seemed provincial and boring, with little to recommend it. Recalling Prince Heinrich's invitation, she decided to write
him a note announcing an impending journey to Leipzig.

The German prince had just arrived at his palace when he received
a letter from one Mrs. Montez. At first he did not remember who
she might be, but then he recalled Lola, the exuberant young Spanish
woman. Delighted to hear of her imminent arrival, he prepared to give
her a warm welcome. Heinrich was the lord and master of a small
principality with only twenty thousand subjects. His tranquil life was
spent hunting, inspecting his lands, and partaking of frequent feasts. By
tradition, all the men in his family were named Heinrich, so numbers
were used to indicate their birth order and to distinguish them from
the other males in the Reuss dynasty. His Highness Heinrich LXXII
did not receive many visitors; eager to impress his guest, he ordered
the gardens to be tidied and new flowers to be planted in her honor.
He also sent a luxurious carriage pulled by six white horses to collect
the dancer for the journey to Ebersdorf, the capital of the principality.

The servants charged with escorting Lola quickly found her behavior
to be completely inappropriate. Bored by the long, tedious journey, she
asked them to sit next to her and speak in French so they could share
court gossip. At one point she even climbed up to the coachman's box,
wanting to take the reins of the carriage. Seeing her intentions, the
coachman flatly refused to give her his seat. Furious, Lola took off one
of her gloves, slapped him in the face, and retreated indignantly into the
vehicle. The journey continued uneventfully until they pulled up outside the doors of the residential palace of Ebersdorf, where the prince,
attired in his white dress uniform, came out to meet her as a drum roll
signaled the honor guard to present arms. Lola emerged from the coach
with a majestic bearing and greeted him with an exaggerated curtsy.

"My dear Madame Montez, it is an enormous pleasure to have
you as a visitor. I hope you will find your days here unforgettable," the
prince said, kissing her hand.

"I am honored," Lola responded, startled by the grand reception.

"Come," he said, gallantly taking her arm, "I will introduce you
to the most distinguished members of the court and then we will dine
together at the palace."

Mrs. Montez made a splendid impression. At a reception that evening, she appeared elegantly dressed in a low-cut ivory silk dress with
flounces and her hair pulled up in a high bun with a few loose curls falling across her forehead, in the latest Parisian fashion. She was charming
and merry, responding in perfect French to all the questions about her
successful debut at Her Majesty's Theatre. At first she was surprised by
how friendly people were. She also had the chance to ride on horseback
and relished galloping through the leafy forests near the palace.

In short order, however, the eccentric artist and the prince began
to clash. Lola saw her host as an aristocratic character straight out of
an operetta, ludicrous and vain, and boring to boot. He wanted people
to call him "Serenissimus," and his grand airs provoked mockery from
his guest. Lola started making rude jokes about him, which shocked

the members of the court. Her favorite entertainment was playing with Turk, Heinrich's huge Saint Bernard, and they would stroll together through the formal gardens. One day she used her riding crop to cut some tulips, with which she fashioned a wreath to place around the neck of the prince's horse. The prince was not amused by this bit of whimsy. Fed up with his outlandish guest's antics, he only wanted to see the back of her as she left. But Heinrich had to keep up appearances in front of his subjects, so he arranged a visit to his beautiful hunting lodge, Waidmannsheil, where they would be served a hearty breakfast and could spend a pleasant day in the countryside. Lola was invited to sit at a table under a large oak with the other members of the party. Everything was proceeding normally until a musical band of unrefined forest wardens and miners started playing a melody, occasionally going out of tune. Rather than feigning approval, Lola started making faces and covering her ears with her hands. When a chorus of children joined the band to sing a folk tune, she couldn't take it anymore.

"Oh, that's awful!" she cried, leaping to her feet. "Get rid of that rabble!"

"Please calm down, madam. I love this music, and I am the master here."

"And I am the mistress," Lola replied scornfully.

At that unfortunate remark, the prince immediately excused himself from the table. He asked those present to remain seated and continue enjoying the performances. Lola apologized and started telling amusing anecdotes about her life as an artist. But Heinrich refused to disregard the incident. Upon returning to the palace, he called an urgent meeting with his advisers. Somebody suggested that Lola Montez would leave only if he offered her a lucrative engagement as an artist. The prince knew Karl Reissiger, kapellmeister at the court of the king of Saxony in nearby Dresden, and thought that he might help him. Heinrich wrote a letter of recommendation to the musician and had one of his aides deliver it to Lola that very evening. The envelope was addressed to Mrs.

James, a detail that she failed to notice. The dancer gave the prince's aide a pair of castanets, saying, "Here, a memento of my visit to your corner of the world."

After a week in Reuss-Ebersdorf, Lola packed her bags and climbed into a less elegant carriage that would take her to Dresden. The dancer arrived in the city in early August and got a room at the Hotel de Wien. With the letter of recommendation in hand, she called on Reissiger, who agreed to hire her. Like Lumley, the kapellmeister thought that a performance by a real Spanish dancer might make an entertaining addition to the intermissions. Lola debuted once more with "El Oleano," which had been such a raging success in London. But the audience in Dresden preferred Wagner to boleros and could not make head or tail of this strange dance. Opinions were sharply divided, but overall, her beauty made more of an impression than her artistic talent. She knew she needed to make good contacts and cultivate a healthy group of admirers. Again she tried to win over the press, giving several interviews in which she invented new lies. At the time, she was calling herself Doña María Dolores Montez, a Spanish dancer at Her Majesty's Theatre who was currently on her way to Saint Petersburg. She enjoyed claiming that she had triumphed on the stages of London and had not only hobnobbed with the nobility but also been invited to Buckingham Palace by Queen Victoria herself. She noted that, after they'd had tea together, the monarch had asked her for a private performance; Lola had sung *bulerías*, accompanied by a Spanish guitar. All these tales were published in the country's most prestigious press outlets, sparking the public's interest in this extravagant and unknown artist.

Lola Montez said farewell to Dresden with a final performance in which she danced "Los Boleros de Cadiz" for the first time, with scant success. She had rehearsed the act in London but never had the chance to debut it before her artistic career was interrupted. In less than a week, she'd managed to collect a large group of admirers who tossed bouquets from the boxes and applauded her enthusiastically. But opera was the most popular entertainment on Dresden stages, and a dancer had no place in that society. Once more she packed her bags and embarked on a new adventure. Thanks to her influential friendships, she'd obtained important letters of introduction and headed to Berlin. Her arrival there coincided with a dramatic incident that rocked the city. On the night of August 18, 1843, the majestic opera house was completely destroyed by fire. It was one of the city's most cherished monuments, an architectural gem erected by the Prussian king Friedrich the Great. The performances scheduled for the season were moved to the Schauspielhaus. The recommendation letters Lola had brought immediately bore fruit. Within a few days she had been hired as a guest performer at the royal theater. As always, she soon assembled a substantial group of hangers-on and journalists who published positive reviews of her art and beauty.

The dancer debuted once again with "El Oleano," but she wasn't a sensation this time either. One critic wrote, "If it is said of Taglioni that she writes world history with her feet, so can it be said of Donna Montez that she writes Casanova's *Memoirs* with her whole body." Her performance, which lasted only ten minutes and was accompanied by a monotonous melody, garnered a chilly and indifferent reception from the audience. Critics acclaimed her voluptuous beauty but questioned her talent. Lola was stunning in a close-fitting black velvet bodice, a checkered skirt, and a Córdoba-style hat fastened at the base of her head, with red and white camellias in her hair.

In the days that followed, she performed other pieces from her repertoire, such as "La Sevilliana" and "Los Boleros de Cadiz," but she was unable to inspire much interest, with audiences complaining that all her dances looked the same. But she remained popular in court circles, and one night she again performed her "Spanish dances," this time for the king of Prussia, Friedrich Wilhelm IV, at the theater in Potsdam. During the show, aides informed the monarch that his brother-in-law, Tsar Nicholas I of Russia, had arrived in Berlin on an official visit, whereupon Friedrich Wilhelm immediately left for the capital to greet him.

The visit of His Imperial Majesty the tsar was a huge event, and a series of military maneuvers and parades, banquets, and cultural activities were organized in his honor. The king hosted a gala lunch in the sumptuous palace of Sanssouci, in Potsdam, and invited a small group of dignitaries and members of the court. After the feast, Nicholas and Friedrich Wilhelm, trailed by their retinue, crossed through a leafy park of statues and marble fountains to reach the Neues Palais. The massive complex's south wing contained a rococo theater. That day it was presenting a memorable performance of Donizetti's opera *La fille du régiment*. When the first act ended, Lola appeared onstage to offer a dazzling rendition of "Los Boleros de Cadiz" for the tsar of Russia, the king of Prussia, and several members of the court. After the show, Lola delighted the jewel-bedecked ladies with risqué jokes and amusing anecdotes about her experiences on the London stage.

Nevertheless, over the next few days, the artist would become caught up in a new scandal. During her stay in Berlin, she had rented a spirited black horse and enjoyed riding it through the countryside on the outskirts of the city. On September 17, Nicholas and Friedrich Wilhelm presided over a large military parade in Friedrichsfelde, where the Prussian troops were going to show off the full extent of their might. Numerous checkpoints were set up to maintain security and prevent the public from entering the section reserved for the royal court and other prominent figures. Lola arrived astride her horse, dressed in a flattering riding outfit and a top hat with a veil. Seeing the assembled crowd, she tried to push into the restricted area to get closer to the array of dignitaries onstage. A Prussian officer, seeing her intention, galloped over and stopped her horse by grabbing its reins.

"How dare you! You don't know who I am," Lola protested, striking him with her riding whip.

"Desist, madam!" he exclaimed, bewildered at her violent reaction. "I give the orders here. Please follow me."

"I promise you, you'll regret it. His Majesty the king will hear about this!" she replied.

Her objections were of no use. Lola was forced to retreat as onlookers laughed and hissed. The next day, a judicial officer came to her door and delivered a summons. According to several witnesses, she flew into a rage, tore up the document, and stomped on the shredded paper. This behavior garnered a new charge: contempt of court. The accusation was a serious one, involving a possible sentence of five to thirteen years in prison. Thanks to her connections, the matter went no further, but it served as fantastic, unexpected publicity for the dancer. The story of her attacking the officer spread like wildfire in the foreign press and caused an uproar in the major capital cities of Europe. A number of papers published a cartoon of Lola on their front covers that depicted her brandishing her whip and grabbing a Prussian officer by the arm as if he were a child. After the incident, to escape the charges pending against her, she decided to leave Berlin. She told her admirers that she needed to continue her journey to Saint Petersburg. One morning, without saying goodbye to anybody, she climbed into a coach and left for Warsaw.

Around this time, Lola's stepfather, Patrick Craigie, who had been promoted to adjutant-general, received orders to leave Calcutta to help establish a new headquarters in Allahabad. Eliza and her husband packed their things and headed up the Ganges with a small fleet. A few days into their journey, Craigie fell ill, and they stopped in Dinapore so he could be seen by the army doctor stationed there. Eliza was forced to disembark once more in the very place where, twenty years earlier, she'd been widowed. Fortune did not smile on Patrick Craigie any more fondly, and he passed away on October 8, 1843. He was forty-four years old, and he was buried with military honors in the same cemetery where Edward Gilbert's remains lay. Lola would not find out about his death until several months later, and the news affected her deeply. Her stepfather had been her only remaining emotional link to a past that was becoming more and more remote.

Lola arrived in Warsaw in late October and stayed at the Hotel de Rome. As usual, she was armed with numerous letters of introduction that would open the doors of the theater world. The country was in turmoil, living under a terrible dictatorship. The Russians had invaded, and Poland's fate was in the hands of Tsar Nicholas I. In 1831 an uprising led by a group of young Polish officers had been brutally quashed. The territory was now governed by the tsar's prince regent, Ivan Fyodorovich Paskevich, the same general who'd crushed the insurgents with his army. He was a cruel, sinister man who implemented the orders he received from Saint Petersburg with an iron fist. The Polish nobles had been exiled to Siberia, and students who protested were deported to the Ural Mountains. Though the atmosphere in the streets was tense, people still attended the theater to forget their troubles for a few hours.

Within days, Lola already had a circle of loyal admirers that included such influential figures as the banker and industrialist Piotr Steinkeller and the editor of the *Warsaw Gazette*, Antoni Lesznowski. Just as she'd done in London, the dancer won over the press with her beauty, boldness, and charm. One critic listed in an article the twenty-six (of a possible twenty-seven) "perfections" that Lola possessed, including her calves, which the critic compared to "the lowest rungs of a Jacob's ladder leading to Heaven." On the morning of her debut, the *Courier* published a lengthy piece extolling the dancer's art, outlining her noble Spanish origins and describing the spell she cast on her audiences.

With this kind of publicity, it's no surprise that people were eager to see the celebrated artist from Seville's Teatro Real and London's Covent Garden who had come to Warsaw as part of a tour that would take her to Saint Petersburg. Lola signed an initial contract for five performances at Warsaw's Grand Theatre, one of the most spectacular venues in the world. The president of the Warsaw Theatre Directorate, General Abramowicz, was the prince regent's former comrade in arms and the

city's chief of police. A man of fifty with bushy sideburns and an imposing bearing, he was a great aficionado of opera and dance, as well as
of beautiful women. Lola immediately charmed him and made her
debut at the theater by dancing a cachucha during the intermission of
Il barbiere di Siviglia. Gracefully shimmying her hips and mischievously
lifting her skirt to the rhythm of the castanets, she was able to win over
the audience. But the idyll between the officer and the dancer would
be a fleeting one.

On the night of her debut, General Abramowicz offered to accompany her to the hotel in her carriage. During the short journey, he made
uncouth advances, and Lola ordered the vehicle to stop and made him
get out.

"What are you thinking? I am an artist!" she yelled in a fury. "If
you are ever so crude with me again, I will not hesitate to denounce
you in the press."

"You've lost your mind; you don't know who you're talking to. I
can have you arrested right this minute and expelled from the country
without a second thought. You'll regret this, I promise you that," the
officer cried, angry and perplexed.

"Driver, take me to my hotel at once," Lola instructed without
looking back.

In the middle of a heavy snowstorm, General Abramowicz had
been kicked out of his own coach and was forced to walk home in the
freezing cold. The fallout from this incident, which swiftly became a
favorite subject of gossip in Warsaw, didn't take long. Lola performed
as scheduled, and though the more sophisticated audience members
considered her dancing an insult to good taste, her dynamic personality and presentation drew applause from everybody. Hopeful and a bit
naive, she thought that her contract might be renewed and that she
could stay a while longer in the city.

While Lola was preparing to give her final scheduled performance in Warsaw, dancing other Spanish numbers from her repertoire,

Abramowicz was obsessing over how to get rid of her. This shameless, disrespectful woman had humiliated him, and he didn't exactly appreciate her political opinions or the flock of young Polish radicals with whom she associated. In interviews, she claimed to be against Russian oppression and extolled the courage of the Polish people in the face of having lost all their freedoms. In addition, Lola had requested that her protectors hire a claque to applaud wildly at all her events; on nights when she performed, Steinkeller would send the workers from his factory and Lesznowski a large group of typesetters from his newspaper, all of them with instructions to cheer for the dancer.

The theater director arranged for a subtle act of vengeance. On Tuesday, November 14, when Lola finished dancing "La Sevilliana," the audience's enthusiastic ovation was countered by the hisses and jeering of men hired by Abramowicz. For her second number, she danced "Los Boleros de Cadiz" as if nothing had happened—until the curtain fell. Then she reappeared in the middle of the stage, her face indignant, and demanded that the orchestra stop playing. In French, Lola thanked those who had applauded her performance and welcomed her to Warsaw. Then she pointed at the box where Abramowicz and other grandees were sitting and exclaimed, "*Messieurs et mesdames,* one man alone is responsible for this insult! There is the scoundrel who seeks revenge upon a poor woman for refusing to submit to his scandalous proposals!"

Silence fell over the theater, and then the audience burst into applause, with some shouting "Brava, Lola, brava!" If the theater director's aim had been to take the artist down, he had achieved the opposite.

The news of Lola's denunciation of the city's highest authority spread like wildfire through the kingdom. Now the general needed to get rid of her before she became a symbol of struggle for young Polish nationalists. He issued an order that she be held under house arrest. Whenever she found herself penned in, Lola always reacted violently. This time, she pulled a dagger on the officer posted at the door of her room. When Paskevich, the prince regent, learned what had happened, he ordered her expelled from the country immediately, though he warned his men, "Remember, she's a Spanish woman. They've always got a dagger stashed in their garter."

The powerful prince regent had his own motives for wanting her gone. After a performance one night, he'd invited her to a private room to drink a glass of champagne, to seduce her. She found the bald, charmless, and toothless sexagenarian repulsive. After examining her as if she were a racehorse, he exclaimed out loud, "Well, there's nothing special about you." Lola responded coldly, "Your Excellency, if you think you've just told me something new, you're mistaken. I've heard it before in London and in Berlin." Paskevich didn't take the hint and showed up at her dressing room the next day with a bouquet of flowers and a leather pouch containing a magnificent pearl necklace. She rejected the gift and demanded that he leave. Poland's most powerful and feared man would not forget the incident—nor would he forgive it.

At first Lola refused to leave, but upon reflection, she decided to comply with the expulsion order for fear that she might be thrown in jail. On the cold morning of November 22, she was escorted in a coach by one Officer Rospopov to the Prussian border at Posen. Even this young man, under strict instructions not to speak with his charge, succumbed to her charms. He wrote ecstatically of her in his memoirs: "Lola Montez was beauty itself, perfection incarnate. She had blue eyes, thick black lashes, finely arched eyebrows, abundant, thick black hair with bluish highlights, a supple figure. In addition, she was full of charm, gay, amiable, seductive, and at the same time naive as a child." A few admirers, having learned of her departure, attempted to follow for a few miles, running after the carriage and calling her name.

Despite how it ended, Lola always remembered her time in Poland fondly and identified with its brave people's struggle. She was not the only victim of the repressions that resulted from her scandal. The police arrested a large number of people who had clapped for her at the theater, along with her influential protectors, the banker Steinkeller and the newspaperman Lesznowski. General Abramowicz would not allow anyone to undermine his authority.

In the first days of 1844, Lola continued toward Saint Petersburg, where she planned to dance for the tsar and his family. On January 4, she arrived in the walled city of Königsberg, where, historically, the kings of Prussia had been crowned. Her reputation preceded her, and all her performances drew capacity crowds to see her Spanish dances, which were little known in those parts. A review published in a local paper after her debut gives an idea of the positive reception: "Donna Lola Montez has conquered us. Königsberg need not be ashamed that it pays homage to the beautiful dancer from the fiery South, that Northern eyes glowed brighter at the sight of her and offered her the flowery wreath of full approbation, which such a favored daughter of agile Terpsichore deserves." From there, she traveled by coach through the snowy Baltic winter, enduring the unaccustomed cold. She still had hundreds of miles to go.

As it turned out, her letters of recommendation were of no use in the capital of the Russian Empire. She had no friends or protectors to rely on. Tsar Nicholas I, one of the richest and most powerful men in the world, was an autocrat known for the strict control he maintained over his vast territory. Before Lola arrived in the city, he'd already heard about her scandalous comportment in Warsaw. Though he had seen her perform in Berlin and admired her grace and beauty, he wasn't about to allow a revolution to break out in his territory.

And so Lola Montez never made her debut on the stages of the legendary Bolshoi Theatre in Moscow. Nor was she invited to the tsar's court, the most luxurious and opulent in all of Europe. The press, which operated under heavy censorship, did not mention her presence in the capital. She was immensely frustrated. In Russia, the great Marie Taglioni had achieved enormous success as a principal dancer of the Imperial Ballet and charged a hefty sum for each performance.

Dejected, Lola was forced to recognize that her trip had been a complete failure: "I feel humiliated by the treatment I've received in Russia. I thought that Tsar Nicholas, an opera lover, would be more sensitive with artists. The Romanovs lack good manners and have no education."

The return journey to Germany was exhausting, and Lola found the monotony of the vast plains blanketed with snow and raked by wind to be depressing. Over the course of a month and a half, she traveled more than a thousand miles in slow carriages and stopped in an endless succession of squalid inns. Few women ventured alone into these dangerous regions. She was perpetually cold because she'd come unprepared for such an extreme climate, and she did not always have the opportunity to eat a warm meal or sleep in a good bed. In those interminable gray days, she had time to reflect: "I must learn to control myself and be more prudent. My reputation is in tatters, but I still have my ambition. Numerous gentlemen stand ready to pay my bills, and I refuse to give up. Never." Very soon she would add to her list of lovers a musical genius who was acclaimed all across Europe.

CHAPTER 4

The Lioness of Paris

Lying in bed and slowly smoking a cigarette, Lola was overcome with nostalgia. Whenever she felt lonely, she would close her eyes and travel to the magical settings of her childhood in India. In those moments, she yearned for Denali, her sweet voice and her tender attentions. She hadn't forgotten the smells of smoke and damp earth, the hot monsoon wind, the humidity that had clung to her skin, those vibrant landscapes where she'd grown up unfettered and carefree. By now her mother had learned through the press that she was a dancer. Her response had been to don mourning garb and inform all her friends in Calcutta that her daughter was dead, that they would never see each other again or be in touch. With all her soul, Lola hated the selfish, superficial woman who'd never loved her. She still remembered her mother's words during the dazzling gala in Simla: "You were born to get on my nerves."

Nearly four years had passed since she'd left India, and it felt like an eternity. She imagined what her life would have been like if she hadn't ditched Thomas, if she'd resigned herself to being the perfect wife of an East India Company officer. She was glad to have left that hollow life behind. Though her behavior had caused pain for the people she loved, she didn't regret a thing. At that time, strong, independent, passionate women were a threat, a provocation.

She'd just arrived in Dresden and hadn't yet recovered from the long, humiliating trip to Saint Petersburg. She was almost out of money, with just enough left to pay for a hotel room for a few nights, but she still had some jewels that had been gifts from friends and protectors. With her pride injured by Tsar Nicholas's disdain, she pondered how to revive her artistic career. She was twenty-three years old, at the height of her beauty, and had performed on the world's most important stages, but she hadn't achieved the triumph she dreamed of. She felt defeated and frustrated because the press chattered more about her scandals and love affairs than it did about her talent. And after the events in Warsaw, she now had a reputation as a rebellious, violent woman that would only make her future more difficult.

While leafing through the newspaper one day, she read that the famous Hungarian composer and pianist Franz Liszt was on tour and would soon be giving a concert in the German city of Dessau. She decided to meet him in the hope that he would help her find success.

Lola had set her sights high. The man she hoped to win over was an international celebrity, the best paid musician in all of Europe. Liszt was thirty-two years old and at the peak of his career. He was given honors, his tours drew a devoted public, and royalty competed to entertain him. From a dull, pale child prodigy who could barely sit on a stool when he gave his first concert at age nine, he had become the greatest pianist of all time, a man who not only played with unprecedented virtuosity but also was a composer, conductor, and benefactor of other emerging artists, such as Richard Wagner. Along with his enormous talent, he had a magnetic physical attractiveness that stirred people's passions. Slender and well dressed, with elegant manners, a melancholy air, and medium-length blond hair, he looked like a prince from a fairy tale. Lola knew of his reputation as a ladies' man and his weakness for beautiful, intelligent noblewomen. High-society ladies fought over his silk handkerchiefs and kidskin gloves, which they preserved as devoutly as holy relics. Some swooned at his concerts, tossed flowers in his path, and shouted compliments at him. Lola had heard that in Saint Petersburg a group of frenzied women had surrounded his carriage and the police had been forced to intervene so he could reach the theater safe and sound.

On February 24, 1844, Lola and a few friends traveled to Dessau to attend Liszt's recital and saw for themselves the mass hysteria he inspired. Sitting in a crowded theater box, she waited eagerly for the artist who was so universally lauded to appear. Liszt paid attention to every detail in his performances and greeted the auditorium with a majestic bow, which was received with cheers. The musician had a prodigious memory and could recall any music, no matter how complicated. As he performed his impassioned melodies, he shot seductive glances at the ladies seated in the first rows. He was so irresistibly magnetic that his most devoted admirers threw jewels onto the stage and screamed hysterically.

Lola was deeply moved when she heard Liszt play his new version of the Paternoster that evening. She'd never felt anything like it in her life. His concerts were works of showmanship in which the musician shone like a massive star. After the performance, the audience burst into thunderous applause. At evening's end, a mutual friend introduced the dancer to Liszt; when their eyes met, the two immediately felt drawn to each other. Liszt, always a sucker for feminine beauty, was incredibly gallant to the Spaniard. Lola was stunning in a low-cut emerald-green velvet dress that left her shoulders bare. Her long hair was pulled back in the current fashion, with a center part and a bun on either side of her head, giving her a girlish air.

"Mr. Liszt, you are enormously talented," Lola said.

"I am flattered that you enjoyed my concert. It has been a very special night for me. The audience was so engaged," he said, gazing at her steadily.

"I understand that you will soon be touring through my country; perhaps you would find it interesting to learn about Spanish customs. I would be happy to teach you a few things."

"I am very interested in Spanish music. It will be a pleasure to chat with you. You know where to find me, Madame Montez," he said, kissing her hand.

Liszt was unaware of Lola's scandals and the reputation that preceded her. To him, she was only another female admirer with whom to enjoy himself. The next day, the dancer met him at the theater, and they took a long buggy ride through the forest. After nightfall, they shared a romantic dinner at an inn, and Lola told him her life story. She described her happy childhood in Seville and how she'd learned to dance flamenco from a Romany woman. Her lies were so convincing and told so vividly that the musician never doubted her for a moment. The pair spent the rest of the night together. After the crudeness and violence of her husband, Thomas, and her brief relationship with George Lennox, who'd shown her off like a trophy, Lola was captivated by the musician's sensitivity and refinement.

Within a few days, Lola and Liszt were seen together all over town, and newspapers across Europe were soon discussing the romance between the Andalusian dancer and the genius composer. Impulsive as usual, she suggested that they unite their artistic paths, and he agreed to have her accompany him on his European tour. Lola moved her belongings into a room adjoining his. "I want you to love me. I want you to love no one else more than you do me. Like all my countrywomen, I do not know what compassion is," she wrote, baring her heart to him.

Liszt was at a painful crossroads in his personal life. His relationship with his lover and companion, the countess Marie d'Agoult, had gone cold. In 1835 the beautiful aristocrat with blond locks and porcelain skin had left her husband and family to follow the young musician, whose baby she was carrying. For ten years they'd had a passionate, stormy romance, living much of that time in Switzerland and Italy. They had three children, but now Marie, tired of his long absences and dalliances with other women, had left him and returned to Paris with the little ones. She had been the great love of his life so far, and his most enduring relationship. Lola had heard about the countess and felt a degree of sympathy for her. The fearless, liberated, and highly educated woman—she was publishing books under the pen name Daniel Stern—reminded her of herself. Marie hadn't hesitated to give up her marriage and social standing to run into her lover's arms.

In Dresden, Lola accompanied Liszt to his rehearsals and attended a memorable recital at which he performed Beethoven. As usual, when the performance was over, the composer found himself surrounded by female admirers demanding autographs. In public, he acted haughty and aloof; he never kissed ladies' hands, expecting them to kiss his. For the first time in a long time, Lola wasn't the center of attention. Nobody noticed her; she had become the musician's shadow. The unfamiliar experience wasn't entirely agreeable. "They worship him as if he were a god; I've never seen anything like it. I don't know how he feels about me, he's so enigmatic and silent, but I do know that no man has awakened such passion in me before this. I love him and want him to be mine alone," she confessed to a friend.

On February 29, Liszt invited Lola to join him in attending Wagner's great opera *Rienzi*, which was being presented in his honor. He had crossed paths with the German composer a number of times, admired his talent, and was his primary promoter. Lola found the five-hour work, set in medieval Italy, interminable. Unable to understand German, she nearly fell asleep. During one of the multiple intermissions, the couple left their box to congratulate the tenor for his outstanding performance in the main role. In his dressing room, they ran into Wagner, and Liszt enthusiastically praised his great operatic work. The German maestro recalled the encounter in his biography: "Liszt's curious lifestyle at the time, which constantly surrounded him with distracting and annoying elements, kept us on this occasion from achieving any productive rapport." The distracting element was Lola, who was clinging to the virtuoso's arm and whom Wagner described as "a heartless, demonic being."

A few days later, Liszt gave a benefit concert for his good friend the Italian tenor Luigi Pantaleoni in the hotel ballroom. Lola accompanied him and again witnessed the passion the musician aroused. The tenor wasn't the best—he had a weak voice and used too much falsetto—but Liszt shone. Though she'd never been the jealous type, it drove Lola crazy to watch his irritating gaggle of admirers follow him to the hotel with love letters that he would read and toss into the fireplace. Lola was also jealous of the Countess d'Agoult, believing that Liszt was still in love with her and hoped they would reconcile. The dancer wanted to leave Dresden as soon as possible and continue on to Leipzig, where Liszt was supposed to give another concert. But their relationship began to deteriorate. They were both arrogant and temperamental, and they weren't used to taking orders from anybody. Liszt expected women to submit to his will and play a discreet second fiddle. He found his lover's aggressive personality and moodiness disconcerting. He started acting out by returning to the hotel later and later and spending very little time with her.

During his stay in Dresden, a group of distinguished members of high society organized a banquet lunch in Liszt's honor. Though Lola wasn't invited, she managed to persuade the musician to let her join him. When they arrived at the restaurant, the dancer realized that the tenor Pantaleoni hadn't been invited either and insisted on sending for him. When Pantaleoni arrived at the gathering, he seemed upset to have been included only at the last minute. He was rude to those present and even came to blows with Gottfried Semper, the architect who had designed Dresden's opera house. Lola was so shocked that she berated him in front of everybody. The man looked at her with scorn and said, "Madam, do not trifle with me. I am not a Prussian gendarme like the ones you are accustomed to intimidating."

"I am sorry about your manners," she responded. "You are very upset and don't know what you are saying."

"Lola Montez! My good friend Liszt may not know who you are, but I know you've been expelled from several European cities because of your scandalous behavior. What makes you think you can give me lessons?"

"If I did give you lessons, they would be music lessons. You have a terrible voice and a terrible stage presence," she said mockingly.

Not content with having delivered that acerbic remark, she slapped him with her glove.

Pantaleoni replied with a gesture so coarse that Lola nearly fainted. The guests couldn't believe what was happening. They got up from their tables, indignant, and the gathering came to an ignominious end. Liszt watched the entire dispute without intervening, not wanting to embarrass Lola in front of his friends. But the unpleasant incident opened his eyes. He was a free, independent man, and Lola was smothering him with her demands. Nor was he willing to be involved with a volatile woman who put his career at risk.

The next day, the musician awoke very early, quietly packed his bags, and stole out of the hotel room while Lola was still sleeping, locking the door behind him. Fearing her violent reaction, he summoned the hotel manager and told him what was happening.

"I'd like to ask you a favor. Take this money and don't open Miss Montez's door until lunchtime," he said, pressing the key and a few bills into the manager's hand.

"Mr. Liszt, please, I don't want your money. I'll do as you ask—we've known each other a long time."

"You don't understand," he insisted. "When my beloved discovers I've left her, she will fly into a rage, and I am concerned she may destroy some of the furniture. This money is an advance on any damages that occur."

"I understand. Get into your carriage and don't worry. You know I'm a discreet man."

And the musician left.

A few hours later, Lola woke up and found that Liszt's belongings were gone and that he'd locked her in her own hotel room. Desperate, she pounded on the door and tried to jump out the window. Just as the composer had imagined, Lola then unleashed her fury on the furnishings and smashed everything she could get her hands on, including several pitchers. Nothing could calm the rage she felt in that moment.

Sobbing, she reviled Liszt for his cowardice. Now she had no idea what to do or where to go next.

Once she had calmed down, she noticed an envelope with her name on it on the desk. Inside was a substantial sum of money and several letters of introduction from Liszt to his influential friends in the Paris press. In addition, the musician promised to arrange her debut at the Paris Opéra when he returned to the French capital in early April.

Though it took Lola a while to forgive him for not saying goodbye, neither of them spoke ill of the other. In his memoirs, Franz Liszt recalled Lola with these words: "You have to see her! She is ever new, ever changing, ever creative! She is a true poet! The genius of charm and love! All other women pale beside her!" Lola didn't want to stay a day longer in the city where she'd experienced the greatest humiliation of her romantic life. The next morning, she bought a ticket on the stagecoach to Paris.

Lola arrived in the French capital in mid-March. Though she found the city to be bustling and impressive, it did not yet have the splendor it would achieve during the Second Empire. Louis-Philippe I was king at the time, and the city was a chaotic, foul-smelling place with more than a million inhabitants crowded into miserable slums. There was no sewage system or potable water, and most of the population lived in extreme poverty. The streets were poorly paved, and a powerful stench permeated the entire city. On the Île de la Cité, the houses were still made of mud, and the alleyways were so narrow that the roofs touched. Epidemics of typhus and cholera frequently swept through the neighborhoods. Despite these grim circumstances, Paris was the dance mecca and cultural center of Europe. Artists, bohemians, and intellectuals came from all over the world seeking fortune and entertainment. It was also the capital of pleasure, and its most famous courtesans held court at parties, balls, and salons.

At first Lola found a room in a modest hotel on the boulevard des Italiens, near the Church of Notre-Dame-de-Lorette. The neighborhood, with its damp old houses, was frequented by prostitutes—known as *"lorettes"*—and was home to renowned artists. The painter Eugène Delacroix had his apartment and studio at number 54 on the same street, and not far away, the writer George Sand was sharing a garret with her lover, the pianist Frédéric Chopin. Lola wasted no time and immediately went around handing out Liszt's letters of introduction to journalists and prominent men from the theater world. She soon discovered that in Paris a beautiful, bold, and seductive woman like herself would have no trouble making friends.

Her first interview was with Jules Janin, the powerful—and fearsome—critic from the *Journal des débats* and one of Liszt's close friends. As usual, to make a good impression on the critic, she selected one of her most alluring dresses. Fascinated by her dynamic personality, Jules offered to write a flattering column to introduce the Spanish dancer to Parisian society. In the piece, which was published on March 18, before he had even seen her perform, he spoke glowingly of "her unmatched artistic talent."

Lola knew that competition in Paris was fierce and that the world's most prominent ballerinas dominated the city's stages. The audience was still spellbound by the charm and sensitivity of Marie Taglioni, whose performance of *La sylphide* at the Paris Opéra in 1832 had made her a star. She had unintentionally become a trendsetter by being among the first to dance en pointe. The ladies of high society loved her pale skin and fragile appearance; they wore their hair like hers, "*à la sylphide*," and her ballet outfit, with its white bodice and sheer skirts—the precursor to the classic tutu—became all the rage. When they attended a play or a dance performance, women would swath themselves in clouds of gauze and tulle to look like nymphs or fairies. Taglioni was forty years old, and though she didn't perform often, she still embodied a myth for her devotees.

But the great diva of the moment was Carlotta Grisi, nicknamed "the lady with the violet eyes." This beautiful, elegant Italian dancer was about the same age as Lola and had achieved enormous success with the ballet *Giselle*. Few could compete with her grace and technical skill. Though the Spanish dances in Lola's repertoire sparked some interest, nothing could compare to the great Romantic-era ballets. In addition, several popular dances were in vogue. The polka was at its zenith, and the cancan, a frenetic, unabashed dance in which young women showed their undergarments by lifting their skirts as they shouted and kicked in the air, was scandalizing respectable ladies. Lola, who had always compensated for her lack of talent with the art of seduction onstage, now had to compete with beautiful women who danced in very little clothing and shamelessly flashed their garters.

Despite the many distractions the city offered, Lola focused on her career and prepared to conquer Paris as a dancer. She started taking lessons from Hippolyte Barrez, a choreographer at the prestigious Paris Opéra. Jules Janin had promised to pull strings to get her an audition with the theater's director, Léon Pillet. In the meantime, thanks to her charisma and her letters of recommendation, she was able to meet other influential men, some of them members of the famous Jockey Club, an elite group of wealthy gentlemen who loved horse racing as much as they did beautiful women. These aristocrats were regular patrons of the theater and opera and enthusiastically supported their favorite ballerinas, many of whom were also their lovers. Lola, an excellent rider even if she could not afford anything so luxurious as a horse of her own, attended the lively races the club organized in the Bois de Boulogne, a stomping ground for the crème de la crème of Parisian society. Joseph Méry, a novelist, poet, and playwright, was one of her great supporters. Lola had never met such an erudite and brilliant man. It was a pleasure to listen to him because "he knew everything" and had an incredible memory and an exuberant imagination. He knew something of Lola's past, having witnessed the incident with the Prussian officer in Berlin. Méry introduced her in the capital's artistic and intellectual circles and initially helped pay her bills. He was eager to have her meet his dear friend Alexandre Dumas. The celebrated and prolific novelist was a mainstay of Paris's literary scene. Extravagant, endearing, and prodigiously talented, he was the center of attention at the fashionable salons. His latest novel, *The Three Musketeers*, would make him rich and famous. Dumas, yet another man with a weakness for beautiful women, soon became Lola's friend and one of her protectors.

One night Méry invited her to dinner at the Café de Paris, where the literati met every week. Located on the corner of the rue Taitbout, it occupied the entire building and was the general headquarters for all of Paris's players. The place was famous for its food, and its loyal clientele included princes, artists, millionaires, aristocrats, and prominent politicians. For this special occasion, Lola chose a striking black silk dress with a square neckline and flounces, and she wore two red carnations in her marvelous dark hair. As accessories, she had her ever-present fan and a stunning Chinese silk shawl draped over her shoulders. The young woman made her triumphal entrance on Méry's arm, and everyone immediately turned to stare. There they were, not just Dumas but all of the most widely read and influential authors of the moment: Théophile Gautier, Alfred de Musset, Honoré de Balzac, and George Sand, among others.

"Dear friends, this is the friend of Liszt I've told you about, the famous Lola Montez. Let's give her a round of applause!" Méry exclaimed as his guest took her seat with the group.

"I understand that you are a lady of a most intrepid nature," Dumas commented, looking her up and down.

"My dear Dumas," Méry responded, "here you have a real musketeer! In Berlin, this beautiful Spaniard faced down a Prussian officer, and she defied a Russian ruler in front of an entire theater audience in Warsaw."

"It is clear you don't lack courage, Madame Montez," the famous critic Théophile Gautier noted. "But if you want to triumph at the Opéra, you must be at the level of the great women of classical dance. I'm looking forward to seeing you perform."

Lola would never forget that lively dinner with Paris's most celebrated authors. Among those present, she found George Sand to be the most fascinating. The famous writer—her given name was Aurore Dupin—was fond of Liszt and so was very kind to Lola. At the time, she was forty years old and living with Frédéric Chopin, a sickly, temperamental young man whose talent was starting to flourish. Lola described Sand as "a large, masculine woman with coarse features" and was startled to observe that she dressed like a man. That night, Sand was wearing a long jacket cinched at the waist with a thick gold cord, a wool waistcoat, trousers, a silk tie, and a wide-brimmed felt hat. She was attractive and passionate, with huge black eyes and short, *garçon*-style hair, which men and women alike found alluring. She had divorced her husband, and her long list of lovers was the talk of Paris. Like Lola, she smoked tobacco and was an excellent horsewoman. They were able to chat for only a little while, but it was inevitable that they would get along smashingly. The two were both free spirited and transgressive, refusing to accept the limits placed on women at the time. Late into the night, having downed several glasses of champagne, Lola ventured to ask why she was wearing men's clothing.

"It's not a costume, darling," Sand replied, smiling. "It's an attitude toward life. It's cheaper and easier to dress like this. Plus, I can go unnoticed and spend time in places that are forbidden to women. You should try it one day. Men's clothing is very comfortable, and corsets don't let you breathe. They're suffocating."

"You are indeed right about that, but we female dancers must sacrifice to be beautiful. I seduce my audience with my physical appearance, and I think most men prefer me in a skirt."

"You seduce with your personality, Lola; you are fearless and you know how to stand up for yourself. You're a real lioness, and you'll soon have Paris in the palm of your hand," the writer said.

In that lighthearted, convivial atmosphere, Lola was in her element and won everybody over. As the evening came to an end, she thanked those present for the warm welcome they'd extended. Right then and there, her hosts promised to help her secure a theater engagement. Before parting, Alexandre Dumas murmured in her ear, "Three months from now, we'll be clapping for you at the Opéra, you can bet on it." George Sand raised her glass in a toast, and the entire table shouted her name in unison: "To Lola Montez, the lioness of Paris."

That successful introduction into Parisian society would soon bear fruit. Her new friends immediately launched a pressure campaign, waged via the papers, on Pillet, who flatly refused to invite a dancer distinguished only for her beauty onto the Opéra's stage. On March 24, the young journalist Pier Angelo Fiorentino, one of Lola's devoted admirers, published an article in *Le corsaire* in which he complained that "even though Lola Montez dances the most voluptuous boleros and is probably the only woman who can perform that gypsy dance with such fiery passion," she was being denied the opportunity to perform. That same day, the *Journal des théâtres* declared, "There is no hope of seeing Lola Montez dance at the Opéra, but is this the only stage on which Europe's most enlightened public may applaud a talent that merits admiration?" For his part, Alexandre Dumas asked Rosine Stoltz, a mezzo-soprano at the Opéra and Pillet's lover, to intervene on Lola's behalf. This captivating artist with an incredible voice was friends with the most powerful men of the era and was delighted to do a favor for the novelist.

Just a few days later, Méry gave Lola the news she so longed to hear. With great excitement, he told her that on Wednesday, March 27, after the evening performance of *Der Freischütz* at the Paris Opéra, the choreographer had added a short piece in which Lola would perform her Spanish dances. Titled "Le bal de Don Juan," it would allow her to show off her grace and mischievous spirit. She had been in the city only two weeks, but she was about to make her debut in the great temple of dance.

On the night of the show, Lola felt genuine stage fright. The theater was large and opulent, with a capacity of more than a thousand and excellent acoustics. Its interior was luxuriously fitted out with silk-draped boxes, red velvet seats, and a giant crystal chandelier that hung from the vaulted ceiling. Though her friends had hired the services of the famous Auguste Levasseur, the Paris Opéra's "claque king," who supplied artists with guaranteed applause, she was concerned about the devotees of Elssler and Taglioni who were lying in wait. The city was full of theaters, but Lola had chosen to perform at the most prestigious, one with a demanding and ruthless audience. If she failed, it would mean the end of her career as a dancer.

In her dressing room, she tried to relax by drinking a glass of champagne while doing her makeup in front of the mirror. The die was cast, and there was no turning back. The house was packed that night, and the overflowing audience included her loyal friends from the Café de Paris and the debauchees of the Jockey Club. When she appeared onstage, in a tight red bodice and a white skirt with gold sparkles that bared her knees, the orchestra played the first notes of the cachucha. Lola began to move and leap to the rhythm of the castanets. Immediately, she was aware of the public's chilly reception and the smiles of a few gentlemen in the first row, which she interpreted as mocking her. At one point in her performance, feeling that she wasn't being taken seriously, she

stopped short and, with an agile movement, removed one of her garters, tossing it scornfully into the audience. A young man, Alfred de
Bellemont, caught it as his seatmates laughed and held it high as if it
were a prized trophy. Though the incident caused a commotion in the
theater, Lola kept dancing as if nothing had happened.

When she returned to the stage to perform "Los Boleros de Cadiz,"
she was received with wan enthusiasm and a few hisses. The audience
was impatient for the polka that was scheduled to be performed by
Monsieur Coballi and Mademoiselle Marie as the final act. The dance
had burst onto the great theater's stage only two days earlier, with enormous success. After the performance, Méry went to her dressing room,
where he found her teary eyed and defeated.

"My dear, you were wonderful. You captivated everyone," he said
to cheer her up.

Lola let him get no further. "Don't lie to me, Méry. This stupid,
arrogant audience was against me from the start. I saw their grimaces,
their smirking faces. They were mocking me. I gave them what they
deserved."

"Don't be upset, you knew something like that might happen. But
chin up—other doors will open. There are other theaters in Paris that
are sure to appreciate your art."

"The press will attack me mercilessly. I don't even want to think
about what they're going to say about me tomorrow . . ."

"Lola, in Paris what matters is that they're talking about you,
regardless of what they're saying."

Just as she feared, all the papers were buzzing about the incident. *Le
siècle* highlighted the unique way Lola Montez had managed to insert
herself into the history of the Paris Opéra:

> Mlle. Lola moved toward the footlights once more,
> waving between her fingers the ribbon that had just
> encircled her leg, and, fortifying herself with her most

rebellious graces, threw the ribbon to the spectators.
Mlle. Fanny Elssler is content to throw kisses to the
audience when she dances the cachucha, but Mlle.
Elssler is only a Spaniard from Berlin; Mlle. Lola Montez,
a Spaniard by blood, throws her garter to her admirers,
which is quite another Andalusian style.

Another critic remarked, "The beautifully agile woman with the
flashing eye was warmly received, but the dancer was rejected, and Lola
Montez will not appear at the Opéra again." Only Fiorentino, the critic
at *Le corsaire* and one of her closest friends in Paris, declared, "Mlle.
Lola Montez's debut lived up to her brilliant and multifaceted reputation, which arrived here well before the remarkable dancer did. She
astounded and charmed the public."

Despite the scandal, Léon Pillet didn't cancel the scheduled performances by the "celebrated Andalusian dancer Lola Montez." Two days
later, she reappeared on the opening night for the opera *Le lazzarone*,
which was attended by the most eminent theater critics. She was more
rational and professional this time, skillfully performing the Spanish
dances in her repertoire. The evening went off without a hitch, and at
the end of her act, she bowed and left the stage with her head held high.
But the public did not hide its discontent this time, and shouts began
to ring out: "You're a terrible dancer! Long live Grisi!" "Focus on the
cancan, you've got nice legs!" The reviews, too, were merciless, some
of them mocking her lack of talent: "Lola Montez is a very beautiful
woman endowed with a lovely figure and the most beautiful eyes in the
world. If that were sufficient, she would have enjoyed complete success.
Unfortunately . . . Mlle. Lola Montez doesn't know how to dance; she
is unfamiliar with the most basic elements of choreography."

Her powerful supporters Dumas and Méry were unable to halt the
flood of negative commentary. Even her friend Théophile Gautier, who
knew her folk dances well because he'd traveled in Spain, did not give

her a flattering review. The renowned novelist was secretly in love with the dancer Carlotta Grisi and seized any opportunity to discredit pretenders to her reign. He saw Lola as an impostor who was besmirching the Paris Opéra's good name, and his criticism was harsh:

> Lola Montez has nothing Andalusian about her but a pair of magnificent black eyes. She hablas very mediocre Spanish, barely speaks French, English only passably.—What country is she really from? That is the question.—We may say that Mlle. Lola has dainty feet and pretty legs.—As for the way she uses them, that's another matter. It must be admitted that the curiosity aroused by Mlle. Lola's run-ins with the police of the North, her conversations via horsewhip with Prussian gendarmes, was not satisfied . . . Knowing of her equine exploits, we suspect Mlle. Lola is more at home on a horse than on the boards.

When Franz Liszt arrived in Paris on April 5 after his successful European tour, he was startled to hear of the uproar that Lola had caused. During his stay, he made every effort not to cross paths with her, fearing her reaction and not wanting his name to be associated with such a controversial performer. On April 16, he gave a piano recital at the Théâtre des Italiens, but Lola Montez did not appear on his list of invitees.

After his long absence from the city, Liszt was grappling with more serious matters. Marie d'Agoult, who lived with their children in a lavish apartment on the Champs-Élysées, knew about his romance with the Spanish dancer. She'd always been tortured by jealousy, but now things were different. When she learned that the artist would be performing at the Opéra, she felt betrayed. When Liszt visited her, they had a fierce argument and Marie broke with him for good.

"You're utterly shameless," she told him. "You not only slept with that vulgar, notorious woman, but you introduced her to our friends. You've humiliated me in front of everyone."

"Calm down, Marie. She didn't know anyone in Paris, so I gave her a few letters of recommendation. You've thrown these jealous fits before."

"Yes, but this will be the last one. I left everything behind for you, but now I want my freedom back. It was never important to me to be your lover, but I refuse to be just another woman any longer. I don't want to see you again."

For Liszt, the breakup was a harsh and unexpected blow. Marie had been the most important woman in his life: his muse, his companion, and the mother of his three children. When Lola found out that the countess had left Paris with the children, she felt terrible.

For her part, Marie would never forgive Liszt. Later, when she had become a famous writer, she would get revenge by publishing a thinly veiled autobiographical novel, *Nélida*, under the pen name Daniel Stern. The book, based on her stormy relationship with the musician, caused a huge scandal. Its male protagonist was a painter named Guermann, a brilliant and seductive but emotionally immature artist who, like Liszt, inspires far more love than he himself is capable of feeling.

Though the savaging she'd received from the critics had done serious damage to her artistic reputation, Lola refused to give up the idea of performing on Parisian stages. Méry was right: the doors of the Opéra may have been closed to her, but every night there were shows that drew a less snooty public looking to have a good time. There was the Ambigu-Comique, where the best humorists of the day performed; the Théâtre des Variétés; the Vaudeville; the Gymnase; and the Porte Saint-Martin. Every night, to enormous success, this last theater presented light comedies that interspersed musical numbers with acts of pantomime, magic, and acrobatics.

Meanwhile, Lola was taking dance lessons and meeting in cafés with her journalist friends, hoping that the larger public would forget about the scandal. Thanks to the generosity of Méry, who made a lot of money and lent it to everyone, she was able to lead a good life. But in July 1844, her name appeared in the papers once more, thanks to her skill as a gunslinger: "Mlle. Lola Montez . . . has left a card at the Shooting Gallery of Lepage . . . entirely perforated with pistol balls from firing rapid double *coups*. The most famous shots in Paris declare themselves vanquished by the fair Andalusian's prowess."

In the months that followed, Lola enjoyed a hitherto unknown freedom. Without a steady lover or a performance on the horizon, she spent time perfecting her French and continuing her dance classes. She also appeared regularly in fashionable clothing shops, always on the arm of some well-known writer or journalist. She learned to dress and style her hair to fit in with the women with whom she was rubbing elbows. Among the Parisian elite, social rank was less important than dressing well. If she wanted to go to the horse races, the theater, the Opéra, or the most exclusive restaurants, she needed an extensive wardrobe and to change outfits at least four times a day. In those places, the women wore splendid gowns and gleaming jewels and scrutinized one another from head to toe. Lola couldn't compete with their wealth, but she got attention with "her extravagant, daring gowns, which she wore with style." She still had a porcelain complexion with rosy cheeks, intense blue eyes, fleshy lips, shiny dark hair, and a shapely figure owing to her daily exercise. When she sat on the café terraces or strolled alone down the boulevards, draped in showy cashmere shawls, men stared with admiration and desire.

At the end of summer, rumors began to circulate that Lola Montez would be appearing at the Porte Saint-Martin with an amusing vaudeville show written specially for her. While most of her friends had fled from the city's unbearable heat, she spent August rehearsing. Still, the competition was fierce, and directors were reluctant to get involved with an artist with such a problematic reputation. It would take several months before she was able to perform onstage again.

In the meantime, she attended the most exclusive literary salons on the arm of Alexandre Dumas and successfully pushed her way into that superficial society of snobbish dandies and pleasure-seekers. At one of those gatherings at the Café de Paris, she met Alexandre Dujarier, who was introduced by a mutual friend, the journalist Gustave Claudin, another of Lola's admirers. In his memoirs, recalling those vibrant years in Paris, Claudin describes her as an adventurer of exquisite beauty who "possesses something provocative and voluptuous that makes men lose their heads, but lacks any talent as a dancer." The event also was attended by Joseph Méry, Théophile Gautier, and Eugène Sue, the hot French author of the moment.

The young, handsome Dujarier—known to his friends as Henri— was the culture editor and co-owner of *La presse*, the most influential newspaper in Paris. Though he'd grown up in modest circumstances, Dujarier had entered the world of finance as quite a young man and become very wealthy. By twenty-five, he had already acquired an immense fortune and led an extravagant lifestyle. In 1839 he partnered with Émile de Girardin, one of the most prominent figures in French journalism. Dujarier invested part of his money in getting the bankrupt paper afloat again. One of his smart decisions was to sign exclusive contracts with some of the most popular writers of the era, such as Dumas and Balzac, and to publish their novels in installments.

Henri fell hopelessly in love with Lola the moment he saw her. Shy and somewhat reserved, the newspaperman barely spoke to her, but he was struck by her beauty and rebellious nature; she seemed so different from other women. "A fierce and indomitable spirit," he thought. Lola, too, was drawn to the tall, lean, well-dressed man with narrow sideburns and tousled dark hair. They exchanged glances all night, and when it came time for her to leave, he offered to accompany her home in her carriage.

"I see you've made good friends in Paris and have plenty of admirers. It's no surprise—you're an unforgettable woman, seductive, mysterious . . ." he said as they drove through the empty streets.

"You're very kind," Lola replied, "and I appreciate the compliments. *La presse* has always been good to me. What I need right now, though, is an engagement with a theater."

"You can count on me. This is a tough city for an artist, but I know what doors to knock on."

After Liszt's rude treatment, Lola wasn't looking to start a new romantic relationship, but Dujarier was different. Soon after they met, she moved into an apartment near his, at number 39 rue Laffitte. And so Lola became the lover of one of the city's most highly regarded journalists. She was living in a splendid neighborhood very close to elite shops and boutiques. She had several servants, a cook, a magnificent carriage, and a man who was devoted to her. She acted as hostess in Dujarier's home and accompanied him to the lively literary cafés where he met each day with friends and fellow journalists. From time to time they went to dinner at Maison Dorée, the best restaurant in Paris. Located a short distance from her apartment, it had a sumptuous interior with mural-covered walls, large gilt mirrors, and its famous *cabinets*, private rooms where the wealthy took their lovers and courtesans to enjoy an intimate dinner. They then would head to the Champs-Élysées and visit the gardens of the popular Bal Mabille, where the celebrated courtesan Céleste Mogador was causing an uproar with her provocative manner of dancing the polka, raising her legs to heights previously unseen. It had been a long time since Lola had been so happy, with a man who loved her and refused her nothing. It was the kind of life she'd always dreamed of.

Through Henri Dujarier, she met characters from Paris's wild bohemian scene. She wasn't bothered that her lover frequently dined with painters' models, *lorettes*, beautiful aspiring actresses, and famed courtesans. She accepted it as part of his professional duties. She sometimes accompanied him to these carefree gatherings, where music hall dancers flirted and sniped at one another while the men discussed politics.

Lola was soon introduced to the famous French courtesan Marie Duplessis, whose life would inspire Dumas's son to write his novel *Camille*. Marie was very beautiful, with a melancholy gaze, though she had a strikingly pale complexion and faint bluish circles under her eyes. She was ill with tuberculosis, but she had not lost a whit of her verve and fun-loving spirit. Despite her youth, she had a lengthy list of wealthy and aristocratic lovers. One of her protectors, the elderly Count von Stackelberg, had rented a luxurious mezzanine-floor apartment for her on the boulevard de la Madeleine, where she hosted dinners and literary salons. On one of those evenings, the two women exchanged confidences.

"I've heard a lot about you, Lola, and I wanted to meet you. A person has to be very brave to do what you did at the Opéra," Marie said with a teasing smile.

"I'm a Spaniard by blood; I'm proud, and I don't tolerate mockery from anybody," Lola replied, lighting a cigarette.

"I think we're very much alike. We've both fought hard for what we have and nothing scares us. After all, a lot of people wrote me off as a dead woman, and here I am. I live my life and I'm not afraid of anything."

Marie Duplessis had experienced harsh poverty and exploitation as a child, and now she was one of the most glamorous women in the city. Lola had seen her driving through the Bois de Boulogne in her beautiful blue brougham drawn by purebred horses. Her final conquest, before she died at age twenty-three, would be none other than Franz Liszt, whom she would meet in November 1845. Their romance was to be short, and the musician would abandon her without saying goodbye, just as he had with Lola.

On March 6, 1845, Lola made her debut at the popular Théâtre de la Porte Saint-Martin in a staging of Pierre Gardel's *La dansomanie*, an amusing comic ballet about a clumsy gentleman from the provinces who loved dance. The work allowed Lola to show off by dancing a cachucha and several boleros. Almost a year had passed since her unfortunate performance at the Paris Opéra, and she was nervous to face the city's public again. But her circumstances had changed. Lola now had the support of Dujarier, who could exert his influence, via *La presse,* to ensure his beloved's success. In addition, over the previous few months, she'd managed to charm a number of critics and had good friends at other newspapers. What's more, the Porte Saint-Martin was a theater in decline. In the past, its ballets had been superior to those at the Opéra, and it had presented plays by Victor Hugo, Honoré de Balzac, Alexandre Dumas, and George Sand. Now dance numbers and mime shows alternated with vulgar, low-quality theater pieces.

On that chilly opening night, the theater was packed. When Lola appeared onstage wearing a tight-fitting Spanish gown of black silk, with a long lace mantilla draped from a comb in her hair, the audience cheered. Before the performance was over, the stage was covered with a carpet of flowers and Lola barely had room to dance.

Mademoiselle Montez may have won over the audience at the Porte Saint-Martin, but she didn't entirely convince the critics. Though more indulgent than the previous year, most focused more on her showy and unusual wardrobe than on the quality of her Spanish dances. The critic from the *Rabelais* was the most positive, but he called into question her abilities as a dancer: "There is something lasciviously attractive, voluptuously enticing in the poses she takes; and then, she's a pretty, very pretty, extremely pretty person, and she throws you kisses so complete that you applaud at once, only to ask yourself afterwards if it was right or wrong to applaud. Go see her: it's singular, it's funny, it's entertaining." Théophile Gautier, who a year earlier had cast doubt on her Spanish origins and suggested she stick to riding horses, now enthusiastically described her cachucha:

> She dances with an uninhibited audacity, a wild ardor,
> and a fierce vitality that shocks the lovers of classical
> pirouettes and *ronds de jambes*; but is dance so seri-
> ous an art that it allows for no invention, no caprice?
> Must it be constrained by inflexible correctness, and
> isn't it enough that a woman be beautiful, young, lis-
> some, and graceful? . . . Rigorous souls will say she lacks
> training, that she permits herself things that the rules
> prohibit. So what!

It wasn't a complete triumph, but the audience appreciated her novel and seemingly authentic Spanish art.

In Dujarier, Lola had found the ideal companion. With him, she enjoyed a stable, peaceful kind of love that she'd never experienced before. Thanks to his influence and economic status, she'd managed to wrangle a return to the stage and garnered respect in his exclusive circle of friends. He was a good, generous man and a brilliant journalist who was unconcerned about her past and accepted her as she was. What's more, he was deeply in love with her. One night, as they were walking home after a romantic dinner at the Café Riche, he whispered in her ear, "You were marvelous, Lola, and the audience adores you—as do I. You should start thinking about your wedding dress because one of these days I'm going to get down on my knee and ask you to marry me."

"Stop joking around," she said, rebuffing his kiss. "We're very happy as we are. We don't need to sign a piece of paper. Anyway, I don't think your mother likes me. I'm sure she thinks her only son deserves better."

"Don't be silly, she'll love you once she gets to know you. Dumas and Méry have given their seal of approval, and the four of us could go to Spain on our honeymoon—what do you think?"

Lola said nothing, but he again suggested that they set a date for their trip to the altar. Suddenly she imagined how hurt he'd be if he found out who she really was and that she was barred from remarrying even though her ex-husband was thousands of miles away. Once again her past was intruding on her happiness. Dujarier had stopped gambling and socializing with people of ill repute, to spend as much time as possible with the woman who now occupied his heart. That night, though, he felt rejected and wounded. Still, he thought that Lola simply needed more time and would change her mind.

The next day, Dujarier was invited to a dinner at the restaurant Les Trois Frères Provençaux, nestled under the arches of the Palais-Royal. Lola wanted to go with him, but he refused, arguing that she would be uncomfortable at a gathering of libertines who had been friends for years. In fact, however, Anaïs Liévenne, a well-known actress from the Théâtre du Vaudeville, was hosting the evening for her friends from the press and her fellow actresses. Among the guests was the young Alice Ozy, an actress, painter's model, and "friend of all men," famous for having been the lover of Prince Henri d'Orléans, son of King Louis-Philippe. After the lively meal, a table was set up in a drawing room with cards for playing lansquenet, an old German card game that was fashionable at the time. The beautiful Anaïs had made the mistake of seating Henri Dujarier at the same table as the journalist Jean-Baptiste Rosemond de Beauvallon, an attractive twenty-six-year-old who was the critic at the rival paper *Le globe*. The two men hated each other and spent the entire evening exchanging contemptuous glares and insults. Dujarier lost a lot of money but kept gambling, hoping his luck would turn. It was six o'clock in the morning when he stumbled out of the restaurant, aided by a friend, the novelist Roger de Beauvoir. Thoroughly inebriated and pleased at having recovered some of his losses, Dujarier was oblivious to the problems that his jabs at Beauvallon would bring.

That afternoon, Dujarier, bleary eyed and still hungover, went to work at his office at *La presse*. Two well-dressed gentlemen stopped in and introduced themselves as the Count of Flers and the Viscount of Ecquevilly.

"I am very busy, gentlemen. What do you want?" he asked impatiently.

"We have come on behalf of Monsieur de Beauvallon, who demands either an apology or redress via arms for your rude remarks yesterday."

"I have no intention of rectifying anything I said," Dujarier declared. "Two of my friends will contact you tomorrow; in the meantime, leave my office."

He clearly would have no choice but to participate in a duel. For a man of his position, refusing the challenge would mean social ostracism. The idea of going through with it, however, was a distressing one since, unlike Lola, he'd never held a gun in his life. The dispute was a proxy for a settling of scores between *Le globe* and *La presse*, the latter of which had increased its circulation, much to its rival's discontent. Beauvallon, who was known for being a superb duelist, had found the perfect excuse to kill his archrival. When Dujarier described the situation to his good friend Alexandre Dumas, the novelist was concerned. Seeing the seriousness of the matter, Dumas advised Dujarier to accept the proposal for sword combat, convinced that Beauvallon would be satisfied with disarming his opponent. But Dujarier, unwilling to back down, opted to use pistols. He named as his seconds Baron Charle de Boigne, a journalist, and Arthur Bertrand, a founding member of the Jockey Club.

From the start, Henri tried to hide the situation from Lola, but she guessed what was afoot. Though she was aware he was going to engage in a duel, she did not know the details. Futilely, she wept and pleaded with him not to risk his life. He reassured her that everything was going to be all right and that it would be a fight between gentlemen.

The duel was set for March 11 at ten o'clock in the morning. The night before, Lola was to perform at the Porte Saint-Martin. Dujarier said he couldn't attend but that they would have breakfast together. That evening, alone in his study and filled with foreboding, the editor of *La presse* wrote his will, then addressed a letter to his mother in which he explained his reasons and said goodbye with these words: "Honor is everything; if you are to shed tears, dear Mother, better you should shed them over a son with honor equal to yours, rather than over a coward." The next letter was harder to write, as the words were addressed to his beloved and he knew the hurt they would cause her:

> My dear Lola,
> I am going out to fight with pistols. This explains why I wanted to sleep alone and also why I didn't come to see you this morning. I need all my calmness and must avoid the emotions that seeing you would have caused me. At ten, it will be over and I'll run to embrace you, unless . . .
> A thousand tendernesses, my dear Lola, my good little woman whom I love and who will be in my thoughts.
> D   Tuesday morning

That night, Lola barely slept. At seven o'clock in the morning, she instructed her maid to look for Henri and have him come to her before he left for the duel. The maid found the journalist already dressed in the obligatory black clothing and eating some soup. Unable to work up the courage to say goodbye to Lola, he gathered his overcoat and a bottle of wine and left the house in silence. On his way out, he sent his servant Gabriel to give Lola the letter he had written.

Dujarier left in his coach accompanied by his two seconds and a doctor. They drove to the place known as the *chemin de la Favorite* in the Bois de Boulogne. It had snowed all night, and a few flakes were still falling. The rules of the duel had already been set the day before. The adversaries would stand face to face at thirty paces apart. At the agreed signal of three claps, each man could advance five paces and fire. Once the first opened fire, the other had to stop advancing and respond. The group arrived at the appointed place at the established time, but there was no sign of Beauvallon or his witnesses. Dujarier attempted to ward off the chill of the gloomy morning by pacing back and forth in the forest and drinking a few glasses of madeira. "How strange," he muttered, "to be about to fight to the death and not know why." Though his seconds informed him that his opponent's absence meant he could return to the city with his honor intact, Dujarier decided to wait. Beauvallon and his entourage appeared an hour later, offering all sorts of absurd excuses. To avert bloodshed, Boigne tried to reconcile the two young men, but they both were determined to see the duel through.

Everything happened very quickly, and the outcome was inevitable. Dujarier, pale and trembling with cold after the long wait, fired first. His hand was shaking so badly that he could barely hold the pistol steady, and the bullet missed its mark by several yards. Then, instead of turning in profile to give his adversary a smaller target, he stood frozen, waiting for the return shot. Beauvallon raised his arm and aimed at his opponent. A loud bang broke the silence, and the bullet struck Dujarier in the face, sending him tumbling backward onto the ground. His seconds ran to him, lifted him up, unbuttoned his overcoat, and unknotted his tie. Dujarier was still alive, but the doctor deemed the wound to be fatal. Working together, they managed to lift his inert body into the coach, which raced off toward the rue Laffitte.

Upon reading her lover's letter, Lola rushed out of the house to look for Dumas. As one of Dujarier's closest friends, the novelist had to know what was happening. When she found him, she looked him in the eye and said, "Please don't lie to me. I just want to know which man he will be dueling."

"Beauvallon, his rival," Dumas replied.

"Then there's nothing to be done—he is going to die!" she said, sobbing.

"Don't say that. We mustn't get ahead of ourselves. Maybe they reconciled at the last moment."

Lola returned to the apartment to wait for news. She was full of despair, unable to do anything for Dujarier and with nobody to turn to. For long hours she hovered by the window, waiting for his carriage to appear. It was still snowing; the Parisian sky was gray and dull. She smoked one cigarette after another while pacing impatiently around the drawing room. At noon she heard the squeak of a coach's wheels stopping before her door. Recognizing Henri's black brougham and his driver, Lola rushed downstairs to meet him. In the street, she opened the carriage door and found her beloved's bloody corpse. With a hair-raising scream, she clutched him and covered him with kisses as the doctor tried to pull her away. She instructed the servants to place his lifeless body in his bed and inform his mother. Two hours later, several policemen arrived at the home to open an investigation into Alexandre Dujarier's murder.

The funeral took place on Thursday, March 13, in the Church of Notre-Dame-de-Lorette, which overflowed with friends and figures from Paris's artistic and literary worlds. A funeral carriage pulled by four richly arrayed black horses and followed by a long procession moved along the boulevards toward Montmartre cemetery. Honoré de Balzac, Dumas, Méry, and Émile de Girardin served as pallbearers. Not far away, Lola listened to the tolling of bells that signaled mourning for the dead newspaperman. Standing next to a large window in her front room, she gazed absently onto the street. She felt as if the bullet that had killed her lover had snatched her life away too. She hadn't been able to attend the ceremony out of respect for Dujarier's mother and sister. She felt sorry for the elderly woman, who'd been so devoted to her son and lost him too young in a ridiculous duel. But as far as his family was concerned, Lola was only the latest in a string of lovers, a dancer with a frivolous life and a scandalous past, and they wanted nothing to do with her.

After her lover's death, Lola was in no condition to fulfill her con-tract to perform again, nor did she feel up to rehearsing her role in *La biche au bois*, an amusing vaudeville number she'd been planning to debut in a few weeks. Without Henri Dujarier's influence or economic support, the theater director was not interested in keeping her on. Just ten days after the funeral, the newspaper *Le corsaire-satan* announced that the Spanish dancer Lola Montez was no longer part of the company at the Porte Saint-Martin.

Yet again her artistic career was being cut short, but her biggest concern was a lack of money. Lola had to deal with a lot of expenses and pay her creditors. In his will, the editor had left his most valuable possession, his share of *La presse*, to his beloved mother and his young nephew. His friend Alexandre Dumas inherited most of his personal assets, including his magnificent horses and the luxurious furnishings from his apartment. Lola received only seventeen shares of the Théâtre du Palais-Royal, which were worth less than a thousand francs. This sum was better than nothing, and in early April, she went to court to try to collect. But the judge decreed that the law granted Dujarier's brother-in-law, the executor of the will, more time to distribute the assets. The dancer was forced to move out of her home on the rue Laffitte to a small hotel next to the boulevard des Italiens. As usual, she managed to survive and turned to wealthy protectors who would pay for her lodging in exchange for her company.

She could regularly be seen dressed to the nines at the horse track, in the finest restaurants, and in a box at the Opéra, always in good company. Though she tried to seem cheerful and carefree in public, Lola had changed. In the past, she had emerged unscathed by life's vicissitudes, but now her career was over. The theater doors were closed to her, and without Dujarier's love, she was just a dancer fallen into disgrace. Her health began to fail; the migraines she'd long suffered grew worse, and she felt very lonely and isolated. Her intellectual and artist friends no longer invited her to the Café de Paris or to the salons, where she used to glow with her own light. People who once toasted her and called her "the lioness of Paris" had now forgotten even her name. She tried to ignore the snubs, but she was very hurt by the cruel rumors going around. Some said she'd sent her wealthy lover to die in order to collect an inheritance. Others branded her a black widow, a beautiful, fiery young woman who used her seductive wiles to drag her lovers into ruin. Alexandre Dumas himself, deeply affected by his friend's death, even remarked that Lola was a *femme fatale* who brought only bad luck and misfortune to men. She was convinced she'd reached her lowest point, but she mustered the strength to serve as a witness against Beauvallon at the trial for Dujarier's murder.

A year later, on the warm morning of March 26, 1846, Lola Montez appeared right on time at the Palais de Justice in Rouen, in northwestern France. Gathered around the enormous gothic building was a large crowd eager to see the parade of famous witnesses—including Dumas and Balzac—courtesans, and music hall stars who would be testifying. Wearing a filmy black silk dress and with a thick veil covering her face, Lola eclipsed all those present. One witness who watched the trial said:

> Though the room was full of the most prominent personalities of the literary and art world in Paris, nobody got more attention than she did. Even the severe president of the court and his advisers stared at her with their mouths agape. She was dressed in mourning, though not entirely, because she was wearing soft silks and laces, and when she raised her veil and removed her glove to be sworn in, a murmur of admiration spread through the room. She had made a long journey from Paris to Rouen, but she was certainly compensated for it.

When it was Lola's turn, she testified that she was twenty-one—subtracting four years—and that her profession was "*artiste* of the dance." Visibly upset, she said that she had wanted to go to the dinner at Les Trois Frères Provençaux but that Henri hadn't let her. The president of the court asked for the goodbye letter Dujarier had written to her, and she reached into her bodice and handed it over to be read into the record. Upon hearing her lover's final words once more, she broke down and began to cry. The public felt compassion for her and was also struck by her bravery when she said, "I should have taken my beloved's place in the duel; unlike him, I am good with a pistol." Had she known that the duel was to be with Beauvallon, she would have called the police, she said.

She also remarked that, in the weeks leading up to the duel, the journalist had been spending time with friends with dubious reputations and seemed anxious and ill tempered. The prosecuting attorney, Léon Duval, representing Dujarier's mother and brother-in-law, asked the witness why she hadn't mentioned these details a year earlier when she was questioned. Feeling that she was being accused of concealing information, Lola exclaimed, "I couldn't talk about it. I was sick, in bed, surrounded by doctors and policemen. I doubt you understand what I went through. It was I, sir, who received his bloody body. I opened the door of the carriage . . . I'd had a feeling for several days that he was going to participate in a duel, but he didn't tell me anything and I saw that at night he was getting together with people who were bad news . . ."

"And who were those disreputable people?"

"My God! Monsieur, I repeat, I opened the carriage door and he fell stiffly into my arms. He was dead—with his face destroyed by a bullet—and you ask me about disreputable people. You have no compassion." A stricken expression on her face, the dancer lowered the veil again and left the witness-box.

The parade of witnesses lasted two more days, and though Lola was convinced that Beauvallon would pay for what he'd done, she was unfamiliar with the country's laws. French juries never applied the murder statute to a duel unless the combat had failed to respect the traditional code. On Sunday, after night had already fallen and in a room crowded with people, Lola heard the verdict of not guilty. It had taken the jury only ten minutes to exonerate him.

After the trial, she returned to Paris, sad and bitter about the victory of the man who'd murdered her lover and destroyed her life. She was done with Paris and began to prepare to leave the city as soon as possible. She sold a few personal objects—mantillas, lace fans, and out-of-fashion dresses. Once again she went to Dujarier's executor in an attempt to collect her inheritance, but he gave all kinds of excuses for delaying the handover of the stock. Penniless and with creditors hounding her, her best option was to leave. It still seemed impossible that the months of happiness she'd shared with Dujarier had evaporated in an instant. She wasn't sure where she might go at first, but then she met Francis Leigh, a young English officer from the Royal Hussars regiment who was on leave in France. The handsome soldier, with blond hair, dark blue eyes, and a slim figure, invited her to spend a delightful summer together on a long tour through the spas of Europe. In June, a rail line had opened between Paris and Brussels, and her new lover bought them two first-class tickets.

Once more Lola was traveling in style, with several trunks, hatboxes, and a chest in which she kept her only assets, the jewels given to her by wealthy admirers. For the next few weeks, they visited Ostend and enjoyed the tranquil beaches of the North Sea. At the end of June, they left Belgium and headed for Germany's most fashionable destinations. But their paths soon diverged. Lola was spotted in Heidelberg in the company of a Russian aristocrat, Baron Georges Meller-Zakomelsky, who introduced her to a new influential admirer, Robert Peel, a diplomat working as secretary to the British ambassador to Switzerland. The young man of twenty-three—who would inherit a barony one day—was the eldest son of former British prime minister Sir Robert Peel, who had recently retired from political life.

Good-looking and brilliant, but very immature, Robert Peel the younger was the black sheep of the family. After working for two years in the British embassy in Madrid, he'd just been transferred to Bern, where he led a dull, monotonous life. Meeting the merry and uninhibited Lola was like a gift from heaven. They spent a few weeks together, and in mid-August, she traveled alone to Bad Homburg, a serene spa city north of Frankfurt. The press announced that the famous Spanish dancer Lola Montez would be performing as part of the summer festival program. But on August 29, to everyone's surprise, the artist packed her bags and left before the show. Peel had invited her to join him in Stuttgart. The king of Württemberg was preparing a splendid celebration to welcome his son, Crown Prince Charles, who was returning from Russia with his new bride, Grand Duchess Olga Nikolaievna. If Lola wanted to meet important people and rub elbows with princes and noblemen, this was her chance.

She spent the month of September going from party to party in the German city surrounded by rolling hills and vineyards. At Robert Peel's side, she attended balls, receptions, and banquets and went horseback riding through the leafy forests. The warm weather and thermal springs were restorative for her health. She had a wonderful time and managed to forget her sorrows for a time. But as autumn began, her relationship with the diplomat grew chilly. He was fed up with his lover's antics, her violent moods, and her expensive whims. For her part, she was considering relaunching her artistic career, and now that summer was over, theaters were looking for new shows. Lola decided to try her luck on the stages of Vienna, a city acclaimed for its music and dance. On the way there, she would make a brief stop in Munich, which would be celebrating Oktoberfest. As always, fate had a surprise in store. As she was packing her bags in preparation to take an early stagecoach, Lola had no idea she was about to be involved in a scandal that would change the course of history.

CHAPTER 5

The King's Lover

After a grueling stagecoach journey, Lola Montez arrived in Munich on October 5, 1846. As usual, she found lodging in one of the best hotels in the city center, the Bayerischer Hof. Loaded down with her voluminous luggage and an inseparable lapdog, Zampa, she took a room with views onto a square shaded by leafy trees. From her window she could see the beautiful red-brick cathedral with its two tall towers topped by domed cupolas. It was a sunny fall day and Munich surprised her with its splendid buildings and tidy flower gardens. The streets were bustling and the terraces and taverns serving the famous Bavarian beer were overflowing with people who'd come from throughout the region for Oktoberfest. The small, peaceful city was being reborn thanks to the efforts of its extravagant king, Ludwig I of Bavaria, a devotee of beauty and the classical world. The monarch dreamed of building an immaculate metropolis inspired by ancient Greece and Rome. Visitors who strolled its avenues and quiet squares came across triumphal arches, obelisks, statues, and large neoclassical buildings decorated with friezes and colonnades. The year that Lola arrived, Munich was thrumming with activity; churches, mansions, palaces, rotundas, art museums, libraries, public gardens, and theaters were being built in every neighborhood.

But the city had other attractions too: it was affordable, it had a lively cultural scene, and it was said that King Ludwig not only was a poet and lover of the arts but also had a weakness for beautiful women.

Unlike in Paris, Lola had no letters of recommendation, but she headed straight to the Court Theatre on Max-Joseph-Platz that very afternoon. She was impressed by the magnificent building, which was inspired by a Greek temple. Some of the world's most famous operas had been debuted in its large auditorium. With her ability to charm powerful men, Lola was convinced that her name would be appearing very soon on its programs. The general director of the royal theaters was Colonel Baron August von Frays, the king's right-hand man. Despite being a military veteran toughened by a thousand battles, he loved opera and took pride in hiring only great stars for his theater. What Lola did not know was that authorizations for guest artists were not easy to come by and that the king always had the last word. As she stormed out of the theater after the director refused to see her, she realized that it wasn't going to be easy to win him over with her beauty and that it could be several months before she got an answer. She had to find a way to reach the monarch directly, skipping over the stultifying protocol.

The next day, Lola ran into Baron Heinrich von Maltzahn, a former admirer she'd met in Paris who was staying at the same hotel. The aristocrat, a wealthy, well-connected man, had been chamberlain of the Bavarian court. At fifty-three years old, he was a handsome widower with graying hair, elegant and courteous, and a lover of earthly pleasures. It was a lucky encounter, since Maltzahn did not often visit his city of birth. Owner of a luxurious mansion on the rue de la Madeleine in Paris, he preferred the freer, more exuberant life he led in the French capital. King Ludwig enjoyed his company, and though the baron rarely returned to Munich, he was always well received at the palace. Lola complained to Maltzahn that the unpleasant August von Frays had refused to see her, and the baron, wanting to help, agreed to write a letter of introduction to King Ludwig, requesting that he have a private audience with the baron's friend.

Lola was eager to meet the king whom everybody described as an affable, intelligent, sensitive man, decent to a fault and a bit of a workaholic. King Ludwig I belonged to the House of Wittelsbach, an ancient and powerful German dynasty that had ruled Bavaria for seven centuries. He'd been born in Strasbourg in 1786 and was the godson of King Louis XVI of France and the unfortunate Marie Antoinette. He'd ascended to the throne at thirty-nine, after the death of his father, King Maximilian I. As a young man, Ludwig traveled to Greece and Italy, and even before his coronation, he was dreaming of turning his city into a new Athens. In October 1810, he married for political reasons, wedding Therese of Saxe-Hildburghausen, considered "the most beautiful princess in Europe." The populace so enjoyed the marriage festivities that they were repeated on the royal couple's anniversary, giving rise to the famous Oktoberfest still celebrated in Munich even today. Therese had nine children and was a devoted, selfless wife who threw body and soul into making her husband happy. From the start, though, Ludwig made it clear that he would pursue romantic flings. The newlyweds had little in common; he was brilliant and erudite, with the soul of an artist, whereas Therese had received only a limited formal education. She was not his intellectual equal or the muse he needed at his side. Yet despite his constant infidelities, which Therese reluctantly accepted, the couple remained united. The queen was still moved to recall the sincere words her husband had written to her on their twenty-fifth wedding anniversary: "I have never met another woman I could love more than you, nor anyone I'd rather have as a wife . . . You belong to me. And I would be happy if I could belong to you. To you alone. But I am ardent by nature. God forbid that this natural condition of mine should destroy your happiness." The week that Lola arrived in Munich, they had been married thirty-six years and were arm in arm when attending the dances and horse races organized during Oktoberfest on a large field known as the Theresien Meadow, in the queen's honor.

Three days after her arrival, Lola met with the king, who granted private audiences in late morning. Ready to present the image of a lady from the Andalusian aristocracy, she selected quite sober attire. After trying several outfits, she opted for a demure black velvet dress with a white lace collar. She pulled her hair back in a bun held by a gold mesh net, leaving her slender neck bare, and covered her head with a black mantilla. Her lace fan and a few drops of jasmine perfume, her favorite fragrance, were also inevitably present. Though the hotel was not far from the palace and she could have walked, she hired a horse-drawn carriage.

The Residenz, the official palace of the kings of Bavaria for four centuries, was a huge complex of baroque buildings and palaces with about two hundred inhabitants. It was surrounded by ten large open courtyards and geometric Italian gardens with beautiful bronze fountains. When her carriage pulled up in front of the palace's imposing facade, Lola felt butterflies flood her stomach. If she didn't manage to win over the king and secure permission to dance at the Court Theatre, she would be in serious trouble. Though the city didn't hold a candle to Paris, Lola liked Munich, but she was unable to lead the lifestyle befitting "a renowned dancer from the bolero school, belonging to an illustrious Spanish family." She could barely afford to pay the rent for a good house and hire a maidservant.

Lola walked down a long, richly decorated gallery with silk-upholstered walls hung with dozens of portraits of distinguished ancestors from the Wittelsbach dynasty, some of them infamous for their cruelty, madness, and excesses. It was rumored that a streak of insanity ran in the family's veins and that Ludwig himself had inherited a few quirks. When she arrived at the crowded anteroom, she handed her letter from Maltzahn to the king's chamberlain, Count von Reichberg. "His Majesty is very busy today and doesn't have much time. Be brief and concise in your request," he instructed her. A moment later, the massive golden doors of the king's chamber slowly opened. Lola made a deep curtsy as the chamberlain pompously announced her name. The monarch, seated at his worktable, was engrossed in reading the memorandum that the director of the Court Theatre had just sent over. With a wave of his hand and without looking up, he invited her to take a seat while he continued reading the message from Baron von Frays:

> The Spanish dancer Doña María Dolores Porris y Montez, better known as Lola Montez, has arrived in our lands and requested to dance on the stage of Your Majesty's theater during intermissions. She is requesting half of net proceeds or fifty louis d'or for each performance. Seeing that, for one, this kind of guest artist offers no real advantage for box office receipts and that, furthermore, in various places where said dancer performed previously the police have been forced to intervene because of the public affronts she caused, this obedient and devoted servant of Your Majesty leaves the matter to your consideration.

Lola waited in silence, admiring the luxurious room from which the king directed the destiny of his little kingdom. Ludwig was proud of being the earliest riser in court, and for the past twenty-one years, the lamp in his study was the first in the city to be lit each morning. The Pompeii-style chamber, in red and black, was decorated with busts and sculptures from classical antiquity. But what visitors found most striking were the extraordinary frescoes that stretched around its soaring walls, reproducing designs that adorned the wealthy Roman houses of Pompeii. The elderly monarch wasn't much to look at, but he had a fascinating personality. He was tall, lean, and well-proportioned, with tousled hair and informal attire. On his thin, pockmarked face, his expressive blue eyes and long, sharp nose stood out. Though he had a rather unattractive cyst on his forehead at the time, his good humor and charisma outweighed his physical flaws. The chamberlain had warned Lola to speak loudly when addressing the king—His Majesty had been slightly deaf since boyhood.

When Ludwig set down his pen on the table and finally raised his eyes, his face lit up and his cheeks flushed. At sixty years of age, he was overcome by Lola's voluptuous beauty, like that of a Botticelli Virgin Mary. With clumsy movements, he drew nearer so that, in the soft light bending through the large windows, he could survey her features in greater detail: the perfect oval of her face; her large, intense blue eyes and thick arched brows; her straight nose; her lush red lips; her sublime neck; her firm breasts and slender waist. He felt his whole body tremble and could barely speak.

"Doña Lola Montez, my good friend Baron von Maltzahn has spoken most highly of you. And from what I can see, he has fallen short in his description. You don't know how delighted I am about your visit. I have few opportunities to practice my modest Spanish, and I love that country so fondly . . ."

"Your Majesty, I am honored to be here today with you, a ruler who appreciates beauty and the arts. Please allow me to introduce myself. I am a renowned Spanish dancer, and I have performed in the best theaters in Europe."

"Yes, I know," the king broke in, unable to take his eyes off her. "Baron von Frays has brought me up to date. Still, you must understand that you are not well known here, and the Court Theatre has a superb reputation . . . But come, sit next to me and let's talk."

The audience stretched longer than usual, to the consternation of the chamberlain waiting on the other side of the door. Though the king had never visited Spain, he was passionate about the country, which seemed to embody a romantic dream: a land of poetry, guitar serenades, fiery women, and forbidden loves. He told Lola that he often read Cervantes and Calderón de la Barca, and that his favorite book was *Don Quixote*. He was delighted to be able to practice the language with a Spaniard of such noble lineage. Ludwig, who spoke quickly and energetically and gesticulated a great deal, was so spellbound by Lola that she had to gently remind him of the reason for her visit.

"Señora Montez, tomorrow I will speak with the head of the theater and instruct him to have you debut on our stage as soon as possible. I am eager to see you dance . . ."

"Your Majesty, I cannot thank you enough. I hope I will not disappoint you and that this visit will be the beginning of a fine friendship." Lola said goodbye to the monarch with another bow, and he kissed her hand effusively in an effort to prolong that moment of pleasure.

The dancer left the chamber with a majestic bearing, leaving a dazzled Ludwig behind her. On his most recent birthday, the king had felt an enormous void, as if his life were slipping through his fingers. His wife, Therese, had told him months earlier that she wanted to sleep alone, but he had no intention of giving up sex and continued to visit his former lovers, actresses from the Court Theatre who helped him to forget his tedious responsibilities. But the king, a hidebound romantic, longed to fall in love again, to woo a beautiful young woman and devote himself to her. When he saw Lola, he was certain that fate had led him at last to the woman of his dreams.

When the chamberlain came into the room to announce the next visitor, the king asked to be left alone for a few minutes. Another of his passions was poetry, and he had been writing sonnets and odes that explored his most intimate emotions since he was very young. Remarkably, Ludwig also published his poems, unashamed to bare his soul to anyone who cared to read them. Now he felt the urge to pick up his pen and write a few lines to his new muse:

> *Love dwells within her.*
> *Luminous regions.*
> *Sun and ecstasy.*
> *That is where she can be found.*

The next day, Ludwig woke up at five as usual, said his prayers, wrapped himself in his old green dressing gown, and spent several hours poring over the papers and documents piled on his table. He was obsessed with keeping his kingdom's finances in order. He hated waste and forced his family to lead an austere lifestyle. His subjects were startled to observe that in both summer and winter he wore the same frock coat, with no overcoat, and his old felt hat. His appearance recalled a "nutty old professor" more than a European monarch. But his attention to cost went out the window when it came to beautifying his beloved city or scouring Europe for paintings and sculptures by the most celebrated artists to augment his museums' holdings. That morning he could not stop thinking about Lola and sent for Baron von Frays to discuss the details of her performance. In addition, he was intrigued by her "scandalous" past and wanted to hear all about the skirmishes in Warsaw.

"Your Excellency, judging by the press reports, you should not trust Lola Montez," the baron warned. "Her bad reputation precedes her, and I fear this woman has the power to seduce men and lead them to their utter ruin."

"Surely you're exaggerating? I've met her, and she seems to me a charming, well-mannered lady," the king replied.

"No, Your Majesty. She hurled a glass of champagne at the head of an officer who made a pass at her in a restaurant in Berlin. She spent fourteen days in jail for striking a gendarme with her whip at a military parade, and in Warsaw, having gotten a chilly reception from her audience, she responded with insolent gestures and displayed her rear end."

"Perhaps these are only baseless rumors."

"Your Majesty, believe me, this Montez woman—"

"Excuse me, call her by her name, Madame Montez."

"Your Majesty, Madame Montez is just a fortune hunter. Still, if you do allow her to dance as a guest performer, the box office will not punish you for it; the lady's reputation will draw many gawkers."

After hearing the director's assessment, Ludwig found Lola even more irresistible. She was beautiful, audacious, rebellious, intelligent, pure fire—only a genuine Andalusian woman could react that way to men trying to take advantage of her. The king ordered Frays to speak to the artist immediately to nail down the terms of her honoraria and the number of performances. In addition, he insisted that he wanted her to dance only during intermissions and that she must wear Spanish clothing. In a fit of generosity, he decided to offer her half of the box office receipts, rather than the usual one-third. The two men agreed that her Andalusian dances would fit perfectly during the intermission of the comedy *Der verwunschene Prinz* by Johann von Plötz, scheduled for October 10 as part of the events commemorating His Majesty's thirty-sixth wedding anniversary.

Two days after her meeting with the king of Bavaria, the dancer was set to debut at the great Court Theatre. Ludwig loved the theater and Italian opera and frequently appeared at the Court, where he assessed his popularity by the applause he received when he entered his box. As he had a hard time hearing the performers, he liked to study the scripts and librettos in advance. Rumors flew around the Munich court, and on opening night a good portion of the audience already knew that the guest artist had conquered the king's heart. Widespread curiosity about His Majesty's new favorite, a blue-blooded beauty with a scandalous past, meant that the performance was completely sold out.

On opening night, Lola waited impatiently in the wings. She was more nervous than usual, knowing that Ludwig and the most distinguished members of his circle would be there. At the last minute, Queen Therese had begged off attending, blaming a severe headache. Though she endured her husband's affairs with high-society ladies, his romances with actresses and performers humiliated her before her subjects. As usual, Ludwig took a seat in a box on the second tier, in the area reserved for courtiers and nobility. He was bored by pomp and protocol and preferred to sit with family and friends, rather than presiding over the sumptuous royal box, which was decorated in purple with adornments fashioned in gold and ivory.

When the first act ended, the orchestra started playing the opening chords of "Los Boleros de Cadiz." The curtain lifted and Lola appeared alone in the middle of the stage. With the whole auditorium lit up, she could clearly see the king in his box and greeted him with a respectful bow. She was wearing a Spanish dress of silk and lace that highlighted her lithe figure and bared her long, shapely legs. Raising her arms, she began to dance energetically to the staccato rhythm of her castanets. The king hung on every detail, using a pair of opera glasses to follow the undulating, sinuous movements of her body. He had never seen a Spaniard perform the country's dances before, but he felt transported to that land of fire and passion. Lola's energy, grace, and indomitable spirit won him utterly. When the performance ended, the theater, led by the monarch, burst into thunderous applause. As usual, the more sophisticated members of the audience criticized the dancer's lack of formal training, but comments on her sensuality and beauty were on all the gentlemen's lips.

The audience grew more dubious during the second intermission, when Lola danced "El Oleano." The pantomime with the spider left the critics speechless. This time the applause was less enthusiastic, and a few hisses were heard that the king was unable to silence. Furious at such rudeness, Ludwig stood up with a dignified bearing and applauded the dancer with all his might. She bowed to him and then fled the stage. Deeply embarrassed, he left his box and went to Lola's dressing room to offer his support.

"My dear, you can't imagine how sorry I am about this," the king said, crestfallen.

"I feel humiliated, insulted. How could they treat me this way, and in Your Majesty's presence?"

"You will not dance in this theater again—they do not deserve you. They are incapable of appreciating your authentic, passionate art."

"Of course I will perform again," she exclaimed, her voice rising. "If I give up now, they will think they've bested me. They'll laugh at me. I intend to fulfill my contract and dance one more time, and then . . . Oh, what will become of me?"

"And then, divine Lola, you will retire from the stage for good and we will travel to Spain; we will see the world and you will have my love wholly," Ludwig said, kissing her hands.

A few days later, Lola returned to the stage to perform her traditional dances after a staging of the play *Der Weiberfeind*. To protect her from any attacks from her detractors, the king ordered the acting chief of police, Baron Johann von Pechmann, to place agents strategically in the first rows of seats. Pechmann, who had been in his job only a few months, did not dare to defy the king, though he found the request perplexing. Baron von Frays also took measures and asked members of the theater to sit in the orchestra pit. In reality, Ludwig knew that the audience's protests were directed at him. When Lola arrived in Munich, his popularity was at one of the lowest points of his reign. Over time, the king who promoted education, the arts, and commerce had become an autocrat who ruled the country with an iron fist. Early in his reign he had enjoyed the affection of his people, who considered him a good ruler, honorable and unostentatious, and forgave him his flaws. But around 1840, as revolutionary movements began to swell and triumph across Europe, he had become increasingly absolutist. The people, the press, and the university began to protest the lack of freedom, and Ludwig had become convinced that he could remain on the throne only through force.

On October 14, Lola Montez reappeared at the Court Theatre, where she performed "El Oleano" again and danced a fandango. There were many empty seats, but, swallowing her pride, she continued with her act. Just as with her earlier performance, the critics were bewildered by her unorthodox dancing style, though they agreed that she possessed a remarkable "savage beauty." The security forces could do nothing to prevent the hisses and jeers that rang out when the curtain fell. Furious, King Ludwig ordered Pechmann to identify the instigators and give them their just desserts. When the king returned in his carriage to the Residenz, he couldn't get the dancer out of his head: "Oh, my dear Lola, they punish you because they know it hurts me, but I will not let anything or anybody tear us apart."

That night, in his little notebook, the king began to compose his first poem in Spanish: "*Yo te quiero con mi vida, con mis ojos, con mi alma* . . . I love you with my life, with my eyes, with my soul, my body, my heart, with my entire being. Your black hair, your blue eyes, your graceful figure . . ." Thinking about her irresistible exquisiteness, he decided that Lola had to pose for his Gallery of Beauties, which was housed in the large ballroom adjacent to the Bavarian royalty's summer residence, Nymphenburg Palace, with its sumptuous gardens. The walls of this unique gallery, which was famous across Europe, were hung with more than thirty commissioned portraits of the beautiful women of the era, all completed by the great court painter Joseph Karl Stieler. It was the king's homage to feminine beauty, though wagging tongues referred to it as "His Majesty's harem." Some of the women had been his lovers, but the collection also included members of his family, such as his daughter and his daughter-in-law. Most were ladies from the German aristocracy, but there were also representatives of every social class, from the lovely daughter of a Munich cobbler to Princess Sophie of Bavaria, mother of Emperor Franz Joseph. The king enjoyed strolling through his gallery—which was open to the public on a set schedule—to gaze at the array of beauties from which he drew so much inspiration.

It had been four years since Ludwig had charged Stieler with painting a portrait for the gallery. The last subject, Caroline Lizius, had been a young commoner with an "artless pastoral beauty" who had won the king's heart and briefly become one of his lovers. Now he was in love again and wanted to add his beloved Lola to the collection as soon as possible. Impatient to get started, he rushed to the painter's studio on Barerstrasse to work out the details of the painting.

"Your Majesty, what a delightful surprise! I wasn't expecting you today," Stieler said.

"My dear Joseph, I have come with a very special assignment. I've met a young Spanish dancer who deserves a place of honor in my gallery."

"You don't mean Lola Montez, Your Majesty?"

"Yes, in fact I do. I want her portrait to reflect her fiery personality, for it to portray a real Andalusian beauty of noble lineage."

"Forgive me, Your Majesty, I thought that the ladies chosen must be not only beautiful but of the most unimpeachable and exemplary character."

But the king refused to hear more.

"Don't argue with me, Joseph," he retorted. "There are a lot of unfounded rumors flying about the poor girl. It's settled. She will begin sitting for you tomorrow. Oh, and take as long as you need to finish the painting," he added, exiting the studio with a look of satisfaction on his face.

The king no longer made any effort to disguise his love for the dancer and started visiting her at her hotel. He would stroll there on foot, sometimes in the afternoon or at night, and often twice a day. Having decided that the city of Munich should have a fine hotel like the ones in Paris and London, he'd hired his favorite architect, Friedrich von Gärtner, to design the Bayerischer Hof. It had opened in 1841 with a banquet attended by prominent figures from all over the country. Since there were no bathtubs in his palace, the king would visit the hotel twice a month to take a relaxing bath in one of its suites. Nobody found it odd to see him wandering alone through the cobbled streets of the historic city center. He enjoyed chatting with people, especially young women, and gazing proudly at the harmonious beauty of the city's monuments. Even though his counterpart, Queen Victoria of

England, had survived several assassination attempts in recent years, he refused to give up his old habits. Those furtive visits to Lola, always with a bouquet of flowers or a box of her favorite bonbons in hand, cheered the dancer's spirit after her rejection onstage. When Ludwig suggested that she pose for his famous gallery, she felt immensely flattered. It was a great honor to be chosen by the king of Bavaria to appear alongside the most notable beauties of the era. Until then, no Spanish lady had enjoyed the privilege. The king assured her that "her dazzling beauty and flawless features would bedim the radiance of her noblest fellows."

The sessions in Joseph Karl Stieler's studio began on the appointed day, though not without complications. In general, the models for the gallery were clothed in sumptuous medieval- or Renaissance-style costumes. Some were dressed as characters from plays by Schiller, the king's favorite author. The portraits, which were done in a static neoclassical style, represented the ideal of feminine beauty that Ludwig so admired. Though Stieler was one of the greatest painters of the era, Lola found his paintings cold and lifeless. She flatly refused to wear a costume, wanting to pass into posterity as a genuine Spanish dancer. As such, she chose to sit in an austere black velvet dress with a high openwork collar and a full scarlet skirt. Her long, curly hair was hidden by a fine mantilla made of black lace that fell to her waist. At twenty-five years old, Lola was at the height of her beauty.

Stieler did not have an easy time dealing with the restless, temperamental woman. For decades he had been doing portraits of timid, docile young ladies who respected and obeyed him. Lola, by contrast, would show up at his studio with Zampa, who never sat still, sniffing the canvases and chewing on the paintbrushes. She didn't have the patience to hold a pose in the painter's chilly, uncomfortable studio. For the king, however, these sessions were the perfect alibi to enjoy Lola's company out of view of indiscreet gazes.

Ludwig knew that, in the short time she'd been in Munich, Lola had already collected a small entourage of admirers, most of them young military officers who joined her on her morning walks. One was a good-looking artillery lieutenant, Friedrich Nussbammer, who had come to her aid when some locals insulted her on the street. In gratitude, Lola invited him to visit her at the hotel one afternoon. He soon became her devoted companion, and the two of them could be seen strolling through the city together. A rumor started that the king was trying to get Lola married to Nussbammer in an effort to regularize her status in Bavaria.

During breaks, Lola and the king would relax together on the painter's red velvet sofa, and the old king would chat animatedly in French, mixing in the occasional word in Italian or Spanish. Sometimes she would strum a few chords on the guitar and sing an Andalusian verse. Lola wasn't a good singer, but Ludwig thought she was perfect: "I adore the music of your voice, and I bow down before your art," he would tell her. Caught up in the romantic atmosphere, the king would be transported back to his idle years as a young man in Italy, when he was the handsome Prince Luigi who rubbed elbows with artists and students and lived for love and beauty alone.

One day, while posing, Lola tossed Ludwig a rose. He caught it and kissed its petals, grateful for her spontaneous gesture. On his way back to the palace, the king realized he had left the flower at the studio. He immediately sent one of his servants to retrieve it, with a handwritten note to the disapproving painter:

> I beg of you to send to my residence at once, in a sealed envelope, the rose that I left at your studio. Tomorrow I will personally check to make sure that you have complied with this request.
> Ludwig

Lola enjoyed His Majesty's attention but was not yet aware of the intensity of his feelings. Though her stint at the Court Theatre had been disappointing, she had no desire to give up on dance. One evening, when the king visited her hotel, she mentioned that she would soon leave Munich to perform in Augsburg. Ludwig refused to accept it.

"My divine Lola, I cannot live without you," he implored her. "Don't you realize, we are soul mates who seek the reason for our existence in art and beauty."

"I am very happy with you, but I am an artist and I must earn my living. I will travel to Augsburg and then return to spend a season here."

"No, no, no, Lola, you do not understand. You will break my heart if you leave now. What I feel for you is something I've never felt about anybody."

"Nor have I," Lola murmured, her eyes welling with tears, "and now I know I have a reason to stay." And she changed her plans.

After this moving confession, Ludwig breathed easier. The dancer was not only staying in Munich but had admitted to feeling something for him. Perhaps in the not too distant future she would even love him as a man and not just as a king. He was so absorbed that day that he was unaware of how time had slipped past. When he finally said goodbye, the hotel's front door was already locked. He caused such a commotion in the lobby that the manager had to come running. In the morning, Lola received one of the first gifts from her fervent admirer: a sumptuously bound edition of his poems, with an emotional dedication written in his hand. She could not understand the poems, but Ludwig could translate some into French; if she remained in Munich, he would teach her some German.

"I feel like an old romantic Quixote who has found in Lola his Dulcinea," the king wrote in his diary.

Everything about her fascinated him. Her arresting beauty and vibrant personality were irresistible. She was not meek and submissive like most of his lovers; indeed, she reminded him a great deal of himself. Ludwig was charming, fun loving, and good hearted, but also proud and selfish. If he discovered he'd been betrayed or his orders were not obeyed, he would fly into a rage and could be crude and even violent.

In his euphoria, he wrote a letter to an old friend, Baron Heinrich von der Tann, to tell him of his new joy:

> What will you say, my dear Tann, when I tell you that this man of sixty has awakened the flame of passion in the heart of a beautiful, intelligent, spirited, good-hearted, nobly born, twenty-two-year-old young woman of the South . . . The admiration (it is immodest to repeat it, but it is she who said it) that she first felt for me later turned to love. And I can compare myself to Vesuvius, which seemed to have gone extinct until it suddenly erupted once more . . . I am entangled in passion like never before. Sometimes I couldn't eat, couldn't sleep, my blood boiled feverishly in my veins, I was lifted to heaven's heights, my thoughts became purer, I became a better person. I was happy, am happy. My life has a new vitality. I am young again and the world is smiling on me.

Lola Montez was about to become the official lover of King Ludwig of Bavaria. She had arrived in Munich nearly penniless and fleeing her past. Now, she would have an important place in history. The monarch—thirty-five years her senior—awakened tender, almost maternal feelings in her. It was a new kind of relationship for the dancer, based more on friendship and mutual support than on sex. The king compensated for his age and his lack of physical attributes with complete and utter devotion. Lola found him the most refined, pleasant, and generous man she had ever met in the course of her tumultuous love life. No one—not Franz Liszt nor George Lennox nor her great love, Dujarier—had treated her with such respect. For the first time in her life, she felt truly powerful; she had a king who worshiped her and granted her every whim. Those who had previously assumed their relationship to be merely a passing fling now began to fear her influence. In the court, rumors and lies began to circulate. They said she was depraved, an impostor, an enemy of the Jesuits, and a social climber who was only after the king's power and fortune.

Though Ludwig was known for his stinginess and for maintaining tight control on every florin in the royal coffers, he was lavish with Lola from the start. Just weeks after they first met, he began to secretly give her ten thousand florins a year in monthly installments, a considerable sum considering that a minister's annual salary was around six thousand. As time went on, Lola enjoyed even more privileges. In addition to generous financial support, he promised her a carriage and a house in Munich's most elegant neighborhood. He also gave her a seat in the lower boxes of the Court Theatre so she could attend all the premieres. But Lola was discomfited by the curious and condemnatory stares from the audience in the orchestra seats. Annoyed by the way Munich high society looked down their noses at her, she persuaded Ludwig to give her a seat in one of the nobility's boxes on the second tier. She then promptly had its walls reupholstered in red velvet to make it even more splendid.

Riding high in her new role as the king's favorite, Lola began to display an arbitrary, authoritarian side. The first request she made of her generous protector was to have her own retinue. Crescentia Ganser, a language teacher and the wife of a sculptor Ludwig patronized, was hired as her companion and interpreter. Lola chose Berta Thierry, a dancer at the Court Theatre, and her sister Mathilde, an actress, as her ladies-in-waiting. The two young women lived with their father, and the incomes they made as performers were not enough to support the family. Lola convinced the monarch to give the Thierrys a monthly salary equivalent to what they normally earned in a year. While Ludwig was in such a giving frame of mind, she suggested that a noble title would make her very happy. She deserved it, she argued, since she came from a family of ancient lineage. To mollify her, the king promised he would name her countess at some later date.

It was clear that Lola had complete possession of Ludwig's heart. A few weeks later, not content with all he had given, he decided to revise his will and add a codicil naming her. In a letter to his wife, Therese, he said:

> I would not be a man of honor and would be unfeeling if I made no provision for her who has given up everything for me; who has no parents, no siblings; who has no one in the entire world except me. At no point has she sought to make me remember her in my last wishes. I do this completely of my own accord. Knowing her has made me a better, purer man. Therese, my beloved, good and noble wife, do not condemn me unjustly.

Ludwig also ordered his executor and heir to, in the case of his death, "give Lola the most recent oil portrait made of him before he died and 100,000 florins, unless she has married, and to award her an annual salary of 2,400 florins for life or until she marries."

Now that Lola was going to live in Munich, the ruler's greatest concern was finding a suitable house. The dancer had argued with the manager of the hotel where she'd been staying and had moved to an apartment attached to the Goldener Hirsch, another luxury hotel in the city, even closer to Ludwig's royal palace. Although the king continued to visit her openly every day, he wanted to have a love nest shielded from prying eyes. He decided to place this highly delicate matter in the hands of the man who had transformed Munich, the court architect and director of urbanism, Leo von Klenze. Though Klenze was retired, the king visited the architect at his home and spoke frankly.

"Esteemed Leo, I need your help in a delicate matter of the highest discretion."

"Your Majesty, I have always been at your service. You can rely on my complete loyalty," the architect replied.

"My dear friend, the Spanish dancer, Lola Montez, will be living in Munich, and I want to acquire a beautiful, comfortable mansion for her, with a small garden and in an elegant neighborhood."

"I understand, Your Majesty. It will be my pleasure to assist you. I must inform you, however, that this type of property requires complete renovation, and the cost could be quite high."

"Money is no issue. The house will be purchased in my beloved Lola's name. I want her to be the owner so that she can seek Bavarian citizenship, and I shall have any and all necessary refurbishments made."

After much consideration, Ludwig bought his lover a mansion at number 7 on the elegant Barerstrasse, next to Stieler's studio. It was a charming Italianate villa, two stories high, with tall windows and a wrought iron balcony overlooking the street. A marble staircase led to a sumptuous vestibule, and all the rooms were flooded with light. In the back was a lovely garden with ancient trees, hidden behind a high wall. Though the country was currently rocked by discontent in the midst of a grave economic crisis, the king of Bavaria spent sixteen thousand florins to buy the house, and twice that on remodeling it. Ludwig himself oversaw the work. To shield himself from gawkers and guarantee his safety, the king had a police gatehouse set up behind a fence. The news that the monarch, always so upstanding and austere, had given a house near the palace to his favorite only increased popular hostility toward Lola. People accused her of having bewitched the king with her occult powers and of seeking to rule Bavaria.

Though Ludwig may have been blinded by love, he soon saw that Lola didn't know the first thing about managing money. Concerned about the young woman's profligacy, he decided she needed someone trustworthy to oversee her finances. An old friend, Baron Carl Wilhelm von Heideck, a widowed former military officer who had always been loyal, came to mind. The king invited the baron to tea in the apartment where Lola was still living. The three of them had a lively conversation in French. The baron greatly enjoyed her amusing anecdotes, many of which were fabrications. Heideck had lived in Spain as a young man, and he swiftly fell for the vivacious dancer's charms.

"As you can see, my dear friend, Lolita is a great artist but she doesn't understand figures, and as with most women, money slips through her fingers. I'm afraid that, now that she owns a home and will be renovating and decorating it, there are those who will try to take advantage of her, being young and a foreigner. I would like you, my good friend, to review all the invoices to avoid any possible abuses."

"I will do so gladly, sir. I have plenty of time now, and if Mrs. Montez will allow it, I will be her attentive and loyal financial manager," he said, looking at Lola and nodding slightly.

But Heideck soon regretted accepting the delicate assignment. His placid retired life was upended by the dancer's capricious demands. Lola began patronizing the city's finest fashion halls and jewelry shops. She knew that all eyes were on her, so when seen in public, whether riding horseback, attending the opera, or strolling through the Nymphenburg Palace gardens on the king's arm, she wanted to look as elegant as the ladies at court. To his dismay, Heideck discovered that the young woman had told everyone to send the invoices straight to him, when she was the one who had the money. The old general spent more and more time dealing with Lola's financial matters. Not only were the bills piling up, but she also consulted him on practically everything, from how much she should pay her new servants to which of Munich's doctors would be best for treating her migraines. But what most bothered Heideck was having to also act as a cover for the couple's regular meetings. Occasionally the king would send him a note inviting him to Lola's rooms just so Ludwig could meet up with her without raising suspicion.

Since there were many people seeking to destroy her reputation, Ludwig warned his lover to be discreet and choose her friends wisely, but she paid him no heed. On the freezing night of November 15, Lola was waiting for her friend Lieutenant Friedrich Nussbammer, and when he didn't show up, she decided to look for him. It was past midnight when she and her maid, Jeanette, walked through the deserted, poorly lit streets of the city center until they reached the building on Frühlingstrasse where Nussbammer lived. Lola, irate and inebriated, rang the bell of every apartment. The commotion awoke the building caretaker, who told her that the young man wasn't home. Lola ignored her and continued shouting for her friend until she finally passed out drunk; her lady's maid, unable to carry her back to the hotel, requested help. A neighbor invited them in and offered Jeanette a cup of tea. When Lola came to, they walked back home just before sunrise.

The next day, Lola Montez's nighttime visit to Frühlingstrasse was the talk of the town. But instead of lying low and waiting for the gossip to blow over, she decided to return to the building. When she found the caretaker, she started insulting her, and the woman replied in French, "Please don't shout at me, girl, I'm not deaf."

"I'm no girl!" Lola yelled in a fury. "I am a lady, and what's more, I'm the king's lover!"

The incident soon reached Ludwig's ears, and he rushed to her side to learn the details. Lola, still furious with Nussbammer, tearfully told the king that the officer had insulted her, provoking her to forget her manners. She begged Ludwig to promise that the young man would be sent from Munich immediately. Back at the palace, the monarch shut himself in his private offices and wrote an order to his war minister. The following day, Nussbammer received the unexpected news that he was being transferred to the Würzburg artillery regiment and must leave the city as soon as possible. Ludwig, who was very jealous, was thrilled to get the handsome young officer away from Lola.

Oblivious to the scandal, Lola attended the premiere of a concert at the Court Theatre that night. King Ludwig, his wife, and some of his older children, as well as other illustrious visitors from the Dutch and Swedish royal houses, were in attendance. Lola's arrival caused a huge stir. In a striking burgundy satin dress with a fine shawl over her shoulders, she took her seat in the box. It had been rumored she would be in attendance, and the seats around her were empty as a sign of disdain. During the first intermission, Ludwig left Queen Therese and his guests to go to his "good friend." There was obvious consternation in the theater when she remained seated as the king conversed with her. Finally, Ludwig made her understand, with a subtle gesture, that she should stand when he spoke to her. Lola stood, and he informed her that Friedrich Nussbammer would soon be far from Munich and would not be bothering her again. When the curtain rose, the king returned to his box with his family as if the situation were the most natural in the world. Therese was embarrassed by the incident, and as they were returning to the palace, she reproached him for his unseemly conduct.

"You know that I am patient and discreet. I am well aware of your tendency to fall in love easily, and I respect your weaknesses; but today you took things too far."

"Forgive me if I've offended you, my dear; I had to inform my friend Lola of a matter of the utmost urgency."

"No, Ludwig, do not say another word. I ask that you not humiliate me again in public. I don't want to ever be in the same room with that woman again, and I only hope that you do not completely lose your head and remain aware of your responsibilities." With that, she withdrew to her chambers.

When Nussbammer received the order to leave Munich, he immediately understood whom he needed to turn to. He showed up unannounced at Lola's apartment and asked for her clemency. With tender words, the officer explained that it had all been a misunderstanding, and she decided to forgive him. She sent an urgent note to the king asking him to annul the order, saying that she would explain the reason in person later. Ludwig interpreted this change of attitude as an example of her kindness, that she had decided to be just and not punish the officer after he'd repented. The monarch retracted the order but begged his beloved not to see Nussbammer again.

Lola also had another important matter to discuss. A policeman investigating the Frühlingstrasse altercation was asking questions that could be compromising for her. Indignant at the rumors circulating in Munich, she was determined to address the topic with the king himself.

"It's incredible," she told him. "Some policeman has had the gall to question my maid, and he keeps prowling about the hotel, and people believe these terrible stories that are going around about me."

"Lolita, dear, I warned you that your position would not be easy, that you would be the subject of intrigues and malicious rumors. People are jealous because they know you mean everything to me."

"But I am innocent. Someone pretended to be me just to tarnish my reputation. You must put an end to this infamy."

"Don't worry, I will make sure these lies are stopped once and for all. You go and rest, and tomorrow I will come by to see you, my beloved Lolita. By that time everything will be resolved."

The chief of police, Johann von Pechmann, met with the king every Friday to present his weekly report on safety in the capital city. At thirty-seven, he was a respected jurist and an upstanding man committed to the rule of law. He came from noble, old Catholic lineage. His relationship with Lola Montez had been strained ever since she had arrived in Munich. He had had to ask her repeatedly to come to police headquarters to fill out the registration paperwork required of foreigners, and when she finally did, she had failed to present a single document confirming her identity or legal situation, claiming they had been stolen from her in Paris. But Pechmann, who took his job seriously, decided to ask his peers in Paris, Berlin, and Warsaw for information about her. He was sure that she was the one responsible for the Frühlingstrasse incident, but none of the witnesses dared to accuse her. According to his investigation, Lola had bought the silence of the neighbor who had helped her; when questioned, he had denied everything.

Now Pechmann found himself obligated to tell the king that his lover was an impostor and a liar. But when he arrived at the palace early that morning, he discovered that the king had his own opinion about what had happened.

"As sure as I stand before you, she is not the one responsible! Someone is trying to sully her reputation! That's how my subjects are—I know them well! And the most respectable ones are the worst!"

"Your Majesty, I have no desire to contradict you, and your anger is understandable, but you should know that Miss Lola Montez has disrespected you by baldly asserting in the plain light of day that she is your lover."

"No, Lola could never say that; she is intelligent and well mannered. It is true that I love her, I won't deny it, but having a lover is something different. One thing elevates a man and the other degrades him. This situation is merely a vindictive plot against her."

"Well then, what would Your Majesty have me do?"

"Drop the investigation, stop questioning Lola's servants, and file the case away in the archives as soon as possible. You will soon receive a charming visitor. Lola will come to see you and explain everything herself."

Pechmann left the king's private offices very concerned. No one else dared to tell the monarch the truth about Lola's past, but Pechmann was determined to unmask her. To that end, he recruited a spy inside the dancer's apartment: her companion and interpreter, Crescentia Ganser, who was charged with giving him daily reports on Lola's visitors and the conversations they had. In the face of such irrefutable evidence, maybe the king would come to his senses and expel Lola Montez from Bavaria.

That same afternoon, the police chief received a visit from the dancer, in the company of Ambros Havard, the owner of the Goldener Hirsch, who was there to act as interpreter. The meeting was very short. Lola demanded, in an imperious tone, that the policeman who had questioned her maid be banished from the city. She also told him that Nussbammer's neighbor could confirm that she wasn't even there that night, then added that it was a personal affront to His Majesty to continue investigating his good friend when it was abundantly clear that she had not been involved in the disturbance. Pechmann listened without a word, startled by her aggressive stance and the fury in her eyes. She was clearly a volatile woman who could go from violence to tenderness with hardly a change in her facial expression. As she bid him farewell, she held out her hand for him to kiss, saying seductively, "Mr. von Pechmann, our relationship got off on the wrong foot, but I would love for you to pay me a visit. Now, I'll leave you to ponder what steps to take. Do your duty. Good day."

Ludwig was irritated with his people. As he saw it, the passion he felt for Lola did not keep him from being a good ruler, and he devoted a great deal of time and energy to governing. In fact, he constantly repeated to his closest confidants that, because of Lola, he was becoming a happier man and a better monarch. He wrote another letter to Baron von der Tann, the only one who knew the true nature of his feelings:

> Dear friend,
> Lolitta (as I call her) is being and will always be subject
> to terrible slander. The mere fact that she is a foreigner
> who wishes to settle in Munich, a beautiful, spiritual
> foreigner who enjoys the king's love, is enough to pro-
> voke gossip, hostility, and harassment against her. But
> all of this will end and the truth will shine forth. Lola
> is not only a woman who loves me, but a good friend
> who has promised to always tell me the truth.

Despite the multiple scandals, Ludwig continued to believe in his beloved's good character. The promise of sincerity that she had made to him was all he needed. Though the pamphlets circulating about his relationship with the Spanish dancer had wounded him deeply, he continued to fulfill his obligations. The monarch arose as usual before dawn, dealt with piles of documents and memoranda, signed decrees, inaugurated museums, received his subjects in audience, and oversaw his ministers. As he told Tann, he was convinced that his people would eventually come around to Lola and respect her as she deserved.

But by late 1846 hostility toward "the Spaniard" was only growing. The few friends she did have advised her to use her influence over Ludwig to defend some noble cause and so improve her public image. Lola had heard that schoolteachers had been asking the king for a raise and that their demands enjoyed popular support. She persuaded Ludwig to better their precarious economic situation by arguing that they were the "true pillar of education." She was so convincing that Ludwig immediately agreed to increase their salaries. But the gambit did not produce the outcome Lola had expected. Instead, it demonstrated that the king's lover could interfere in political matters and influence his decisions. Furthermore, she made the mistake of detracting from the king's authority by announcing that she had persuaded Ludwig to increase the teachers' pay a week before he signed the directive. It was abundantly clear to the Bavarian people that Lola constituted a grave threat to the established order. Her increasingly arrogant, assertive, and outlandish behavior was earning her many enemies.

Despite all that, she continued to enjoy the king's unconditional love and generous gifts. One day she received an unexpected surprise. Stepping out to the street, she found an elegant black coupé upholstered in gold-trimmed white silk that the sovereign had instructed Maltzahn to buy for her when he returned to Paris. Ludwig also gave her two splendid horses from the royal stables so she could travel in the style of a grand lady. Lola had other moments of happiness in those days as well. Stieler had finished her portrait, which hung in a prominent spot in the palace's Gallery of Beauties. None of his paintings had ever aroused such anticipation, and long lines of curiosity seekers formed.

Only one incident cast a pall over the happy day that her portrait became part of the famous gallery. At the announcement that Lola Montez's likeness would join the exhibition, Count von Arco-Valley—a fervent Catholic and leader of the Bavarian opposition—asked that the painting of his wife be removed from the royal collection. Ludwig did his best to hide this from Lola, but it was no use. When she heard, she became furious, feeling rejected once more by the Bavarian nobility. When the king appeared at the usual time with a bouquet of flowers and a poem under his arm, Lola was at her wits' end. "Let's leave here, Luis," she told him, sobbing. "I beg you to abdicate and flee with me to Spain. Just the two of us."

"Lolita, of course I would love to travel with you to my beloved Spain and stroll together through the gardens of the Alhambra, but you must understand that I am the king and have a duty to my people."

"You yourself complain that your people used to love you but now have turned their backs and only seek to drive us apart," she insisted.

"My dearest," the monarch replied, trying to calm her down, "this will all soon be resolved. You will have your own house and servants, and you will be accepted by all those who now look down their noses at you. Have patience, my divine Lolita. You know that my love for you is pure and true."

During that harsh winter, Lola's greatest hope was to be able to show off the lovely house on Barerstrasse that the king had given her. For the first time in her life, she had her own home, and it felt like she was living a dream. Thanks to the costly renovation, her new place was elegant and very comfortable. The main entrance was crowned by two spectacular caryatids, to the king's taste. In the center of the garden, a marble fountain with four sculpted dolphins greeted visitors. It was perfect for Lola, small and welcoming enough for her to feel at home, but decorated with the utmost refinement. It had a grand hall, a main sitting room, a dining room, a ladies' parlor, a "Don Quixote" room named by Ludwig, and a yellow and a green room, both decorated in the Pompeian style. Most impressive was a gleaming crystal staircase that led to the bedroom, dressing room, and boudoir. The king had helped her with the decorating, choosing paintings and art objects with his exquisite taste. He lent Lola an Etruscan vase from the royal collection for her to display proudly in her sitting room beside the fireplace, along with a valuable Madonna by Raphael and a selection of books from his private library. The king felt very lucky, even though the original budget for the house had been doubled by its owner's whims and demands.

One of Lola's first guests was her friend George Henry Francis, a journalist and editor at the *Morning Post*. Lola had met him in London, and he came to Munich to write an article about the new life of the Andalusian dancer who had become the mistress of the king of Bavaria. He found her new residence "quite unique in its simplicity and lightness" and "supplied by French elegance, Munich art, and English comfort."

Lola was living a fairy tale. She was the owner of a small palace, with her own servants, a carriage at her disposal, a stable of fine horses, and a king who loved her madly. Europe's most famous courtesans—even Madame de Pompadour, the favorite of Louis XV, for whom the French monarch had built the Petit Trianon at Versailles—had nothing on her. She dreamed of being the perfect hostess, organizing parties and starting her own salon that featured talented artists, politicians, and intellectuals. During that happy period, Lola learned from Baron von Frays that Marie Taglioni was set to arrive in Munich. The classical ballet legend had been invited to perform at the Court Theatre and at Nymphenburg Palace. The news revived sad memories for Lola. She hadn't forgotten the success of her debut in London at His Majesty's Theatre, nor the rave reviews she'd garnered on her opening night, even if her aspirations had gone up in smoke after someone in the audience had recognized her. Now the presence of Taglioni, to whom she'd always been compared, reminded her of that painful failure. She decided to organize a private party in her "rival's" honor and show Taglioni the spectacular advance she'd made in becoming King Ludwig I's official lover.

At forty-two years old, Marie Taglioni was on her final European tour before retirement. Her Munich appearance was highly anticipated, and all the tickets quickly sold out. In her debut performance at the Court Theatre, she would be dancing the role that had made her famous in *La sylphide*. Lola, who had only heard of her legendary feats, decided to attend the opening. When the curtain lifted and the ballerina, stunning in her gauzy white dress, appeared in the center of the stage, Lola was overcome by a wave of emotion. The set evoked a gloomy Scottish forest wrapped in mist, and Taglioni was an ethereal sylph silently gliding en pointe with perfect technique. When the show ended, she had to make several curtain calls, and Lola tossed flowers from her box. Taglioni was an intemperate, arrogant diva who'd never been able to tolerate rivals, and after seeing her dance, Lola felt a mix of envy and admiration. She would have given anything to have had her success on the stage and have won the Munich public's affection and respect. But she consoled herself with the thought that she had the friendship and unconditional love of a king who lived only for her.

At the party she hosted for the ballerina, Lola spared nothing for her illustrious guest. Though Baron von Heideck begged her to keep to a budget, she ignored him entirely. In an effort to dazzle the ballerina, she ordered fresh floral centerpieces for the entire house and purchased a complete silver tea set, fine Bohemian glassware, an antique crystal punch bowl with cups, and a very expensive set of porcelain dishes from Paris that she had emblazoned with the emblem of the nine-pointed crown, the symbol of a countess. She didn't yet hold that noble title, but she knew that Ludwig couldn't bring himself to deny her. She also had her servants' flashy uniforms updated.

When a footman opened the door to Marie Taglioni and her small entourage, the ballerina was amazed by Lola's exquisite home. For the occasion, her hostess had chosen a two-piece gown of green silk taffeta that matched her magnificent emerald necklace, a gift from the king. Lola looked stunning, a fact confirmed by the gentlemen clustered around her. They were men from the theater world, society chroniclers, businessmen, dancers, and choreographers. Lola was unfailingly sociable, charming, and generous with her guests—even with journalists who had criticized her in the past. The evening was a resounding success, and after a sumptuous meal served by the fireplace in the dining room, the guests raised their glasses to toast the grande dame of the dance world with French champagne. The next day, all they talked about was Lola Montez, the true queen of Munich.

CHAPTER 6

Scandal in the Court

Each morning the king practically skipped as he made his way from his palace to Lola's house. It was only a ten-minute walk, and he thrummed with anticipation of the moment he could hold her in his arms, hear her velvety voice, and smell the soft fragrance of her skin. On his way to his trysts, he was amazed to contemplate how his life had changed since meeting his lover. He was a new man, passionate and full of dreams. That day he'd gotten up early as usual and, thinking of Lola, had grasped his pen and written in his diary: "Beloved Lola, thanks to you my life has been ennobled; my life without you was lonely and empty; your love feeds my heart, I would die without it. All the feelings that other women inspired in me have been extinguished before you. Because my eyes read in yours: love."

Ludwig never showed up empty handed; he always brought a bouquet of her favorite flowers, into which he would tuck one of his poems or a piece of jewelry. Lola would be waiting for him in the sitting room with the fireplace lit, sometimes reading Homer or languidly strumming the guitar. They never got bored together, and the servants often heard them laughing.

She gave him Spanish lessons and he taught her a few words of German. They talked about art, politics, dance, and literature, and they confided in each other. When it was sunny, they would sit under the pergola in the garden behind the house, shielded from prying eyes. Lola would smoke a cigarette, and the king never tired of admiring her untamed beauty.

Though the Bavarian press had been forbidden to mention the name Lola Montez, offensive pamphlets about the Spanish dancer were circulating, along with cartoons depicting Ludwig as a satyr or as a donkey wearing a crown on its rump. It was said that the king was being manipulated by a "devil woman" who wanted to wrest the throne of Bavaria away from him. Some Catholic schools in the city recited prayers that His Majesty would regain his sanity. Ludwig deplored the attacks, and he decided to do something about them. One morning he sent for Maurus Harter, a loyal subject who had served Ludwig's father, King Maximilian I. The venerable old man of seventy had been the head librarian for decades. When Ludwig had transferred the university at Landshut and its library of more than three hundred volumes to Munich, Harter was charged with protecting and cataloging that priceless patrimony. Now, tired of hearing cruel calumnies, Ludwig made a request that stunned his longtime collaborator.

"My dear friend, you have been in my service for many years, and I would like for you to carry out an order from this now-elderly king whose people will not allow him to be happy. Starting today, I would like you to collect and archive all the pamphlets and libelous documents about my relationship with Lola."

"Sir, I have heard the rumors and lies about Your Majesty and your Spanish friend, but you should remain above all that and not give it any attention. Why would you want to keep them?"

"Oh, my friend, because in the end justice will be done. I want to preserve for posterity these displays of disloyalty to the king."

"I will do as you command, but I fear that this will not appease your rage and indignation; quite the contrary, reading this offal will do you no good. As we speak, people are claiming that Lola Montez is a British spy and—"

"Nonsense!" Ludwig interrupted, pounding the table with his fist. "She simply makes me happy, and my selfish, puritanical people can't understand that."

At the end of the icy January of 1847, Munich awoke one morning blanketed in a thick layer of snow. The children pulled out their sleds, and for a few hours the city was filled with cheer. Lola had the king's ardent love, but she was unable to win the affection of his people. Her most loyal companion in those days was a large, ferocious-looking black mastiff. She called him Turk, in memory of Prince Heinrich von Reuss-Lobenstein's Saint Bernard, with whom she'd pillaged the prince's gardens of lilies and tulips. When she went walking or shopping in the city center, her mere presence was a provocation. Sure of her rank, she was arrogant about being the king's lover and demanded the privileges she believed she deserved. If one of her desires was not met, all of her charm vanished in an instant and her temper exploded without warning. Lola was given to shouting at, slapping, or brandishing her whip against anyone who confronted or displeased her.

On one occasion she visited the Meyerhofer workshop to buy a set of cutlery. When the silversmith explained that, on orders from Baron von Heideck, he was unable to extend her any further credit, she flew into a rage and punched her fist through the glass front of a cabinet. A physician had to be summoned to tend the resulting cut on her hand. This incident greatly displeased Heideck, who complained to the king about Lola's bizarre, violent behavior.

"This sort of reaction is making your friend a persona non grata in the city," the baron warned Ludwig. The king, who had been informed about the incident by the police, merely responded, "This time Lolita has punished herself, and it was well deserved."

Since moving into her house, Lola's social life had been practically nonexistent. The king visited her every day and felt so comfortable there that the two hardly ever went out. In part, Ludwig feared his subjects' reactions if they saw him in public with his young lover. The members of the nobility no longer concealed their disdain for her; they refused to invite her to their parties and no longer acknowledged her on the street. All of Ludwig's efforts were futile. The Art Association, more than three thousand members strong, rejected Lola's request for admittance, even though the king was her main patron. The Museum Society, Munich's most exclusive social club, also unanimously denied her. But what wounded him most was that all his advisers opposed granting her Bavarian citizenship. Shielded from the rejection she provoked by the cocoon of the king's protection, Lola enjoyed Ludwig's complete devotion and his extravagant gifts. The most recent of these had been a unique white-gold bracelet set with diamonds and sapphires, along with one of his poems:

> *Let the poet sing praises anew,*
> *without love, the blood goes cold.*
> *Let it warm itself once more*
> *with love's eternal fire!*

> *On the ether's brilliant heights,*
> *the transfigured soul soars*
> *when I am beside you,*
> *when bliss surrounds me.*

But the dancer was starting to grow bored. She couldn't bear the idea of having come so far only to sit idle. She thought longingly of Paris, where joy, pleasure, and desire had reigned. She yearned for that worldly life so different from conservative Bavaria. She missed her liberal and progressive journalist and writer friends, who had been part of a powerful opposition. She had read in the papers that revolutionary winds were blowing in the French capital, where King Louis-Philippe's support was plummeting. She would have liked to have been there and experience firsthand the changes that, in the next two years, would bring down two monarchs and a dozen autocratic governments across Europe.

To survive in the hostile atmosphere, she decided to start her own literary salon. In Paris, through Joseph Méry and Alexandre Dumas, she had been to the most exclusive salons, most of them led by famous courtesans. There, those mistresses were real celebrities, sophisticated and vivacious women who were close friends to kings, emperors, and wealthy financiers. They set trends and inspired artists. Lola wanted to host a group of prominent figures to engage in lively literary and political discussions in her home. When she excitedly proposed the idea to Ludwig, he expressed hesitation.

"My dear Lolita, how can I put this: Munich isn't Paris. That sort of salon doesn't exist here. But invite your theater friends over for tea if that will amuse you, and—"

"It's not a matter of being amused," Lola broke in, annoyed. "I want to welcome talented people into my home—politicians, artists, writers, men and women who share my progressive views."

"I'm an elderly king who's hopelessly in love with you, but I cannot and must not support you in your every desire. If you discuss politics during such salons, you will be undermining me. Don't look for more enemies than you already have," he said.

As the king's official lover, she thought she had the right to receive visits from whomever she wished and to establish a refined salon characterized by "gallantry, reading, frivolity, and reflection." When her friend George Henry Francis, the London journalist, visited Munich, she invited a number of prominent local figures to breakfast at informal gatherings attended by artists, academics, and foreign visitors. Francis witnessed Lola's charisma and described her as a lady with fine manners, an attentive, hospitable hostess who dressed with style and elegance. Yet he also observed how the young woman could fly into a rage if contradicted. In an article on the life of the celebrated Lola Montez in Munich, he wrote the following:

> She loves power for its own sake; she is too hasty, and too steadfast in her dislikes; she has not sufficiently learnt to curb the passion which seems natural to her Spanish blood; she is capricious, and quite capable, when her temper is inflamed, of rudeness, which, however, she is the first to regret and to apologize for.

Those breakfasts with which Lola sought to increase her political and social influence lasted only a few weeks. Her lust for power, her ferocious temper, and her dark past earned her ever more antipathy. She soon discovered that she had only enemies around her. The representatives of the old aristocracy detested her, and the high-society ladies had no wish to interact with her and jeopardize their own reputations. Overcome by nostalgia, she wrote a long letter to her friend Pier Angelo Fiorentino, the Parisian journalist who had always stood by her:

> Well, dear Fiorentino, I left Paris at the beginning of June as a lady errant and raced about the world and *today* I'm on the point of receiving the title of *countess*! I have a lovely property, horses, servants—in sum, everything that could surround the official mistress of the king of Bavaria.
> Here I am, surrounded by the homage of great ladies, I go everywhere, all of Munich waits upon me, ministers of state, generals, great ladies, and I no longer recognize myself as Lola Montez. The king loves me passionately; he's given me an income of 50,000 francs for life and has already spent more than 300,000 francs on my property, etc., etc.

. . . The king publicly shows his great love for me . . . Every week I have a great party for the ministers, etc., etc., which he attends and where he can't do me enough homage. I know, dear Fiorentino, you always wished me well and that this news will please you. That's why I'm writing, because, although surrounded by all the glories and homage of my most ambitious hopes, alas, sometimes I dream, I think of Paris. Dear Paris!

In truth, there isn't real happiness in grandeur. There is so much envy, so many intrigues. You always have to play the great lady and measure your words to each individual. Alas! my joyful life in Paris!

But I'm resolved. I won't leave this world to which I find myself elevated as if by a miracle. The king has a passion of true love for me. He's never had mistresses before. But my character pleased him. He is a man of remarkable talent. A true genius and one of the most elegant poets in Europe today. My slightest whim is a duty for him, and all of Munich is confounded.

Farewell, dear friend. I send you a kiss. Thank God you aren't here because I can have neither friend nor . . . [ellipsis in the original] Grandeur is so difficult!

Your ever affectionate,

Lola

Though she sounded exultant in her letter, the reality was quite different. While it was true that Ludwig loved her passionately, the nobility and the bourgeoisie increasingly opposed her. The few friends she had were harshly criticized and pulled away for fear of possible retaliation. Lola's favorite baker complained to the king because his association with the young woman had substantially harmed his Christmas sales. As compensation, Ludwig named him court chocolatier. The doctor who treated the dancer also complained that he was losing patients because they didn't want to run into her in his waiting room. In a letter, he requested that the king give him a salary to compensate for his losses. Many people were trying to avoid Lola Montez's company, and she found herself increasingly isolated. She openly blamed the Jesuits for being behind a campaign to bring her down, as the rise to power in 1837 of the brilliant politician Karl von Abel had enabled the order to exert a great deal of control over life in the country. Abel, one of King Ludwig's closest advisers, was a staunch Catholic and a sworn enemy of the kingdom's Protestant subjects.

Lola's fixation on the Jesuits had begun during her time in Paris. The year of her arrival in the French capital was one of great protest against the Society of Jesus. The press at the time was full of articles about the Jesuits' efforts to bring down governments, influence kings, and destroy any who opposed their power. Though Lola pretended to be a devout Catholic in order to make her Spanish noblewoman character more believable, she publicly accused them of conspiring against her. One day with the king, she broke down.

"I can't bear to live this way. I am disliked and insulted behind my back so I can't defend myself," she said. "And the Jesuits hate me—they make my life impossible and are trying to run me out of Bavaria. You must take measures against them immediately."

"Lolita, my dear, you are the one who declared war on them, and they will not forgive you for it. I don't like their plotting either, but they will continue to attack you because they consider you a threat. We must remain more united than ever and fight for our love."

"What good are your love and your gifts when I'm not even a Bavarian citizen and cannot have a noble title?"

"Be patient, Lolita, you will have everything you desire. I will never let you down, and I'll stand with you always."

To cheer his lover, the king commissioned a new portrait of her from the court painter, Stieler. It wasn't that he hadn't liked the first one, but he wanted her to pose the way she'd been when he met her— wearing the same black velvet dress, with red carnations in her hair and a simple lace veil. He didn't want to remember her as a dancer but as the beautiful, demure young woman from the Andalusian aristocracy whom he'd fallen in love with at first sight. Every day Ludwig went to the studio to chat with her or read a Goethe poem to her. It was very cold and the king had two woodstoves installed to heat the room. The effort was worthwhile: this second portrait of Lola Montez would be one of the celebrated painter's most esteemed works. Though he didn't much like his model, Stieler managed to capture her sparkling eyes, her proud bearing, and her vibrant "Spanish" temperament better than any other artist. Despite the annoyance and worry she caused the king, Lola still knew how to keep him interested. In return for Stieler's portrait, she gave Ludwig a gift that he treasured: a life-size marble carving of her own foot, created by Johann Leeb, the court sculptor. Upon receiving the sculpture from the artist himself, Ludwig wrote his beloved a note, enclosing one of his love poems:

> Heart of my heart, my Lolitta,
> You have given me great pleasure with your lovely sur-
> prise of sending me your foot carved in marble. Your
> foot has no equal—it appears to be an antique ideal.
> Once Leeb had left, I covered it with ardent kisses.
> Many thanks. I wish to thank you in person, which I
> will do at noon today. Your ever faithful
>   Luis

The king gave the sculpture a place of honor in his private chambers. He kissed it often, and it became a pet object that gave him unusual pleasure. In thanks for the gift, Ludwig had Leeb make a marble reproduction of the king's august hand holding a pen and writing a poem.

As the king's obsession with his beloved Lolita grew, a new scandal rocked the peaceful kingdom. The chief of police, Pechmann, was still looking for evidence to expose Lola as an impostor. Though Ludwig had told him to drop the investigation, Pechmann had decided to take the delicate matter to his superior, the minister of the interior, Karl von Abel. So far, that astute politician had not interfered with the king's relationship. For ten years he had served the king faithfully and knew of his weakness for beautiful women. But now Abel was increasingly concerned. For the first time, Ludwig appeared to be truly in love, and Abel feared the sway that Lola might hold over the king.

Pechmann went to Abel's office and asked him whether he should continue his efforts to reveal the dancer's true identity, or if it was better not to irritate His Majesty any longer.

"Talk to the king," the minister of the interior told him, "and tell him everything you've discovered about the Spaniard."

"Sir, I fear his reaction. He refuses to hear the truth."

"It's true, he will fly into a rage, but I know him well. Afterward he will calm down and he will be grateful for your loyalty. When he sees that your frankness is born of a loyal heart, he will not hold it against you."

The chief of police decided to speak honestly to the king during his weekly audience. Without beating around the bush, he informed Ludwig that Lola faced increasing rejection at every level of society. Even some of his most faithful and devoted subjects considered her a threat to the crown.

"I know," the king told him. "And it doesn't bother me a bit. All of this will blow over. There's nothing but spite behind it."

"Your Majesty, the biggest problem is that Lola Montez defies feminine decency and speaks openly of the favors she receives from you."

"Absolutely not. That is mere idle talk. What could she say about me? I don't even have that kind of relationship with her. That's just envy and jealousy at work."

"She is also accused," the chief of police continued, "of boasting about exerting a certain influence in affairs of state, and she has expressed her wish to make some changes in Your Majesty's government."

"No chance of that happening. I know very well who is in charge in Bavaria, and nobody is going to talk me into anything."

After a pause, Pechmann lowered his voice and murmured, "As Your Majesty's subject, I am obliged to tell you the whole truth. There are rumors all through the city that Lola Montez allows men to visit her at night and, specifically, that she is visited by Lieutenant Nussbammer."

"Enough! Now listen: she promised to always tell me the truth, and I believe her with all my heart. These absurd rumors are pure libel. Poor Lola—she is beauty, purity, and sincerity incarnate."

The king pulled himself together and thanked the chief of police for speaking frankly. Patting him on the shoulder, he added that Pechmann had done the right thing. Then, without saying goodbye, he spun on his heel and exited the chamber.

Pechmann hadn't been able to provide any proof of Lola's immoral behavior, but his words sowed doubt in Ludwig for the first time. When the king went for a stroll with her a few hours later, he didn't say anything about it. For the moment he only wanted to keep this wonderful dream of love alive and enjoy a rejuvenating passion.

The next day, Crescentia Ganser went to Pechmann to tell him she could no longer endure the situation at Lola's house. She refused to keep spying and wanted no part of any conspiracy. The police chief told her to go directly to the king and tell him everything she'd learned about the dancer. Before she left, he handed her copies of the daily reports she'd submitted to the police.

Ludwig was engrossed in work when it was announced that Crescentia Ganser wanted to see him about an urgent matter. He had known her for years; her husband, Anton, was a skilled sculptor who worked in the court, and he was fond of the family.

"What do you have for me, my dear Crescentia?" he said warmly.

"Your Majesty has been betrayed!" the woman cried out, sobbing.

"By whom? Surely you don't mean Lola?"

The king read over the reports and fell to his knees with his hands clasped and tears running down his face. Mrs. Ganser begged him to get Lola out of his life and never see her again, since she would bring only misfortune. Deeply upset, he went over to his table and, with a trembling hand, wrote a note for Baron von Heideck:

Happiness is not made for this world. Here I have been happy, but now I see that I am being expelled from my paradise. The unthinkable has occurred. I thought I would spend the years remaining to me in a state of exalted love. It has all been a dream . . . and now it is over. But let us not be unnecessarily hasty. The bearer of this note, the wife of the sculptor Ganser, will show you the proof. You will have the calm that I lack. After leaving me to reflect a while, I will go to your house today at about half past one. I think it is best that Lolitta meet with me there. If I must break things off with her forever (I fear there is no other solution), then I want to see her one last time. There is no need to fear any violence on my part. The king is ashamed that tears are welling up in his eyes as he writes this, but the sixty-year-old man is not.

He who only an hour ago was still happy,

Ludwig

After signing the note, he ordered Mrs. Ganser to take it and the reports to the residence of Baron von Heideck immediately. The old general was having breakfast and still in his dressing gown when the woman burst into the house and pressed the king's missive on him. Heideck asked her to sit down and briefly questioned her over a cup of tea. He then dismissed her and told her not to tell anybody about the matter. Next he began poring over the papers and found himself overwhelmed by a great feeling of unease. On those pages were listed all the visits and conversations that had taken place at number 7 Barerstrasse over the past few months. Again and again, the names of Lieutenant Nussbammer and other gentlemen appeared, their visits taking place at hours at which a respectable woman would never have been alone with a man. Crescentia was unable to say what had happened during these encounters, but she considered them immoral. The reports also included Lola's comments about various locals who had attended her parties, and if they were true, it was clear that she was an arrogant, outlandish, trifling person disposed to use her power over the king to achieve her own aims.

Heideck was still recovering from his anger when the king arrived unexpectedly. He looked pale and anxious, with bloodshot eyes. Ludwig hugged Heideck and wept bitterly on his shoulder.

"Joy will no longer be mine," he moaned. "I thought I had found a woman who would be my friend for the rest of my days, someone who would fill my empty hours with an intimate, spiritual happiness and whose tranquil inspiration and company would make me forget problems of state. I love and honor the queen, but her conversation is simply insufficient for my intellect, and my heart needs female companionship. I thought I'd found that woman in Lola, and she has betrayed me."

"Your Majesty, you must pull yourself together and think about your health and your duties as a ruler. Stop tormenting yourself. I beg you not to suffer over her any longer; Lola deserves only your disdain. You must not see her ever again."

"No, Heideck, I cannot do what you ask," the king replied. "But I will not see her until you have spoken with her first."

"I fear for your health and how much it might affect you to see her again."

"Maybe she is innocent or at least not so guilty as this woman claims. Think about how gravely she is being accused, about how profoundly harmed she and I have been. No, I will not condemn her without hearing what she has to say. Her disloyalty has already caused enough pain deep in my soul; there is no need to add self-recrimination for having been unjust to her."

Ludwig asked his friend to summon Lola and show her Mrs. Ganser's reports. He would meet with her later to hear her version of events. The baron could not refuse, but he was nervous about talking with the dancer. He didn't know how she would react upon discovering that she'd been spied on in her own home. It was rumored that the Spaniard carried a dagger hidden in her garter and that she always had a pistol at hand in her mansion. He decided not to meet with her alone; one of his servants would keep watch to ensure his safety.

After a few hours, Lola Montez arrived at Heideck's home. He told her that he had summoned her to discuss a confidential matter. Lola, sitting comfortably on the sofa, lit a cigarette and asked what was so urgent. Heideck mustered his courage and told her that Mrs. Ganser had been spying on her and was accusing her of comporting herself in a manner unbefitting of a lady. A stern expression on his face, he reproached her for her behavior and demanded that she confess. As he'd anticipated, Lola stood up in a fury and hurled the silver tea service to the floor.

"How dare you judge me? I swear on my father's grave that I am innocent. I can't believe that the king, who is well aware of my pure spirit and loyalty, has taken such false reports to heart. I will take a stagecoach to Paris straightaway tomorrow and he will not see me again." She stalked toward the door.

As Heideck tried in vain to placate her, King Ludwig entered, pale and downcast. He had been listening from the other side of the door. Upon seeing him, Lola's eyes widened.

"I will never forgive you!" she cried. "Spying on me is a very low blow! You have betrayed me, your Lolita who has always been so faithful and devoted to you."

Ludwig was devastated and didn't know how to respond. Once she had calmed down, he asked Heideck to leave the parlor. The baron retreated to an adjoining room and waited to hear what would happen next. Lola collapsed and started sobbing as the king tenderly held her. They spoke in Spanish, which Heideck could not follow, and the king promised that he would continue to love her just as he had from the very start. After a while, the baron peeked into the room and pointed to his pocket watch to remind Ludwig that it was almost three o'clock and his wife, Therese, would be waiting for him at the palace. Ludwig waved him away.

Eventually the couple reconciled. After hearing her arguments, the king sincerely believed her, and she agreed not to leave Munich. Calmer now, she strode past the baron with her head held high and, without saying goodbye, marched out the door. As Heideck helped Ludwig into his coat, he remarked, "Well, now Your Majesty has seen her in a rage. I must admit I've never seen such a devil before. I imagine you won't be seeing her again."

"Actually," the king answered, a slight smile on his face, "I promised to visit her later this afternoon."

"But Your Majesty, you must stay away," the baron insisted.

"I made her a promise, and I'm not about to let anyone tell me what to do."

The king left, reassured and more relaxed, but Heideck was bewildered by what he'd just witnessed. "I feel sorry for His Highness—he is so hopelessly in love that he is incapable of seeing what that woman is really like and how she is manipulating him to her own ends," he thought, trying to calm his nerves. When Ludwig visited his lover in the afternoon, she convinced him that Mrs. Ganser's reports were false. The king asked the baron to return the devastating letter he'd written that morning so that Lola could see that his feelings hadn't changed. He felt closer than ever to her and swore to himself that nothing and nobody could tear them apart. He wrote to his loyal friend Tann, "We have reconciled. Lolitta is not going to leave me. Even if all the accusations had been true and she had remorsefully confessed her guilt, I would have forgiven her because of how passionately I love her."

The next day, Ludwig received a letter from Heideck asking the king to accept his resignation. He claimed to be too old for such trying work and that his health was suffering because Lola was uncontrollable. He wanted to go back to his former retired life and have time for his hobbies. The king reluctantly agreed, but he knew the young woman needed a loyal, understanding friend by her side, ideally someone widely respected. Only Maltzahn, who knew her well, could fulfill that role.

Maltzahn had been in Paris since November, and Ludwig wrote to him at once. He asked him to return to Munich as soon as possible because his dear Lola needed him. Maltzahn replied that he would comply, but he had conditions. He wanted to be named His Majesty's aide-de-camp and to be allowed to spend the summers in Baden-Baden. The king hastily acquiesced and wrote, "Love, honor, and duty bind me to Lolitta. There is a conspiracy brewing here to drive us apart, but they've only managed to make us closer than ever."

Still, Ludwig could not conceal his unease about the way she behaved sometimes. In his diary, he wrote, "She is sticking her nose into private affairs of state. Despite the concessions I've made for her, she wants even more. Where will this end?"

Ludwig had assumed that, after the business with Mrs. Ganser, his favorite would be more discreet, but Lola's behavior did not change. The king had asked her not to see Lieutenant Nussbammer without his permission, and he'd made it very clear to the officer that, if he kept pestering Lola, he'd be kicked out of the city. But the two young people were very attracted to each other and decided to ignore the ruler's orders. Just as the secret reports had claimed, Nussbammer continued to visit Lola at her home on Barerstrasse, and appearances suggested that they were lovers.

One afternoon the king arrived at Lola's residence earlier than expected and found the officer sitting in an armchair by the fireplace.

Nussbammer had just returned to Munich after a long leave in Ansbach, where his superiors had sent him to get him away from the seductive dancer's charms. Ludwig, very upset, ordered him out of the house. After the officer left, Lola tried to calm the king and convince him that he was misinterpreting the situation. Her voice forlorn, she begged him to listen to her for once.

"Luis, this is all a huge misunderstanding. You know me; you know I am kind by nature. I let Nussbammer keep visiting because I felt sorry for him. The poor man is madly in love with me, and you know I don't love him, but I couldn't refuse to see him. I told him he has to forget me, and he is deeply hurt."

"Lolita, I adore you, but inviting that man into your home, even if it was for noble reasons, was an audacious thing to do. Listen to me, sweetheart, your reputation is at stake. All eyes are on you," he pleaded.

"Darling Luis," she replied, laying her head on his knees, "forgive me, you know I don't have anybody in this world and gave up everything for your love. It won't happen again if it makes you uncomfortable."

The dancer's words, uttered as her eyes brimmed with sincerity, touched the king deeply. Ludwig forgave her and they spent the rest of the afternoon together, having tea and chatting by the fire. He could never be angry with her—she always got her way. But the king was worried about her obstinacy and her unwillingness to heed his advice. None of his previous lovers had provoked as much contempt among his people as Lola. The police had given him a copy of a flyer that had been posted throughout the city; it began with "Montez, you great whore, your time will come soon" and concluded: "The hell with the royal house, our loyalty is running out. It brings us only humiliation and scorn; may God have mercy on us." He also learned that priests were ordering their congregations to pray "for the redemption of the great, gray man," and some rumors claimed that, in the confessional, they were instructing their parishioners to pray for the king to leave the "treacherous Spaniard."

Lola was even an object of mockery for the city's street urchins. When she went walking in the mornings, groups of them would trail after her, hissing and jeering. They'd even fling horse dung and stones as she passed. Ludwig assigned two agents to protect her. He also ramped up the security at her home, where two police officers alternated shifts in the little booth by the gate. But she continued to act as if she were the queen consort, and the Bavarian people detested her arrogance.

During that same period, Lola was involved in another serious incident. She went to the post office and entered the restricted area in an attempt to retrieve a letter that Lieutenant Nussbammer had sent to her. When an employee stopped her, she slapped him in a rage and pushed him to the floor. Once word of the matter reached Pechmann, he had his men open an investigation. The next morning, one of his agents questioned Jeanette, Lola's maid, and her friend Berta Thierry, both of them suspected of having been accomplices in the attack. Indignant, the dancer sent the chief of police a note in which she demanded that he leave her alone or she would complain to the king. In response, Pechmann sent a summons requiring her to appear within the week to address her "abusive conduct at the post office." The war had only just begun.

That afternoon, one of Lola's liveried servants brought Pechmann a curt reply:

> Sir, I do not speak or understand German, so I cannot read the summons you have sent. I request that you drop this unpleasant matter. Affectionately,
>   Lola Montez

But the chief of police refused to back down and replied that Bavarian officials issued their documents solely in German and that she should have someone translate for her. A while later, Lola's servant returned and handed over the summons, which had been ripped into pieces. That was the straw that broke the camel's back. Her reaction was an act of contempt against the judicial process, and Pechmann wasn't about to let it go unanswered.

Later, as Pechmann rested at his home on Sommerstrasse after a draining day, a messenger appeared with an urgent note from His Majesty:

> With the utmost vehemence I command you to leave my dear Lola Montez alone. She is unfamiliar with our local customs and you must not be so demanding of her. Do not forget that you are only the acting chief of police, and I expect nothing but obedience from you.
> Ludwig

Pechmann, a man of steadfast principles, refused to let the king twist his arm and continued to dig. According to the Bavarian constitution, the king had no right to call off a criminal investigation. Ignoring His Majesty, Pechmann instructed his men to interrogate everyone who had witnessed Lola destroying the summons. When she reported this to Ludwig, the king ordered his interior minister, Abel, to have the police chief transferred to the city of Landshut at once. "Pechmann alone is to blame. It's time that government officials learned that they cannot defy the king with impunity, nor be negligent in fulfilling their duty," he wrote in his diary. A new joke began to spread through Munich: "What's the difference between Prussia and Bavaria? In Prussia the police expel Lola Montez, and in Bavaria Lola Montez expels the chief of police."

Until that point, no member of the royal family had interfered in Ludwig's love life, but his sister Karoline Auguste, widow of the Austrian emperor Francis I, wrote a letter from Salzburg that wounded him deeply. A distinguished and devout woman, she was very concerned about reports from the Bavarian court:

What sort of example are you setting? The world forgives this kind of behavior in the young, but not in the old. Think of your subjects. Brother, have mercy on your soul, on your country, and on me for writing these things to you, but I want to be able to look at you with pride. Let go of her hand, fill it with money, with lots of money if necessary, but make her leave. Every word of this letter pains me greatly. Use your head, use your will! I pray to God to help you. Your true friend, your devoted sister.

Annoyed, Ludwig sent a brief note in reply:

Each person must attend to his own affairs, and people should know me well enough to realize that I will brook no interference with my own.

The king needed somebody by his side who could help him improve his public image. But when Maltzahn arrived in Munich, he found that the situation was not as he'd anticipated. He wrote to the king asking not to be named aide-de-camp:

My life is at Your Royal Majesty's disposal, but not my honor. The situation here is completely different from what I believed; unfortunately, during my absence, Lola has insulted every rank of society, she has offended everybody, and the city and nation are so indignant that even with the best of intentions it is too late—it is impossible to improve your position, or at least I am too weak to manage it. I beg Your Royal Majesty, with utmost humility, to grant me an hour in which we can speak uninterrupted to discuss what can still be done.

That February morning, when King Ludwig received Maltzahn in his audience chamber, the baron told him soberly that the situation was untenable.

"Your Majesty, I know that my words will wound you, but you cannot imagine the level of indignation, scorn, and even hatred that your beloved Lola provokes throughout Bavaria."

"I know that she has acquired many enemies in Munich," the king acknowledged, "but I didn't realize circumstances were so dire. She does not deserve to suffer so because of my love."

"Sir, you can combat this defamation campaign, but I have no support. I have not lived in Munich for more than thirty years; people accuse me of being the person who brought the Spaniard here."

"But what else can I do? I am bound to her," Ludwig replied mournfully.

That afternoon, Heinrich von Maltzahn visited the dancer. It was a short visit, as the aristocrat berated her for her offensive and shameless conduct. He then offered her a lifetime pension of fifty thousand florins a year if she left Bavaria and promised never to return. Lola, who hadn't expected such a proposal from a person she thought was loyal to the king, ordered him to put his money away and get out of her house. When she told Ludwig what had happened, he was speechless. He couldn't believe that his old chamberlain would attempt such a bribe. Later he learned that the baron had had a long conversation with Karl-August von Reisach, archbishop of Munich and a loyal ally of the Jesuits. Maltzahn, fearing King Ludwig's reaction, left the city in a rush, claiming that family matters required his presence in Paris. After this incident, the king was even more convinced of Lola's goodness. Her refusal had proved that she did not love him for his wealth, as people claimed, but out of noble feeling. "It is the confirmation of love!" he wrote in his diary, full of joy. "She would not leave me even if they were aiming a pistol at her heart."

But the Jesuits did not drop their efforts to drive him and his favorite apart. Melchior von Diepenbrock, the prince-bishop of Breslau, whom the king respected because he wasn't an extremist like the archbishop of Munich, wrote to him in the following terms:

> King Ludwig, a poisonous tree is growing above you and its deadly perfume lulls you to sleep, blinds you, dulls your senses, and beguiles you so that you fail to see the abyss yawning before you, the open chasm that threatens to swallow your honor, your reputation, your family's happiness, your land, and your life as well as the salvation of your soul. King Ludwig, awake from your dream! Do not sully your name, which has been so noble up to this point, as did the French Ludwig [Louis XV], whose life of transgressions itself dug the pit of the Revolution.

For a week, Ludwig pondered how to respond. He now realized that the Jesuits weren't going to stop until Lola had been driven out, and they wouldn't hesitate to use all of their influence to achieve that end. He took his time to explain in a clear and honest manner:

> Appearances are deceiving. I have never taken a mistress, nor have I now. I have loved only friendship, which has been my best protection against sensual passions. I have a poetic nature that cannot be measured by the normal standards. I give you my word of honor that for the past four months I have not been intimate with any woman, not my wife or any other. I want to prove to my people that they have no reason to be scandalized. I cannot break off this friendship. If I did, I would be unable to respect myself. Do not ask me for the impossible.

The king gave a copy of his reply to the dean of the Munich cathedral and ordered him to send it to all the bishops in the kingdom, believing that a sworn statement about his sex life would be enough to put a stop to their opposition. But the Jesuits took another swing. They managed to get the pope himself to send the unruly king of Bavaria a harsh rebuke. On February 9, 1847, Pius IX wrote to Ludwig:

> Heretofore, the King of Bavaria has always been a solid pillar of the Catholic Cause. Upon hearing, nevertheless, that Our Beloved Son has strayed from the path of virtue, We realize that, owing to a change of great magnitude and grave consequences, this support has rotted and is bringing shame and disgrace to the Catholic Cause rather than supporting it with its aid and honor. Having given careful consideration to all of these circumstances, We admonish Our Dear and Beloved Son Ludwig I, King of Bavaria, and beg of him, by virtue of our Duty, that he return to the path of righteousness and honor.

The letter from the Holy See only infuriated Ludwig further and had the opposite of the intended effect. The pope's meddling in his private life showed him clearly that he had to nip in the bud the ever-growing power of the Jesuits and Karl von Abel. Though he considered Abel the best statesman in the kingdom, he now watched him with a distrustful eye. Then, quite unexpectedly, King Ludwig announced an important change in the government. Religious and educational matters that were currently the domain of Abel, as minister of the interior, would thenceforth be under the remit of the minister of justice, who was more tolerant and less conservative. "I would not be surprised if they blamed my poor Lola," he said. And indeed they did.

Amid the uproar, King Ludwig commissioned another renowned court painter, Wilhelm von Kaulbach, to make a new portrait of his lover. The artist, like most of the Bavarian people, despised the dancer. The king asked the painter to create a preliminary sketch with the young woman dressed in a Renaissance-style gown, suggesting that she should resemble Mary, Queen of Scots, a famously persecuted Catholic. Kaulbach, who owed much of his career to the king's ambition of turning Munich into a Teutonic Athens, could not refuse. A few days later, he presented a charcoal sketch that showed Lola with a somber expression, black flowers in her hair, a belt of serpents, an ax, and an executioner's stump in the background. On the table, the artist had placed a newspaper open to a page that talked about the trial of her lover Dujarier. Ludwig thought the joke in very poor taste, "a perverse fantasy," but he persisted in his desire for Kaulbach to paint her portrait.

Lola had no desire to pose for long hours for a painter she didn't like. She was irritated by his scowl, his haughty air, and his self-importance. But since Ludwig was so excited about the project, she tried to be polite and obey the artist's instructions. The king wanted to immortalize his lover in a full-length, life-size portrait in which she would wear a sumptuous black velvet dress and a wide Elizabethan ruff. The sessions began in the painter's studio beside a beautiful English garden that extended on either side of the Isar River. Ludwig visited every day to encourage Lola and keep her company.

One day Zampa, the dancer's mischievous lapdog, slipped into the garden, where Kaulbach had a small collection of animals and birds that he used as models in his still lifes. Suddenly the dog started chasing six peacocks, which fled into the street. Passersby were dumbstruck to see the famous Lola Montez, garbed in a Renaissance gown, the celebrated painter Kaulbach, and Ludwig I of Bavaria himself chasing a half dozen peacocks and a dog. The next day, the whole city was talking about the eccentric behavior of the king and his lover, "who were amusing themselves by chasing some harmless birds."

When Kaulbach completed the portrait and showed it to the king, his patron was not pleased. Ludwig informed the artist that his dear friend bore no resemblance to the gloomy-faced, even menacing woman who appeared on the canvas.

Ludwig didn't demand that the painter make any changes, but he refused to pay. The massive portrait languished in the painter's studio. When Josephine von Kaulbach, the painter's wife, saw the painting years later, she wrote him these lines:

> I have finally seen the portrait of the Spanish woman, and after contemplating it for a long while I can only tell you that the woman's entire biography is contained in this painting. It is impossible to look at this work and joke about the sitter. One cannot laugh—it conveys a feeling of gravity and sadness that is overwhelming. It reflects her destiny, yes, but an incredibly somber and tragic destiny. My darling husband, you sound the depths of people's souls, and that is what makes your portraits classics.

Not wanting Lola to see the unfortunate rendering and fly into a rage, Ludwig made some excuses and then asked the sculptor Johann Leeb to carve a life-size marble bust of his beloved instead. The sculpture, which pleased both Ludwig and Lola, was installed in the audience hall so that all visitors could admire Lola's classic beauty and the perfection of her features.

At that time, another topic was worrying the king. For a while he'd been petitioning the Council of State to grant Lola Bavarian citizenship, which would allow him to offer her privileges such as landownership or a noble title. After several meetings, his advisers unanimously refused to formalize his lover's status. In addition, given how the kingdom's citizens felt about her, they deemed it inappropriate for the king to declare the dancer Bavarian, as "it would be the greatest calamity that could befall Bavaria." Losing patience, Ludwig summoned the council to vote, and warned that he would interpret their rejection as an assault on his authority.

Just as the king had feared, only the loyal Georg Ludwig von Maurer, the council's sole Protestant member, voted in his favor. The respected jurist suggested that Ludwig decree his friend naturalized and have one of his ministers sign the document. When Karl von Abel heard about this, he announced his resignation. In his letter, he informed Ludwig that all the other ministers shared his view and that the entire government was prepared to back him up:

> Since last October the entire nation's eyes have been directed toward Munich, and all over Bavaria people have been talking about what is going on here, so much so that it is practically the only topic of conversation in family circles and in public places. Based on these opinions, a highly alarming popular feeling has developed. Respect for the monarch is becoming ever more eroded in the minds of his subjects because all they hear are expressions of bitter reproach and manifest disapproval. At the same time, the pride of the nation has been gravely offended because Bavaria finds itself being governed by a foreigner whom the people see as a marked woman, and however many facts you present to refute their view, it cannot be altered.

Though Ludwig was surprised and asked his minister of the interior to rethink his resignation, Abel stood firm. A few days later, the king wrote to his friend Tann:

> Abel has been quite categorical. He will resign; the Jesuits' mandate has been broken. I have felt a pleasant calm and joy yesterday and today. Lolitta knows nothing as of yet. I am pleased that Abel resigned and that the people have learned of it; it is good that he has withdrawn. I acknowledge the great service he has given us and believe he is an upstanding man. Things have changed a great deal here, and as far as the

question of whether the king or the Jesuits should govern the country, I have now answered it.

On Lola's birthday, the king appeared at her house with a bouquet and a fine pearl necklace. After wishing her a happy birthday, he announced that his government had resigned en masse. The dancer embraced him effusively and told him that the news was the best gift he could give her. At long last the monarch was imposing his will, and she had contributed to this political change. Years of liberal agitation had been unable to put an end to Jesuit control in Bavaria, but a single woman had managed it overnight. Lola had won the battle against her sworn enemies and was ready to collaborate closely with the king in forming his new government. That same afternoon she presented him with her own list of candidates for the ministerial posts and told him that she would like to chat with the people chosen and be present for their audiences with the king. Smitten though he was, Ludwig was not about to give up his role as an autocrat, even if he found some of her ideas intriguing. Lola was a Bavarian citizen now, and it seemed that the path was cleared for her fondest dream to become reality: she could be elevated to the Bavarian aristocracy.

In the following days, Ludwig worked frenetically to reform his government. Wanting a break with the past, he named Maurer chief minister. The press dubbed the new cabinet the "Dawn Ministry." After a decade of conservative Catholic rule, many welcomed these winds of change.

But not everybody was pleased with the arrival of a more progressive government. At the Catholic and conservative University of Munich, the professors and students lamented the resignation of Karl von Abel, who had always supported them. In mid-February, at a meeting of the university's governing council, Ernst von Lasaulx, a professor of philosophy and ethics, suggested that the minister should be honored for his valiant defense of the dignity of the crown. When the king learned of this proposal, he considered it a provocation and, determined to show who was in charge in Bavaria, unceremoniously fired the professor. On the morning of March 1, notice of the professor's dismissal appeared on the university's announcement board, and a large group decided to march to his home in a gesture of solidarity.

At around ten o'clock in the morning, several hundred students gathered outside Lasaulx's residence, singing anthems and cheering for him. The group broke up peacefully, but at noon pamphlets began to circulate calling for a protest outside Lola Montez's residence. When word of this protest reached the king's ears, he immediately sent a note to the newly appointed chief of police, Heinrich von der Mark, to ensure his friend's safety.

At the appointed hour, a group of students followed by a large crowd appeared at the end of the street and stopped outside her gate. The dancer was waiting for them in one of the windows, accompanied by four friends, among them the indefatigable Lieutenant Nussbammer. For a moment she observed the crowd with a mocking smile. Then she asked her servant to bring her a glass of champagne and raised it in the air.

"A toast to all of you! To the young people of Munich—you are the future!" she cried.

"Go back to Spain, you conniving witch, we don't want you here!" a few men shouted.

A rock sailed through the air and grazed her head. Nussbammer seized her by the waist to pull her away from the window, but Lola struggled and slapped him to make him let go.

"Three cheers for you, you cowards, trying to injure an innocent woman for her liberal ideas!" she continued loudly.

"Please, ma'am," her maidservant begged her, "come inside, it's very dangerous."

"I can take care of myself, Jeanette, these people don't scare me," she replied as she tossed candy to the crowd.

The king, unaware of this turn in events, had finished his work and was preparing to visit his lover as he did every afternoon. The new minister of the interior, Johann Baptist von Zenetti, arrived in time to warn him that there was a commotion in front of the dancer's residence and that it would not be prudent to go. Fearing for Lola's life, Ludwig rushed out. When he reached Barerstrasse, he found complete bedlam. The police were trying to disperse the students, who were angered by Lola's provocations; she was still in the window, now brandishing a large knife. The king made his way through the crowd; upon recognizing him, many removed their hats in respect. When he managed to get inside and find Lola, she showed him one of the large stones that had been hurled at her. The king went out onto the balcony and cried indignantly, "Return to your homes, all of you! I am ordering you to go home!" Then he clasped Lola in his arms. "Nobody is going to get me to renounce the thing I love most in this world—you, Lolita."

The crowd broke up, but a few headed toward the palace and began throwing rocks at it. Queen Therese, who was visiting a friend across the street, worried that her carriage would be attacked and asked her driver to go back to the palace alone. Hiding under a large hat and overcoat that her maid lent her, she returned home on foot and slipped in through a rear entrance.

When Ludwig learned that his home was under attack, he left immediately. As he rushed through the streets, people whistled and jeered, mocking his relationship with the Spanish dancer and cheering for Queen Therese. The king was irate and bewildered. He didn't recognize his people. By ten o'clock that night, the streets were calm once more, though some protesters had destroyed street lanterns and store windows as they withdrew. Despite the tremendous uproar, Ludwig ended the evening playing his usual game of cards with his wife. They didn't talk about what had happened, and though he seemed at ease, he was roiling with emotions, furious and eager for revenge. "My nobles, the Jesuit party, and the priests have incited demagogues to insult me and wound me, but I'll show them who's in charge," he thought.

Calm reigned the next day, but Ludwig could not forget the terror he'd felt. He'd witnessed his people's hatred and contempt. Many of the young men who'd insulted Lola were the sons of noble, pedigreed families, boys educated at a renowned university. He'd never dreamed the situation could devolve into violence. He was disillusioned, weary, and sad but also worried about Lola's safety. New rumors were sweeping the city. People were claiming she'd tried to open fire on the crowd but that her lover, Nussbammer, had prevented it. In another version, she'd picked up the stones they'd thrown at her, juggled them, and then hurled them back. Others claimed she'd bared her breasts to provoke the students.

After the events of March 1, Lola saw herself as a heroine. She had routed the Jesuits and bravely faced down extremist students demanding her expulsion. She was the talk of Europe, with many sympathizers abroad. Ludwig indulged her every whim—except one: "The king must keep his word and offer me the noble title I deserve. Nobody will look down on me anymore, because soon I will be a countess and those who now criticize me will kiss my hand."

CHAPTER 7

The Uncrowned Queen

The king remained devoted to his lover, but the recent tension had taken its toll. His body was covered in sores, and at night his bones ached. He was so disfigured that he didn't want anyone to see him until the infection subsided. When Lola found out, she sent a note begging him to let her come. Ludwig was touched that the young woman wanted to keep him company and was unfazed by his unpleasant appearance.

Every morning Lola would arrive at the Residenz and go to the monarch's chambers via a secret staircase. For the first time in a long time, the two of them were at peace. Having Lola there every day, reading him *Don Quixote* and looking after him without anybody interrupting them, alleviated his suffering. On occasion, passersby on Max-Joseph-Platz were surprised to see them sitting next to the window drinking tea. The king was able to calm his nerves and forget about the cruel rumors.

For six weeks Ludwig was confined to his rooms and bore his illness with admirable stoicism. He would later remember that period as the happiest in his relationship with Lola. Only the arrival of another letter from his sister the empress of Austria, Karoline Auguste, broke the spell. In it, his sister appealed to his pride as a sovereign:

Ludwig, who was once so strong and independent . . . ruled by
a winsome little girl! I wanted to tell you this with all my heart,
without any hope of success, but so that you at least understand how I feel, I who love you and am your ever-loyal sister.

    Karoline

Ludwig tore up the letter. He refused to heed any advice, much less
allow his favorite sister to mock his most intimate feelings.

Around that time, the king noted with satisfaction that Lola's attitude had changed. She was more discreet and affable, controlling her
temper. The king's most loyal subjects liked the fact that she visited him
every day. Her public image had improved; people no longer rebuked
her on the streets. Her influence over Ludwig had increased too. A
number of politicians and businessmen started coming to her to seek
the king's favor. One standout in her circle of admirers was Franz von
Berks. The notorious charlatan and conniver had been minister of the
interior prior to Karl von Abel. When the conservative Catholic regime
came to power, Berks had been relegated to the provincial government
in Landshut. Now, the ambitious politician was brazenly cozying up
to Lola in an effort to secure a post in the new Bavarian government.

After the student revolt and the resignation of all the ministers,
the French and British press called Lola the shadow queen of Bavaria.
With Ludwig's permission, the young woman sent letters to the London
Times and Paris's *Le national* claiming to have been the victim of a malicious Jesuit plot. Lola insisted that she'd had no hand in the change
in government, though she approved of His Majesty's decision. "I no
longer have any intention of enduring these insults and attacks that
damage the image of a generous king and present me as a cruel and
manipulative woman. They call me the Spanish Messalina. Envy and
human wickedness are capable of anything!"

On March 20, 1847, the *Pictorial Times* published an article that
was mostly accurate. It claimed that she was twenty-seven years old, that

she'd married a Lieutenant James from the British East India Company's army, that she'd lived in India, and that she was famous for her volatile temperament. The article was accompanied by an engraving that depicted her holding a whip and facing off against an angry crowd. Lola feared that she might be unmasked. If Ludwig learned that she was an impostor, her privileged life in Bavaria and her dream of becoming a countess would evaporate.

At the end of March, Lola sent several letters to major European newspapers. In them, she defended her noble Spanish lineage and accused her defamers and doubters of lying:

> Sir—
>
> In consequence of the numerous reports circulated In various papers regarding myself and family utterly void of foundation or truth, I beg of you through the medium of your widely-circulated journal to insert the following:
>
> I was born at Seville, in the year 1823; my father was a Spanish officer in the service of Don Carlos; my mother a lady of Irish extraction, born at the Havannah, and married for the second time to an Irish gentleman, which, I suppose, is the cause of my being called Irish and sometimes English, "Betsy Watson,""Mrs. James," &.
>
> I beg leave to say that my name is Maria Dolores Porris Montez, and I never have changed that name.
>
> As for my theatrical qualifications, I never had the presumption to think I had any. Circumstances obliged me to adopt the stage as a profession: which profession I have now renounced forever, having become a naturalized Bavarian, and intending in future to make Munich my residence.

While Lola was cleaning up her image in the press, King Ludwig was keeping up to date on affairs of state and reading the weekly reports his ministers sent him. He also used his convalescence to write and was preparing the fourth volume of his published verse. In one poem, dedicated to Lola, he expressed his absolute devotion and loyalty:

If you have renounced any tie because of me,
so too have I broken all because of you,
my dearest one. I am yours—I am your slave—
I will make no pact with your enemies.
Their calumnies have no effect on me,
no cunning exists that could drive me away from
*   you,*
the power of love lifts me above them.
With you my wanderings on this earth will come to
*   an end.*
Like the union between body and soul,
Just like that, my soul is bound to yours until death.
In you I have found what I never found in any
*   woman,*
Your contemplation has given me new life.
All my feelings for any other have withered,
Since my eyes read love in you!

On April 26, the king appeared in public, seemingly hale and in excellent spirits. To celebrate, he attended the Court Theatre, which was presenting a special performance in his honor. The audience gave him a standing ovation, except Lola, who remained seated. Ludwig never managed to get his lover to obey protocol; she believed that their relationship allowed her to take any liberty she wished. The seats around her emptied in a gesture of repudiation, but Ludwig considered it a minor gaffe.

Now that spring had arrived, Ludwig spent many evenings with his consort in the Renaissance-style gardens of Nymphenburg Palace. Lola's favorite spot was the enormous greenhouse made of wrought iron and glass, which was full of tropical plants from all over the world. Palms, giant fig trees, ferns, bamboo, hibiscus, orchids—the heat, the humidity, and the fragrance of the flowers took her back to her childhood in India. They would also spend evenings at her house, where they listened to live musical performances, read poetry, and drank tea in the garden. Ludwig enjoyed watching her sitting under the pergola, cigarette in hand, relaxed and deep in thought. So great was his euphoria that in her honor he allowed smoking in public throughout the city.

The royal family usually left Munich during the summer and returned just before Oktoberfest. This year Queen Therese announced that she intended to travel to Franzensbad, a popular hot springs resort in northeastern Bohemia. Ludwig had other plans. First he would spend a few weeks with Lola in Bad Brückenau, one of his favorite places. There he could breathe pure mountain air, exercise, and enjoy the thermal waters. Afterward he would travel to Aschaffenburg, a city with a sunny, temperate climate, leafy gardens, and Renaissance castles on the banks of the Main River. Though his advisers tried to convince him not to take Lola, it was no use. He was excited to introduce her to Baron von der Tann, who had a summer villa in Bad Brückenau. In a letter, the monarch asked his friend, "How do you picture her?" The baron replied teasingly that he was "somewhat fearful of falling in love and making Your Majesty jealous," and added that he was also afraid of "her dog, her slaps, the whip, dagger, and pistol that she wields so ably."

After his convalescence, Ludwig found that his popularity had increased. Some of the measures approved by the new government were well received. When he walked through the city, his subjects greeted him warmly as they once had. In addition, he had Lola all to himself—Lieutenant Nussbammer had been in a riding accident and was confined to his bed. Though the king had always insisted on the purity of his "innocent love for Lolita," now he desired her more than ever. In mid-June, Queen Therese and the children left for Franzensbad. Two days later, Ludwig was able to spend the whole night with Lola for the first time. Lying in her rosewood bed and embracing her naked body, he felt like the luckiest man in the world. The next morning, the young woman found a rose and a note on her pillow: "I am yours for always; you are for always mine! How vast the happiness that, like a wave, renews itself in its own eternal source!"

Around that time, some young men belonging to a student fraternity, the Corps Palatia, visited Lola at her residence on Barerstrasse. Ludwig Leibinger, Jacob Härteiss, and the leader of the group, Elias Peissner, were eager to meet the woman who had faced off against their conservative schoolmates with such courage and determination. Lola was delighted to have young men with romantic, liberal ideals come calling. She showed them her library and offered them a glass of liquor. Peissner barely spoke and stared at her, spellbound. He was a shy, attractive young man of twenty-one and a brilliant law student. As she chatted animatedly with them, other university students walking past the house spotted the scene through the large windows. The news spread swiftly, with serious consequences. Elias Peissner and his companions were kicked out of the student society. The professors called their behavior a "dishonor for the University of Munich."

At the beginning of June, the king had everything arranged for their trip to Bad Brückenau, but the plan hit a snag. Lola had learned that Lieutenant Nussbammer had just undergone surgery. Fearing for his life, she rushed to the hospital. She even persuaded Ludwig to accompany her one day, and the king waited in a room next door for more than an hour, to the amazement of the medical staff. When Lola was certain that the young man was recovering well, she took leave of him until the end of summer.

On June 22, she left Munich early in the morning. The lovers had decided to travel separately so as not to raise suspicions. Lola first took the train to Nuremberg, traveling comfortably in the first-class car. When she reached that beautiful walled medieval city, she was greeted at the station by the most prominent local personalities and welcomed with traditional songs and bouquets; she also had time to tour the narrow streets of the historic city center and admire Nuremberg's elegant monuments. The city pulled out all the stops, hoping she would encourage the king to order the construction of a direct train line between Nuremberg and Würzburg.

She then continued to Bamberg, where the municipal authorities' welcome was less lavish. She was tired and in a bad mood. It had been a long trip, and the small city, which claimed to be one of Germany's prettiest, struck her as dirty and sad. Lola communicated as much to her hosts, who were bewildered by her rudeness. To top it off, she asked the burgomaster if there were monasteries in Bamberg, and when he said that there were two very important ones, she replied, "I should have known, sir. It's obvious that the Jesuits are in control of this city, and that's why I am not a welcome visitor." This offended people even more, and they chased her carriage to the Bamberger Hof, where she would be lodging. On the way, Lola was treated to a shower of insults, jeers, and even rocks and horse manure. Once night fell, she decided that she did not feel safe even in the hotel and asked her driver to take her to Würzburg and straight to Bad Brückenau from there.

When Lola told the king how she'd been treated in Bamberg, he ordered the city authorities to send a delegation to apologize. Ludwig had arrived in the spa town the previous day and wanted nothing more than to enjoy his "honeymoon" with her, but now he was having to endure her towering rage. His son, the crown prince Maximilian, and his wife were visiting Bad Brückenau. Forced to divide his time, Ludwig asked Baron von der Tann to look after Lola.

Since the last night they'd spent together, Ludwig had been ruled by the desire to make love to her. But they couldn't see much of each other for the moment, so the king asked his favorite to send him pieces of flannel that she'd worn under her clothes, in direct contact with her skin. These intimate "gifts" aroused his imagination and inspired a number of erotically charged poems. Lola, who had expected to enjoy a few romantic days with the king, was upset and irritable. The little time they spent together only rubbed her face in the fact that he prioritized his family above her. In public she was haughty and demanding. She'd managed to get the king to name Berks a member of the Council of State, but now she was insisting that Ludwig fulfill his promise to make her a countess. She kept telling him that it was the only way to make Bavaria's nobility accept her. One evening, when Ludwig came to her room, Lola flew into a rage.

"You've lied to me! You promised me I'd be a countess, but you don't have the courage to stand up to my enemies, who should be your enemies too. And I thought you loved me!"

"Lola, darling, please don't talk to me that way," the king broke in, pale and nervous. "I have always stuck up for you. I made you a promise and I intend to keep it, but everything in its time. You must be patient."

"I won't wait a minute longer! They don't respect me; they treat me like a courtesan. They think I'm just a way for you to pass the time. You're the only one who can change all of that and prove to me with this gesture that your love is genuine."

Ludwig found himself faced with a huge dilemma. His advisers and Maurer had begged him to wait until fall to raise his lover's station. They hoped that, by then, people would have forgotten her scandalous behavior. But Lola kept pressuring him mercilessly. One evening they argued and the king said he was sick of her demands. He stalked out of the room and slammed the door. Tann, who had witnessed the incident, reproached the dancer, and rather than apologizing, she became even angrier. Her shouts were audible on the street, and a worried Ludwig sent one of his servants to find out whether she'd suffered another nervous attack. That night, the king sent a note to the baron so he could show it to Lola:

My dear Tann,

The brusque tone I used with my beloved Lolitta was
quite harsh, I admit. Please tell her that. My feelings
were wounded by the tone she took yesterday, and not
only yesterday, a tone that was the opposite of loving
sentiment. That explains my reaction, but does not
justify it. I hope that she forgives me, but also that
she treats me differently, not like one of her servants
but like someone who loves her deeply and is a true
friend. If I am still welcome by her side, I hope she
will let me know.

She did not reply to the note and left Ludwig sunk in uncertainty.
The next day, the young woman had her trunks loaded into the carriage and spread word that she was leaving Bavaria for good. In reality,
the trunks were empty. When the news reached Ludwig, he rushed to
find her. Lola was waiting for him calmly in the sitting room, reading
a book of poems. She looked stunning in a tight-fitting dress of dark-
green velvet that fell in ample folds around her hips and plunged at the
neckline. She was wearing the pearl necklace he had given her on her
birthday. The king stared for a moment, entranced, and thought how
sad and dull his life would be without her.

"Lolita, you can't abandon me like this," he implored, his voice
trembling. "I don't deserve it. I've asked for your forgiveness—what
more do you want me to do?"

"I am surrounded by spies and enemies—I can't live like this. You're
going to have to choose."

"Choose? I don't know what you mean."

"Yes, choose between your dear friend Tann and me. I can't bear
having him scold me as if I were a little girl and meddle in our relationship. I want him gone as soon as possible."

Seeing the fury in her eyes, Ludwig realized there was no reasoning with her. His lover would get her way once again. The king ordered Tann to go to Aschaffenburg, where he would meet up with him in a few weeks. Once Tann had left, Lola's mood improved and she became affectionate and kind. That same day she accompanied the king to lunch, and in the evening the two went into the countryside in an elegant landau upholstered in blue silk. There, in a green field by the river, they enjoyed a romantic picnic together.

But the idyll didn't last long. Lola fell ill, with a high fever and chills. She told Ludwig not to worry, that it was a relapse of the malaria she'd caught in India. His Majesty's personal doctor treated her successfully with large doses of quinine and recommended that she rest for a few days. In early August, Lola was feeling better and started preparing to return to Munich. For his part, the king would continue on to Aschaffenburg, where he would meet up with the queen in the fall. Upon reaching the city, his first act was to pick up his pen and write an urgent note to Maurer instructing him to name Lola Montez a countess immediately and saying that he didn't want to hear any objections. To his beloved, now on her way to Munich, he sent a letter sharing the happy news that the title would be conferred by his birthday, and for her to keep it a secret.

When he read the king's missive, Maurer panicked. If he approved the title, it would mean the end of his career. The minister replied that he would prepare the document but warned Ludwig that it would be seen as an insult. He knew that the aristocracy would never accept a foreign social climber. In addition, Maurer argued that, after all the sacrifices he'd made for the king, he deserved to be chosen as a noble member of the High Chamber and be granted land in accordance with his rank. He also suggested that it would be appropriate that his son be named professor at the university, with a generous annual salary.

Ludwig was enraged by what he considered extortion. His reply was swift: "I demand obedience especially from my ministers. You seem not to realize that, if you don't do it, I will do it anyway, even if it harms my own interests. I will not bend. I order you to send me Lola Montez's countess title at once, with your signature and all the details in order." Maurer had never seen the king so obstinate and immediately signed the document and sent it off that very night.

On her way back to Munich, Lola stopped in Würzburg to visit its baroque palace and the famous gardens. On the king's instruction, Berks had come from the capital to introduce her to the local authorities. That afternoon, Lola and a small entourage decided to take a stroll through the radiant gardens. A large crowd gathered outside the grounds to gawk at the Spaniard who was the talk of Bavaria. At the entrance gate to the palace, a soldier was standing guard. Seeing that the lady was accompanied by her dog, he pointed to a sign that prohibited smoking, stepping on the grass, and bringing animals into the gardens. Lola held Zampa in her arms, but it wasn't enough. The dancer protested, and the soldier, who didn't speak French, tried to grab the dog. Lola stepped back and slapped the guard in the face. Berks tried to placate her, and the group entered the garden to the sound of jeers.

The details of this dispute spread swiftly across Würzburg, and locals began to gather outside the dancer's hotel. As night fell, she was forced to use a service door so she could get to her carriage and make it on time to the dinner being held in her honor. The shouts and whistles persisted the entire evening. Her host, Baron von Ziegler, sent Lola's empty carriage back to the hotel to trick the noisy crowd and lure them away. Once she was finally in her room, Lola burst into tears and took some laudanum to calm down. She wrote a letter to King Ludwig informing him that more than five thousand people had tried to attack her and that it was all the work of the Jesuits and their leader, the bishop of Würzburg.

Back in Munich, the dancer received an unexpected visit from Elias Peissner, wanting to discuss an urgent matter. Lola liked this bohemian young man who actually looked rather similar to King Ludwig: tall and slender, with tousled hair, a delicate goatee, and lively blue eyes. He told her that he and his friends had been kicked out of their fraternity but that they'd formed a new association, Alemannia. It was made up of fifteen students who were ready to protect her from enemies and serve as her honor guard. They would escort her on walks and follow behind her carriage, to prevent incidents like the one in Würzburg. Flattered, Lola assured him that she would convey the good news to His Majesty. As he took his leave, Elias gallantly kissed her hand and, overcoming his shyness, told her, "Mrs. Montez, you are a woman capable of making a man lose his head."

The king's sixty-first birthday was approaching, and Lola would finally see her dream of nobility realized. Ludwig had considered and reconsidered his decision. He couldn't give his lover the title of an actual county in his kingdom because its inhabitants would object, perhaps violently. One day he scribbled the word Landsfeld in his notebook. He had combined the first letters of the city of Landshut, where he'd banished his hated police chief Pechmann, and those of the alpine village of Feldberg, whose high, snowy mountains he had frequented as a young man. "Lola Montez, Countess of Landsfeld"—the name sounded majestic, and his lover would never bother to find out where the supposed county was located. The title, a calligraphic masterpiece several pages long, was ready on the appointed date. The king gave it to a messenger to be delivered to Lola that same morning of August 25, along with a letter.

King Ludwig's birthday, a national holiday in Bavaria, was an unforgettable day for Lola. She rose early, and as she breakfasted in bed, His Majesty's messenger arrived with a large, wax-sealed envelope. When she opened it and saw the title Countess of Landsfeld, tears sprang to her eyes. It was mounted on blue velvet, and on the page facing the king's signature was a hand-painted image of her coat of arms. Above it appeared the nine-pointed crown that marked her rank.

Very carefully, she placed the title on a sideboard in the main salon, where everybody could see it. Then she sat down and read the letter that had come with it:

> Countess of Landsfeld, to me, my ever-beloved Lolitta, On my birthday I am giving myself the gift of granting you the title of countess. I hope that it helps you improve your social station, but it cannot change the government. Lolitta cannot love, much less admire, a king who is unable to govern, and your Luis wants to be loved by his Lolitta forever. Your enemies, and especially your female enemies, will be furious when they see you've been made countess, so it will be even more necessary that you be modest and prudent and avoid any possibility of scandal, that you avoid places where there are a lot of people. Your enemies may try to create a commotion so they can make an attempt on your life. Be careful!

Lola was delighted. To the surprise of witnesses, she was spotted entering St. Peter's Church that same morning. Though she never attended mass, she wanted to make a symbolic gesture to thank Ludwig for his generous gift and to shut up a few critics at the same time. That night, she organized a celebratory dinner. As the evening drew to a close, Lola invited the guests to come to the back garden, which was lit with torches. There, gathered around a marble bust of the king, she surprised everyone with a fireworks display while a band played traditional Bavarian music.

Still in Aschaffenburg, the king was sorry he couldn't share the special day with his favorite. But that night he wrote to the newly fledged countess that the first thing he'd done on his birthday was kiss her portrait: "Except when I am asleep, breathing and thinking about you are one and the same for me," he confessed. "It is true that absence destroys a passion if it is weak, but it increases it if it is strong. In all the world there is no one capable of driving Luis away from his Lolitta."

She was triumphant. Those who used to insult her now owed her respect. With a smile, Lola imagined the shock of the snooty ladies of the Bavarian nobility who had reviled her when they'd learned she was being made a countess. But her ambition knew no limits. That night, as she brushed her long, curly hair at her dressing table, it occurred to her that there were other favors she might yet obtain. The aristocrats might still refuse to visit her residence or invite her to their social events. She needed to be presented at court so they would finally accept her.

Rumors began to spread that not only had the king gotten Queen Therese's permission to name his lover countess but that the queen herself was going to award her the Order of Theresa, one of the highest distinctions a woman could receive in Bavaria. Though the story wasn't true, the public believed it. Ambassadors spread the tale, and the foreign press reported it. When Queen Therese, who was still at her summer residence, learned of this, she immediately rebutted the rumor. Though usually kind and patient, she clearly was very upset with her husband.

Lola's happiness lasted only a week. A friend mentioned that the title she so prized would not be valid until it was published in the official gazette. She wrote the king a stern letter telling him that she refused to accept a title under such circumstances and that she had been deeply wounded to learn the truth. Angered by this new setback, the king instructed his adviser Berks to make the title official immediately. Lola was thrilled: the king had acceded to her every whim, and that made her feel even more powerful.

Though Ludwig had asked her not to meddle in affairs of state, Lola started writing letters haranguing him about his ministers or informing him of conspiracies being hatched against her. With Berks's help, she made sure that her most loyal friends received awards and privileges. Lola was generous with the people who supported her, but she knew how to punish her enemies. With the king away, she would show up unannounced in the offices of the new minister of the interior, Zenetti, to present complaints or ask him questions. On one occasion he lost patience and declared that he didn't have time to deal with her personal problems. She was so offended that she wrote to the king to tell him that Zenetti was in league with the Jesuits and he should keep an eye on him. Maurer, who had initially supported her, also was not exempt from her criticisms and attacks. In a letter, Lola informed the king that she found his trusted aide incompetent and complained that, because of Maurer, none of the cabinet ministers ever came to visit her.

In the daily letters that the king wrote to Lola, he avoided discussing politics. Ludwig preferred to talk about how much he longed for her, about the erotic dreams he had of her, and about the pleasure he felt when he received the pieces of fabric that she sent to him. The dancer, for her part, never wrote about her feelings, and the few notes she did write were full of praise for Berks and other courtiers, as well as criticisms of his ministers. The monarch was annoyed, and a few days before he returned to Munich, he confessed in a letter that, although he liked hearing her ideas, even if they differed from his own, it made him very unhappy to talk of nothing but politics.

At the beginning of October, Ludwig put his personal accounts in order. Though he'd spent a fortune since he met Lola Montez, he thought he owed her even more. He ordered his personal secretary to double the Countess of Landsfeld's allowance to twenty thousand florins a year, effective immediately. Since she was now a member of the nobility, Ludwig felt that she needed to maintain a lifestyle in keeping with her position.

On the evening that Ludwig returned to the Residenz, he got a pleasant surprise. Lola had decided to move up the reunion they'd set for the next day. Wearing a beautiful purple silk gown and a matching feathered hat, she'd made her way in secret to the royal apartments. The king was delighted. After two months apart, they had a great deal to tell each other and much to celebrate. It had been only a year since their fates had crossed in Munich. The elderly king was just as enamored as he'd been that first day, but he sensed that something in her had changed. The new countess, whose name was now Marie von Landsfeld, was even more arrogant, demanding, and temperamental than she had been as Lola Montez.

One afternoon, when they were alone in her house on Barerstrasse, she rested her head on the king's knees and, sighing, confessed, "My darling Luis, I couldn't be happier because you have shown me how much you love me. But some of the nobles continue to scorn me. They ignore me completely."

"Lolita, what did you expect? They will never accept you, but you have no reason to worry about that. You have a title that nobody can take away."

"I know, but I'd like to be presented at court, before your wife, Queen Therese."

"What you ask is impossible," the king said, downcast, "but I will try if it matters that much to you."

After only a week back in Munich, the king received a letter from his wife. Though they saw each other every day, Therese had decided to address in writing an issue that threatened to tear the family apart:

> My beloved husband,
> It is my duty as your loyal wife to maintain your conjugal happiness and dispel any problem that might mar it. This is something that should have been quite clear to you during the final weeks of our stay in Aschaffenburg, because of the news I read in the *Gazette*, which relayed something that I, knowing you as I do, would never have believed possible and that wounded me keenly. I will not reproach you—that is far from my aim. The purpose of these lines, instead, is

a simple and sincere warning to prevent you from irre-
mediably destroying the peace and well-being of your
family. As an honorable woman—my honor is more
important to me than life itself—I must warn you that
that woman, whom you have elevated to a rank that
you never should have even considered, must never
hope to be received in the court. It does not matter
what you may have promised her; you can tell her on
my behalf that the queen, your wife, the mother of
your children, will never receive her.

Given the turmoil this causes me and to avoid
future conflicts, I believe it my obligation to inform
you of this irrevocable decision. Not another word,
either written or spoken, on this painful matter. As
always, you will find me happy and grateful for the joy
you give me and always ready and on the alert in order
to maintain for you, my dear Ludwig, the peaceable
harmony of our home. Your
Therese

For the moment Ludwig decided to keep his wife's decree secret;
he didn't want to risk one of Lola's terrible rages. The king longed to
find a bit of peace and harmony, but now he was barely seeing his
favorite. The happy times were behind them. Lola was always very
busy and had no time for him. One morning, as he met with one of
his ministers, she burst into his office.

"My dear Luis, you should know that not all of the university
students are against me. There is a group of brave liberal youths—
Protestant, of course—who stand ready to defend me with cape and
sword. They have founded a new fraternity known as Alemannia."

"Yes, I know. I will compensate these young men for their loyalty
and they will always be well received in the court."

"They will be my three musketeers, and I will use my own funds to help them with their expenses," Lola said. "These young men adore me and we share the same ideals. I no longer have anything to fear. They will watch over me day and night," she added proudly, giving the king a winning smile.

Ludwig was happy to know that Lola had the support of students who appreciated not only her beauty but her ideals. But as the days passed, the king noted with irritation that a group of handsome members of Alemannia was accompanying his lover everywhere. They spent the afternoons gathered in her sitting room or at their favorite haunt, Rottmann's Café. The young men accompanied her shopping and even on her countryside jaunts. Lola had designed for them a striking uniform of white leather breeches, a fringed black velvet jacket, and a red cap embroidered in gold. On the street, people referred to the "Lolianer," or "Lola's harem." The dancer loved their company; they were young like her—wild, entertaining dreamers. Her joie de vivre was restored, and she felt safer than ever in Munich. But the nobles took great affront at seeing the Countess of Landsfeld striding proudly through the streets flanked by liveried lackeys, a privilege reserved for Queen Therese and the crown princess. And Lola caused an even greater scandal when she attended the Court Theatre and the Alemannen sat dispersed throughout the audience to eavesdrop on what people were saying about her.

The Duke of Leuchtenberg, nephew of King Ludwig and son-in-law of Tsar Nicholas I, visited Munich in early November and tried to make the king see reason. The prince, who was married to Grand Duchess Maria Nikolaievna, spent a few days in the city, where he visited its main monuments and museums and attended a special performance held in his honor at the Court Theatre. At his farewell dinner at the palace, Queen Therese signaled for the courtiers to leave the royal family alone. The duke, on his feet and with his face solemn, begged Ludwig to allow him to communicate to the tsar the happy news that the Countess of Landsfeld no longer lived in Munich. The king's children joined in, tearfully pleading with their father to leave Lola Montez. The king was moved by their reaction. After a pause, with a knot in his throat, he replied, "I am grateful to all of you for this show of your affection for me, but I can respond only that you do not know her, she is wonderful."

At around that time, the Austrian ambassador in Paris sent a letter to Prince von Metternich in Vienna in which he offered the following assessment: "Lola Montez is a person without education, ill-mannered, whose capricious game cannot last. She is more uninhibited and novelty-addicted than depraved and grasping." Metternich, the strongman of the Austrian Empire, a defender of Europe's old monarchies, considered Lola "a serious threat to the Bavarian crown."

Lola started spending more and more time with Elias Peissner, the leader of Alemannia. He'd never met such a captivating, bold, and passionate woman. They shared an enjoyment of literature, travel, and German fencing. Elias was an expert in the sport and showed the countess how to wield a double-edged sword. Many afternoons they could be found in her garden, practicing as they chatted and laughed. Lola was very gracious to her "first musketeer," as she called him; she even asked King Ludwig to grant him a private audience. The king offered the fraternity his full support and assured its leader that they had His Majesty's protection. When she mentioned that all of Munich was saying that Peissner was Ludwig's bastard son because of their resemblance, Ludwig took it in good humor: "My dear Lolita, if I had to worry about all of the illegitimate children attributed to me, I would go mad."

The dancer flirted freely with Elias, who was five years her junior, and was flattered by his besotted devotion. One morning he arrived at her home bearing a large bouquet of white roses. As the countess regally descended the marble staircase, the young man could not take his eyes off of her. Though she hadn't expected him so early, she happily invited him into the sitting room. Lola lit a cigarette and lounged seductively on the sofa. There was a long silence, and he finally dared to speak.

"I apologize for showing up like this, but I can't stop thinking about you and I'm dying of jealousy because the king loves you too," Elias confessed, flushing.

"You know that the only thing that joins me to His Majesty is a close friendship; he is like a father to me, and I am very grateful to him for all of his help and understanding."

"Lola, I've loved you since the first day I saw you, and I will defend you with my sword if anyone dares touch a hair on your head."

"Hush," she interrupted, sealing his lips with a kiss. "I feel something for you, too, but for the moment you have only my heart; do not ask for my body yet."

That unexpected kiss changed Elias Peissner's life forever. He'd never dreamed that a woman like Lola Montez could be attracted to him. He was prepared to die for her. One afternoon, when the king informed the dancer that he wouldn't be coming to visit because he was going hunting, she invited the student to dinner. Peissner didn't realize that it would be an intimate evening, just the two of them. Lit by candelabra and fueled by wine, they talked about their dreams, about politics, about the power of the press, and about the revolutions that had toppled ancient monarchies. After dinner, Lola opened a bottle of champagne and they toasted to Alemannia and a Bavaria free of Jesuits and conservatives. In the wee hours of the morning, the young man was about to leave when the countess, with a sultry smile, suggested he come upstairs. In her beautiful rosewood bed hung with gauzy curtains, their bodies intertwined on a wave of desire. The king required her warm presence, tender words, and indulgent gestures, but with Elias she felt the fire of passion.

It was almost noon when they awoke. The lovers consumed hot chocolate and brioche in bed as the sunlight streamed through the window onto their naked bodies. Feeling happy, Lola suggested that they take a walk through the city. It was a gorgeous day, and the king wouldn't be back till the next day.

After that unforgettable night, the couple saw each other frequently, and Elias slept at Lola's house many nights. At the end of the month, she installed her young lover in a room in a building adjoining her residence that the servants used. That way he could visit at any time, and if the king arrived unexpectedly, he could sneak off quickly.

The comings and goings of Alemannia's leader and the Countess of Landsfeld's meetings with the other members of the fraternity late into the night did not go unnoticed by her enemies. Rumors began to spread about the parties she hosted for her friends, where the beer flowed freely. There was talk of orgies and bacchanals in the wooden house she'd set up as a social space for the Alemannen at the far end of the garden. Some witnesses claimed to have seen her dancing naked while the students crowded around, clapping.

Though the members of Maurer's cabinet had felt obligated to name Lola countess, they were reluctant to be seen in her company. The so-called Dawn Ministry's days were numbered because of its ministers' desperation, the king's discontent, and Lola's constant accusations that they were plotting against her. At the end of November 1847, the countess convinced Ludwig that it was time for change and that Maurer be dismissed. A new council formed, headed by one of the few liberal-minded aristocrats, the ambitious Prince von Wallerstein. Serving as minister of the interior was Franz von Berks, whose son was an Alemannen. Across the city, people joked that it was only a matter of time before a "Lola Ministry" would be formed.

The king began to have doubts about Lola's increasingly rebellious "musketeers." He wanted his beloved all to himself and was frustrated to find that she preferred their company. For his part, Prince von Wallerstein was trying to convince the Bavarian aristocracy to accept the Countess of Landsfeld—and finding that the same band of rabble-rousers was one of the main obstacles. The minister promised the king that he would keep a close eye on the students and inform him of their every move. He also wrote an etiquette guide for the countess and sent it to her through one of her close acquaintances. It was accompanied by a note that began, "If you wish to be countess and the friend of a monarch by the grace of God, you must adhere to social conventions and avoid compromising situations." Lola reacted with anger. Nobody needed to give her lessons on urbanity, much less somebody like Wallerstein: "The arrogant fool has forgotten that he's prime minister of Bavaria thanks to me. His days are numbered. I swear he'll be stripped of his position before spring."

Even more vexing to the king was the fact that Queen Therese was holding firm in her refusal to ever meet the Countess of Landsfeld. She also refused to receive anyone who frequented the Spaniard's residence. Lola kept pressing the king to have her presented to the court, but Ludwig always changed the subject. In the meantime, he tried to protect her from the relentless rumors and criticisms. The people of Munich were forbidden to utter Lola Montez's name, and the police warned citizens that they must refer to her as Marie, Countess of Landsfeld. But these measures were of little use, and the local press in other German cities published cruel cartoons mocking the couple. One of them depicted the young, beautiful Countess of Landsfeld with a dog at her feet wearing a crown on its head.

Official efforts to win over the city's noble families were thwarted a few days before the start of the new year. Lola organized a raucous, beer-soaked party for the Alemannen. According to witnesses, the young men stripped off their trousers and wandered through the house in their shirts—or even naked. At dawn, some were carrying the countess around the salon on their shoulders, singing and chanting her name. Unfortunately, Lola ran into a bronze lamp that was hanging from the ceiling. She tumbled to the floor, unconscious, and cut her head. The policeman charged with guarding her called a doctor, who treated her wound. Her reputation, though, was irretrievably injured. The year 1848 was off to a bad start for her.

The king heard about Lola's injury that same night. He would have rushed to her, but Therese was waiting in his chambers for their daily card game. Worried, he dispatched a servant to ask about Lola's condition. The servant assured him that she was fine, but when Ludwig learned the details, he grew indignant and ordered a secret investigation.

The next day, the king ran into Peissner on the street. To his surprise, the young man spoke of the countess with a familiarity and admiration that Ludwig found suspect. The king's suspicions grew when someone in his inner circle informed him that the countess was having intimate relations with Elias in her home. Ludwig, who had so far refused to believe that his dear Lola could be unfaithful, grew more and more jealous as he listened to the many stories about her love affairs. Aware of the damage she'd done, Lola sent him an apology: "I beg you to forgive me for what happened last night and come this afternoon at 5:30 to visit your loyal and fervent Lolitta."

That afternoon he went to her house and invited her to stroll in the English garden along the Isar River. Walking arm in arm, they stopped in a Greek-style temple atop a small rise.

The king gazed at the beautiful landscape and then, turning to her, asked, "Do you still love me, Lolita?"

"Luis, what a ridiculous question," she replied, surprised. "You know I don't love anyone the way I love you."

"No, my dear, you no longer care about me of late. We hardly see each other, and you turn to me only when you need something or want me to intercede for one of your protégés. You have no consideration for my feelings or my reputation, and you humiliate me before my people."

"This is absurd. You yourself say that we need to put a stop to the rumors defaming me. So how can you listen to these lies that only aim to destroy our happiness? If you are referring to Peissner, he is like a brother to me. There is nothing between us."

"Lola, you have condemned yourself all on your own, and I'm sorry with all my heart because I still love you. I warned that making you part of the nobility would mean that your behavior had to be unimpeachable. But you are incapable of understanding the gravity of your actions."

They continued to walk in silence until dusk fell. Lola had never seen the king so hurt, nor had he spoken to her so frankly. She felt for him: he was her best support, her most loyal ally. Thanks to the king, she was not a mere courtesan; she had independence, money, and a good social position. It would be very foolish to throw away everything she'd managed to achieve. "This very night I'll write him a letter and ask forgiveness for having wounded his pride, and I'll promise to behave more decorously," she thought. "We will go back to being good friends and sharing laughter, caresses, and confidences."

After the student party fiasco, hostility against Lola increased. The king asked Wallerstein to ensure that his lover found a new, more respectable group of friends. The prince thought the dancer should organize a weekly salon and encouraged His Majesty to ask one of his most loyal ministers to have tea at the Countess of Landsfeld's home. After much deliberation, they selected Baron von Hohenhausen, the minister of war, for the task. The old soldier was very grateful to the king for having awarded him the knight's cross of the Order of Civil Service.

Two days later, at a palace dinner, Ludwig casually mentioned that he would be very pleased if one afternoon the minister would visit the noble Spanish lady. Hohenhausen was a bit surprised but interpreted the invitation as an order and accepted. At five thirty on the dot, he appeared at the residence on Barerstrasse, and his hostess regaled him with a lovely afternoon tea party. Having heard that the minister did not like tea, she had prepared a hot punch that her guest very much enjoyed. But the next day, the general formally tendered his resignation, offering no explanation. King Ludwig was upset, but there was nothing he could do.

After Hohenhausen's resignation, the military's support for the king began to falter. In early January, Ludwig complained to an army commander that it was a disgrace that his officers refused to greet the Countess of Landsfeld on the street. The soldier replied that his men would greet her only if they received a written order from His Majesty himself. A Bavarian general told the king that he couldn't guarantee that his officers would obey if they were called on to defend her. Ludwig was no longer sure that his troops would defend him in the event of an uprising.

On the afternoon of January 12, Berks and Wallerstein were meeting to try to find a way to improve the countess's situation when a delegation of Alemannen arrived. The students had come to invite them to an official banquet they would be hosting thanks to a generous donation from their benefactress. The lunch would take place at the Bayerischer Hof hotel on Saturday night. Wallerstein diplomatically informed them that it was not prudent for anyone from the government to have a direct association with student groups and that he must kindly decline the invitation. Lola took the refusal as an affront and immediately showed up at their office.

"Minister von Wallerstein," she began, "hear me well. You have taken me for a fool by offering such an absurd excuse for refusing Alemannia's invitation to a banquet that will be attended by university authorities and administrators. I wonder what His Majesty will think of this insult."

"Forgive me, Countess, but perhaps I have not explained myself well. Under the current circumstances, I do not think it appropriate for the ministers to give support to the fraternity, however laudable its aims. You know what a violent climate is brewing at the university; this banquet is a provocation."

"That is ridiculous. I will speak to His Majesty and you will regret it if you do not attend. You have no idea how far I'll go to crush your

brilliant career." Before he could respond, Lola spun on her heel and
stalked out.

Wallerstein wrote an urgent message to the king, telling him what
had happened and adding that the banquet would only anger the other
students. Berks, though, saw no problem with attending the event. The
banquet hall, presided over by an enormous portrait of His Majesty
Ludwig I of Bavaria and the student association's coat of arms, was
packed. Though it was a men-only celebration, Lola could not resist
appearing briefly to greet her faithful followers. The University of
Munich's administrators and professors were also among those invited.
In his speech, Berks noted that the students loyal to the Countess
of Landsfeld were an example of manly virtue that was sorely lacking among the degenerate youth of the time. Elias Peissner thanked
the minister and raised his glass to toast the fraternity. The festivities
stretched on until dawn.

Just as Wallerstein had foretold, the conflicts between the student
societies intensified after the banquet. Any time an Alemannen appeared
at the university in his characteristic red cap, he was received with jeers
and whistles. When they went to class, all the other students walked
out, and professors refused to lecture with most of the students absent.

By late January, the situation had become untenable and Peissner
asked the king to intervene. The king's response was decisive: he decreed
harsh punishments for any students discovered harassing other students
or causing trouble.

After these measures, a seeming calm settled over the university,
until a new scandal erupted. At the end of January, Joseph von Görres,
one of the university's most respected intellectuals, passed away. The
elderly professor, Catholic and ultraconservative, was a sworn enemy of
the Spanish dancer, whom he considered "the female Antichrist." The
large funeral took place two days later, and as the long procession moved
toward the cemetery, the marchers saw the Countess of Landsfeld walking her dog in the street. A few young men started hissing at her and

muttering threats. "Down with the Spaniard!" someone yelled. "Out of Bavaria, witch! We don't want you here!"

Rather than retreating, Lola responded that they'd better show her respect or she'd see to it that the university got shut down. The police intervened to prevent further escalation, but the students would not forget her threats.

By the gloomy month of February, the Countess of Landsfeld had begun complaining that her life had shrunk to fit within the four walls of her beautiful residence. The literary evenings she'd been so excited to organize were a complete failure. Nobody in their right mind would dare invite social ostracism by visiting her. The new minister of war, Heinrich von der Mark, was also compelled to have tea with her, but the visit wasn't a pleasant one. On the few occasions that Lola attended a performance at the Court Theatre, she had to endure stares and whispers. One Sunday night she was spotted arriving at her second-tier box. Her stunning diamond tiara, necklace, and bracelet caused a commotion. The ladies exchanged hushed speculations about how much the jewelry must have cost. Despite everything, Ludwig was still trying to win Lola's affection with magnificent gifts.

As the winter dragged on, the brawls between students became more frequent. One day a number of Alemannen were attacked on Odeonsplatz, in downtown Munich. Pursued by a furious crowd, Lola's followers were forced to seek refuge in Rottmann's Café. Peissner sent a message to the Countess of Landsfeld, who immediately grabbed her pistol and leaped into her carriage. When she entered the large square, which was thronged with nearly three thousand people, a mob surged toward her, and she fled amid insults and shoves. She sought shelter in the nearby Austrian embassy, but they denied her entrance. Then some in the crowd began hurling manure, and she brandished her pistol at them in defiance. With a final effort she managed to hide in the baroque Theatine Church, but even there, people swarmed after her. The priests asked the assailants to respect the holy place and leave immediately.

They also pleaded with Lola to go, saying they could not guarantee her safety. Soon, mounted policemen dispersed the crowd, and she was escorted safely outside.

The next day, Ludwig summoned Wallerstein. "I asked you to protect the Countess of Landsfeld, yet a frenzied mob nearly killed her. The things that poor woman has suffered are beyond the pale: insults, shoves, blows—and all in broad daylight. Where is this going to end, Wallerstein?"

"Your Majesty, I warned you that the banquet was going to cause trouble, and the countess strolls through the city with that grand air as if she were queen, always looking to rile people up—"

"I forbid you to continue speaking of her in this manner," Ludwig said vehemently. "I have written a draft ordering the immediate closure of the university, and all students who do not live in Munich will have to leave the city within forty-eight hours."

"I'm begging you, sir, don't do it. If you sign this decree, a revolution will break out. The people support the students and they will rise up against Your Majesty."

"If it troubles your conscience, you are welcome to step down."

Ignoring Wallerstein's advice, the king closed the university the next day. Hundreds of young people gathered in front of Wallerstein's ministry in a show of support, raising their fists and unfurling their fraternities' flags. Though it was a peaceful gathering, the police charged violently. Officers struck students with their clubs, seriously injuring some. This only made the situation worse. There were shouts calling for the removal of the minister of war and the chief of police, and for the immediate expulsion of Lola Montez.

Early that afternoon, the city's most prominent officials met in the Rathaus, the ancient city hall, to discuss the university closure and its serious economic implications for Munich. They selected a delegation that would ask the king to revoke his decree and force Lola Montez to leave the city. They all agreed everything was the fault of the Spanish dancer alone and that her influence was immensely harmful to Ludwig. They needed to end the chaos racking Munich once and for all. After a long, tense meeting, the attendees headed for the royal palace, led by the burgomaster. When they reached the wide esplanade of Max-Joseph-Platz, the doors of the Residenz swung shut and mounted soldiers took up positions.

As the hours passed, a crowd gathered in the square, and soon more than two thousand people were spilling down the Court Theatre stairs and waiting under the arches of the post office. The protestors were told that Ludwig would not be returning to the palace until dinner, but they decided to wait. What they did not realize was that the king was currently in his private chambers with Lola. As tension mounted outside, Ludwig recounted the most recent developments. Lola was pleased that the king had ousted Wallerstein and closed the university, "a breeding ground for insurgents and ingrates." But she objected when she learned that the decree to leave Munich would apply to the Alemannen as well. The king refused to make an exception and was in fact relieved that her faithful "musketeers" would have to return home. Ludwig was eager to see the back of them, especially Elias Peissner. Unable to change his mind, Lola told him that she intended to host a farewell party for her dear students that very night to thank them for the courage with which they'd defended her.

Ludwig refused to receive the delegation waiting outside his doors, but his son Prince Luitpold, with tears in his eyes, begged him to listen to what the men had to say. At last the Residenz's doors swung open and the grand marshal of the court led the burgomaster and his committee into the audience hall. The king, wearing a general's uniform, received them coldly. The crowd's presence in front of his palace was a show of defiance that he had no intention of tolerating.

"Gentlemen, no mob is going to scare me into changing my mind. You can take my life from me, but not my will. Giving in would be a sign of weakness. If the citizens don't behave peaceably, they will force me to move the court elsewhere," the king exclaimed.

He assured the committee that they would receive a written response to their petition the next morning. The members of the delegation left the palace and returned to the Rathaus. The citizens who had waited for hours in the freezing air returned home. The streets of Munich were empty, but the calm was taut and fragile. Soon, a hundred people headed to Lola's residence to demand that she leave the city at once. They found the countess out on her balcony, chatting with the guards in the sentry box. Her student friends would arrive soon, and she was dressed for the occasion. At first the protestors just shouted and whistled, but at some point a few rabble-rousers armed with bats attempted to scale the garden wall. The guards reacted violently, and panic ensued. Several people were wounded before the crowd dispersed. Lola, still standing on the balcony, clapped her hands and shouted in French, "*Très bien, très bien!*"

At nightfall, Minister von Berks arrived at the Rathaus with a message from the king. Upon seeing that the citizens had left the square peacefully, Ludwig had signed a decree that the university would reopen in summer as long as the people of Munich continued to conduct themselves respectably. But this was not enough. Angry voices rang out, and a unanimous cry filled the vaulted, torch-lit hall: "We want Lola Montez out of Munich! We will take up arms and burn her house!"

From his chambers, the king gazed through the windows at the deserted square. He was calmer now, convinced that his subjects would appreciate his gesture of goodwill. In an effort to show that he had everything in hand, he went to the Court Theatre, which was presenting a performance of the comic opera *La sirène* to a nearly empty house. After the first act, he returned to his rooms, where he found a note from Lola that read:

If you wish to continue being as noble and great as you have been so far, now is the time to prove it. Always yours and faithful until death,

   Lolitta

Ludwig felt disillusioned and overwhelmed. Berks brought him up to speed on the people's demands, and he was afraid of what might happen the next day if he didn't give in to the insurgents. While Lola was enjoying herself at the students' farewell dinner, he picked up his pen and wrote his lover a letter, which he rushed over by messenger. It read:

I just received a note from Berks informing me of the enormous discontent that reigns in the city. If not for the police holding firm and the assistance of a squadron of cuirassiers, your house would have been attacked. "Tomorrow will be a very dangerous day," he writes, and if you remain there you will not be safe. I am entreating you, if you have ever loved me and still love me, leave the city. The best thing would be for you to leave at first light, without a word to anybody, for Lake Starnberg; I repeat: without a word to anybody. If possible, tell me at what time I can go see you at your home before you leave. You will be able to return the next day. Though it would be better if you left this very night. I know you are not afraid of anything—you have already shown that. I fear not for myself but for you. If blood is spilled in your name, hatred will explode and your situation will become untenable. We must ensure that this does not happen. You know that nothing in the world could drive me away from you. I beg of you to heed my advice. Lolitta will always love her

   faithful Luis

A short while later, the messenger returned from Barerstrasse with his lover's reply:

Your Lolitta has no intention of leaving Munich or of giving in to extortion. My place is here beside you, and nobody will make me change my mind.

CHAPTER 8

Countess on the Run

Throughout that long night of February 10, 1848, Ludwig had nightmares.

He was terrified that Lola, like his godmother, Marie Antoinette, might be murdered by a furious mob. He had always hated violence. He was an artist, an aesthete, a poet-king who asked only that his people let him love and be loved. But now he had no choice. To defend his lover, he was prepared to stand up to his people, his family, and the entire government. Not even Queen Therese's pleas had any effect. The king could not understand his people's outrage. It was true that the young woman behaved arrogantly on occasion, but she didn't deserve to be treated like this. "Nothing and nobody will separate me from you. Lolita, you are my whole life, my inspiration, my reason for existing. I would leave everything for you," he repeated to himself.

At dawn, thousands of citizens and students surrounded city hall, where the delegates were still meeting. Though the burgomaster asked that no one take justice into his own hands, the more violent elements threatened again to burn down Lola Montez's house if the king did not accede to their demands. Seeing the direction things were taking, Minister von Berks went to the palace to inform the king.

"Your Majesty," he said, "the situation in the city is quite serious. I fear that an uprising may break out against you, with unforeseeable consequences. The life of Mrs. Montez and indeed the future of the crown are at stake. You must act swiftly and order that the countess be expelled."

"I will not!" he exclaimed. "I asked that her safety at her residence be ensured. If necessary, call up more men to protect the Countess of Landsfeld!"

"Your Majesty, I have only two thousand men to reinforce the police, and that is not enough. I beg you to accede to the public's demands; she must leave immediately, and I swear that she will be escorted safely to the border."

"I will not sign an order to expel my friend from Bavaria! I could never forgive myself for such disloyalty. But I promise that I will do everything in my power to see that she goes of her own free will. Now leave me be."

When Berks left, the king sat down and wrote a brief missive to Lola. His hand shook as he picked up the pen, and he felt as if he couldn't breathe: "You must leave Bavaria today for your own safety." The dancer replied that she'd just gotten up and that she would have breakfast in her room as usual.

Ludwig was restless; he'd never been so frightened before. The minister of war had informed him that, if he received orders to use the army to defend Lola Montez against the people, he would shoot himself in the head. The king, ignoring the warnings of his wife and children, decided to go see his lover to try to convince her before it was too late.

News of the Spaniard's imminent departure spread swiftly, and thousands of jubilant citizens headed to Barerstrasse. They didn't want to miss the sight of the king's detested lover being humiliated. The dancer, oblivious to all that was occurring, was about to get dressed when her loyal musketeers burst in. Elias Peissner and his two companions had managed to muscle their way into the besieged house

This was the first portrait of Lola Montez, commissioned by King Ludwig I of Bavaria from the court painter Joseph Karl Stieler in 1845. The dancer was twenty-four years old and at the height of her beauty. Lola Montez, c. 1845 by Joseph Karl Stieler, National Portrait Gallery, Canberra, Australia/Album/Alamy Stock Photo

Lola Montez had a brief, passionate romance with the composer and pianist Franz Liszt. He abandoned her because he found her violent temper unbearable. Heritage Images/Getty Images

Lola met the writer George Sand at a dinner in the Café de Paris. They were both rebellious, tempestuous, transgressive women. It was Sand who dubbed Lola "the lioness of Paris." World History Archive/Alamy Stock Photo

The celebrated novelist Alexandre Dumas, author of The Three Musketeers, *was a friend of Lola Montez and introduced her to the Parisian literary and art world during her time in Paris in 1844.* GL Archive/Alamy Stock Photo

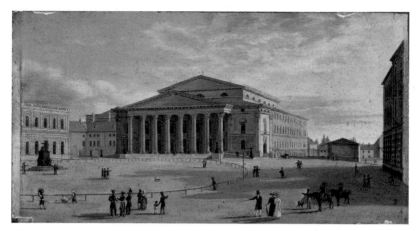

When Lola Montez arrived in Munich in 1846, the city was being reborn thanks to its king, Ludwig I of Bavaria, who dreamed of building a perfect monumental city inspired by ancient Greece and Rome.
Culture Club/Getty Images

The author, Cristina Morató, posing in the famed Gallery of Beauties, in Munich's Nymphenburg Palace, next to the most famous portrait of Lola Montez. © José Diéguez

Lola Montez was never a great dancer and was depicted in countless mocking cartoons like this one over the course of her lifetime. The Picture Art Collection/Alamy Stock Photo

King Ludwig I of Bavaria met Lola Montez in October 1846. The sixty-year-old monarch was instantly smitten. Blinded by love, he lost his people's trust and was forced to abdicate to his son Maximilian. De Agostini Picture Library/Getty Images

Lola Montez charmed King Ludwig, who was besotted with her "fiery Spanish beauty," though in
fact the young woman had been born in Ireland. Many considered her the "shadow queen" of Bavaria
because of her influence in state affairs. The Picture Art Collection/Alamy Stock Photo

Cartoons like this one and offensive pamphlets about King Ludwig's relationship with the dancer circulated all through Munich. INTERFOTO/Alamy Stock Photo

King Ludwig granted Lola Montez the title of Countess of Landsfeld. This document is a calligraphic masterpiece that features the monarch's signature and coat of arms. Naming Lola to the nobility set off a profound political and social crisis in Bavaria that culminated in the 1848 revolution and the king's abdication. © Bayerisches Hauptstaatsarchiv

Lithograph by Marie-Alexandre Alophe from 1844 that shows the dancer Lola Montez dressed in the Spanish style, with a lace mantilla and a hand fan. INTERFOTO/Alamy Stock Photo

Cartoon of Lola Montez that shows King Ludwig weeping at his lover's hasty departure from Munich in 1848. Her next adventure was in the Americas. Alamy Stock Photo

The author during her visit to the mining town of Grass Valley, in front of the cabin where Lola Montez lived for two years as a real pioneer. © Ana Lara

In 1853, drawn by the gold rush, Lola Montez arrived in San Francisco, where she enjoyed great success among the unrefined miners with her provocative "Spider Dance." Bettmann/Getty Images

This is a poster for the legendary movie Lola Montès by the director Max Ophüls, starring French actress Martine Carol. In this film, Lola appears brandishing a whip. The real Lola Montez was a great horsewoman and was known as "the lady with the whip" because she wielded one against men who dared to contradict or mock her. Lola Montés (1955) © Gamma Film (France) and Union-Film-Verleih (West Germany)/Everett Collection, Inc./Alamy Stock Photo

Lola Montez was a legend in her era, and inspired one of the great directors of cinema's golden age, Max Ophüls, who filmed a biopic about the famed courtesan's life: Lola Montès (1955). Martine Carol played the title role. In this scene, Lola smokes a cigarette. Although it was frowned upon in the nineteenth-century United States for women to smoke, Lola Montez enjoyed appearing in public with a cigarette in hand, defying social conventions. Lola Montés (1955) © Gamma Film (France) and Union-Film-Verleih (West Germany)/Album Images

During her audacious life, Lola Montez passed herself off as a famous Spanish dancer born in Seville and ended up performing in the world's best theaters across Europe and the United States. In this scene from Max Ophüls's Lola Montès, *actress Martine Carol does a Spanish dance while wearing the traditional flamenco garb that the false Spaniard Lola Montez wore with such panache in her performances.* Lola Montés (1955) © Gamma Film (France) and Union-Film-Verleih (West Germany)/AA Film Archive/Alamy Stock Photo

In the movie The Blue Angel *(1930), by the director Josef von Sternberg, the actress Marlene Dietrich plays the seductive cabaret dancer Lola Lola. The character was the prototype of the femme fatale, a young woman who drags men to their doom just like the real-life Lola Montez. Lines from the most famous song from the movie, "Ich bin die fesche Lola" ("They Call Me Naughty Lola"), say, "I'm the lovely Lola, the favorite of the season! I have a pianola at home in my parlor." At her home in Grass Valley, California, Lola Montez organized musical gatherings at which she played the pianola for her gentlemen guests.* The Blue Angel (1930) © Universum Film A.G. (Germany) and Paramount Pictures (United States)/AF archive/Alamy Stock Photo

In 1852, during her American tour, Lola Montez posed defiantly for a portrait, holding a cigarette. This is one of the earliest extant photographs of a woman smoking in the mid-nineteenth century.
Pictorial Press Ltd/Alamy Stock Photo

Lola Montez's grave in the Green-Wood Cemetery, Brooklyn, New York, circa 2019. Dennis K. Johnson/Getty Images

LOLA MONTEZ   S 355 - 6

An undated portrait of Lola Montez by an unknown photographer, circa 1852. Alpha Stock/Alamy
Stock Photo

to beg her to leave. They were surprised to find Lola sitting serenely in the parlor, talking with Lieutenant Weber, an officer loyal to the countess who had also come to help. She thanked the young men for their unconditional support but told them that she had already made a decision.

"I have done nothing wrong and have no intention of fleeing like a fugitive. I will resist and will die with my head held high if necessary, but I will not surrender. The king knows I'm not afraid of anything."

"Lola, please see reason!" exclaimed Peissner. "The house is surrounded; the agitators want you dead. Get into your carriage and flee without looking back. Do it for me, I'm begging you! I would never forgive myself if something bad happened to you."

Though she'd ordered the maid to close the shutters, they could still hear the insults hurled by the crowd: "Get out of here, harlot!" "Death to the king's whore!" "Witch, you'll burn in hell!" Peissner warned that a number of protestors had started climbing over the rear fences and the garden wall. Lola threw the front door wide open and, raising her pistol, shouted to the agitated crowd, "Here I am! Kill me if you dare!"

For a moment there was silence as the people stared in astonishment at the defiant countess. Then they started throwing rocks.

"You missed! If you want to kill me, you have to hit me here!" she added, pointing to her heart.

The students had to drag her back into the house. At that point Lola seemed to realize the gravity of the situation. Her voice trembling, she asked, "Are they never going to leave me in peace? Fine, then—I don't want a single drop of blood spilled because of me. Have the driver get my carriage ready. I will leave immediately."

She didn't have time to pack or even change her clothes. Despite the hasty departure, however, she made sure to bring along her title as countess, one of her most prized belongings. Saddest of all was having to leave behind her dogs, Zampa and Turk, but her friends promised to take care of them. Within minutes, her driver had hitched the two black horses to the carriage and climbed onto the box; the countess clambered in with Lieutenant Weber beside her, ready to escort her to the border. Though trying to be cheerful, she looked downcast and anxious as she said goodbye to the loyal students who had so heroically defended her. The heavy iron gates swung wide, and the black landau sped through the furious protestors, who began to leap and shout with joy.

The dancer did not want to leave without saying goodbye to the king, so she ordered the driver to try to reach the palace by going through the English garden. But it was no use: all points of access to the Residenz were closed off, and agitators were patrolling the square beside it. The Countess of Landsfeld's carriage, its curtains drawn, disappeared into the labyrinth of cobbled alleyways and passed through the Sendlinger Tor city gate, headed south.

While Lola Montez was fleeing Munich, the king was trying to reach her house on Barerstrasse, thinking he might still find her there. He ignored Berks's exhortation that he not go out alone. With great difficulty, he managed to make his way through the crowd choking the wide avenue. The king had to go behind the house and climb the garden wall, only to encounter a disturbing scene. After his lover's departure, the frenzied mob had managed to break inside. In the main drawing room, where he'd shared such wonderful moments with his beloved, men had flung books to the ground, torn down the velvet curtains, and shattered the Chinese vases. Ludwig raced upstairs to find a woman slashing the silk cushions and gauzy muslin canopy of the rosewood bed with a knife. Another young woman, laughing wildly, was pulling petticoats, corsets, and silk stockings out of the drawers. Ludwig went downstairs and was crossing the courtyard when a rock aimed at one of the windows struck him on the arm. The guards rushed to protect him.

Ludwig went to the main entrance and stood at the top of the stairs. "Listen to your king!" he shouted. "This very morning I have issued the order to reopen the university. In addition, the police chief has been removed from his post. I have made this decision freely, as yet another demonstration of my benevolence."

"Long live the king of Bavaria! Long live His Majesty!" the crowd chanted.

"I hope," he continued in a commanding tone, "that you will now respect this house, which is also mine, and that those who love me will return to their homes."

Mollified, the citizens began to scatter. From the maidservant, Jeanette, Ludwig learned the details of Mrs. Montez's hasty escape, but nobody could tell him where she had gone. In the parlor again, surrounded by overturned furniture and broken mirrors, tears came to his eyes. Everything he loved had vanished in an instant. Even the flowers he'd given his friend the day before were on the floor. Ludwig gave instructions for the house to remain under guard to prevent further damage. Crestfallen, he returned alone to the palace on foot. He couldn't remember how many times he'd made this same journey—happy times in which he'd believed he'd finally found the muse and companion with whom he would share the final stretch of his life.

When he reached Max-Joseph-Platz, the crowd there cheered. The king, his expression grave and weary, waved to his subjects and walked through the iron gates of the royal residence without saying a word. How he hated those people who had destroyed his happiness.

In his chambers, he went to the window and stared pensively at the jubilant crowd below. Queen Therese took his arm and said, "Ludwig, you've done the right thing. You are the king, and you owe your people."

"No, I cannot smile at them. They have humiliated and extorted me. I will never forgive them."

"Yes, Ludwig, you must. A king has to be above his feelings. You saved the crown today. Forget this woman—she has brought us only misfortune."

But Ludwig could not hear his wife's sensible words nor the people's ovations. He felt alone and demoralized. "Everything is lost," he mused. "I am but the shadow of a king."

Early in the afternoon, the countess's carriage reached Gross-hesselohe, a town five miles from Munich that was a popular tourist spot during the summer but nearly deserted in February. They stopped at an old inn, where the owner offered her a room where she might rest, a good wine, and a simple dinner.

Lying in bed, she pondered how to reestablish communication with the king, imagining that he could simply sign an order authorizing her return and everything would go back to the way it was. She thought about her charming mansion, her beautiful gowns, her magnificent jewels. In her rush, she hadn't been able to retrieve even her emerald silk robe with Chantilly lace that the king loved so much. Lola picked up a piece of paper and scrawled a note telling Ludwig she was safe in the company of Lieutenant Weber and her driver. She added that she would wait for him in Grosshesselohe until the city had calmed down. The old driver, George, changed his livery and fine velvet breeches for some peasant garb and rode off on horseback with his mistress's message. When he reached the city, he managed to give the missive to an acquaintance who had access to the palace. Then, certain that nobody would recognize him, he went into a tavern downtown to have a beer before returning to the inn. But he was recognized and people began beating and yelling at him. George managed to escape before the police arrived and spent the night at the home of some friends.

In Grosshesselohe, the countess's patience had already run out. Though Lieutenant Weber tried to convince her it was too risky, she refused to sit idle. She asked the innkeeper's wife to help her with a disguise and selected a discreet peasant dress. With her hair pulled back in a bun and powdered white, Lola was unrecognizable. The innkeeper hitched his horses to a cart and, with his young daughter sitting next to the camouflaged countess, they headed to Munich.

It was nightfall when they reached the city, and Lola went to the home of the Günthers, a married couple who had supported her in difficult times. There she learned that a dozen of the Alemannen had taken refuge in Blutenburg Castle, an old fortified hunting lodge a few miles west of Munich. The countess, seeing that it was impossible to reach the heavily guarded palace, decided to look for her musketeers. When she reached the castle late that frigid, starry night, her friends were dumbfounded. Peissner, who was the first to recognize her, embraced her and invited her into the main sitting room, where she could warm up beside the large fireplace. Lola was exhausted—it had been a very long day and the tension had worn her out. After dinner, she retired to one of the bedrooms with Peissner. She lay down to sleep on a sofa under several blankets, and her lover settled in a nearby armchair to keep vigil.

Early in the morning, Ludwig received Lola's note. The king was relieved to learn that she was safe and sent for his interior minister, Berks. The most hated man in Munich because of his friendship with Lola had become his closest adviser and the only person he still trusted.

"My dear Berks," Ludwig said, "I finally have news of Mrs. Montez. She is well and safe, but it is too dangerous for her to stay in Bavaria. I want you to come with me at once to the inn where she is lodging."

"Your Majesty," the minister replied, "things are calm now in the city. But if anybody finds out that Your Majesty has gone to meet her, I cannot guarantee either your safety or hers."

"I have to say goodbye," Ludwig insisted. "She will need money and a letter of safe passage. If we leave now, we will be back by lunchtime."

The king decided that Lola should cross the Swiss border and settle in Lausanne, where he would join her later. But when Ludwig and his minister arrived in Grosshesselohe, Lola was nowhere to be found. The innkeeper explained that he had taken the countess, disguised as a peasant woman, back to the city; that he'd left her at the home of some friends; and that he hadn't heard from her since. Ludwig knew that Lola would do anything to be reunited with him, but he never dreamed she would be this reckless.

In the meantime, the proprietor of Blutenburg Castle had decided to tattle on his problematic guests. In Munich he'd gone to Berks, who reassured him that the Countess of Landsfeld was simply waiting for her luggage to arrive before continuing her journey. He promised to send some police officers to Blutenburg to escort Mrs. Montez to Lindau, where a steamboat would take her to Switzerland.

A few hours later, when two policemen entered the Blutenburg sitting room, they found Lola writing a letter to the king in which she requested that he move the royal court to Nuremberg as punishment for the way the people of Munich had treated her. Lola, furious at the intrusion, shouted in German, "*Raus! Raus!*" (Out! Out!). She then threatened the officers with her pistol, and when they showed her their order to escort her to Lindau, she tore it to shreds.

In the end, Peissner was able to talk some sense into her and promised to accompany her to Switzerland. The countess, three of the students, and the two policemen climbed into a carriage to head to the nearest train station on the Augsburg line. From there they would make a long journey by coach to the picturesque village of Lindau, on the shores of Lake Constance. Before leaving, Lola wrote the king a letter to tell him that she was heartbroken. She also complained that she did not have clothes to protect her from the cold and snow.

A boat was waiting to transport the Countess of Landsfeld to the other side of the lake, but at the last moment, she refused to board. Lola didn't want to leave Bavaria without her dogs, her servants, and her personal effects. Waiting to hear from the king, she and her three friends took rooms at the Hotel de la Couronne, the best in town.

As calm returned to Munich, the king hardly left his office. He was consumed by a combined feeling of rage and impotence. He stewed over the fact that Lola hadn't been satisfied with being his official lover and enjoying the privileges of that position. Her obstinacy and volatile temperament had ruined everything. She always wanted more; not even the title of Countess of Landsfeld had been enough. "Lolitta, darling, you wanted the crown of Bavaria and even to govern in my name, but flying to such heights was your perdition," he wrote in a letter he never sent.

She was still writing to him about politics and warning him not to trust anybody, not even his closest advisers. Minister von Berks was the only person in whom he still had any confidence and to whom he could bare his heart. All over Europe, news of the uprising in Munich was on the front pages. The year 1848 was bringing winds of change to Europe, and Bavaria seemed to be headed in a worrying direction, with the people demanding greater freedoms and democracy.

In Lindau, the countess still refused to leave the country. Though she had pleasant companionship and the hotel was comfortable, she rarely went out in public, to avoid being recognized. During those uncertain days, she wrote the king a long letter in which she complained of her harsh and unjust "exile":

> I feel like a fugitive criminal . . . I am in a deplorable physical state; my emotional state is even worse because who knows whether, now that I am apart from you, our enemies and false friends may tell you lies about me. Now I know why that person unknown to me told you that outrageous lie about Peissner, the student, and you, my poor, dear Louis, believed it! . . . I beg of you not to forget how much I have suffered for my Louis, because I did not wish to deceive you like the others, but have always told you the truth about other men, even when it went against my own interests. That is enough to reassure you that I love you infinitely—but now I am so unhappy . . .
>
> Though everybody here is very nice to me, I think that only in the grave will I find rest. To pass my time in exile, I want to study German, and soon I hope to be able to write to

you in your own language. Nevertheless, my dear Louis, I cannot wait all this time . . . It truly is not possible—this country is so dreary in winter, and cold. The idea of living in Switzerland fills me with fear and horror. Send me another passport with an English name and I will leave for Palermo at once. Yesterday I got my period and I feel quite out of sorts. While here, I am trying not to go out to avoid the public's prying eyes. Goodbye for now, my dear Louis. Until I receive a letter from you, and my dogs, servants, and belongings arrive, I will wait here, and from the bottom of my heart I send you thousands of kisses from your faithful

Lolitta

Do not forget me, and do not be unfaithful to me.

With every day that passed, the king regretted more and more having allowed his lover to leave. He pined for her and lost any joy in living. Every night he kissed her marble foot and imagined her swathed in her exquisite silk robe. Although initially the people had praised the measures he'd taken, now his subjects eyed him warily. He resented them and wanted nothing more than to bring his beloved Lola back to Munich. Though he tried to seem calm and collected in public, his heart was in pieces. A recent pamphlet titled "The Night at Blutenburg" had people in an uproar. The pamphlet gave a satirical account of the countess's stay with the Alemannen at the hunting lodge and even of the fact that she and the devoted Peissner had spent the night together. For Ludwig, who never wanted to believe such rumors, it was a devastating blow. He could not forgive Lola for being unfaithful and throwing herself into her young lover's arms in such a moment of crisis. Enraged, the very afternoon he first read the pamphlet, he wrote a harsh letter ordering the students to stay away from her, saying that under no circumstances were they to accompany her to Switzerland:

> My dearest Lolitta,
> As you know, the entire world is unable to drive me
> apart from you—only you can do that. The moment of
> truth has arrived. If a student travels with you or joins
> you on your journey, you will never see me again—we
> will be finished. Lolitta, you inspire in me a love that
> no one has provoked in my life. I have never done for
> anyone else the things I have done for you. With your
> love, it wouldn't matter to me to leave everything else
> behind. My beloved darling, think about the last six-
> teen months, about how your dear Luis has behaved
> in this time we've known each other. You will never
> find a heart like mine. Lolitta must make a decision.

Like many other letters he wrote to Lola, this one was never sent. Though the constant rumors about her affairs had wounded him deeply, the king could not stop loving her. In another unsent missive, he said that, even though she'd betrayed him, he forgave her with all his heart: "You know that I will never be able to be apart from you, only if you ask it of me. Is that what you want, Lolitta? Oh, if only it were possible for you to be faithful to me at every moment, or at least honest, with a boundless honesty!"

In her letters, Lola continued to defend herself against the libel that sought to destroy her reputation: "I am weeping now, and can no longer see the paper through my tears. It seems to me that the world wishes to slowly break my heart. I should take my own life in a moment—that would be preferable to my constant heartache." Ludwig still wanted to believe her, but the students would have to leave her before she would hear from him again.

Despite his anger, he sent her maid, Jeanette, to accompany her to Switzerland and bring her some of her belongings. Far from being happy to see her, Lola lashed out. The countess accused Jeanette of having stolen her beautiful cashmere shawls, jewelry, and a valuable prayer book the king had given her. She wrote several letters to Ludwig accusing the young woman of theft and demanding that she be brought to justice. Jeanette was aghast to see her mistress so agitated and returned to Munich the next day.

In late February, Lola Montez said goodbye to her gallant escorts. Elias Peissner and his two companions were forced to join the rest of the Alemannen in Leipzig. She would miss their company, their laughter, and their support—not to mention the bravery and loyalty they'd shown as her personal guard. But the person most deeply affected by the separation was Elias Peissner. In his naivete, the romantic young bohemian had believed they could one day get married and live happily in some remote corner of Germany. Now he was seized by the bitter realization that he had been only a passing fancy for her.

"I would have given my life for you, Lola," Peissner lamented, gazing into her eyes. "Ever since we met, you have been the most important thing in my life. By giving me hope, you have broken my heart many times. But despite everything, I would do it all again."

"My dear friend," Lola replied tenderly, "I know you will always be my most loyal musketeer, but now our paths are separating. I am not good company for you—misfortune dogs my heels and you deserve better."

"I wanted so much to stay with you!" the young man exclaimed, embracing her. "I would follow you to the ends of the earth. You know that, if you need my protection, I will race to your side."

That night, alone in her room, Lola recalled Peissner's final words and realized that she could have been happy with him. He was a young man with a brilliant future, brave, and a marvelous lover. Because of her he'd been expelled from the university and was unable to finish his studies. Now she feared that in Leipzig he might face some sort of reprisal from her enemies. At daybreak she wrote to the king: "To make you happy, I have now separated from all my friends. I am ready to travel alone. Given the bizarre ideas you've concocted regarding the students, I have made them leave to satisfy you."

On February 24, at nine o'clock in the morning, Lola Montez went down to Lindau's docks, where a hundred curious onlookers were waiting to watch her leave. There were no shouts or insults, and men doffed their hats as she passed. The lady boarded the steamboat *Ludwig* to cross Lake Constance. Once in Swiss territory, she hired a carriage to take her to Zurich and in the evening checked into the Hotel Baur, in the city's historic center, surrounded by a private garden and with lovely views of the lake and the snowy Alps. The Spanish dancer registered as the Countess of Landsfeld and instructed the hotel staff to address her by that name.

Lola spent several days resting in her elegant suite, trying to recover from the stress of recent days and to think about her future. The migraines were back, and she barely had an appetite. But then she received an invitation from her old friend Robert Peel to visit him in Bern, where he was the British chargé d'affaires. With her good mood suddenly restored, she excitedly prepared her luggage. The diplomat welcomed her with open arms. He organized a large dinner to introduce her to prominent Bern personalities. Lola, delighted to be the center of attention again, enjoyed regaling an eager public with tales of her Munich adventures and her relationship with King Ludwig I of Bavaria.

That same month, King Louis-Philippe and his family fled the Tuileries Palace with nothing but the clothes on their backs, and the French Second Republic was installed. On February 27, Lola wrote to Ludwig, "The scene in France is very bad. I am worried for Munich. Above all, keep Wallerstein by your side. If you love me, prove it to me and be very diplomatic with him. Though he is a bad man, he is the only one who can keep the situation under control. Most important, offer him some public attention. If he leaves, your Lolitta will never be able to return to Munich."

Ludwig took his lover's advice seriously, though he remained mistrustful of all but Berks. Word spread through Munich that Lola was still sending letters to the palace. Given the hostile climate, Berks tried to tender his resignation on March 2, though the king persuaded him to take a year of leave instead. That night, a crowd attacked Berks's apartment on Ludwigstrasse. Fearing for his safety and that of his family, the minister fled at dawn, wearing a disguise. The residents of Munich and other Bavarian cities put together petitions demanding that the king grant them greater liberty, abolish press censorship, sign a new election law, and have the military swear a loyalty oath to the constitution rather than to the king. To buy time, Ludwig dissolved the parliament and called new elections. On March 4, the capital's armory was captured; Bavaria was on the brink of revolution. Mobs threatened to attack the palace, and barricades went up in some neighborhoods. Ludwig found himself forced to capitulate and reluctantly signed a proclamation conceding to nearly all of his citizens' demands.

The next day, the people of Munich spilled jubilantly into the streets and gathered in Max-Joseph-Platz. Once more, Ludwig was applauded by his subjects, but he was indignant and furious at having given in. Only the hope of reuniting with his lover in Switzerland helped him endure the humiliation. Far from Munich, all Lola was thinking about was how she could return to Bavaria. Thanks to her friend Peel, her stay in the Swiss capital was very pleasant, so much so that she decided to remain there rather than continue on to Lausanne. In the hotel where she was lodging, the countess ran into another old friend, Baron Georges Meller-Zakomelsky, a Russian aristocrat she'd met in Heidelberg.

Though Bern was a tranquil city with a provincial feel and hardly any social life, Lola was able to enjoy an agreeable lifestyle there thanks to her friends' generosity and the king's. But now she was worried about her future; her economic well-being depended on an elderly monarch who could not last if a revolution broke out.

On March 8, Lola made a decision that would have dramatic consequences for the king and for Bavaria. Tired of not hearing from Ludwig—who didn't know she was in Bern and had been writing to Lausanne—she decided to disguise herself again and return to Munich. This time she chose to wear men's clothing, hiding her hair under a hat and donning a large cloak. Though he thought the idea insane, Baron Meller-Zakomelsky offered to accompany her. To avoid arousing suspicion, they left Bern at night by carriage and headed north toward the Bavarian capital. They arrived in Munich in the middle of the night and hastened to the home of Caroline Wegner, one of the countess's loyal friends. Lola started ringing the doorbell insistently and shouting to the young woman. The noise alerted a policeman on patrol; he found the sight of two cloaked figures hurrying into the apartment suspicious. There were rumors that a group of agitators was planning an attack on a munitions storehouse, so the policeman reported what he'd seen. Within minutes, two officers appeared at the Wegner home and insisted on searching the apartment. Caroline, very nervous, told them that the strange men had left, but then they heard a noise and discovered one of them hiding under the sofa. To their surprise, the policemen found that the young man was wearing a fake beard and was actually a beautiful, blue-eyed woman, the despised Countess of Landsfeld. They immediately sent an urgent message to the police chief, who speedily dressed and rushed to the palace at one o'clock in the morning. The chief was perplexed and frightened; if people learned that Lola Montez had returned to Munich, the consequences could be deadly. He felt no sympathy for the Spanish dancer, but he knew that the king would not forgive him if he kicked his lover out of the country without informing him first.

At the palace, Ludwig was sleeping peacefully when his valet woke him and announced that the police chief was waiting for him in the antechamber. The king donned his velvet robe and went to meet him in embroidered slippers, his nightcap still on his head.

"This must be a matter of vital importance," the king said curtly.

"Your Majesty, I have some news for you and I don't know how to say it because I know it will upset you and—"

"Tell me what this is about!" Ludwig broke in.

"Your Majesty, your friend Mrs. Montez is in the city; she has disguised herself as a young man, but a policeman found her and she is being detained at the main police station."

"There must be some mistake. The Countess of Landsfeld left Bavaria some time ago and I haven't heard from her since."

"Your Majesty, please do not go to see her, it's very dangerous. If you authorize it, I will personally make sure that she is deported immediately."

"Wait here, I'll get dressed and you can take me to her." With that, the king hurried out of the room.

Ludwig couldn't believe what he had heard, but he knew that Lola was capable of anything. As his carriage sped through the empty streets, he felt befuddled, his heart pounding. When they arrived, for a moment he didn't recognize her; sitting there on a bench with her hair hidden under a felt top hat, she looked like one of the young students she was so fond of. Even dressed as a man, she was powerfully alluring. The king studied her carefully; she was wearing riding boots, tight black pants, a white shirt, a silk vest, and a jacket with bone buttons that concealed her figure. Lola threw herself into his arms, and the king asked that they be left alone.

"My darling Lola, what have you done?" he asked sorrowfully. "It is reckless. If you are discovered, what will become of you?"

"Luis," she replied, resting her head on his shoulder, "I was feeling desperate because I hadn't heard from you. I thought you'd forgotten me, that you were angry with me. Who knows what my enemies have told you . . ."

"Lolita, my love, how could I forget you? Since you left there hasn't been a single moment that I don't wish I'd stopped you from going. I wrote to you every day, and I'm sorry to hear the letters didn't arrive."

"We must be together," Lola said. "I can't bear this separation."

"Though it pains me deeply, I must tell you the truth: you will never be able to return to live in Munich; if you did, they would kill you."

"Then come with me, leave Bavaria. Your people no longer love you—they do not appreciate what you've done for them. Leave them and come live with me. Leave the thankless burden of your crown; only then will they realize all that they have lost."

For three long hours the king and his lover were able to talk alone. Lola kept pushing him to run away with her, and though he was tempted, he couldn't abandon the throne, his wife, and his family. Ludwig assured her that he would continue to be generous with her, even at a distance. The dancer pleaded with him to sell her house as soon as possible and send her belongings. She also begged him to dismiss his prime minister, Prince von Wallerstein, despite her earlier urgings to the contrary. Filled with emotion, Ludwig listened, wishing he could prolong the encounter indefinitely. His Lolita had risked her life to see him, but now they had to separate for her safety. The couple embraced, and the king kissed her on the lips. He was certain he'd soon be able to meet up with her in Switzerland and spend a few weeks away from all the turmoil. The policemen escorted Lola and Baron Meller-Zakomelsky back to the city center, where they clambered into a post office coach that was heading west. Day was breaking in Munich, and the tenuous rays of the sun were illuminating the churches' red roofs and slender steeples. Lola refused to look back, but she sensed that it was the last time she would set foot in that place.

The news of the countess's return soon spread through the capital. When the people found out that the king had spent a few hours alone with her, they felt deceived and offended. Because she had not been assigned an official escort to accompany her to the kingdom's border, many questioned whether she had actually left. Fearing renewed upheaval and determined to demonstrate his authority, Ludwig finally dismissed Prince von Wallerstein. He accused him of disloyalty and claimed that he was behind the serious events that had taken place in the city before Lola's departure. On March 15, a mob tried to occupy the royal palace of Fürstenried on the outskirts of Munich. A rumor had spread that the king was hiding the dancer there. The disturbances throughout the city became so serious that the new interior minister, Gottlieb von Thon-Dittmer, felt obligated to ask the king if he knew the countess's whereabouts. Ludwig replied that, lamentably, he did not.

The next day, the king furtively visited the apartment of Caroline Wegner, where his lover had been discovered. He wanted to thank the woman for her loyalty and find out whether she'd had any news of Lola. Despite his precautions, Ludwig was spotted, and people became convinced that the Countess of Landsfeld was back again. A furious crowd surrounded the building, and the police had to perform a thorough search of all the apartments to calm people down. That evening, while the king was attending a performance of Mozart's *Die Entführung aus dem Serail*, a crowd occupied the police station where Lola had been held several days earlier. In the mayhem, several officers were injured. When Minister von Thon-Dittmer went to the scene to try to calm the demonstrators, he was struck in the head by a large rock. In his box at the theater, Ludwig was informed of what was happening and immediately returned to the palace to meet with a crisis task force. Over the course of that long, eventful night, troops were deployed to prevent a bloodbath.

Chaos now reigned on the streets of Munich. After another tense meeting in the Rathaus, the assembly sent a delegation to demand that the interior minister make the king forbid the countess from returning to Bavaria, and to have her arrested if she did. Startled by this request, Ludwig responded indignantly that it was unconstitutional to exile a

Bavarian citizen. The ministers, in turn, advised the king to revoke her citizenship. They reminded him that revolution was spreading across Europe and that, if he wanted to remain on his throne, he was going to have to make greater concessions. A few days earlier, similar disturbances in Vienna, the capital of the Austrian Empire, had forced the powerful Prince von Metternich to resign and flee to England. Ultimately, Ludwig gave in. Full of remorse, he wrote the following letter:

> My dearest Lolitta,
> The love in your heart for your Luis reassures me that you would wish me to make the sacrifice of revoking your Bavarian citizenship. Revolution has reached Vienna, and in Munich something terrible will happen this afternoon, if not earlier. Therefore, and convinced of your love for me, your citizenship has been canceled. I have declared that you no longer have it, at the insistence of those heading up the ministries, who have requested this of me. I did it with the anticipatory certainty that your love will make this sacrifice for me. But it is clear now that my beloved Lolitta was right, that Luis is no longer beloved, that the only love remaining to me is that of your heart. You yourself told me that you felt you could not return to Munich. They would kill you if you returned. Even without citizenship, you are still the Countess of Landsfeld—that has not changed. It is possible, though I cannot guarantee it for now, that I will abdicate the throne, though in this critical situation it seems to me an act of cowardice to do such a thing. My much beloved Lolitta, you are ever adored by your faithful
> Luis

It was the first time that Ludwig had mentioned the possibility of abdication, though he had been contemplating the idea for days. He resented making so many concessions to stay in power, especially when they affected the woman who still occupied his heart. He believed that renouncing the crown would make it easier for him to reunite with her. He faced a difficult dilemma that left him sleepless and anxious. Before making a decision, he met with the crown prince. Maximilian was an artistic young man, highly educated, brilliant, and ready to take on the royal mantle.

"For twenty-three years I have ruled this country, devoting my life to my people's well-being," the king said. "But now they want me to do nothing but sign their laws. My hands are tied. I am unwilling to rule at any price. I have decided to abdicate, my son; your moment has arrived."

"Father, you have been a good sovereign and a model of uprightness and devotion," said the prince. "You still enjoy your people's affection—you cannot renounce the throne. I ask you to reconsider. I know that you are still thinking about that woman who has brought us only misfortunes, and I keenly lament the pain she has caused you."

"My son, you know I love your mother above all else, but in Lola Montez I have found a companion, a loyal friend whom I cannot, nor wish to, stop seeing. One day you will understand. I have nothing to be sorry for. The House of Wittelsbach will continue to rule the Bavarian people."

Maximilian, who had not expected such a confession, embraced him and they wept together.

The next afternoon, Ludwig called the whole family into the throne room and announced that his decision was final. The crown prince kneeled and asked for his blessing. Therese, who was still much beloved by the people, could not believe what was happening. That Sunday, March 19, 1848, her darling husband was abdicating his responsibilities. The queen knew that Lola Montez was behind it. That impostor had ruined the life of a good, just king who was admired by his people. She blamed the dancer for all the kingdom's ills and thought how naive she'd been to look the other way while Lola was taking possession of his heart and his will. Therese did not realize that, at that historic moment, the deflated king still wanted nothing more than to return to his lover's arms.

When Ludwig was alone once more, he let out a sigh of relief. He had given his life to his people, and now he was free of responsibilities. Despite the suffering he was causing his wife and children, he had no regrets. Filled with the excitement of the moment, he wrote another letter to Lola:

> My dearest Lola, to whom I am so entirely devoted, I have just now abdicated the crown, freely, without anyone having persuaded me. My plan is to return to your arms in April in Vevey and live there a while by your side. Afterward I will rejoin my family in Aschaffenburg. Without a single one of my ministers realizing it, I have declared my abdication in the presence of all the princes of my house. My son Max has kneeled and asked for my blessing. The five of us burst into tears. Today I feel good. As soon as I declared that I wished to abdicate, I felt happy. Happy if he ends up being with his Lolitta, your faithful
> Luis

When the people of Munich learned of their king's renunciation, they were bewildered. The streets were full of glum faces, and some were unable to hide their tears. Ludwig was abandoning his throne, but he had negotiated very favorable terms. He would retain his properties throughout the kingdom and an annual income of five hundred thousand florins; he could establish his residence outside of Bavaria; and he would continue to be referred to as "His Majesty, King Ludwig of Bavaria."

The countess was surprised and hopeful when she received word of his abdication. She did not doubt that the king would be able to join her in Switzerland at last. In a letter, she congratulated him for his decision and added, "I hope with all my heart that it is true, because that way you will have preserved your dignity and have retired from public life with honor and your head held high." She also reassured him that she harbored no resentment over his having revoked her Bavarian citizenship and sent him her naturalization certificate to give to King Maximilian with a note stating that she had no wish to return to his kingdom. The note did not reach the young monarch; instead, Ludwig stored it in his personal archives.

Lola was back in Bern, and her primary preoccupation was, as usual, money. In most of the letters she sent to Ludwig during that time, she discussed the topic openly. She was worried that the king would forget about her, or that something might happen to him and she would be forced to "beg on the streets." More than once she told him that, if he couldn't offer her the amount she required, she would rather take her own life. For his part, Ludwig, who had previously been so lavish with his favorite, now warned her that his annual income would be much lower after abdication. Again and again he said to be prudent with the money he sent to her: "I beg you to keep your affairs in order and pay your bills each month. Do not make unnecessary expenditures and do not accumulate debts. My wallet is no longer in a position to be able to pay it." The king continued to send her twenty thousand florins a year, but he could no longer cover the bills for her "unforeseen expenses" as he had in the past.

But the Countess of Landsfeld was unwilling to adjust her opulent lifestyle, and when the king announced that he would soon arrive in Switzerland, she set out to find appropriate accommodations. Her friends Robert Peel and Baron Meller-Zakomelsky accompanied her to Lausanne, but all the properties she saw seemed both overpriced and unexceptional. Then she went to Geneva and got a suite in the

Hôtel des Bergues, located on the shores of Lake Geneva. Its owner, Mr. Rufenacht, was honored that such a distinguished lady had elected to stay at his establishment.

Finding Geneva to be clean and charming, Lola started searching for a residence worthy of a king. In early April, she found what she was looking for in Pregny, outside the city. It was love at first sight. The property was a sumptuous two-story mansion with stone walls and a slate roof topped by two towers, and it was known as "the Empress's Castle" because Napoleon I's beautiful wife had resided there. After Napoleon had repudiated her when she could not give him a son, Empress Josephine had purchased the semi-abandoned medieval fortress and transformed it into a pleasant palatial villa where she spent the summer months. Located in the middle of the countryside, the castle was surrounded by tall, centuries-old trees and was reached via a wide avenue flanked by lindens and chestnuts. It had impressive views of snowy peaks, and it cost a fortune. Peel advised his friend to rent the property until the king could see it and approve the purchase. Lola agreed and rented the place for six months. Unfortunately, the villa was unfurnished and in great disrepair, and Lola still had not received her belongings. She would need a lot of money to get its ancient rooms ready and decorated to her taste.

Reports that Lola Montez had set up shop in a Swiss castle while waiting for the king to arrive caused a stir in Munich. Once more the citizens met in the hall of the Rathaus. They were heard to avow that, if King Ludwig left Bavaria to go see that woman, he would be prohibited from returning and his annual income would be canceled. Tensions were running so high that King Maximilian went in person to talk to his father.

"Father, I am begging you not to leave the city to meet that woman. I fear that, if you do, a revolution will break out. It is the only subject on people's lips, and our subjects are irate."

"I am no longer king!" Ludwig exclaimed. "They should leave me in peace and stop meddling in my private affairs. Why do they care what I do? It is unfair for them to punish me like this; I am their prisoner."

"I am begging you for all of us—think of your family, of your son who has just been crowned king," Maximilian entreated. "You still have responsibilities."

"All right," Ludwig said. "I won't leave yet, but I want you to know—and I'll tell your mother this too—that I will not give up being with my faithful friend."

Ludwig felt aggrieved and cheated, but his family breathed a sigh of relief. Over the next few days, the king and his wife moved to a palace in the city center. Upon leaving behind the large, luxurious Residenz complex, the king felt a great weight lifted from his shoulders. Maybe now his actions could go unremarked, and he would be free to pursue his desires and enjoy his grandchildren's visits. However, the days dragged on and his beloved occupied all his thoughts.

In Geneva, the Countess of Landsfeld was still at the hotel, waiting to be able to move into her new house. A portion of her belongings had arrived from Munich, some sixty or so trunks weighing a total of eight tons. She asked the king to cover the cost of transport, since once again her debts were accumulating, but she didn't want to move without furniture. Rufenacht, the hotel proprietor, wrote in secret to the king. Ludwig learned that she had hired several servants and two lady's maids, and that she had acquired a fine carriage and horses and was remodeling her new home in grand style.

On May 24, Lola was finally able to move to her villa. The remodeling project was not yet completed, but most of her furniture was now there. Some of the pieces had been badly damaged during transport and needed to be repaired. Among her belongings, she found one of the portraits of her by Joseph Karl Stieler, in which she was dressed like Andalusian nobility, and she hung it in a prominent spot in the main salon. It was the king's favorite portrait, but after abdicating, he had decided to give it to Lola so she would not forget "the happy times of yore."

A few weeks later, the countess was forced to take to her bed with fever. Her creditors were hounding her, and many stores in the city now refused to allow her a tab. Again she wrote to the king and pressed him for money:

> To me, life and death are equally appealing. I fear you will be angry with me when you receive this, but I must tell you: you know that everything was damaged on the journey here from Munich, and I have had to purchase rugs and curtains and candelabra and sets of crystal and porcelain dishes (the majority were completely destroyed) and repair the stables. With tears in my eyes and death in my heart, I see your outraged face before me, but these things were indispensable. I cannot pay for everything on my own. My monthly stipend is only enough to cover the house, the stables, and the servants. I have had to cancel my harp lessons and return the harp and piano I had rented. Yesterday they sent a sheriff to see me . . . And in addition to all this, the Jesuits continue to conspire against me. An American gentleman told me the other day that I could earn a great deal of money dancing there because my name is well known on that continent. Dear Louis, leaving you would be my death, but what can I do?

Moved by her words, Ludwig paid the outstanding bills and sent some cash so she could cover her expenses. By now he understood that the countess's extravagances would exceed any amount he set as an allowance. He told her frankly, again and again, "Lola, you're terrible when it comes to money." But he still needed her and loved her desperately. It had been more than a year since the night they'd been able to spend together at her house on Barerstrasse, and Lola had agreed to have sex with him only once since then. The king had only her letters, full of reproaches and threats but also promises of love. He clung to them to keep his dream alive, and after the stymied encounter in April, he planned to see her in the summer instead.

At the end of May, he wrote her a note asking whether, when they saw each other again, she would like to sleep with him. Lola, who had received the king's promise that he would pay all her bills from the Hôtel des Bergues out of his own pocket, replied at once:

> How can you ask such a thing? You know I am as devoted to you as is humanly possible, that I love you more every day for everything you have sacrificed for me. Of course I want to, and I am delighted to think that my beloved Louis might still love his Lolitta. I am more in love with you than ever, and now my health is fully restored. I am much, much better than when I was living in Munich. My dear Louis, I beg of you to be faithful to me until then and you will be able to love me with great satisfaction and pleasure. My heart is yours and my self entire.

Again and again Ludwig reread this letter as he strolled through the Nymphenburg Palace gardens or the woods of the English garden, his cherished place of refuge where they had spent so many wonderful moments together. Fearing that such intimate confessions might fall into the wrong hands, he inserted small slips of pink paper into his letters, on which he wrote, "Burn this immediately after reading it."

Lola urged the king to visit her in summer, when the weather would be warmer. In the meantime, the seductive Countess of Landsfeld had acquired a new coterie of admirers. These Swiss gentlemen, some with dubious reputations, began to frequent the Empress's Castle, just as the Alemannen had made number 7 Barerstrasse their headquarters. The splendid mansion had many bedrooms, and her male visitors sometimes spent the night. The countess was once more defying all the norms of decorum. The residence had its own dock on the shores of Lake Geneva, and Lola decided to buy a large sailboat, to enjoy its placid waters. She also acquired several smaller craft so her friends, whom she dubbed "my corsairs," could row along behind her. The neighbors, scandalized, started to complain.

Around this time Lola met Auguste Papon, an outlandish character who used the title of Marquess of Sarde. He claimed that his father had been the adjunct director of the French Treasury and that his mother was from Provençal nobility, but the truth was quite different: Papon was a grifter who had learned his craft from his father, an infamous con artist in southern France. Auguste had studied for the priesthood but ended up settling in Marseille as a lawyer. After accumulating staggering debts and developing a terrible reputation, he lost his license. Fleeing his creditors, he had arrived in Switzerland, where his parents were living in a villa in Nyon, on the northern shore of Lake Geneva.

The fake Marquess of Sarde and the Countess of Landsfeld met at the Hôtel des Bergues, where he had been living for several months. Short in stature, with a tanned face and sparkling eyes, he spoke Spanish well and was a fixture in Geneva's high society. When the dancer moved into the castle, he invited her to his Nyon villa, Mon Répos, to meet his parents. Her friends the corsairs took her on her sailboat to the residence, where she was greeted by the Papons and the local parish priest. In July, King Ludwig began to notice that his beloved was writing less frequently, but he was as yet unaware of the existence of the crafty marquess. At the end of the month, Papon moved into the castle in Pregny at the countess's invitation.

Lola resumed corresponding regularly with the king, but now she was obsessed with recovering the jewelry she'd had to leave behind in Munich. Ludwig told her that it wasn't safe to ship the jewels and said that he'd bring them himself. The king threw himself into travel preparations, choosing a place for their encounter where they would not be recognized. Malans was a small town midway between Geneva and

Innsbruck. Ludwig planned to spend his vacation in Berchtesgaden and then to travel to Innsbruck to visit some relatives. From there he could make a quick incognito trip to Malans and spend some time with his lover. But his plans were delayed and the tryst was pushed off to early September.

In the meantime, Papon was acting like the lord and master of Lola's castle. The countess's maids were uncomfortable in his presence and fed up with their mistress's wild whims. One day Lola berated them for refusing to spend the night aboard her boat with her and her friends. The corsairs, too, found themselves being shunted aside by the marquess, who treated them like servants. Rufenacht, who'd become a friend of the dancer, was no longer welcome at the castle.

On August 25, Ludwig was celebrating his first post-abdication birthday. The date was a sad one for him because it coincided with the first anniversary of Lola being named Countess of Landsfeld. The king put a lot of stock in these symbolic dates and hoped to receive tender well wishes from his lover. The letter he received that morning did not even mention his birthday but, instead, informed him that Lola was broke and needed a thousand francs to be able to meet him in Malans. He was so excited by the thought of seeing her again that he forgot his annoyance. The date of the reunion was set for September 2.

The countess had to borrow money from Rufenacht for the journey, and the hotel owner made her sign an IOU. Wanting to dazzle the king, she selected a maroon taffeta dress with a square neckline and Venetian lace, and set out in her carriage at dawn. She was accompanied by her maid and two of the corsairs. It was a long, uncomfortable journey. Upon reaching her destination, she had an unpleasant surprise. In Malans she found not Ludwig but his valet, who gave her two thousand francs, a few poems, and a letter from His Majesty:

Tears are welling up in my eyes, because instead of clasping you to my heart and telling you of my feelings, I am forced to write. Since my last letter I have discovered the cause of the disturbances in Munich. The revolutionaries have been circulating the story that I gave you diamonds that belonged to the state. (Your Luis, a thief!) The rumor started because the treasury department does not display them to the public. New bloody conflicts and dire consequences will surely follow if I go to Tyrol now. People who are very loyal to me and are not your enemies have assured me as much. It is a terrible situation. Do not stop loving me—it is not my fault. I say again, the entire world has not the power to keep us apart.

Lola became very upset. She believed that Ludwig was just making excuses and was distraught at not having been able to recover her valuable jewelry. But the violent clashes that Ludwig mentioned were a very real threat. Newspaper front pages were announcing that the king had left for Switzerland, and once more voices began to clamor for him to be denied the right to return to Bavaria and for his income to be revoked.

The countess's reply was hardly compassionate; she reproached him, complaining that, after all her preparations for the journey, the king had backed out at his family's behest. She also said she was considering leaving for Rome and living, if His Majesty allowed it, in his beautiful palazzo there, Villa Malta. Ludwig swiftly disabused her of the notion. He could only imagine the outcry if word reached Munich that he had set his lover up in his Roman villa. But he did send along her jewelry via a banker. In response, Lola wrote him a loving letter thanking him for the gesture. She was delighted to have the jewels in her possession again at last.

After their thwarted encounter, the king grew increasingly melancholy. His joviality ebbed, and he seemed weary and older. The information he was receiving from Geneva kept him awake at night, and he was worried about Auguste Papon, whom the countess frequently mentioned. Ludwig warned her that, even if Papon seemed like a distinguished gentleman, he might take advantage of her. Unsettled by the influence that this strange man was wielding over Lola, he asked the hotel owner to keep him posted about the marquess's movements. To his surprise, Rufenacht's reply mentioned that a young man named Elias Peissner had arrived in the city and was staying at the hotel. The countess had invited him because she was starting to feel uncomfortable about Papon's presence at her villa and thought she needed her most loyal friend to protect her from a man she was beginning to mistrust. In a note, the king, consumed with jealousy, said, "It seems to me that you want Luis for love, Papon for conversation, and Peissner to sleep with."

Elias barely recognized Lola when he arrived at the castle in the Pregny countryside. She had grown thin, dressed sloppily, and yelled at the few servants who had remained. She was under Papon's spell and surrounded by a small circle of lazy, spendthrift youths who were living off of her money. She received her old lover indifferently and put him up in a rear room of the castle. Peissner was dismayed to see what had become of the woman to whom he had pledged eternal love. She seemed to have lost her mind—she told him that she intended to return to Munich and that he should go with her to protect her. She was penniless, creditors were camped outside her door, and everyone in the village wanted her gone. After a week, Elias gathered up his things and left without saying goodbye. They'd had a heated argument the day before because Lola refused to pay back some money she owed him. They would not see each other again, though he would never forget her or speak ill of her.

Upon his return from vacation in Berchtesgaden, the king was surprised when one of his footmen brought him a note from a Marquess of Sarde written that very morning in Munich. In it, the marquess explained that he was a good friend of the Countess of Landsfeld and included an urgent letter from the king's lover:

I know that you will save me from a misfortune worse than death (my God, what has become of my self-respect?). The Countess of Landsfeld finds herself in a terrible situation, without security, without anything, and in a hellish, horrible country. Please open your door to this man who, in my moments of misery, offered me his services. He is a man of his word. He is a freemason, which says everything.

For a moment the king considered not seeing him, but curiosity won out. Ludwig was angry with Lola, who wrote to him only to ask for money and seemed unconcerned about his well-being. When Auguste Papon stood before him, the king was on the defensive. But the marquess knew how to win over his victims. He began praising the harmonious elegance of the buildings in the city, which, in his view, was among the most beautiful in Europe thanks to His Majesty's good taste and artistic sensibility. Ludwig, who had been quite downcast for weeks, was pleased by his visitor's praise. More relaxed now, he asked about Lola, and Papon's face fell. "Your Majesty, I must convey to you a harsh reality. Mrs. Montez is in the most absolute ruin; she has had to pawn all her valuables, and her creditors are poised to confiscate the villa's furnishings."

"I am sorry to hear that," the king said glumly, "but I warned the countess that she must manage her money well. She is an adult and is responsible for her actions."

"Forgive me," said Papon, "but the worst part isn't the lack of money but her fragile health. A few days ago she began coughing up blood and has been forced to take to her bed. She loves you just as she did the first day—she always talks about Your Majesty and knows that you will not abandon her."

The Marquess of Sarde left the monarch awash in pain and confusion. Ludwig refused to give the man any money, but he was worried that Lola might be gravely ill. A few days after Papon's visit, the king received a letter from his lover in which she responded to his accusation that she loved him but was sleeping with Peissner:

> One day all the secrets of this world will be revealed before God, and then, my dear Louis, you will be convinced of my fidelity and of the sincere love of your much-vilified Lolitta. Dear Louis, death invades my soul. Without you I am wretched in this world, friendless in a country that is terrible for foreigners, in Geneva. If you do not come to my aid, I will be the world's laughingstock; my honor will be utterly lost. What can I do? Everything is so terrible and my health is always so delicate . . . But God is good and you, my dear Louis, are too devoted to me to abandon me.

Touched once more by her words, Ludwig sent twenty thousand francs to ensure that she had enough to live on and to prevent the furniture from being repossessed. He was unable to send her any more until the parliament's budget session had finished and his assigned income had been authorized. To the king's relief, the countess moved out of the castle in Pregny at the end of October and rented a house that she shared with Auguste Papon and his elderly parents. Though she was now living more modestly, her problems didn't end there. Faced with the chilly autumn weather, the lack of money, and the marquess's ever-increasing control over her, Lola became listless. The only bright spot was that her new lodgings were close to Geneva, so she could have a bit of a social life.

At the theater one night, Lola spotted Baron Meller-Zakomelsky among the audience members. She also noticed a tall, dark-haired young man, very distinguished, who was seated in a box near her own. At intermission she asked her old friend to introduce her. The handsome Lord Julius had recently turned twenty and belonged to a noble family of ancient lineage. His parents were dead, and it was rumored that he was set to inherit a large fortune when he came of age. The young man was enchanted by the Countess of Landsfeld, who was nearly eight years his senior, and people began seeing them together in public. In the meantime, her relationship with Auguste Papon grew very tense. The marquess, who intended to keep living on the countess's dime, opposed the relationship and refused to allow Lola's new admirer into his house. She and Lord Julius began meeting in secret in rooms that the Baron Meller-Zakomelsky had rented at the Hôtel des Bergues.

As the days passed, she attempted to pull away from Papon, who was monitoring her every move and had become quite abrasive. Whereas a month earlier the countess had told Ludwig that she found the Marquess of Sarde to be a noble, trustworthy friend, she now described him as a cunning and deceitful enemy:

> I do not feel boundless trust in him, though he is (I think) a very worthy man. You know how unusual it is to find a truly sincere friend who is not out merely for his own interest. Many people have told me not to trust him completely because he is a man of great ambition and vanity, two things that could be said of most men, and it seems that he is no exception. I also think that he is banking on the chance that I may one day return to Munich and you will compensate him for his assistance to me. In addition, since he is in the Jesuit camp, at the moment I find him to be a very necessary but also very dangerous man. My servants claim that he has intercepted documents addressed to me. One thing is for certain: he is not terribly honest.

What the countess did not know was that the wily Papon had started exchanging letters with Ludwig, and the king thought him a trustworthy man who was concerned about his friend's future. This correspondence between the two men was interrupted when Lola, tired of the marquess's manipulations, kicked him and his parents out of her rented house. To ensure that the king would not listen to anything Papon might say about her, the dancer told him that the fake marquess was in fact a depraved libertine who had been caught having sexual relations with a young man in a public park. She also discovered that he'd had run-ins with the law and that in Marseille he had been convicted of fraud.

With Papon and his family gone, Lord Julius continued to woo Lola. Seeing the direction their relationship was taking, the young aristocrat's tutor asked the police to investigate Julius's new friend, who, he claimed, "was exerting a bad influence on the boy and trying to ensnare him to seize his fortune." Julius was considering buying his beloved an engagement ring when he was sent to Chambéry to separate him from the countess. It seems he had expressed his desire to marry Mrs. Montez and live with her in a castle in the French countryside.

Though no charges were filed against her, Lola made the sudden decision to travel to London. She was afraid that Swiss authorities would uncover her true identity, prompting the king to withdraw his support. Though Ludwig had begged her to adopt Swiss citizenship to secure residence in the country, she roundly refused, saying that she was "unwilling to lose her right to call herself the Countess of Landsfeld." Lola had been in Switzerland for nine months, but she did not like the country, finding it sad, boring, and devoid of cultural attractions. She had a number of friends in London, a vibrant city she had always enjoyed. She longed to be on the stage again, and now that her reputation preceded her throughout Europe, she was convinced that the doors of its major theaters would open to her.

One cold, rainy winter morning, Lola Montez and her maid left Geneva, escorted by Baron Meller-Zakomelsky. Wrapped in a wool coat and a fetching fur cap that matched her cuffs, she stared out the carriage window at the snowy landscape that paraded before her. She felt frail, and a difficult journey lay ahead. As they sped away, she felt a shudder run through her body. She realized that she would never see Ludwig again. Their paths were diverging for good. She sighed, thinking about what she was leaving behind. For nearly two years she had had it all: fame, glory, and power. But once again fortune had eluded her. "They never loved me," she lamented, holding back tears. "I was always 'the Spaniard' to them, but I still have their king's unconditional love."

CHAPTER 9

Starting Over

On the deck of the ship bearing her to the port at Dover, Lola pondered her uncertain future. Of late, the days had been stormy and the sea very rough, and the west wind blew in powerful gusts. It had been more than five years since she had fled London, alone and hounded by scandal. With a smile on her lips, she recalled her passionate romance with George Lennox. Their days had been a succession of parties, romantic candlelit dinners, and buggy rides in Hyde Park. But the dream had evaporated when somebody recognized her and the press pounced mercilessly. Now she was the celebrated Countess of Landsfeld. She would make a space for herself in high society and resume her artistic career.

As she walked down the ship's gangplank, she swore to herself that she would not be brought low again.

During the voyage, Lola had taken the opportunity to write the king several letters full of laments and reproaches. She begged him not to abandon her and to maintain her generous allowance. She also confessed that, during her time in Geneva, Lord Julius, a very handsome and wealthy young man, had asked for her hand in marriage. To soothe him, she added that she had emphatically refused because her heart belonged to her beloved king alone and she would not dream of betraying him. Ludwig replied that he admired the way she had held firm in the face of temptation but that, if she was in love with her attractive suitor, he did not wish to stand in the way of her happiness. "Even if you marry," he wrote, "I will never feel any passion for another woman." In truth, the king had already been informed by Auguste Papon of how the young heir had been sent to Chambéry.

For the first time, Ludwig resigned himself to not seeing her again and was seized by a deep melancholy. Though he was still obsessed with his Lolita and kissed the marble foot nightly, he was increasingly disillusioned. He was surprised when he learned that Lola had left Geneva, because she had reassured him a few days earlier that she was saving money and keeping her expenditures under control. And now she was getting ready to set up shop in London, Europe's most expensive capital. As she put it, her aim was to "escape the attentions of Lord Julius, listen to good music, and look after my health, which deteriorated greatly in the cold and damp." At this point, he didn't know what to believe, and he was hurt that in all her letters her only concern was that he guarantee her stipend and transfer money to a bank in England. But the dancer knew the king well and knew how to keep his passion alive. Sensing that he was having doubts, she replied:

> I am pleased that you encourage me to marry, but you forget that for a woman who is no longer in her first flush of youth, and with all the stories that the newspapers of Munich have written about me, and basically penniless, in the nineteenth century it would be a miracle for her to find a respectable husband. Furthermore, the most impossible of all the impossible things is, after having been the lover of a king, to settle for being with other men. And cruelest of all is that you refuse to grant me an independent and honorable existence with my own name. Dear Louis, if you still love me (though that is something I cannot believe), do this for me and I will finally

be able to breathe!!! What happened in Munich seems like a
punishment from God, just as I now lament the unfortunate
position to which I have been reduced. If I were a few years
younger, I would still be able to dance, but I no longer have the
necessary strength; my health grows worse every day, and it is
all your fault. Every time I look at your portrait, I am keenly
wounded to think of the precarious position you have left me
in. Goodbye. You were my only hope.

Ludwig's trust in his lover was shaken even further by an odd letter he received on December 1. In it, Auguste Papon complained of
the treatment he'd received from the countess and the terrible situation she'd left him in. In a pompous tone, he informed the king that
he did not intend to seek vengeance for Mrs. Montez's ingratitude by
publishing information about her private life. Instead, since he was an
upstanding gentleman, he would be content to return to the king all the
documents in his possession and not publish anything if His Majesty
would grant him the title of lord chamberlain along with ten thousand
francs. Ludwig was not pleased with Papon's high-handed attitude nor
with the attempt at blackmail. By then, he had had the man investigated
and knew about his criminal activities. But he was deeply worried to
think that Lola might have given the unscrupulous Papon his intimate
letters. The king did not reply to Papon and said nothing to Lola about
what was happening.

One sunny morning in January 1849, Elias Peissner came to the
king to ask him to help finance his university studies in the United
States. Though once jealous of the young man, the king now greeted
him warmly but with an ulterior motive.

"My dear young man," Ludwig said, "I would love to help you. I
know you are a brilliant student and that you will secure yourself a good
future there. But I want you to be honest with me and tell me the nature
of your relationship with the countess."

"Your Majesty!" the student exclaimed, blushing. "From the moment I met Mrs. Montez I fell hopelessly in love with her, though at first I held firm and did not succumb to temptation. Later we saw each other again and I felt the same passion. Whenever she spoke to me of Your Majesty, she did so as her 'dear father' or 'elderly friend.' I understood that she was uncommitted and so . . ."

"So, what happened? I want all the details!"

"Your Majesty, she offered to allow me to live at her house on Barerstrasse, in the servants' quarters. I moved in there when I was expelled from the university. One day she invited me to come up to her bedroom and made me feel what I had never felt before."

"Do you mean that you gave in to her caresses?"

"Yes, Your Majesty. That woman was pure fire, and I was a rather callow lad. Afterward we kneeled beside the bed and swore to be faithful to each other. For a time we loved each other madly; she even suggested she would marry me one day, and I believed it. But when I went to see her at her castle in Pregny, she was quite indifferent to me and I left with my heart in pieces. I have not seen her since."

Listening to Peissner's confession, the king felt as if he could not breathe. He was so upset he could barely speak. Thanking the young man for his honesty, he promised to help him pursue his studies abroad. Ultimately, he felt sorry for Peissner. Lola, with her charms and lies, had deceived them both.

Once alone, Ludwig started sobbing like a little boy. He'd convinced himself that the ravishing, vivacious woman truly loved him and that he was the only one who had her heart. Now he realized that Peissner had not just slept with his Lolita multiple times but that he'd done so in her own house. He was tempted to write Lola a letter full of rage and reproaches, but glum and disenchanted, he simply pulled away. Lola immediately noticed that the king was discussing only banal topics such as the weather in Munich or the beauty of the roses in his garden. "It seems to me that you no longer love me so dearly," she complained again and again. But for the moment the king was preoccupied with other matters.

Auguste Papon wrote to Ludwig again, threatening to publish a memoir about Lola Montez that would include the king's correspondence. Ludwig refused to be blackmailed and once more did not reply. But he was anxious about the repercussions the publication of his private correspondence might have. He asked Lola multiple times to tell him whether any letters he'd sent to her had been stolen or whether she'd ever shown them to Papon. She promised that they were all in her possession and that the man had never seen them. Finally, Ludwig offered Papon a sum of money in exchange for the documents and a promise not to publish the book. But it was too late. Papon had grown impatient, and the first installment was already at a printing house in Nyon.

When the book *Lola Montez: Memoirs Accompanied by Private Letters from His Majesty Ludwig, King of Bavaria, and Lola Montez* hit the public on February 7, 1849, the Countess of Landsfeld was quite miffed. Rufenacht sent her a copy from Geneva. Its pages were a series of rumors and half-truths that the author had taken from newspaper articles and anecdotes that Lola had told him at the castle in Pregny. Papon didn't hold back in criticizing his old friend, of whom he wrote, "Once expelled from Munich, she could be seen in many different countries, serving as a high-end courtesan, gathering scandals and libertinism around her, displaying the sad spectacle of madness, vice, and vanity." He also wrote scathingly of Lola's scant knowledge of literature and art: "She confuses Byron with Cervantes and believes that Joan of Arc is a Roman heroine." She replied indignantly that she had good and influential friends in Switzerland and that she would not allow him to "insult her and an old man who cannot defend himself."

In London, the Countess of Landsfeld had rented a small furnished apartment on Queen Street while she waited for her trunks and other belongings to arrive from Geneva. For a few weeks she hardly left her home and avoided appearing in public. She had a persistent cough and dark circles under her eyes, and the doctor recommended that she rest. But she found her gloomy room, which overlooked an interior courtyard, depressing. Everything around her lacked the beauty, luxury, and comfort to which she had become accustomed with King Ludwig. Her greatest happiness in those sad days was recovering her beloved dogs, Zampa and Turk, which friends had sent from Munich.

During her convalescence, she considered writing her own memoirs and publishing them in Paris, where she was still well known. At night, by the light of an oil lamp, she began to fill a diary with sweet memories of her childhood in India, but reality and fiction blended together. Lola had no intention of telling the truth about her origins and began by saying that she was born on a sunny morning in the city of Seville and that she was the daughter of the legendary bullfighter Francisco Montes Reina, known as "Paquiro."

She also planned to return to Her Majesty's Theatre, where she'd enjoyed such success on the day of her debut. But it wasn't going to be easy. Contrary to her expectations, her scandalous behavior as King Ludwig I of Bavaria's lover had closed doors, not opened them. During her exile in Switzerland, one of London's most prolific playwrights, Joseph Stirling Coyne, had written a one-act comedy titled *Lola Montez; or, A Countess for an Hour*. The play opened with great success at the popular Theatre Royal. To avoid violating the law that forbade representations of the monarchy onstage, the character of King Ludwig was named Prince Greenasgras. All signs indicated that the play would have a long run, but it was canceled after three days by the lord chamberlain. Apparently, the Bavarian ambassador himself had requested that Her Majesty Queen Victoria ban the piece. Refusing to give up, the playwright reappeared a month later with the same play, this time titled *Catching a Governor*. The plot was very similar, but it changed the main characters' identities to avoid censorship.

During her first months in London, Lola arranged an interview with Benjamin Lumley, who was still the head of Her Majesty's Theatre. Lumley, though he was just as arrogant as when she'd first met him, knew his business well and did not refuse to see her. She was no longer a naive beginner willing to accept any kind of contract but an international celebrity who proudly bore her noble title. After the success of Coyne's show, she thought she could portray onstage her own life as the king's lover. It was an original and daring idea. Lola selected her most seductive gown and hired a carriage to take her to the theater; she had sold some jewelry and was still able to indulge in certain luxuries. She proudly strode into the office where Lumley had so rudely fired her years ago. His final words still echoed in her head: "As long as I am the director of this theater, you will not tread these boards again." She had to swallow her pride and act sweet and charming when she walked in and said, "Mr. Lumley, thank you for seeing me. It's been a long time, and I, as you can see, have changed."

"My dear Mrs. Montez," the director responded, observing with surprise that she was as beautiful as ever, "I have followed your adventures in Munich with great interest. No doubt it has given you a great deal to talk about—"

"I will get straight to the matter that brings me here. I know that Mr. Coyne has mounted with great success a play about my life, which, by the way, had an awful title and a number of passages of dubious taste. I would like to propose something better: having me play the part of the person I once was, the shadow queen of the Bavarian court. Naturally, the figure of King Ludwig will be given the respect he deserves."

"Forgive me, but you're knocking on the wrong door. Since you left, Her Majesty's Theatre has hosted performances by the most important stars of classical dance, and the maestros Verdi and Mendelssohn have debuted operas here with Queen Victoria in the audience. Do you think a piece about your scandals in Munich has a place in an auditorium of this caliber? You are the personification of sin and immorality.

The queen would find it highly inappropriate for such a work to be performed in her theater."

"That is absurd! There is no reason it should offend Her Excellency—indeed, it would show the more human side of King Ludwig, an old monarch who loves beauty and is an icon in Germany."

"I'm sorry, Mrs. Montez. Try the other theaters. There are a lot of them in London, and I'm sure they'll compete for the play. I am not about to risk either my reputation or my money. Thank you for your visit," he said, without rising from his chair. "I wish you the best of luck."

Lola decided to return home on foot. The cool air would help calm her fury. She was disappointed in this country full of "hypocrites and false moralists." She hated puritanical Victorian England, where chastity was a woman's highest virtue but most happily married men had lovers whom they draped in jewelry. She did not envy their wives in the least, those English ladies surrounded with luxury but subjected to their husbands' tyranny. They couldn't walk through Piccadilly or sit on a bench in Hyde Park except when in someone else's company. Dancing with the same man twice was seen as brazen flirting, and when a lady broke the rules, people gave her a wide berth. In Lola's view, English society was just as caste bound as the India of her youth. Here, the untouchables were women like her—independent, liberal-minded artists.

If anyone had followed Lola Montez's Bavarian adventures closely, it was Sir Jasper Nicolls, her stepfather's friend. The old officer had returned from India in 1843 and was living in the elegant Kensington neighborhood. His diary was full of notes about the child he'd taken in at Captain Craigie's request. At around this time, Nicolls added an article from the *Times* detailing her expulsion from Bavaria. Ever since he had first met her, he believed that the brazen young woman would do nothing good with her life, and now this assessment was reaffirmed. At the bottom of the page, he wrote, "What a hold this miserable witch has obtained over this old, adulterous idiot sovereign. Wretched country to be ruled by such a shameless rogue—but I must remember that Munich is the most abandoned capital in Europe." Luckily for Lola, Mr. Nicolls never gave her away.

On February 11, a year had passed since Lola Montez had been forced to flee Munich. Compelled by nostalgia, the king walked over to the house on Barerstrasse at the same time of day that she'd left the city. The residence had been confiscated by creditors, and the iron gates were secured with a large padlock. Ludwig walked behind the house and peeked in at the abandoned garden, which was full of weeds and broken windowpanes. Seeing his bust in marble, toppled and battered, in an overgrown corner, he mused that the statue was a reflection of his own self. He felt destroyed, humiliated, bereft of his will to live. Until now he had chosen not to tell Lola that he knew everything about her relationship with Elias Peissner, but he could not take it anymore. Sorrowfully, he wrote, "I had suspected that you were unfaithful to me last winter, and now I am sure. You were in love with Peissner and you slept with him on multiple occasions. You cannot deny it." He closed by noting, "Since you have been unfaithful to me, I no longer sign myself 'Your faithful Luis,' but that doesn't mean I'm not. Luis."

Lola generally took a while to reply to the king's letters, but this time she didn't wait even a day:

I have never slept with anybody, except with you, in Munich. You may accuse me, but this is the truth. Everybody may say otherwise, but as sure as there is a God in heaven, that is a lie. My conscience is clear. If I died today, my last words would be that you (since Dujarier's death) are the only man I've truly loved and about whom I've worried, and today as ever I would give my life and soul for you, my noble Louis. Listen to me, these are words that come from the purest blood from the bottom of my heart, and just as everybody has sacred feelings, all the ones in me are those I have for you. May the Virgin Mary lead your heart to believe me. I need her and her divine assistance against my enemies' tricks and plots. I don't believe that the Jesuits have forgotten me; once they're against you, it's for life, everywhere, always.

Ludwig no longer believed a word, but his heart still belonged to her. Sometimes, while visiting his son King Maximilian, he would go to the Gallery of Beauties and gaze raptly at her portrait. The longer he stared, the more he pined for her. He now signed his letters "Your devoted Luis," and though he was disappointed, he wrote to her almost daily.

Lola had been in London only a few months, and in her notes to the king, she complained that the weather was very bad for her ailing lungs, that she hardly ever saw the sun, and that her cough had not improved. She dreamed of going to the south of Spain for a while to convalesce and explore the scenes of her childhood. Ludwig could not understand how his lover, who continued to receive twenty thousand florins a year, could not live comfortably. In reality, since arriving in the English capital, Lola had barely had a social life. Everything was very expensive, and without a protector by her side, London did not seem as fun or charming as it once had. The news that the king had learned of her romance with Peissner had alarmed her greatly.

The dancer arranged to depart Southampton for Cádiz on April 7, but the problem of a passport remained. She could not request one from the Spanish embassy because she was actually Irish. Her Bavarian passport had expired a year earlier. And she was unwilling to admit that her real married name was Elizabeth Gilbert James in order to acquire British papers. Since arriving in Geneva, she'd implored Ludwig to ask King Maximilian for a new passport in her name. The king insisted that he couldn't do anything and that Lola didn't understand the level of animosity against her in Germany.

At the beginning of April, Lola had moved to a house in the exclusive Mayfair district, where she had lived in 1841 when she was George Lennox's lover. It was an elegant two-story brick building surrounded by a lovely garden with a small pond. She wanted to raise enough money to travel to Spain and get rid of the tons of objects and furniture that had arrived in London from Pregny. She had decided to auction off her assets, including some gifts from King Ludwig. On March 22, the famed Phillips auction house on New Bond Street announced the sale of the lot of the Countess of Landsfeld, which included furniture, Persian rugs, tapestries, silverware, porcelain, Bohemian crystal, and silk and velvet draperies. Many objects were engraved with the royal coat of arms of Bavaria. Lola had informed the king that he could purchase the paintings he'd given her, including Joseph Karl Stieler's portrait of her in typical Spanish dress, if he wanted them. But Ludwig let them go to auction, though he later acquired Stieler's small painting, which he hung in his private chambers. Her fine carriage and horses sold for a tidy sum. This enabled her to pay her creditors and tackle the high rent of her new house.

With spring's arrival, Lola's health improved and her good humor returned. She was determined to organize some gatherings. She had a printer make up elegant cream-colored cards with gold lettering that featured her aristocratic title, Countess of Landsfeld. To her satisfaction, many responded that it would be an honor to attend. The male members of London high society were eager to meet Mrs. Montez, the beautiful adventuress who had conquered a king's heart. Lola had just turned twenty-eight, and fatigue and illness had taken their toll. Though her face was thinner and her silhouette less voluptuous, she had a good complexion and her magnificent blue eyes were still striking. And as anyone who had had dealings with her could confirm, her ambition and determination remained intact.

Her salons were attended by Lord Henry Brougham, a leader in the Whig Party and the former lord chancellor of England. This ugly old libertine was a very influential man. Though he claimed to be happily married, his relationship with the famous courtesan Harriette Wilson had been a scandal. The shrewd young woman had tried to extort him, threatening to mention him in her memoirs; the incident had almost ended his marriage. Now seventy years old, the extravagant aristocrat declared himself platonically in love with the Spaniard, prompting all sorts of rumors. Lola was delighted to receive illustrious gentlemen in her home: lawyers, writers, journalists, politicians, and handsome officers from Her Majesty's army.

In Munich, Ludwig was happy to learn that Lola's health had been restored, but he was still worried about the harm that Auguste Papon's book might cause. Around that time, the second installment of Lola Montez's fake memoirs was released; it mocked the king mercilessly, recounting supposed conversations the pair had had in his palace. But the most serious threat to the king's image was that, at a point when parliament was debating not only Ludwig's annual income but also his debts to the state, Papon had included a letter in which the king promised Lola a monthly allowance. The jabs at the king were so exaggerated that, in the end, they achieved the opposite effect. In Switzerland, the few people who read the publication took it as a joke. A literary critic from Nyon's local newspaper, where the fake marquess lived, denounced the author's poor taste in betraying the intimate secrets and trust of a good and generous sovereign. A few weeks later, the Swiss authorities deported Papon and his parents to their native France, accusing him of blackmailing the king of Bavaria and stealing documents.

In early June, the dancer wrote to Ludwig, wanting to see him again. Upon discovering that he'd be spending the summer in Berchtesgaden, she asked if he would allow her to visit him in secret. Lola was unable to accept reality and understand how thoroughly she was reviled throughout Bavaria. Ludwig did not respond, but he agreed to her request to receive three months' allowance in advance. She had not prodded him for money for months. He believed that his lover was finally managing to get a handle on her expenses, but Lola's excuse this time was that she was suffering from migraines again and was hoping to be able to travel to the Isle of Wight during the summer to bathe in the sea and recuperate.

That summer, on one of Lola's strolls through Hyde Park, a tall, slender, blond gentleman caught her eye as he played with a large Newfoundland dog. She went over to stroke the dog and asked the stranger if he would sell it to her. Immediately they hit it off, and though the dog was not for sale, they chatted a while. His name was George Trafford Heald, he was twenty-one years old, and he was an officer in the Second Regiment of Life Guards.

Born in London, Heald was the only son of a powerful lawyer. His mother had died when he was just a boy, and after his father's death, he'd become the ward of a maiden aunt, Susanna Heald. This strict, devoted woman had made sure that he studied at Eton and Cambridge, but in the end, he had bought a position as an officer in one of the most distinguished regiments of Her Majesty's army. When Lola met him, George was living in the officers' residence in Regent's Park, in central London, which allowed him to enjoy the capital's social life.

The next day, they were spotted walking together again through Hyde Park in the company of their respective dogs. The young officer became her constant companion and began to woo her. Lola learned he had inherited a large fortune, but she continued to pursue her plans to leave for Spain. Then, one bright July day, George asked her to marry him. It was during an evening stroll along the banks of the Thames, and the young man had to make a huge effort to overcome his shyness.

"Lola, I love you," he told her, stammering, as he took her hands. "I imagine you must have noticed. But it's not a passing fancy—I have discovered that I truly love you and I'd like you to be my wife."

"Dear George, I am fond of you, too, but we can keep things as they are. We have a nice time together and there's no need to take such a major step. Besides, we hardly know each other," she replied.

"That doesn't matter," he insisted. "Lola, I love you with all my heart. I am not asking you to answer me now; I know it's an important decision. But promise me you'll think about it."

The offer caught Lola off guard, but it was very tempting. The union could offer her the economic independence she longed for. It could also solve a thorny problem: upon becoming Mrs. Heald, she would immediately be eligible for a British passport. On the arm of her wealthy husband, she would become part of the most respectable stratum of London society and might even have the honor of being invited to St. James's Palace by Queen Victoria. But before saying "I do," Lola wanted to inform King Ludwig and get him to promise to continue paying her annual stipend.

In her next letter to the king, she told him that she needed to mention a very important matter and that she wished to be guided in all things by his opinion. She recounted that, by chance, she had met a young officer from a good family and that he had surprised her by asking her to marry him. Lola added that the marriage would solve the problem of her nationality and noted that her fiancé was not wealthy, bringing in an annual income of only eight hundred pounds:

You must believe me, I swear before God. I am not in love with that gentleman—it is something completely different. I respect him for his character and he has a good position, and thanks to that I will not be alone and without protection, at the mercy of any who wishes to harm me. Now it depends on you. Dear Louis, if you do not wish me to marry, tell me. I love you enough to renounce this marriage. However favorable it would be for me. The gentleman is known in the best social circles. All of my friends know him as a good-hearted and very honorable man. But if you allow me to marry, our relationship will be the same as ever. I could never change what I am to you. My life belongs only to you and I am yours with all my soul. A husband would not change the love I feel for you, which will remain with me until death. Please do not delay in writing to me; without your permission and your promise guaranteeing my lifetime income, the family of this young gentleman will not consent to the marriage . . . Thousands of kisses and the eternal love of

    your Lolitta

Ludwig received the letter on July 22 while on vacation in the Bavarian Alps. He had always told her that he would never object to her getting married if it made her happy, and he repeated that now. Nevertheless, before giving his complete consent, he wanted to find out a little more about this Heald fellow and asked his ambassador in London to look into him. In the meantime, the king replied that the eight hundred pounds the young officer received yearly would allow them to live quite comfortably in London and that he did not see why he should continue to pay her pension if she married him. Adopting a protective tone, he also recommended that she ask Lord Brougham's advice on the details of her marriage contract and that she consult a good doctor to see if her lungs were strong enough to engage in sexual relations. He signed "Your devoted Luis" and sent the letter at once. To his displeasure, the next news he received of the Countess of Landsfeld and her fiancé arrived through the press. In a fury, he wrote to his beloved:

You wrote to me on July 16 to tell me that you would follow my advice about the possibility of marrying an officer of the Royal Guard who received no more than eight hundred pounds a year, and whose family would not agree to the union if you did not continue to receive the same income as now. I have learned that this officer is named George Trafford Heald, that he has an income of no less than four thousand pounds a year, and that you married him on the 20th, before I could receive your letter of the 16th, which arrived on the 22nd. This changes things.

    Luis

In reality, Lola Montez had gotten married on July 19, 1849, in St. George's Church in Hanover Square. It was a rainy day, and the wedding was attended by a few family members and witnesses. In the registry, the countess signed as Maria de los Dolores de Landsfeld and stated that she had been born in Seville and was the daughter of Colonel Juan Porris and Maria Fernandez. She added that she was a widow, acknowledging for the first time that she had been married previously. The groom's aunt refused to attend the ceremony. The obstinate old woman had been wary of the flamboyant Countess of Landsfeld from the start and ordered her lawyers to investigate her.

The newlyweds left London for a few days and stayed in a large, Tudor-style mansion in the countryside. For several weeks Lola had a wonderful time riding through the verdant fields, fishing in the river, and allowing George to dote on her. The clean air and contact with nature were restorative. Wanting to enjoy her honeymoon, she made the serious mistake of refusing to receive visits from his family, a long list of uncles and aunts. Back in London, the couple moved into the house that Lola was still renting on Half Moon Street.

At nine o'clock in the morning on August 6, 1849, just as Lola was about to climb into her carriage, she was detained by two police officers. One politely informed her that Miss Susanna Heald was accusing her of bigamy and that they had orders to take her to the station. Surprised, the countess begged them to go into the house to tell her husband. George put down the newspaper he was reading and listened to the policemen in astonishment. It seemed his beloved wife had remarried while her first husband, a Captain Thomas James, was still alive.

"You have no right to detain me!" Lola insisted. "I don't know whether Captain James is dead or alive, and I don't care. I married him under a fake name and it wasn't a legal marriage."

"Madam, please don't make things more difficult," the sergeant said. "You just need to come with us and the rest will be decided in court."

"George, find a good lawyer—this is all a misunderstanding," she told her husband as the officers escorted her out. "I'll explain later."

Lola was taken to the police station on Little Vine Street, where they took her statement and arranged for her to see a judge early that afternoon. News of the arrest spread quickly, and a crowd of gawkers and journalists soon gathered outside the courthouse on Great Marlborough Street. The dancer, who arrived in the company of Mr. Heald, looked calm and cheerful, but she was furious with George's aunt. "This bitter old maid," Lola thought, "has dug through my past like a bloodhound. My marriage to Thomas is in the past, and I'm a free woman." George wasn't having an easy time either. Appearing at a hearing where sordid details of his wife's private life would be aired had him quite upset. But despite his youth, he managed to maintain his composure. The two made a dramatic entrance into the suffocating courtroom, which was packed with onlookers. Everybody wanted a first-row seat to see the celebrated Lola Montez face down the British justice system. The *Times* reporter present at her appearance wrote that she exhibited no signs of remorse and smiled frequently:

> She was stated to be twenty-four years of age on the police-sheet, but has the look of a woman of at least thirty. She was dressed in black silk, with close-fitting black velvet jacket, a plain white straw bonnet adorned with blue, and blue veil. In figure she is rather plump,

and of middle height, of pale dark complexion, the
lower part of the features symmetrical, the upper part
not so good, owing to rather prominent cheek bones,
but set off by a pair of unusually large blue eyes with
long black lashes.

Though the hearing had been set swiftly because Lola and her husband were planning to travel to Spain, the prosecutor had a great deal of evidence to present. He established that Lola Montez was really Elizabeth Gilbert James and that, in 1842, an ecclesiastical court had granted her a divorce from Thomas James of the British East India Company, which meant that neither could remarry as long as the other was still alive. The dancer, who had not heard from her husband since then, learned that he was still active in a distinguished regiment in a remote spot in northern India. In her defense, the countess presented herself as a victim of antiquated laws that prevented people with few resources from being able to remake their lives. As she saw it, her previous marriage had no legal validity.

During the hearing, Mr. Heald sat next to his wife, holding her hands and whispering words of support in her ear. When his aunt took the stand to offer testimony, he stopped speaking to her. For the rest of his life, he never forgave Susanna. At the end of the hearing, the magistrate set Lola's bail at two thousand pounds while they waited for witnesses to arrive from India to provide additional evidence. Mr. Heald paid the astronomical bail—equivalent to the entire yearly income Lola received from King Ludwig—and the couple left without making any statement to the press.

Since the scandal began, George had been very patient, but he was anxious for an explanation from his wife. Lola wanted to wait a few days, until they were feeling more at ease, before addressing such a thorny subject. At dinner one night, she sorrowfully assured him that the evidence against her was a pack of lies. She admitted that she'd been married but that she'd believed her husband had died in India.

"George, please don't judge me," she begged him, gazing into his eyes. "It's true I was married, but it's a mistake I'll regret for the rest of my life. I was only a naive, romantic girl . . . Your aunt is just trying to drive us apart. She's never liked me, and she thinks I'm trying to take advantage of you."

"Don't worry, darling," he said soothingly. "We'll get through this challenging test together. I believe in you and I know my aunt only wants the best for me. She simply can't bear the fact that I am no longer by her side and, in her grief, blames you."

"Sweetheart, we must leave London as soon as possible. The press won't stop hounding me at the moment, but I'm sure this unpleasant affair will be forgotten in a few days. Let's go to Spain as we'd planned. It will be a second honeymoon, and afterward all of this will be over."

Lola had urged her husband to discover the beauty of her "native country," of which she had only vague memories and enormous nostalgia. But at the last moment, the couple changed their plans and went to Paris first. In mid-August, the city was nearly deserted and the countess's old acquaintances had fled the heat. Lola and her husband stayed at the Hôtel Windsor, near the Opéra, and for the first time she found herself bored in this city that had once so enthralled her. George didn't speak French or make any effort to communicate. He had no interest in Parisian cultural life; theater and opera made him yawn, and he wasn't a big reader. He only enjoyed sports: horseback riding, hunting, and fencing. Except when they went out to stroll the boulevards or have dinner in a restaurant on the Champs-Élysées, they spent the rest of the day in the hotel suite. How she longed for the stimulating company of King Ludwig!

One morning Lola left the hotel early without saying anything to her husband. She wanted to visit a place that brought back bitter memories: Montmartre cemetery, where Henri Dujarier, the brilliant journalist and editor of *La presse*—and the only man she'd truly loved—was buried. She placed a bouquet of flowers on his simple white marble gravestone and stood there a while, lost in thought. She imagined what her life would have been like had death not snatched him away so soon. Tears slid down her cheeks as she recalled his sweet kisses, his seductive smile, and the gleam in his eyes as he gazed at her raptly. "I never lied to you. You knew me better than anyone and loved me for who I am. We could have been so happy!" she sighed as she left the cemetery. When she reached the hotel, she got into bed and told George she had a headache. The ghosts of the past haunted her, but she refused to give in.

The Healds continued their long honeymoon by train, carriage, and ship until they reached Marseille. From there they embarked on the steamship *Marie-Antoinette*, headed for Rome. One afternoon during their stay, Lola visited Ludwig's Villa Malta, located in a tranquil, elegant area next to the Porta Pinciana. There, King Ludwig liked to compose poems and surround himself with German painters and sculptors who loved classical antiquity as much as he did. She had little trouble convincing the guard to open the huge entrance gate and let her in to look around. The villa was enormous, a splendid two-story mansion topped with a slender tower. On its ochre-colored facade, three arches supported a large veranda edged by Corinthian marble columns. Intoxicating roses climbed the walls to the windows, balconies, and terraces. Lola was finally able to see all that the king had described to her so many times. Though she had not written to him since her marriage to George, she was still fond of the old monarch. Walking through the luminous rooms richly decorated with tapestries, sculptures, busts, and paintings by the great Italian masters, she felt very close to him.

At the end of August, the Healds arrived in Naples, but a letter with unsettling news was waiting at the hotel. Their lawyers informed them that they must return to London before September 10, when the next hearing had been set. If they weren't back in time, they would lose the bail money. They decided to return at once.

In recent weeks Lola Montez had appeared on more newspaper front pages than she had when she was the lover of King Ludwig I of Bavaria. The international press eagerly repeated the news that the dancer had been accused of bigamy, making her an even more fascinating figure. In the press in England, her situation gave rise to an energetic discussion of the difficulty and cost of obtaining a divorce in Great Britain. Articles on hypocritical Victorian morality also appeared when the Marquess of Londonderry, the officer leading the Second Regiment of Life Guards, decided to expel George Trafford Heald for having married a divorced woman. The elderly Miss Heald had made Lola a bigger celebrity than ever.

The couple arrived in London on September 7 and met with their lawyers to go over the details of the case. Lola learned that the prosecution had proof that Captain James had been alive in India on the day she was married. This was alarming news. She had believed that Miss Heald would eventually withdraw her accusation, but now her situation had become more precarious. If she appeared at court to retrieve the bail money, she could end up in prison. Lola didn't have to think twice. She told George that she was leaving that very night for Boulogne-sur-Mer, in France, on a mail boat that would set sail at dawn from Folkestone. A few days later, he was to join her and send all her belongings from the house on Half Moon Street to the address she indicated.

In the peaceful seaside city of Boulogne, on the English Channel, Mrs. Heald took a room at the Hôtel de Londres, to wait for her husband. Calmer now, she wrote to the king for the first time since August 1. Lola had not heard from him because Ludwig had been writing to an address in Seville that she had given to him. In a few brief lines, she tried to explain the bigamy charge and convince him that it had all been an act of vengeance by her husband's embittered aunt. But that summer of 1849, the Munich press was still trumpeting the news from England about the countess's marriage to Captain James. Ludwig no longer believed anything published about his lover, but he didn't believe her either. Mostly, he was hurt that she hadn't written in a month and a half. The king, as he'd informed her in the letters she never received, had decided to cut off her pension starting in October. In his accounting ledger, where he kept a precise record of the money he sent to her, he now referred to Lola as "Mrs. Heald."

In mid-September, George joined his wife in Boulogne, and a few days later, the couple returned once more to Paris, where they found lodgings in a luxurious hotel on the rue de Rivoli with their small retinue: a secretary, two servants, and three maids, plus the dogs. This time the dancer's only aim was to confirm the purity of her life before she'd married her husband. To that end, she ordered her secretary to send an announcement of her arrival to the most select elements of Parisian society.

Within a few weeks, a wide variety of people were dropping by the hotel to see her: French dandies, English nobles, Russian princes, and some of her old friends from the theater world. In honor of her guests, Lola organized a huge banquet that would introduce her into society as Mrs. Heald. That night, the attendees were amazed when they saw her appear, radiant, arm in arm with George, a man so young that one lady present commented snidely that "he looked more like her son than her husband." To dazzle the public, Lola was wearing a green satin dress that matched her jewelry: a magnificent bracelet and a triple chain of emeralds, from which dangled a cameo with a portrait of King Ludwig I of Bavaria.

At the end of the lively evening, Lola got to her feet and called for a moment of silence. Clutching the pendant that hung from her neck, she said melodramatically, "This is the portrait of the king of Bavaria, who has been like a father to me. Oh, I know full well that our pure friendship has been interpreted otherwise and that both he and I have been the targets of attacks and calumnies. But history will demonstrate the injustice of these hateful lies and prove that the monarch of whom I am speaking, and whose memory I carry in my heart, has been like a loving father who, moved by my misfortune, granted me a noble title and a generous income."

After this unexpected confession, the guests applauded their hostess enthusiastically. Lola declared that, far from being the king's courtesan, she had been his best friend and political adviser for nearly two years. Encouraged by her audience's reaction, she kept going: "Foul lies have attacked me not just during my stay in Munich, but since I came into the world in my native Seville, and they have pursued me in every country I've visited. While living in the independence of celibacy, I paid little heed to the rumors circulating about me, but today I owe it to my husband, and to myself, to refute them. The Countess of Landsfeld is in the past; now I am the happy Mrs. Heald."

Her emotional words seemed to convince not just her husband, who was gazing at her as if spellbound, but also the rest of her guests. The next day, the dancer read with satisfaction several articles that referred to "Mrs. Heald's elegant banquet and brave speech." For the moment she had managed to stop the scandal in its tracks and pretend that she was delighted with her new role as faithful and loving wife.

One brisk autumn day the couple left Paris for Marseille and from there sailed to Barcelona, where they stayed in a sunny guesthouse located in a sixteenth-century mansion in the Gothic Quarter. Though Barcelona was undergoing massive transformation and some neighborhoods were very unsanitary because of the lack of sewers, Lola relished her time there. Her English friends had warned her to be careful with Spanish food, which had strong flavors, with spices and lots of garlic. As she was accustomed to curry-seasoned dishes from her childhood in India, Lola had no problem. Afraid of getting sick, George consumed only well-done steak and beer. In the evenings, Lola would wander along La Rambla, one of the city's busiest pedestrian areas, with its Renaissance-era palaces, streetlamps, flower sellers, and open-air bird market. She managed to persuade George to buy her two parakeets and a parrot, which joined the three dogs already traveling with them.

The famous dancer's presence did not go unnoticed in Barcelona, and a correspondent from the *New York Herald*, James Grant, requested an interview. Lola was flattered by the attention from a major New York paper. When meeting with the reporter, she deployed all her usual charms. Mr. Grant found her impetuous temperament, exotic accent, and deft conversation to be captivating. Lola disguised her shaky Spanish by mixing in English words and French expressions. Once more she changed her biography at will, this time making her mother Irish—since by now people had discovered that Lola was from Cork—and her father a Spanish aristocrat. She claimed to have been brought up in a very austere environment and that her first marriage, to Lieutenant James, had been a mere formality intended to protect her from a predatory guardian.

"Mr. Grant, as I say, all the scandals attributed to me in Munich are cruel falsehoods invented by my enemies, the Jesuits and the ultra-conservatives of the Bavarian court, who refuse to accept that a woman could be a king's political adviser."

"I'd like to know if you are still in contact with King Ludwig since his abdication."

"Of course. He still writes to me every day and continues to send me a generous pension. In addition, my husband, Mr. Heald, has agreed to give me a lifetime income and to provide a significant sum to support our future children."

"Won't Mrs. Heald miss her glorious past as the most celebrated woman in Europe?"

"People change, and I have found a good husband, one who is young, wealthy, and devoted to me. I am a new woman, a faithful and respectable wife to my husband, and I'd appreciate it if you'd make that clear in your article."

"Have you ever considered traveling to my country? America is a land of opportunity where a person's past is irrelevant. A woman like you would triumph there in anything she set herself to."

But even though Lola kept repeating how happy she was, she couldn't fool herself. Ever since they'd left Paris, the couple had been arguing fiercely, and it was becoming more and more difficult to spend time together. George was fed up with her eccentricities, her arrogance, and her terrible moods. The dancer even confessed to a friend, "He is completely incompatible with my way of being . . . Rather than finding peaceful day-to-day contentment by his side, I found myself the wife of a dull, possessive, profligate Englishman."

Though the Countess of Landsfeld was seeking to improve her public image, a serious incident brought her into the news again. On the evening of October 7, 1849, her husband, George, happened to read his wife's imaginative interview published in the *New York Herald*. Annoyed by her shamelessness, her perpetual desire to call attention to herself, and her obsession with money, he stormed up to the hotel room and berated her for airing their private life without consulting him. Lola, who'd been delighted to appear in such an important paper, flew into a rage. George was bewildered when she grabbed a small dagger she'd been concealing beneath her clothing and lunged at him. In the struggle, Lola stabbed him in the shoulder. The wound was superficial; nevertheless, Mr. Heald hastily stuffed some belongings into a valise and left the room, shouting, "You're completely insane! You could have killed me. My poor Aunt Susanna was right, you're an unstable, violent woman. I can't believe I've been so blind. And to think I gave up everything for you . . ."

George went to the British consul, claiming to be afraid for his life. The consul advised him to report his wife to the Spanish police. Mr. Heald didn't dare take that step and, instead, caught an evening train to Mataró, a tranquil coastal city a few miles from Barcelona. A fellow Englishman who owned a textile mill lived there, and George planned to take refuge in his compatriot's home until he'd decided what to do.

Alone in her rooms, Lola paced desperately back and forth. Still agitated, she'd had to take a few drops of laudanum to calm down.

But as the hours passed and George did not return, she was seized by a deep sense of alarm. He had taken his passport and left her very little money. She was certain he would never forgive her and would go back to London. She decided she had to find him before he left Spain. She would beg for his forgiveness and cover him with kisses, and he would forget the incident. Not knowing what else to do, she published an urgent notice in the *Diario de Barcelona* newspaper:

> I am seeking a British citizen who goes by the name George Trafford Heald. He is twenty-one years old, tall and slender, with blond hair and a fine mustache and sideburns. He does not speak Spanish, and I will offer a reward to anyone who can give me news of his whereabouts. His beloved wife, Mrs. Heald.

In Mataró, Mr. Heald learned from his friend that his name was appearing in the press and that his wife was looking for him. Reevaluating his behavior, he decided it was time to go back to her. Lola was alone, in a strange city, with hardly any money. Three days later, he returned and assured her that he still loved her madly. But Lola, who was lounging on the sofa smoking a cigarette, remained aloof.

"How could you humiliate me like this? Running away like a coward so that everybody eyes me pityingly and whispers, 'Look, poor woman, so young and newly married, abandoned by her husband.'" Her words were full of scorn.

"You're forgetting, Lola, that you lunged at me like a wild animal, you were out of your mind. I didn't know what to do; I was aggrieved and frightened. But now I'm back, I'm here."

"All of Barcelona has been talking of nothing but you absurdly making a run for it. You made me look ridiculous. Here, look at the newspaper: 'Lola Montes has managed to trap her unfaithful husband and drag him back to the marriage bed.' Everybody has been laughing at me." Then she changed strategies and apologized: "But maybe I deserve it for the way I treated you. Forgive me!"

Lola embraced her husband and promised to try to control her fits of rage. But despite her good intentions, her kind and apathetic husband was a heavy burden for her. That night, she bared her heart to the king in a sincere letter:

> What a shame that you are not near me to see for yourself the eternal punishment to which I have subjected myself. This man is not just boring, stupid, and brutish, but he also has no heart and insults me before the entire world. How could I, after knowing you, give my love to another? Furthermore, this man is ignorant and unstable, practically a lunatic who cannot take a single action without assistance.

She added that she hadn't written sooner because she had been embarrassed to tell him about the terrible chaos she'd made of her life. Ludwig asked that she send him a lock of hair in her next letter, as she'd done some time back. He had stopped writing to her every morning and was devoting more time to Therese, trying to make up for the suffering he'd caused her.

At the beginning of December, the Heals boarded the steamship *El Cid* to travel along the Spanish coast to Cádiz. It was an uncomfortable journey that lasted twelve days, with brief stopovers in Valencia, Alicante, and Málaga. In all these cities, the dancer visited the main monuments and the local press reported on her arrival. The December 8 edition of Valencia's *Diario mercantil* published the news on the front page:

> The day before yesterday the celebrated horsewoman and adventuress Lola Montez arrived on the steamship *El Cid* and left for Cádiz at five in the afternoon. In this

brief period of time she visited the city's most significant sights, seeming immensely pleased and eager to
come again in the future. It is reported that on her way
back from the Grau neighborhood, the intrepid lady
started driving the old wagon that was ferrying her
and managed to whip the horses into a gallop. It is also
said that she purchased a blanket and a red cap of the
sort worn by farmworkers. We fervently hope for the
return of this remarkable woman, who will no doubt
provide us with plenty of material for a new column.

Being stuck with each other all day in a small cabin did not improve
the couple's relationship. When they finally disembarked at Cádiz's bustling wharfs, Lola was a wreck. Her head hurt, her mood was irritable,
and she blamed her husband for the loss of her parakeets, which had
escaped during the voyage. The Healds stayed at the Fonda Jiménez, one
of the city's most authentic guesthouses, frequented by foreigners from
all over Europe. Lola found Cádiz, with its whitewashed houses, old
taverns, and flamenco shows, immensely charming. Unlike the other
Spanish cities, it had a tropical flavor that evoked the exotic ports she'd
stopped at on her way to India. In her letters to King Ludwig, she
remarked that Cádiz had a rich cultural life, with five theaters and more
than thirty cafés that hosted literary gatherings and salons. The dancer's
presence aroused great curiosity among the city's residents. She told the
journalists who interviewed her that she had learned the Spanish language and typical Spanish dances in 1842 in a dance academy in Seville,
and that she had made her debut as first ballerina at the Teatro Real.

While Lola was enjoying the attentions of the admirers who flocked
around her, George was anxious to leave Spain as soon as possible. He
was still attracted to his wife, but he could not bear her temper and
the way she enjoyed showing him up in front of acquaintances. Since
their wedding day, he had been constantly on the move, and he was

exhausted. He was worried about his health—he had grown thinner and had very little appetite because he found their arguments so stressful.

"The truth is I don't even recognize you. I don't know what you're hoping to achieve, behaving this way with me," he complained one night. "I've done everything you wanted, I've followed you all over, I've bought anything that caught your fancy. When we met, you seemed like a lady, seductive and fun, and now . . ."

"Now what, darling?" Lola asked, her voice cold. "I've disappointed you. Well, I'm sorry, but you bore me and I'm sick of always having to take the initiative. I want to have a good time, and you ruin everything. You don't like wine, you don't like flamenco, you don't like bullfighting . . . You interact only with English people and consider my friends unsophisticated and beneath you. It's clear I made a mistake marrying you."

"Maybe so, but I loved you. Sadly for me, it seems you just wanted a husband who was rich and naive. I was foolish to think a woman like you could love me."

On December 25, Mrs. Heald was excitedly preparing to celebrate her first Christmas in Spain. As usual, her husband went out early to walk Turk, but the hours went by and he still hadn't returned by noon. George had fled again, this time with Lola's cherished dog and one of her servants in tow. The dancer visited every inn and tavern and eventually went to the police to report that he had abandoned her. When she learned that Mr. Heald had gone to Gibraltar, where he planned to board a steamship for England the next day, she felt that this time she'd lost him for good. "There's no use waiting—he won't be coming back," she thought. "Things have gone too far this time."

Mr. Heald sent her a goodbye note from the *Pacha* on his way home: he said that he bore her no ill will, but he could not continue living in exile and missed his homeland. The only ray of hope in Lola's life during that difficult time was receiving a letter from King Ludwig. Though he scolded her for her behavior and the way she'd betrayed him with Peissner, he included checks for the first three months of 1850. The money was a huge relief. Now she could pay her debts in Cádiz and return to London to try to win back her husband's affection. When the king heard that Mr. Heald had run off, he criticized the younger man's behavior. "I was quite dismayed to discover that your husband has left you," he wrote to her. "I am sorry."

In early February 1850, after four eventful months of travel through Spain, the dancer returned to France and settled once more in Boulogne-sur-Mer. To rekindle the king's interest, she sent him a carefully considered letter:

> The first thing I did was send to London for the bundle of all the letters you've written me, and it's a good thing I did so immediately, since two days after they sent me the box with your papers, Mr. Heald went to the lawyer who was holding them and asked for them. When he learned I'd requested them, he grew furious. God knows what he would have done with your letters if they'd fallen into his hands. He is quite depraved and capable of the most vile and dishonorable acts. This gentleman wishes to annul our marriage, but I intend to resist, because the other marriage was not legal. I would very much like to entrust to you all the letters you wrote me, but how can I send them to you? I do not have the money to pay someone to take them to you. If Mr. Heald managed to steal them from me, I am certain he would publish them immediately. I am thinking more about you than about myself, though I can't even afford to buy myself shoes. The monster also took poor Turk from me, my only consolation and friend. I can do nothing but weep, weep all day and night. It is terrible to be alone and to be poor and unhappy, but thankfully your letters are safe. For the love of God, do not abandon me; you are my only hope. Your devoted, your unhappy Lolitta, whom you once loved.

The king replied at once. He had been thinking about how to get the letters back from Lola, wishing to make sure they were safe. He thanked her for her thoughtfulness and advised her to send them as soon as possible through a trusted banker friend of his. He added that, once he had them in his possession, he would send her the checks for April, May, and June early. The king had fallen into the trap, but Lola wasn't willing to surrender her leverage so easily. In her next letter, she had changed her mind:

Why do you write me such cold letters? It is very cruel of you. It is not my fault that I am poor and unhappy. With regard to your letters, now that I am calmer and people are no longer hounding me so persistently, I would like to keep them. I will send them to you only if I begin to travel, which is not likely because traveling requires money, which I do not have. Please, write me more amicable letters. You have a very capricious heart and forget easily, but I am not like you, I remain your devoted and affectionate Lolitta always. Tonight I am going to London in secret—it is very dangerous, but I have to see Mr. Heald to get him to give me money and things that he took from me.

Once Lola received the king's checks, she stopped writing to him for a while. Her priority now was to travel to London to save her marriage. It was a dangerous undertaking: if the English police discovered her, she could be thrown in jail. Despite everything, the journey had a happy ending. When poor George opened his front door in the middle of the night to find Lola standing before him, he pressed her in his arms with tears in his eyes. He couldn't believe that his wife had risked her freedom to come see him. That was proof enough to convince him that she still loved him.

Exhausted after her long journey from Boulogne, she told him, "My darling George, you must forgive me, my nerves betray me. My life has not been easy; I have always had to struggle on my own and I have nobody else. Sometimes I cannot control my impulses—my blood boils and I do not recognize myself. Please, let's put the past behind us."

"I still love you just as always, Lola, and your strength and bravery fascinate me, but I think you need another sort of man by your side. We are not united by the same things, and I sometimes feel that you treat me like a little boy and I am merely—"

"Hush, don't say anything else," she interrupted, kissing him. "I have longed for your caresses so keenly. I do not need any other man by my side."

Once they had reconciled, Lola convinced him that they should return to Paris, where she still had good friends. In late March, the newspaper *Le siècle* informed its readers, "There is a great commotion in Paris. The public is enormously excited. Lola Montez has returned to our city!"

Mrs. Heald, who had given up being called the Countess of Landsfeld, arrived in the city with her maidservant, a butler, and her dogs and took rooms at the Hôtel du Rhin in the Place Vendôme. A few days later, her husband appeared with servants, fifty trunks, five carriages, and seven magnificent horses. He had ignored his aunts and uncles, who had begged him to stay in England, saying that his wife would be his downfall. Lola was happy because she had found an impressive mansion to rent that met her needs perfectly. The Château Beaujon, next to the Champs-Élysées, was a luxurious residence belonging to a wealthy banker, surrounded by a large park and a French-style garden. George signed the fifteen-year lease without flinching. He was ready to remake his life with Lola and start a family.

While spending a huge sum of money on decorating her new home, buying furniture and antiques, Lola took up her social life again. Though distinguished people now turned their backs because of her notoriety, she managed to collect a small circle of snobbish artists and liberal-minded gentlemen who were intrigued by her dark history. They weren't the prestigious figures of before, such as George Sand, Alexandre Dumas, and Joseph Méry, but she found them to be entertaining. She often could be seen riding down the Champs-Élysées, looking like a grand lady in her carriage pulled by four white horses and helmed by a liveried driver. A few meters behind, Mr. Heald would be following in his beautiful black two-seater phaeton.

Around that time, the happy couple commissioned a portrait from Claudius Jacquand, an esteemed artist who worked in high-society circles. They wanted the canvas to portray the moment when George had asked for Lola's hand. Lola appeared sitting on an elegant sofa and George stood next to her, in his striking Life Guards uniform, grasping her hands and gazing into her eyes. On a nearby malachite table lay a jewelry box displaying the officer's wedding gifts to his beloved. When the painting was finished, Lola hung it in a place of honor in the main drawing room where everyone would see it.

Their lifestyle was very expensive, and George started receiving letters from his lawyers urging him to return to London to discuss his expenses and income. At the end of May, Lola wrote to Ludwig for the first time since he had sent her the last three checks. Three months had passed, and she explained the long silence by saying that she had been very sick after suffering a serious relapse of her malarial fevers:

> My life is miserable, quite miserable. Mr. Heald is worse than a tyrant with me. And ultimately I cannot leave him because I do not have anything to live on. I am penniless. I am in an appalling situation. You have begged me to return your letters to you. But you had sworn and promised to send me those small monthly payments for the rest of my life, and now you wish to take everything from me. Nobody who had a heart, not even the very poorest, would be capable of doing that. If I

were independent, God knows I would not say anything. Still, in the critical situation in which I find myself, it is very harsh and cruel on your part. I suffered so very much in your country, and nothing of what you gave me remains to me. I must tell you this. I am constantly being insulted as if I were a fallen woman working the street. The whole time I have been in bed, Mr. Heald has done nothing to look after me. What's more, he has spent all his time outside of the house, at the theater and amusing himself with other people.

Ludwig wrote to his ambassador in France, Baron August von Wendland, and asked him to provide a confidential report on the Countess of Landsfeld's activities in Paris. Wendland told him that the Healds had rented a large mansion and had servants, horses, and several carriages. They could be seen in the most fashionable restaurants, at the Opéra, and patronizing the finest shops.

The king immediately wrote and told Lola that he knew quite well what her new life was like. He accused her of continuing to deceive him and repeated that she would not receive any more money if she did not send him his letters. Lola, outraged, accused Ludwig of spying on her. Furthermore, she insinuated that an editor in London had offered her a lot of money to publish the letters. And she added, "I know that your letters are very valuable to you, but if something happened to me or they fell into the wrong hands, I cannot assure you what would happen." Ludwig did not reply and once more badgered his ambassador Wendland for details of his lover's life in Paris.

At the end of July, the Healds sold four of their thoroughbred horses to cover some expenses, and they tried to return two of their carriages to the manufacturer. Mr. Heald's lawyer was about to arrive in Paris to discuss what measures could be taken to salvage their precarious situation. At that point George decided to abandon his wife for the third and final time. This time he took not only all of his assets but also most of Lola's, including her title as the Countess of Landsfeld, the marble sculpture of King Ludwig's hand, and all the letters she kept in a little chest. Lola was convinced that now she truly had hit rock bottom. She had hardly any cash to pay the creditors who lurked outside her gates and descended whenever she went out. Nor could she pay the rent on her splendid mansion, and the owner was threatening to evict her. The dancer pursued her husband, but this time her efforts were in vain. George demanded that his lawyers draw up an arrangement that would free him for good. Lola's belongings were returned to her, and both spouses' representatives began negotiating for the most amicable separation possible. Mr. Heald agreed to pay the debts accumulated while he had been living with his wife in Paris and to pay her an alimony of fifty pounds a month. It was a laughable sum for a woman so accustomed to lavish spending, but she had no choice but to accept.

Lola wistfully left her beautiful villa on the Champs-Élysées and moved to a small apartment on the rue Saint-Honoré rented to her by a friend, Count Michel de Corail. It was a distinguished neighborhood very close to the Place de la Concorde, and soon everybody in the area was aware of the famous performer's presence. In the mornings, they would see her go into the nearby Madeleine church, to the great surprise of those familiar with her reputation.

After the last four agonizing years, Lola Montez had begun seeking spiritual support. She told one journalist that she wanted to withdraw from public life and that she was seriously considering entering a Carmelite convent in Spain. She received frequent visits from a priest at the Madeleine church, who reproached her for her shameful lifestyle and extravagances, but Lola defended herself by claiming that her behavior was the product of having been abandoned by her parents as a little girl. It was the excuse she'd used for years. Recalling the words that King Ludwig had once said to her—"Look inside yourself for the origin of your misfortunes"—she believed it was time to find peace with herself.

Lola was ready to change, but, as always, her main concern was financial. The king had stopped sending her money in July, and she could not depend on Mr. Heald's monthly payments alone. She needed to earn money, and it occurred to her that it would be a good time to publish a memoir. She'd been pondering the idea for months, but she needed to find someone to help her write it. A writer offered to draft the memoir of her extraordinary life in "elegant and clean" French and to create an entertaining account. The dancer arranged with the editor of *Le pays*, which had high circulation numbers, to publish the text in installments. Lola had not seriously considered including the king's letters in her autobiography, but through a friend, she let Ambassador von Wendland know that "in exchange for an annual pension of twenty-five thousand francs, the countess would be willing to return the king's correspondence to him and abstain from using it in her memoir." The diplomat, startled by what he considered to be flagrant blackmail, went to the French foreign affairs and interior ministers to find out whether anything could be done to prevent it. The ministers called in the editor of *Le pays* and informed him that, if anything he were to publish should damage French relations with a foreign power, he would be jailed immediately. The newspaperman refused to cooperate, saying that laws recently enacted by the new republic protected him from censorship.

On January 8, 1851, the first installment of the memoir of the celebrated adventuress Lola Montez appeared. In the introduction, the author addressed King Ludwig I of Bavaria directly and offered a rundown of the topics that would be addressed in the book:

> Your ideas as a poet, as an artist, as a philosopher, your judgments, sometimes harsh but always valuable, the elevated ideas of a liberal-minded, intelligent, and courteous king are what I want to present to Europe, which now finds itself sunk in a foolish materialism, which no longer believes in anything, thinks about anything,

or even acts. Society does everything it can to make
women hypocrites. We are constantly forced to say the
opposite of what we think. I will reveal many scandalous things that have remained hidden until now.

The dancer's memoir was a mixture of "lies and vanity," as one critic
put it, and not terribly credible. Readers expected to read the confessions of an adventurous woman who had become the lover to a king and
figured in wild scandals all across Europe. What they found instead was
a wistful account of her childhood in India, her triumphs as a dancer,
and her friendship with an elderly monarch, "the most cultivated and
generous man she had known in her life." Lola spun wild fantasies about
her time in Munich, even saying that Queen Therese herself, as a sign
of her high esteem, had given her the badge of the Order of Theresa.
She also claimed that the happiest day of her life had been when King
Ludwig had taken her hand and led her before the nobles of his court
to announce, "Gentlemen, I present to you my best friend."

Lola had been counting on earning a lot from the publication, but
Le pays changed hands and the new owners, ardent defenders of the
French Republic that she described with such disdain, refused to publish any more installments. It was a harsh blow for the dancer because
she had put all her hopes in the project and devoted a great deal of
time and energy to it. Ambassador von Wendland smugly informed the
king that his friend's memoir had not sparked much interest, that the
countess was furious about her failure, and that she hadn't been seen
in public for days.

That spring in Paris was the saddest of her life. Whereas Lola had
once relished the beauty of the city's gardens in bloom, strolls along the
banks of the Seine, and romantic sunsets on the Pont Neuf, she now
felt defeated. She was alone, in debt, and without any projects in the
offing. In late March 1851, her situation was so precarious that she tried

once more to gain the king's pity. An acquaintance who would soon be traveling to Munich offered to carry a letter to Ludwig. It read:

> Oh, Louis, if you only knew what a miserable, if honorable, situation I find myself in. I am poor, very poor, but money obtained through wicked means is always wicked. I prefer to live as I do rather than possessing luxuries thanks to wickedness. Oh, Louis, be charitable, remember that it is Lolitta who is begging you—Lolitta, who is the same as ever to you. Out of the pity you feel for me, Louis, help me recover my dignity. Your letters, which Mr. Heald will not allow me to return to you, are at your disposal. They are sacred to me. I am going to allow a friend of mine to write what will be known as my memoir, but nothing about Munich will be included. Answer my letter, only a few lines—how happy you would make me if you wrote me a few lines. My heart is the same as ever to you.
> Your always devoted
> Lolitta

This time the king did not reply. Hers would be the last of the hundreds of letters they had written to each other over the course of more than four years. Ludwig read it several times and finally tucked it away in a wooden box where he kept notes, poems, and mementos of his beloved. Lola, who claimed to love and respect him so much, had tried to extort him in the foulest manner. He no longer cared what she did with his letters nor whether she humiliated him before the entire world. He wanted only to forget her, though her absence would cause him unbearable pain for a long time.

But Lola was unpredictable. In June, Ludwig was spending a few weeks at Villa Malta, in Rome. One morning he received an unexpected visit. A young Irishman named Patrick O'Brien was claiming to have brought an urgent package from the Countess of Landsfeld. The king was surprised when he saw the package's contents: all the letters the king had been demanding for so long. That night, Ludwig was finally able to sleep easy, knowing that he now had in his possession hundreds of pages of his most intimate secrets. The king sent a note of thanks to O'Brien and two thousand francs for him to take back to Lola. A few days later, Ludwig sent the countess another three thousand francs in recognition of her generous gesture. That was the last time he ever sent money to her.

In Paris, Madame Montez had moved to another apartment on rue Saint-Honoré, one that was larger and brighter. After the failure of her memoir, as Mr. Heald moved forward with their divorce, and without the king's generous allowance, she decided to return to the stage. It had been five years since her last performance, her debut at the Court Theatre in Munich. She had lost weight, her health was poor, and her face showed signs of weariness. But she was still determined to win over the audience with her ardor. In the end, after Queen Victoria, she was the woman who had graced the most newspaper and magazine covers in all of Europe.

Lola placed herself in the hands of the dancer Victor Mabille, who, with his father, owned the Jardin Mabille, a fashionable outdoor ball-room on the Champs-Élysées. Around a bandstand was the dance floor, surrounded by benches and tables. Everything was decorated with garlands, Chinese lanterns, and banners that hung from the tree branches. Wealthy Parisians went there to dance waltzes, polkas, and mazurkas, but the venue also presented some performances. Victor Mabille choreographed several numbers for the countess, including a tarantella and Bavarian, Hungarian, and Tyrolean folk dances. For three months Lola took lessons, and the money King Ludwig had sent for giving back his letters enabled her to pay her dance teacher and buy the splendid dresses she would wear onstage.

During that summer of 1851, the countess continued with her dance exercises. She was thirty now, and though she had not trained in a long

time, her body swiftly gained flexibility. She worked hard, but she also
had fun. At her home she organized gatherings at which she entertained
gentlemen of several nationalities, singing along in a suggestive voice
to the chords of her guitar or dancing a fandango. She had not quit
smoking, and she could be seen in the evenings lounging on the sofa,
inhaling cigarette smoke, and basking in the attentions of some devoted
admirer. One of her ever-present companions during those months was
Edward Willis, a young, enterprising New Yorker who, fascinated by
Lola, insisted she must travel to the United States, where she would
be able to emulate the success that Fanny Elssler had enjoyed there.
Another of her illustrious guests was a brother of the famous newspaperman James Gordon Bennett, editor of the *New York Herald*, who also
encouraged her to try her fortune in his country.

On September 12, Lola Montez reappeared before the Parisian public at the Jardin Mabille. She had sent hundreds of invitations to friends,
acquaintances, and members of the press. Her performance was scheduled for eight o'clock that night, but it was delayed. The artist asked
Mabille to distribute punch, cigarettes, and ice cream to the attendees
to entertain them. Two hours later she took the stage, dazzling in an
elaborate Spanish dress and with her hair pulled back with a beautiful
mother-of-pearl comb. Her short, flounced skirt left her beautiful legs
bare, and her bodice highlighted her small waist and generous bust.
The audience received her with applause and cheers. She performed
three dances in three different costumes, each more striking and exotic
than the last. To her admirers' delight, she repeated the famous garter
moment that had made her debut at the Paris Opéra so memorable
seven years earlier. The critic Théophile Gautier, who had written of
her so harshly in the past, now acknowledged that, thanks to Mabille,
Lola had improved considerably. He noted to his readers that, though
Madame Montez was no longer a young lass, "she maintained her well-
proportioned silhouette, her blazing blue eyes, and her gleaming white
teeth."

After her triumph in Paris, the artist signed a contract with a theater agent, a Mr. Roux, for a long tour through several European cities. In Boulogne, where she had spent a few seasons and was quite well known, she enjoyed rousing success. A local critic wrote of the opening night, "Lola Montez's dancing is poetry in motion, sometimes fantastical, often lustful, and always attractive." She then moved on to Belgium, where an unpleasant incident took place in Brussels. One morning, while staying at the Hôtel de Suède, she was informed by the staff that a gentleman representing Mr. Arnaud, the owner of the local horse track, wanted to see her. Lola received him in the sitting room of her suite.

"My dear countess, forgive me for bothering you—I imagine you must be tired from your tour," he said. "But I'd like to make a proposal."

"I'm listening. But be quick, I don't have much time."

"Mr. Arnaud, a devoted admirer of yours, wishes to propose a very special performance at his horse track."

"I'm sorry, I don't understand. I thought only horses performed at the horse track."

"That's it exactly, madam. Mr. Arnaud wants to hire you as a rider. He will pay you three thousand francs for six performances. All you have to do is round the track at a gallop two or three times each afternoon for the spectators. You will be a sensation."

Lola stared in astonishment. "How dare you! I'm not a circus attraction, I am a great artist! I practice the art of dance and do so with good taste and decorum. Get out of my sight before I lose my temper."

The gentleman slinked out in terror.

After performing in Antwerp one night, she traveled to Cologne, where she was planning a show for early October. But the tour was interrupted when the chief of police announced that the Countess of Landsfeld was not welcome in Prussian territory. The authorities had not forgotten the uproar the Spanish lady had caused in Bavaria. For the dancer, this was a major disappointment and an economic blow because it meant several performances could not go forward, including one in Berlin. Her agent, Roux, had to improvise and quickly managed to secure new engagements. The tour continued through other cities, from Lyon to Marseille, with diminished success because there wasn't time to sufficiently advertise her arrival. By the end, Lola was tired and ill after traveling thousands of miles on trains and slow stagecoaches, lodging in mediocre hotels, and enduring all manner of discomforts.

Upon returning to Paris, she took a few days of rest to recover her health and ponder her career. At this point in her life, she could no longer deceive herself. She knew that her talent as a dancer left much to be desired and that people were coming to see her because of her reputation. If she stayed in Europe, she would end up an itinerant performer, always on the move. At that crucial moment of her life, she recalled the words of James Grant, the journalist who had interviewed her in Barcelona: "America is a land of opportunity where a person's past is irrelevant." And she decided that it was worth a shot.

CHAPTER 10

The American Dream

One windy day in November 1851, Lola Montez headed for New York, ready to start a new life. She was accompanied by her friend Edward Willis, now acting as her agent and secretary. The steamship *Humboldt* set sail from Le Havre early in the morning and crossed the English Channel to Southampton, where it picked up more passengers. One of them completely eclipsed the Countess of Landsfeld: Lajos Kossuth, the Hungarian nobleman who had declared Hungary's independence from Austria's Hapsburgs during the revolution of 1848. Considered a hero, he was traveling to the United States to raise funds and seek support for his cause. Lola, who had become quite the diva, was thoroughly miffed at having to share the ship with a bigger celebrity. She accused Edward of incompetence for having purchased the tickets without checking to see who else would be on board and continued to throw it in his face throughout the voyage.

The fifteen-day journey was not a pleasure cruise, though Lola had a spacious and comfortable first-class cabin. At that time of year, the western wind blew forcefully, storms were frequent, and the sea was very rough. When good weather permitted, she would stroll along the main deck, wrapped in a cashmere shawl and gazing at the horizon as she smoked. Luckily for her, Kossuth got seasick and spent most of the crossing in his cabin. With him out of the picture, the dancer took the opportunity to regale the other passengers with tales of her extraordinary adventures. The ship was a Tower of Babel where every conversation included multiple shifting languages. Most of the passengers were political exiles with whom Lola was able to exchange opinions. She declared herself a committed liberal and fired up her listeners with her sharp criticisms of the tyranny that still prevailed in Old Europe. The *Humboldt* was also carrying entire families of Italian, Irish, Jewish, and German immigrants fleeing from hunger and poverty. All of them, like her, dreamed of making their fortunes across the Atlantic.

When they reached New York, a crowd thronged the dock on the East River, waving flags and handkerchiefs. To Lola's disappointment, she swiftly realized that they were not waiting for her but for the Hungarian patriot, who was received with music, cheers, and salutes as he descended the gangplank.

The countess waited to disembark until the man had disappeared from view, escorted by authorities and journalists on his way to city hall. Watching from the deck, she mused, "I'm in America. I feel happy and reenergized. Soon my name will be glowing on the best marquees on Broadway. Stupid, arrogant Kossuth isn't going to ruin my moment of glory."

The few reporters who remained were surprised to discover that Lola Montez, famed for her violent temper and whip-wielding skills, was a delicate-looking, very feminine woman. Her expressive blue eyes and arresting personality made a powerful impression on the journalists. In her first comments made on American soil, the countess said euphorically, "Gentlemen, I am happy to be in this great nation, the last refuge of freedom and asylum for millions of people fleeing the tyrannies that devastate Europe. Like them, I have come to try my fortune. King Maximilian II has seized all my properties in Bavaria and I have no choice but to return to the stage."

Peering from the carriage that carried her to a hotel, she discovered a chaotic, noisy city with dusty neighborhoods of unpaved streets where children played barefoot. New York was expanding rapidly and already had more than a half million inhabitants. Most lived in deplorable conditions, crowded into slums where crime and poverty reigned. Five Points, an Irish area, was the poorest and most dangerous neighborhood in Manhattan. "Ma'am, no decent person goes to Five Points," her driver told her. "Everybody drives several blocks out of their way to avoid it."

Hearing these words, Lola shuddered. Had she stayed in her native Ireland, maybe she would have been forced to flee the famine like so many unfortunate souls. She knew the Irish weren't exactly welcome in New York. They had a reputation for thievery, drunkenness, and violence. If anyone learned that the famous Lola Montez was Irish, it would be the end of her career.

Her agent had reserved a suite for her at the recently remodeled Montgomery Hotel, in Lower Manhattan. Here the most important public buildings were found, including city hall and the neoclassical Federal Hall, as well as Wall Street, where the major banks had built imposing office buildings. Across the East River, vast fields spread out, peppered with farms, estates, villages, and the summer homes of the New York elite.

The Countess of Landsfeld—as she was calling herself once more after her divorce from Mr. Heald—arrived at the hotel in the company of her young maidservant, Ellen, and two employees carrying her numerous trunks. The lady never let her little leather suitcase out of sight; locked with a heavy padlock, it was where she kept her remaining valuables. For the first few days, she hardly left her room and only gave interviews to the city's two most prestigious newspapers, the *New York Herald* and the recently established *New York Times*. From the start Lola had the support of James Gordon Bennett, who had heard about her from his brother. Bennett, a Scot, was one of the most brilliant and celebrated newspapermen of the time. His *New York Herald* was a sensationalist rag that knew how to capitalize on everyday events. In Lola Montez he had found a real gold mine; her scandals and adventures in America were going to provide him with juicy news that readers would eagerly lap up.

Once she'd recovered from the voyage, she immediately got in touch with Thomas Barry, the Broadway impresario and stage manager. They had been exchanging letters since Paris, and he was impatient to meet the indomitable woman. When Lola arrived at his offices wearing a beautiful velvet dress with fine lace and a hat adorned with feathers, Mr. Barry greeted her politely.

"Welcome, Mrs. Montez!" he exclaimed, shaking her hand. "It's an honor to meet such a celebrated artist, the woman whose name is on everyone's lips. I am certain that New York will succumb to your charms. A lady as adventurous and brave as you will not go unnoticed, I assure you."

"Thank you for those words, Mr. Barry; I am eager to make my debut on Broadway and hope that the American public will appreciate my Spanish dances that have had such success across Europe."

"That's just what I wanted to talk to you about. Americans like musical comedies; your solo act won't work here. The audience wants to see a star, the celebrated Countess of Landsfeld, with a huge supporting cast. They want a show, and you can't disappoint them."

"Excuse me," Lola retorted, annoyed, "but I doubt the New York audience is more exacting than that of London's Covent Garden. I have triumphed in the finest theaters in Europe and—"

"Please, Mrs. Montez, don't misunderstand me. I am familiar with your success, believe me. I will make one of my best choreographers available to you. You will work together, and three weeks from now, we'll see you onstage."

Forced to swallow her pride, Lola said a cordial goodbye to the impresario, thanking him for his help. She was insulted to have to share the spotlight with other dancers. But she was in a country whose customs she hardly knew, and if she wanted to make money fast, she had no choice but to accept Mr. Barry's advice.

She devoted her first weeks in the United States entirely to her dancing. She hadn't performed in many weeks and needed to get back in shape. The countess put herself in the hands of the choreographer George Washington Smith, considered the nation's best dancer. This legend of American ballet had done it all, from circus clowning to dancing the polka during *Hamlet* intermissions. He had partnered with the greatest divas of the time and in 1840 had joined the company of the legendary Fanny Elssler on her US tour, when he'd had great success as principal dancer. Now he was giving lessons and developing choreography for Broadway's biggest theaters. Smith wanted to make the most of the countess's personality, to disguise her technical deficiencies as a dancer. Lola became his most diligent disciple. She was worried about having so little time to rehearse before the opening night, but George promised to create a role that matched her abilities. And so he did: he incorporated dances that Lola had learned with Mabille in Paris along with some numbers of his own creation. The result was a musical comedy called *Betley, the Tyrolean*, in which she played a happy, carefree peasant girl.

Every morning she bundled up and trudged along the snowy sidewalks to the theater to rehearse. In late December, people sought refuge from the frigid air in entertainment venues. Lola loved Broadway, a long, energetic avenue full of major theaters, small variety halls, and dance halls where live bands played. The city had a rich cultural life, and the New York public paid high prices to see an opera or a good melodrama.

Feeling nostalgic, she often recalled her first acting teacher, Fanny Kelly. It had been nine years, but she hadn't forgotten the day she'd met Kelly in her London home, surrounded by her cats, nor her advice: "To be successful, it's not enough to have talent; you have to work hard, be consistent, and push yourself every day." Thanks to Kelly, Lola had become a new woman and had left a painful past behind.

That Christmas, Lola prepared diligently. In addition to her role as a Tyrolean peasant, she rehearsed a number of ensemble pieces that Smith had developed for her, such as "Diana and Her Nymphs," which she performed scantily clad. But without a doubt, his most original choreography was the "Sailor's Dance," in which she played a young sailor who hurried to rescue some shipwrecked people after a storm and returned to dry land with the flag of freedom flapping above him. It was the first time she wore pants onstage. The dance had an impressive musical accompaniment that evoked the roar of the rough ocean and the thunderclaps of the storm. In addition, Smith came up with a complex lighting plan to recreate the shipwreck, something rarely found in the stagecraft of the period. He also transformed the celebrated "Spider Dance" into a wild, joyful display of foot stomping.

On December 29, Lola Montez was thrilled to see her name in large letters on the marquee of the Broadway Theatre. It was the night of her American debut, and expectations were high. The tickets had sold out immediately, and more than three thousand New Yorkers crowded into the auditorium to see the famous, fiery Countess of Landsfeld in person. The audience was mostly male; Lola dubbed it a "black auditorium" because of all the dark suits. There were hardly any women in attendance because word had spread that the show was "indecent and scandalous." Lola was nervous. The show had nearly been canceled because of heavy snow that had fallen all morning. When the curtain rose that evening, a dozen dancers performed traditional Bavarian dances before a set that mimicked the Tyrolean Alps. A few moments later, Lola appeared, perched on a snowy mountaintop. She was greeted with clamorous applause that lasted several minutes as she bowed a number of times in grateful acknowledgment. The orchestra began to play, and she descended to the stage. She was unrecognizable in a blond wig with long braids, a white blouse with a tight black corset fastened around her torso, and a red skirt that came to her knees. The countess began her Tyrolean dance, and the public could see that, though she moved gracefully, her steps were rather unskilled. At the end of the first act, the applause was less enthusiastic. Lola withdrew to change and reappeared dressed in a striking Hungarian officer's uniform, leading a company of soldiers who performed a military march. A loud ovation surged through the auditorium, and she had to return from the wings several times to meet it. "Ladies and gentlemen, I thank you from the bottom of my heart for the very kind reception you have given me, a poor stranger in your noble land. I will never forget it," she said, bowing.

The performance had lasted just forty minutes, and though most of the audience considered Lola Montez a mediocre dancer, they agreed that she was expressive and passionate. A young critic from the British news magazine *Albion*, who watched the show from the front row, wrote enthusiastically that "she threw great spirit into her action and gave inklings to the curious of that latent fiery temper with which rumor has so generously endowed her." Lola was satisfied, though disappointed that nobody had come to her dressing room after the show. In every European capital where she'd performed, flowers had piled up on her dressing table and she'd always received visits from admirers. She wondered if her bold spirit, which had been so widely described by the press, was frightening the gentlemen away. "No doubt this country is different—the men are afraid of self-made women," she mused aloud as her maid helped her undress.

Her initial seven-day run at the Broadway Theatre was extended to three weeks. As word spread that the artist's performance and wardrobe were modest and decent, more women began to attend. Mr. Barry was gleefully delighted with ticket sales, and Lola alternated the amusing musical comedy with new dances Smith created for her. Her first week on Broadway brought in more money than the theater had ever recorded, and Lola became one of the best-paid performers in the country.

But as always, an obstacle arose. Lola accused her agent, Edward Willis, of irregularities in his management of her accounts, and he claimed that she was failing to fulfill her artistic obligations. The press made great hay of the dispute. For several days the two exchanged accusatory and indignant letters that were published in the *New York Herald* for readers' entertainment. The argument peaked with a lengthy missive sent by the Countess of Landsfeld to the *Herald*'s editor, which was published on January 15, just as her performances in New York were coming to an end. Her words had such resonance that the letter was republished by numerous other American papers and managed to win public opinion to her side:

> Mr. Bennett—
>
> I am sure you will not refuse a stranger, and that stranger a woman, a little space in your paper, for an appeal to an intelligent and generous community, against unjust and illiberal attacks upon her, intended to prejudice the people against her . . .
>
> Since childhood, when I first came to know of America, my heart yearned to visit it . . . I studied your institutions, and all my dreams of romance were connected with your happy country . . .
>
> . . . I have been wild and wayward, but, if I know myself, never wicked . . . I have been traduced, and slandered, and vilified more, I think, than any human being, man or woman, that has lived for a century. If all that is said of me were true—nay, if half of it were true—I ought to be buried alive . . .

Lola also seized the opportunity to give her own version of her time in Bavaria, where, she claimed, her only crime had been to open the king's eyes to the corruption of his closest ministers, such as his trusted adviser Karl von Abel. She also emphasized the "innocent" relationship she'd had with the old monarch:

> The populace of Munich were . . . persuaded I was the enemy of the people when, as Heaven knows, all my ambition was to promote their happiness and well-being, and make myself beloved for kind and good acts. A revolution was fomented by the Jesuits, and the good old King was dethroned and exiled. I sympathized with him in his misfortunes, and in his exile, and continue to correspond with him. The King is . . . a poet, a painter, a sculptor, and as virtuous and kind-hearted a gentleman who lives on earth.
>
> This venerable man was slandered with respect to me. I am a poor, weak, little woman. I love him as I would love a father . . . He was my friend, and while I live I shall be his friend . . .
>
> I hope that my simple story, told in my own poor way, will be believed by the American gentlemen and ladies. It is true as I live. I am not the wicked woman you have been told. I have never harmed any one knowingly. I am not the enemy of a single human being living . . .
>
> . . . I know I have erred in life, often and again— who has not? I have been vain, frivolous, ambitious— proud; but never cruel, never unkind . . . I appeal to a liberal press, and to the intelligent gentlemen who control it, to aid me in my exertions to regain the means of an honorable livelihood.

Attentively,

Lola Montez,

Countess of Landsfeld

Nearly all of Lola's claims were lies, but for the first time she acknowledged publicly that her pride, ambition, and frivolity had caused her serious problems. With this letter, she managed to blot out her notorious reputation and win the affection of many American women who identified with her way of thinking.

Though Lola had been warmly received by the New York public, she was worried about her future. She knew she couldn't compete with the young dancers who showed off their long legs on the Broadway stages. When she looked at herself in the mirror before bed at night, she saw a thinner, more angular face, but her eyes sparkled as brightly as ever. The countess knew how to make the most of her beauty; she pampered her complexion with masks and rosewater facial tonics; darkened her long, lush lashes; and used ground orris root to whiten her teeth. She took special care of her long, thick, wavy hair, which she brushed frequently and washed with an egg-white shampoo. Hot baths with oils and flower essences were also part of her beauty routine. "The passing years are unforgiving. I've lived a life of excess, I've lived intensely and loved passionately. How many women I know can say as much?" she mused.

The light comedies that Smith had adapted worked well, but they did not show her to be a great artist. Beauty and seductive poses alone weren't enough, so she decided she would have to triumph as an actress, presenting her own life onstage. "I will turn my life into a spectacle of love, passion, adventure, and power, and America will be forced to recognize my talent," she told herself, dreaming of emulating the great actresses of the era.

Before leaving New York to begin her American tour, Lola met Charles Ware, a young playwright introduced to her by Mr. Bennett.

The countess commissioned a theatrical adaptation of the memoir she'd published in *Le pays* and asked that he respect the original text and dialogue because, she claimed, they were "an exact reproduction of her adventures and misadventures in the Bavarian court."

In mid-January 1852, Lola and her company began a long tour through major East Coast cities. Heavy snow made travel difficult; trains were canceled and traveling by stagecoach was dangerous. Their first stop was Philadelphia, where they had a successful opening at the Walnut Street Theatre, one of the country's oldest. Their reception was similar to that in New York, and the week-long engagement was extended to two. When the dancer went to a local photography studio to pose for a portrait, she crossed paths there with a delegation of chiefs from the Cheyenne, Sioux, and Arapaho tribes who were returning home after an audience in Washington with the Great Father, then president Millard Fillmore. Lola was so struck by their dramatic feather adornments and solemn faces that she insisted that Alights-on-a-Cloud pose with her. The *New York Herald* swiftly published the image of them arm in arm, insinuating that the Native American chief had proposed making her the "queen" of his tribe. The newspaper was forced to issue a correction, but once again Lola had defied convention. The photograph was considered provocative and reinforced her reputation as an intrepid adventurer. Lola said farewell to Philadelphia by participating in a benefit performance for local firefighters. Her generosity was much applauded, and in gratitude the city authorities gave "this distinguished artist of worldwide renown" a portrait medallion of President George Washington.

The dancer returned briefly to New York before continuing on to Washington, DC. The newspapers reported that Lola Montez had earned $16,000 from her performances, a remarkable sum given that a professional earned less than $500 a year. In the nation's capital, where she spent a week, she had the privilege of visiting the halls of Congress, and one of her gallant hosts took her for a ride through the city in his elegant carriage. Next she traveled to Richmond, where she gave three performances before a packed house that included the governor of Virginia and other notable political figures. Lola's popularity was reinforced by her habit in interviews of offering opinions on controversial political topics such as abolition and women's suffrage, which she considered unfinished business for such a freedom-loving society.

The tour continued with full houses, rapturous critics, and the occasional scandal that helped the artist get even more publicity. One of her best-known encounters occurred as she traveled to Boston by train. Comfortably ensconced, Lola lit a cigarette while contemplating the passing landscape. A ticket collector approached and said, "Ma'am, you can't smoke here." With a mischievous smile, she replied, "But you see I can," then blew a mouthful of smoke in his face. The stunned young man complained to his supervisor, but nobody dared disturb her further; she continued smoking for the rest of the trip, to the horror of the other ladies sharing her car. When she reached Boston, knowing that the local papers would report on the incident, Lola headed to a photography studio, where she posed defiantly with a cigarette between her fingers. She did not imagine at the time that this image would go down in history. It is one of the earliest extant photographs of a woman smoking.

Lola enjoyed being provocative, but not everybody tolerated her behavior. In Boston, she was received by some of the city's most prominent figures, who accompanied her on a tour of the principal monuments and educational institutions. Among her kindly hosts was a rich businessman who invited her to visit Boston's public schools, which had a stellar reputation. At the Wells School, an academy for girls, the principal introduced the Countess of Landsfeld to the students in one class, and the artist sat chatting with them for a while. This set off a wave of indignation among the more conservative sectors of Boston society, with some demanding, "Why should innocent little girls be corrupted by a woman of dubious morals?"

The next day, as she had breakfast and perused the local press, Lola couldn't believe the responses to the visit, which spoke of a "notorious person in the public schools" and "dishonor and shame" in the classrooms. Once more she was running up against the puritanism she so reviled, and she was amused to discover that her harmless chat with students had managed to draw more attention than debates over legislation that would establish dry laws in the country.

As usual, she became embroiled in a dispute with the media, firing off a letter to the editor of the *Boston Daily Evening Transcript* in which she accused him of attacking her merely for being a beautiful, ambitious, independent woman.

After four months of successful touring, she returned to New York, where she rented a lovely mansion on Waverly Place. She was tired of staying in hotels and longed to have her own home, where she could entertain friends and admirers. The well-appointed two-story residence reminded her of her house in Munich. Now she wanted only to rest and recover from the draining tour. Her fondest dream became to debut in the play about her life, *Lola Montez in Bavaria*. Though she knew she wasn't a great dancer, critics had always pointed out her dramatic talent and compelling stage presence. She was eager to read the theatrical adaptation of her memoir. With the manuscript in hand, she shut herself in her room and asked not to be disturbed. But after leafing through the pages, she concluded that the writer had altered her entire life. Lola made an appointment with him the next day.

"Mr. Ware, I do not doubt your abilities, but I am disappointed," she said, upset. "I do not recognize myself in these pages."

"Ma'am, allow me to say that your fame the world over is due to your relationship with King Ludwig I of Bavaria. You are a legend, and your name, Lola Montez, is synonymous with scandal, debauchery, misfortune, luxury, audacity, and power," he replied. "I have written a play that shows all of those facets."

"Yes, you are right," Lola said, "but remember, it is a historical drama based on real events. It is not believable to present me as a woman who lashes ministers and governors with her whip or sets off a revolution to save the country from her enemies. In addition, you make the king of Bavaria seem like my puppet. I cannot allow it. If he ever found out, it would break his heart."

"I beg of you to review the text again with some distance; you will see that I have merely adapted your manuscript to the taste of the American public. This play is conceived as a great spectacle, with many different actors and sets. It has to be nimble and entertaining. I am sure it will be a huge success."

Lola knew that Mr. Ware was right: if she wanted to truly win over the public, she needed to go all out. The writer had divided the play into the five stages of her time in Bavaria: "The Dancer," "The Politician," "The Countess," "The Revolutionary," and "The Fugitive." King Ludwig sees Lola Montez dance and is bewitched by the beautiful and sophisticated "Moor." The dancer, seeing that the king is old and easily deceived, warns him to watch out for his minister of the interior, Abel, who is allied with the Jesuits and has the Bavarian people under his thumb. Grateful, the king names Lola countess and invites her to live in the palace. As a sensible and decent lady, she refuses, whereupon Ludwig gives her a beautiful palace and visits her daily. Lola spends her days giving His Majesty sage advice and pushing for the release of political prisoners. This angers the kingdom's Jesuit ministers, who plan a coup. Ludwig learns of the plot and sacks his entire government. On the dancer's advice, the king asks the people of Munich to choose their representatives. The Jesuits then attempt to poison the Countess of Landsfeld, whereupon civil war is unleashed and she is rescued from the barricades by a group of Bavarian students who help her flee the capital. The play ends with the young men carrying the Countess of Landsfeld on their shoulders to the tune of "La Marseillaise" and shouting, "Lola and liberty!"

The next day, she went to visit Thomas Barry, who was eager to present the world premiere of *Lola Montez in Bavaria*. The news of the Countess of Landsfeld's first venture into acting had sparked great interest. It was an audacious idea: the first performance of a historical work in which the protagonist would play herself. Mrs. Montez had been a disappointment as a dancer, but there was no question she was a stage animal.

"My dear countess!" Barry exclaimed. "I am delighted to see you again. I know your tour has been a huge success and received positive reviews despite the occasional scandal."

"I assure you it was no pleasure jaunt," Lola said, her face serious. "Bedbugs and Bibles have been my ever-present companions in hotels up and down the coast. But now I want to focus on my career as an actress. I would like to make some changes to the script—I am not satisfied with it."

"Of course, but I should tell you that I have read it too, and I couldn't stop laughing. It is a very amusing comedy, and you will be wonderful. We will open at the end of the month, and there isn't much time for edits. I have put all on the line for you; it's an ambitious production, with five set changes, wardrobe, and a cast of more than thirty."

"Yes, but I was expecting a dramatic play, and everything seems very artificial and caricatured," Lola objected. "What's more, there's hardly any time to rehearse, and I need to try on my wardrobe. I refuse to go onstage unprepared."

"Mrs. Montez, it seems to me you are a woman who never gives up, am I right? Well, then, you need to make this work. There's no time to lose. We'll kick off a massive publicity campaign that is sure to draw a large audience. With regard to the rest of the cast, they will include the finest actors: H. J. Conway will be Minister von Abel, and I myself will play King Ludwig. We are the same age, and I think I even bear him a passing resemblance."

"My good and loyal friend the king of Bavaria," Lola retorted, "is a handsome, well-educated, and generous man. He does not resemble you in the slightest. Good afternoon, Mr. Barry."

Across the ocean, the real King Ludwig was leading a tranquil life, far removed from Broadway. Though he and Lola no longer exchanged letters, he was well aware of her adventures in the United States. The monarch still got reports from Ambassador von Wendland, which included clippings from the American press. In a letter, the king thanked the diplomat for keeping him up to date on his friend and fretted that Lola would squander all her earnings:

> I see that she gets in as many fights in the New World as she did in the Old. She finds no peace in either. Let me know if and when she returns to Paris. It would be better for her to stay in the fourth or fifth continent. It is not the artfulness of her dancing but the memories of her stay in Bavaria that bring her so much income, but I fear that unfortunately she won't be bringing much of it with her when she crosses the sea again, desirable though that would be since she should invest her profits well. Money slips through her fingers, and she is accustomed to living surrounded by pomp and luxury.

That spring, the king received an unexpected letter from Auguste Papon, whom he had not heard from since the grifter had been deported to France. Ludwig worried that Papon would try to extort money from him again, but he found the man quite changed. Papon was now known as Brother Antoine and had entered a Dominican monastery in Flavigny-sur-Ozerain. Remorseful, the monk informed the king that he had returned all the letters remaining in his possession to Ambassador von Wendland in Paris. Ludwig thanked Brother Antoine. His beloved Lola was part of the past now, and nothing bound him to her. The voluminous correspondence that he kept in a locked chest was just the memory of a late-blooming passion and a few happy years in which he had briefly become young again.

In late May 1852, Lola returned to the stage on Broadway, this time not as a dancer but as the heroine of her own life story. Tickets had sold out, and the first row was occupied by celebrities, critics, and eager journalists. The previous days had been a frenzy. Feeling insecure, she'd had the seamstress alter her costume three times. The stunning gown in which, in a dramatic reenactment of an event that never took place in real life, she was presented in court to Queen Therese had been chosen because it looked "old-fashioned and more fitting to the court of Versailles." When the house lights went out and the curtain lifted, Lola appeared in the middle of a sumptuous set that recreated the interior of the Munich opera house. She was radiant in white and blue—the colors of Bavaria—and surrounded by a group of elegant gentlemen in tuxedos who applauded her performance. Thomas Barry had managed to turn the Countess of Landsfeld's struggle against tyranny and despotism into a huge spectacle. The staging was impeccable, the sets very realistic, and the principal actress's wardrobe worthy of a great star. At the end of the final act, the audience gave her a lengthy standing ovation. Lola had to come out five times to bow and pick up the flowers being thrown onto the stage. The scenes in which she took a whip to the Jesuit ministers caused a furor and more than one guffaw.

The play's Broadway run was only four nights. The New York press was generally favorable, and some critics even wrote that she should give up dancing and take up acting instead. They all agreed that her diction wasn't very good—she had a weak voice and a strange accent—but her personality was irresistible.

Lola packed her bags and, along with her maid and the choreographer Smith, prepared to travel the East Coast by train with her new show. Two days later, she arrived in Philadelphia, where her name appeared in lights on the facade of the Walnut Street Theatre. She was no longer unknown in the city, and her visit excited great anticipation.

Lola Montez in Bavaria was set to open with a completely new cast, except for the star. The countess found it inconceivable that the local companies could produce a play like hers, with five acts and thirty-four characters, with just two days of rehearsal. Lola expressed her reservations to Smith, fearing that the other actors and the staging wouldn't be up to snuff. The choreographer tried to reassure her: "Mrs. Montez, it's the usual thing here in America. Don't worry, most are experienced artists, and the rehearsal aides do their jobs very well. The audience will have the last word, and you'll win them entirely."

Though *Lola Montez in Bavaria* sold out for its week-long run in Philadelphia, opinions were starkly divided. An anonymous writer for the *Sunday Dispatch* gave it a devastating review. He acknowledged that the Spanish lady was a decent actress but said that the show was dull and its plot absurd. Lola knew by now that she inspired hatred and passion alike. Though she often responded to attacks with lengthy letters to newspaper editors, this time she refrained. "I won't lower myself and respond to a man who conceals his identity. The people of Philadelphia have shown me their affection, and that is enough," she thought as she angrily ripped up the paper.

After leaving Philadelphia, the countess returned to Washington, where her play was booked for six nights at the National Theatre. Once again the house was packed and the reviews were fairly good. "There was no straining after stage effect—no mannerisms—all was natural and easy. Her voice is not agreeable, but her acting is good," a local critic wrote. By the end of the week, Lola Montez's infamous reputation had evaporated. Now women constituted the largest share of the audience, loving her comical and mischievous "Spider Dance."

When she reached Baltimore, she learned that a theater near the one where she would be performing was putting on *Lola Montez; or, A Countess for an Hour.* Coyne's play was still enjoying immense success in the English-speaking world. Far from being bothered, she thought it could be a good publicity opportunity. When a journalist asked if she was unhappy to be competing with another work based on her life, Lola, with her usual aplomb, replied, "Not at all, I'm delighted. People can choose between seeing the real Countess of Landsfeld act, or an 'interloper' portraying her life. I believe they will prefer the original."

In Baltimore, as usual, the artist engaged in a spat that would then be described breathlessly in all the papers. To draw a larger audience on the final two nights, she decided to perform an energetic bolero, playing the castanets as accompaniment. This improvisation annoyed her choreographer greatly and made their already testy relationship worse. Smith was tired of his star's whims and volatile moods; she was becoming ever more eccentric and unpredictable.

One day he couldn't take it anymore. "Mrs. Montez, I am this company's choreographer. If you wanted to make a change, you should have talked to me about it."

"My dear," Lola explained, "you don't understand. A lot of the people who come to see my play want to see me dance, and I can't disappoint them. I have tried to make my character more compelling, and I think my bolero was very well received."

"No, it's time somebody told you the truth," he replied, furious. "You're a mediocre dancer, but you're quite good at scandalizing audiences and titillating them with your provocative poses. I have worked with the greatest divas of dance, and I assure you that none of them gave me as many headaches as you do."

"Well, if I'm just a mediocre dancer to you, Mr. Smith, we would do better to part ways as soon as possible."

The six-day engagement in Baltimore had to be cut short because of another confrontation with her dance master. Lola had learned that Mr. Smith was going around saying that she wasn't fulfilling her professional commitments and that she wasn't a serious artist. When she crossed paths with him just as she was about to go onstage, she slapped him soundly. The choreographer reared back in surprise, swearing he would never work with her again and shouting that she was over the hill. A few seconds later, the curtain rose and Mrs. Montez behaved as if nothing had happened. The final performance scheduled for the next night was canceled without explanation, though news of Lola's fury raced through the city.

On June 18, 1852, Lola Montez and George Washington Smith parted ways for good. The countess had just fired one of the most talented artists in the country and would soon regret it. The choreographer, offended and humiliated, went to the press to denounce the Countess of Landsfeld's savage behavior and lack of professionalism, which did nothing to counter her image as a difficult artist. A year later, Smith began working as *partenaire* to the dancer Pepita Soto, whom Lola considered her most direct rival. Soto, a beautiful young woman with black eyes and wild curly hair, could legitimately claim to have been born into an aristocratic family in Seville. She was the first Spanish dancer to find success on American stages. She had arrived in New York that year and, after her debut at Niblo's Garden, had taken her repertoire of popular dances such as the cachucha, the zapateado, and the jaleo up and down the East Coast, wowing audiences with her exotic beauty and authentic art. Critics dubbed her "the Andalusian Taglioni," and Lola avoided talking about her in interviews because she knew she couldn't compete with Soto's talent.

At the end of the month, Lola Montez was back in New York. She had received word that the well-known British businessman and actor Thomas Hamblin had just renovated the Bowery Theatre. It had an elegant neoclassical facade and was one of the largest in the city. Opened in 1826 as the New York Theatre, it was the first to have gas lighting and originally offered high-caliber performances of ballet, opera, and drama. But after the theater suffered several fires and lowered its ticket price to twelve cents, the programming had become coarser, featuring animal circuses, comedians, and minstrel shows. Having carried out a costly remodel, Hamblin needed to win back the public and return the theater to its former glory. As he saw it, *Lola Montez in Bavaria* would be the perfect show to draw a more sophisticated audience. His intuition was correct.

June 28 was an unforgettable night for the Bowery. The house was packed to the rafters, and Lola Montez earned more than $1,000 in the first week alone. She was very satisfied, but accustomed as she was to the refinement of European theaters, she found the atmosphere too popular for her taste. The audience sat on long, backless benches rather than in seats. They were mostly male and uneducated. If the performance bored them, they would start hurling peanut shells at one another and at the actors. The youngest of them, crammed into the balcony, sat with their feet dangling and tossed coins at the stage. Lola, who could win over the most difficult audiences, responded to any provocation, and the jeers almost always gave way to thunderous applause.

Now that summer had arrived, the artist was able to take a well-deserved vacation. Most of the theaters were closed and the heat was suffocating, so she decided to spend a few days in the Catskills. She felt exhausted and had lost weight. A journalist trailing her reported that she enjoyed "climbing precipices, fording the streams, and skipping about the rocks." People were struck by her indomitable personality and strength. Almost every day she would go out riding in the nearby woods and was still a skilled horsewoman. She liked walking, and whenever she decided to climb to the top of a hill, her young maid was unable to keep up. The clean air and rest did her a world of good, and in late August she returned to the city with her energy restored.

Lola began preparing to continue her successful East Coast tour. Over the next few months, she performed again in Boston with *Lola Montez in Bavaria*, and in Philadelphia she opened on October 11 with the "Spider Dance" at the legendary Chestnut Street Theatre before an audience of two thousand. The dance that had made her famous in Europe offended the most conservative members of the public. The critic from the *Daily Pennsylvanian* angrily opined, "The manager of the Chestnut has, during the week, been engaged in the experiment of endeavoring to ascertain how much indecency the public will stand without hissing a performer off the stage." He also noted with horror that "some persons did hiss in the upper part of the theater and the danseuse, with raised finger, defied them."

Reading the reviews, Lola flew into a rage. It was true that, depending on the city and the audience, she bared more or less of her legs. But the dance was never indecent or obscene. The countess wrote the newspaper editor a lengthy letter in which, among other points, she claimed that she had performed the dance before every court in Europe and that she had executed it in the Spanish style, energetic and somewhat impish, as was usual among the women of southern Spain. This review in the *Daily Pennsylvanian* gave her a great deal of publicity, and audiences at her subsequent performances always shouted one request: "The spider! The spider!"

The artist arrived in New Orleans on December 30. She had made a lot of money, and her star was rising in the United States. Her new agent, John Jones, had encouraged her to perform in the south. Lola looked down on the short, portly man, but he knew the business well. He was indefatigable and loquacious, and he knew how to handle wily impresarios. From the start he warned her that the competition in New Orleans was stiff. Dubbed "Little Paris," the city contained a great variety of theaters where prominent artists from all over the world performed. Lola saw it as a challenge to triumph in the place where Fanny Elssler had drawn historic crowds. Smith, who had been part of Elssler's company at the time, had witnessed the furor she'd caused, which verged on hysteria. Some paid as much as $500 to see her perform, and President Martin Van Buren invited her to the White House. Lola knew these tales and dreamed of achieving such fame. "It's not easy to stand out here, Mrs. Montez, but with your legend, beauty, and audacity, you will win over the natives," Jones reassured her.

When the steamship pulled into the port city, she took comfort in the lush vegetation on its banks and the festive air at the docks.

After a cold winter in New York, she was grateful for the humidity and blinding sun. The countess checked in at the Verandah Hotel, where the manager rolled out the red carpet and asked her to sign the book of his most celebrated guests. Lola was tired and wanted to gather her strength. Though the December heat was mild, she was suffering from migraines again. Her spacious room overlooked a courtyard full of tropical plants. The birdsong and the flowers' intoxicating fragrances brought back memories of Calcutta. As she lay in the canopy bed under a gauzy mosquito net, she thought she heard the sweet voice of her ayah, Denali, singing lullabies.

From the start the countess was drawn to this city inhabited by Latinos, Africans, and Europeans. Its rows of pastel-painted houses adorned with wrought iron balconies recalled its rich French and Spanish heritage. Floods were frequent, and yellow fever outbreaks tore through the population; but its privileged position at the mouth of the great Mississippi drew men and women seeking their fortunes. New Orleans also had a more sinister face. Thousands of black slaves toiled in brutal conditions on its sugarcane, tobacco, and cotton plantations. The sight of those men, women, and children tied together in a row by their hands and feet, waiting to be sold to the highest bidder, made a powerful impression on Lola.

"Ma'am, if you would like to visit our slave market, I will accompany you myself," the hotel manager told her. "It's a lively place."

"It's a deplorable business and I only hope that the abolitionists win their fight," Lola retorted, a look of outrage on her face. "It is unworthy of a great country such as the United States."

"Do not be shocked, Mrs. Montez," the manager said. "Slavery has existed in all great civilizations. This city has prospered thanks to cotton and slaves, there is no question."

That evening Lola went to visit Thomas Placide, director of the Varieties Theatre. There was no time to waste; the local company had to memorize their roles in just four days. To her satisfaction, tickets for opening night, set for January 3, were sold out, but Placide was calling for a number of changes. "Mrs. Montez," he suggested, "you will need to adjust to meet the audience. People here are conservative and Catholic, and the attack on the Jesuits will not go over well. You must cut that scene and be respectful about religious matters." When the director invited her to visit the theater, she was very disappointed. Her agent had told her that it was the most beautiful venue in Louisiana, but she found it quite modest compared to New Orleans's St. Charles Theatre.

Upon returning to the hotel, Lola had her first fight with her new agent, who would not last any longer than previous ones.

"Mr. Jones, I just visited the Varieties Theatre. No doubt it is very popular, but I do not believe it is the right place to present *Lola Montez in Bavaria*. I would like to know why we're not opening at the St. Charles before four thousand spectators. Am I not Fanny Elssler's equal?"

"Mrs. Montez, engagements with American theaters are set months in advance, and your show came out of nowhere. The St. Charles and the Orleans both have their seasons fully booked. Furthermore, I have to be honest—theater owners are leery of you. You introduce changes at the last minute, you fired your choreographer, and you never like your wardrobe. You aren't an easy performer."

"I'll remind you, Mr. Jones, that I pay you to arrange the best contracts with the country's most important theaters. If you wish to continue working with me, I suggest you be more selective."

On January 3, Lola debuted at the Varieties Theatre with *Lola Montez in Bavaria* before an enthusiastic audience that had paid double the usual price for their tickets. The artist was a better negotiator than her agent, and she'd managed to secure an increased share of the profits. The house was packed, and to her surprise most in the audience were women. At the end she received protracted applause, and the stage filled with bouquets. The actress offered a few appreciative words of thanks and withdrew. But the next night did not go as well. During the first act, a group of men began talking and laughing loudly. Lola signaled for the music to stop and turned to address the public: "Ladies and gentlemen, I am truly delighted to perform for you, but if there is a conspiracy against me, I will retire." A deathly silence fell over the hall, the gentlemen gestured apologetically, and the show went on without further interruptions.

When Thomas Placide heard what had happened, he had her summoned to his office. With a fatherly tone, he first congratulated her for her successful debut and then said, "Mrs. Montez, I am not certain whether it is customary in European theaters for an actress to interrupt a show because somebody is talking. Here it is unheard of. This is the first time such a thing has happened in my venue. My actors are used to people even throwing eggs or vegetables, and because they are professionals, they keep the show going."

"I'm sorry, but as the leading lady, I cannot allow people to disrespect me, and my colleagues shouldn't accept it either," she said, indignant. "I am not used to such vulgar people."

"My dear lady, I'm sorry the Varieties public isn't up to your standards, but let me tell you a story. Once, the brilliant William Macready was playing *Macbeth* at Astor Place in New York when somebody threw a chair at the stage and it fell just a few inches shy of him. Without missing a beat, he continued the performance, and it was one of his greatest successes. That's exactly what you should do: just act, that's all."

"Mr. Placide, you have no business giving me orders. If you don't like my behavior, I will find another venue. There are plenty of theaters to choose from in New Orleans." She stalked out of the office.

Despite the incident, which was all the city's performers could talk about, the reviews were good. Most, like the one published in the *Courrier de la Louisiane*, noted that her acting was "free, easy, and offhand, unlike the histrionic style of most actresses." During the second week of the run, she decided to round out the performance with her famous "Spider Dance." Upon arriving in New Orleans, she'd arranged for dozens of small spiders to be made from whale baleen and rubber, so flexible that they seemed real. Lola strategically placed the arachnids in her petticoats, bodice, and long hair and caught them one by one with a look of increasing surprise and panic, accompanied by a catchy melody. Her sometimes exaggerated pantomime provoked howls of laughter from the audience.

Audiences loved the "Spider Dance," and the tickets for all the performances sold out. Nobody was scandalized, and everybody, men and women alike, demanded an encore. Lola decided to expand her acting repertoire. She starred in *Maritana; or, The Maid of Saragossa*, written especially for her and inspired by Napoleon's siege of the Spanish city. In it, she played a Spanish girl who disguised herself as a soldier to fight in her cowardly lover's place. The countess also performed her first comic role, Lady Teazle in Sheridan's classic *The School for Scandal*. Critics hailed her grace and expressiveness and predicted a brilliant future for her as a "queen" of comedy.

Though Mr. Placide would personally have loved to see the back of the combative star, he extended her engagement at the Varieties Theatre to four weeks. Lola demanded astronomically high compensation, but her name was synonymous with success. It was her longest run at a theater in her artistic career. When on the night of January 30, 1853, she said goodbye to her audience with a bow and tears in her eyes, Lola Montez had performed for "twenty-eight evenings in five plays and five dances." Offers were piling up on her desk, and the Orleans Theatre, the only one in the country that had its own French opera company, proposed booking her for two performances of her Andalusian dances.

But an article in the *New York Daily Times* forced her to cancel a number of commitments. In the current events section, she read that George Trafford Heald had drowned off the coast of Lisbon, Portugal, when the boat he was sailing foundered in the ocean. Lola was very upset by her ex-husband's premature death and canceled her performances for a few days so she could be alone. George had truly loved her, having been forced to resign as an army officer and stand against his entire family because of her. Now she regretted having been so mean to him. Deep down she had fond memories of George and sometimes still used his name, signing documents as "Marie de Landsfeld Heald." But a few weeks later, Lola read a belated retraction of the sad news. One journalist, in a jeering tone, noted that Mr. Heald was alive and kicking and quipped, "I trust that Lola Montez will bear the disappointment with creditable fortitude."

Lola now became tangled in a new conflict. The performer had been under the weather for several days. She had taken to her bed because of a recurrence of malarial fever, and the inactivity, combined with the "humiliating" debunking of the news of Mr. Heald's death, shattered her nerves. Visibly agitated, she used drops of laudanum to sleep at night. Ellen, her maid, had endured Lola's foul mood for weeks, but her patience had run out. The girl took advantage of her mistress's convalescence to tell her she was leaving. She also reminded her that she'd signed a six-month contract with the promise that her return travel home would be paid. She had fallen in love with a handsome Creole and had decided to settle down in New Orleans. Lola calmly listened to her maid, but when the girl demanded the money for a return ticket to New York, she lost her composure. She leaped out of bed in a rage, called Ellen a thief, and started hitting her. The maid fled the room and immediately went to the police to accuse Lola of abuse. "I thought she was going to kill me," she said, sobbing. "She went completely mad. My mistress isn't in her right mind."

Two police officers went to the hotel with an arrest warrant. They had been warned about the countess's aggressive nature and were surprised to find a well-dressed, attractive woman who seemed eager to cooperate. But when the officers asked her to accompany them to the station, Lola's friendly expression changed. With a wrathful look in her eye and brandishing a knife, she exclaimed, "Sirs, if you dare detain me, rest assured I will defend myself."

One of the policemen managed to distract her, while the other grabbed her by the arms and wrested the weapon from her grasp. Lola, kicking and biting, tried to break free. She caused such a commotion that some of her friends rushed up from the lobby to try to calm her and persuade the officers to let her go. When they released her, she melodramatically snatched up a small bottle from her table and drank it, crying, "It's poison. I swear I'll never have to suffer such humiliation again." Then she fell to the floor in a swoon.

The room gradually filled with people; some raced off to find an antidote, others attempted to revive her, and a small group of hotel guests berated the policemen for the brutal treatment that had driven a good, noble woman to go so far as to take her own life. Amid the chaos, Lola came to and sat in an armchair, where she lit a cigarette. Moments later, she fainted again. In the end, the officers withdrew without carrying out the arrest, and Lola miraculously survived the poison. Her acting had been most believable. After the uproar, she took the night off "to recover from the brutal assault."

A week later, Lola had already forgotten about her maid and was ready to head to her next engagement, in Cincinnati. Aboard the *Eclipse*, the largest steamboat at the time, she traveled up the Mississippi. She arrived at her destination on February 26 and, after three days of rehearsals with the local company, debuted *Lola Montez in Bavaria* at the National Theater. The comedy enjoyed enormous critical and popular success. The city had a significant community of German immigrants, and Lola had been worried they'd accuse her of distorting Bavarian history. Indeed, the critic from the German newspaper *Der Deutsche Republicaner* declared the work a poorly written bit of drivel that gave Americans a ridiculous portrait of the customs and dress of a German court. Still, Lola charmed him, and he called her performance "masterful acting":

> Up to now we could never fathom how it was possible
> for her to achieve such limitless influence over King
> Ludwig, who otherwise was never mild or malleable.
> Now, since she worked her witchery before us on the
> stage, we are fully convinced that poor Louis could
> not have mounted any resistance. Her expressions
> and gestures were completely admirable, she often
> reminded us of Miss Rachel [Félix], who is accepted
> as an unattainable model in this area . . . Her pronun-
> ciation is pure and correct, the audience misses not
> a syllable; that ugly modulation and vibration of the
> voice, that quaking and shrieking that is constantly
> encountered with American actresses is totally alien to
> her, and in this respect she presented a most positive
> contrast with the other ladies in the cast.

Lola stayed in Cincinnati for two weeks, playing to a sold-out house and an increasing proportion of women. She acquired a new agent, Jonathan Henning, a twenty-five-year-old telegraphist whom she hired more for his looks than for his experience. In early April, she returned with him to New Orleans, where she became embroiled in yet another legal incident.

The Varieties Theatre was holding a benefit gala for actors, and Thomas Placide did not invite Lola to participate. But the countess managed to charm the security guard to let her in through a rear door. She stood in the wings watching the performances and waving to her peers. This was common practice among performers, but Lola was unaware that it was prohibited at the Varieties. When the company's elderly curtain-raiser and prompter, George T. Rowe, told her that she had no business there, Lola bristled and started slapping him with her glove while demanding that Henning come to her aid, yelling, "If you're a real man, give him what he deserves!" The young man seized Rowe by his neckerchief and started strangling him. Several spectators had to separate them, and calm was restored when police arrived.

The next morning, Rowe signed a sworn statement accusing the countess and her agent of violent aggression. Upon learning of the charges against her, the artist and a small entourage of admirers appeared in the courtroom. After offering some grandiloquent words in her own defense, Lola accused Rowe of the same charges. The hearing set for April 14 piqued citizens' curiosity. Starting early in the morning, a crowd gathered to enjoy the spectacle. This famously "wild and shameless" artist was guaranteed entertainment.

But they would have to wait. Henning told the judge that the countess was very ill and they were requesting a continuance. The prosecutor refused and sent some officers to her hotel. After some time, Lola Montez arrived, looking stunning. As usual, when it came time to appear in court, she had taken great care with her image and acted like a great lady. She knew that the press would be watching her every move, and she did not disappoint. As a local reporter commented:

> She was neatly dressed in a skirt of straw-colored China glass linen, a black mantilla of Canton crepe, a Tuscan bonnet, smothered in the richest lace, and a white lace veil, star-besprent, that waved at her slightest breath, and like the mists of her own dear and purple Cyreness but half concealed while it adorned a finely chiseled and classic head.
>
>   . . . The target of a thousand eyes, and stared at worse than the zeuglodon, or any other monstrosity, her wit and self-possession did not forsake her. Seeing what a full house she was drawing, she naively remarked that the officers of the law had made a great mistake in not having tickets of admission at two dollars a head.

The artist was the absolute star of the show, and the public applauded her every remark. Even the judge was unable to hold back a smile at her impertinent wit. Rowe once more identified the dancer and her agent as his aggressors, and Lola retaliated by accusing him of having started the fight by kicking her in the shin. Looking at the jury, she noted that he was a violent man of few charms and that he'd made several dishonorable propositions. Her new maid, Josephine, then took the stand and swore that her mistress had returned home with a bruise on her leg. Lola exclaimed drolly, "I could be content to be kicked by a horse, but by an ass . . . !" Laughter and applause filled the room. A number of witnesses testified, including Placide, who admitted he hadn't seen anything and said that, when he'd been informed of the disturbance and had asked Lola to leave, she'd refused and called him "a damned liar, a damned scoundrel, and a damned thief." "And so you are!" Lola shouted, and the public dissolved into laughter once more.

Four hours into the trial, the prosecutor decided that the case should be moved to another court, and the countess's bail was set at $1,000. Lola's lawyer managed to get that cut in half, noting that Mr. Rowe "had been injured neither in hair nor hide." After handing over the money, Lola triumphantly left amid cheers. She returned to the hotel in a coach pulled by four horses, waving at her admirers.

Back in her room and more relaxed now, she acknowledged that she'd burned a lot of bridges in New Orleans. Most of the theater owners refused to book her. Her agent, Henning, urged her to look for new opportunities. "Lola, I have to be honest. You have triumphed here, everybody knows who you are, but it won't be easy to get them to engage you. But in California the theaters will fight over you. The forty-niners are looking to have a good time and are willing to pay an arm and a leg for tickets. What do you say?"

As she listened, Lola thought about the turns her life had taken. A few years earlier she'd been the shadow queen of Bavaria, and now she was about to embark for a lawless land where men sold their souls for gold. One of the most famous women in Europe, she would be performing for unrefined miners in miserable camps. Though it seemed her career was in decline, the proposal intrigued her. "Am I not an intrepid adventurer, a self-made woman unafraid of anything or anybody?" she mused, ordering Josephine to pack their bags. The gold rush excited her imagination, and Lola couldn't resist trying her fortune in the Wild West.

CHAPTER 11

Gold Rush

Lola was about to begin the most dangerous journey of her life. She had decided to take the shortest route to California from New Orleans, crossing the Panamanian isthmus. "Mrs. Montez, I wish you luck. For days you will see nothing but jungle, mud, and thousands of insects," the manager of the Verandah Hotel told her as they said goodbye. The man did not realize that the capricious artist was a seasoned traveler known for her marksmanship and her skill with a whip. She had seen her father die of cholera in India when she was just a little girl, and ever since, she'd faced her life with extraordinary courage and aplomb. Smiling, Lola shook the man's hand and replied, "My dear friend, if I told you what this lady has seen with her own eyes, you surely would not believe me."

In spring 1853 the artist embarked on the mail ship *Philadelphia*, heading toward the Panamanian coast. She was accompanied by her maid, Josephine, her dog, Flora—a gift from an admirer in New York—and her agent, Jonathan Henning. After her most recent problems with the law, her good mood had been restored and she was charming to everybody. The first part of the trip was a pleasant voyage through the crystalline waters of the Caribbean. Dolphins and whales followed the ship's wake, to the delight of the three hundred passengers aboard. After a week, they reached the bustling port of Colón, which presented a

lamentable air of grime and neglect. Every day thousands of men of
all nationalities passed through, all hungry for riches. The travelers
from the *Philadelphia* climbed onto a train, the most reliable mode of
transport to reach the Pacific coast, some fifty miles away. From there,
ships sailed for California, full of adventurers and laden with merchan-
dise. With the mass influx of settlers drawn by the gold rush, an astute
entrepreneur had decided to build a narrow-gauge railway to save those
impatient men a few weeks of travel. But the lack of resources, the
deaths of thousands of laborers from disease, and the difficulty of access
had delayed its opening.

Belching smoke, the locomotive moved slowly down the track into
the dense vegetation. Lola contemplated the dizzying cliffs and deadly
curves as they passed. For a moment she recalled the difficult ascent to
the city of Simla, when she and her husband, Lieutenant Thomas James,
had hazarded a dangerous pass in a litter carried by four Indian porters.
Midway, the train stopped abruptly in Barbacoas, a cluster of huts in the
middle of the jungle. Since construction of the bridge over the Chagres
River was not yet completed, the passengers had to continue the trip
by canoe upriver to the village of Gorgona. Muscled black oarsmen
poled the long, narrow wooden boats. Though strong currents made it
a dangerous journey, Lola had only one worry. Having heard that bandits were common in these parts, she feared for her jewels, which were
hidden in the lining of her bag. She'd been informed that the railroad
company funded a well-trained private militia that lynched robbers, but
off the train, security was not guaranteed. Even so, this was preferable
to the land route from New Orleans to San Francisco, which crossed
inhospitable deserts and where travelers in Indian territory required a
military escort.

Lola arrived in Gorgona at dusk. It was another village with a few
scattered huts, shops selling provisions, and shacks built out of planks.
Her agent, Henning, tried to secure lodging in one of the few hotels
offering shelter from mosquitoes and tropical storms. The New York

Hotel, despite its pompous name, was a modest structure with brightly painted wooden walls that offered "cleanliness, rest, and food." The owner was Mary Seacole, an intrepid mixed-race woman of Jamaican descent who, with her brother, had established two hotels on the route across Panama, capitalizing on the flood of gold hunters. This enterprising woman was renowned in the area for her abilities as a healer. In the Panamanian jungle, epidemics of cholera and dysentery wreaked havoc, and she treated the ailing with medicinal plants.

Mary had heard of the dancer, and from the start she disliked Lola's haughty bearing and demanding nature. Deeming her a troublesome woman, she refused to give her lodging. Lola, who was tired and hungry, tried to win the hotelier over.

"Mrs. Seacole, allow me to introduce myself. I am the artist Lola Montez, and I, along with my representative and my maid, am on my way to Panama City. I need two rooms; I will pay you well for them."

"Mrs. Montez," Mary responded, barely looking at her, "I know very well who you are, but I'm sorry to say my hotel is full. You will have to look for somewhere else to stay. I can offer you something to eat, if you like, but that's all."

"I'm exhausted, I need to change my clothes and take a hot bath, and my dog, Flora, also needs to rest," Lola insisted. "I beg of you to give me your best room."

"It seems you have not understood me," Mary said firmly. "No doubt you are accustomed to always getting what you want, but this is my hotel, and I'm in charge here. Women like you are not welcome. We accept only respectable ladies."

Lola ignored the insult. She was too drained to argue and wanted only to sleep for a few hours and eat a hot meal. Like most of the women travelers who made this journey, she had exchanged her fine petticoats and corsets for comfortable men's clothing. Mary Seacole recalled her jungle encounter with the Countess of Landsfeld in her memoir:

Came one day, Lola Montes, in the full zenith of her evil fame, bound for California, with a strange suite. A good-looking, bold woman, with fine, bad eyes, and a determined bearing, dressed ostentatiously in perfect male attire, with shirt-collar turned down over a velvet lapelled coat, richly worked shirt-front, black hat, French unmentionables, and natty, polished boots with spurs.

The artist had no choice but to try another hotel. Lola introduced herself to the owner as the Countess of Landsfeld and demanded a room for herself and a bed for her pet. When the man said that all the beds were occupied for the night and that he had no intention of making one of his guests sleep on the floor, Lola replied threateningly, "I don't care where or how your guests sleep, but I'd have you to know my dog has slept in palaces—get me the cot immediately, and say no more. I am very tired and frazzled." The hotelier, intimidated by her commanding tone, acceded to her demands without further objection. The next morning, when he tried to charge five dollars for Flora's bed, the dancer pulled her gun and forced him to lower the rate. She then headed cheerfully to the bar and bought a round for all the patrons.

The last leg of the Panamanian route was the one the *Philadelphia's* passengers dreaded most. They would travel twenty-five miles astride saddled mules. It was the rainy season, and the trail was nearly impassable. The animals, overloaded with the heavy trunks and provisions, struggled through the mud and scrub. Attacked by mosquitoes, the travelers tried to ignore the noises issuing from the dense vegetation. Reptiles, howler monkeys, and fearsome pumas abounded.

At last they reached Panama City, a charmless but booming city where stores, restaurants, and banks were opening and elegant brick public buildings were going up. Though Lola published a note of thanks in the local paper praising the crossing of the isthmus, she later admitted that it had been a difficult trip even for an adventurous woman like her.

The countess took a room at the Cocoa Grove Hotel, with views of a white-sand beach and palm trees. For a few days she was able to rest and forget the travails of the journey. Staying in the same hotel was a group of men who'd recently arrived from New York. Some were distinguished politicians from the administration of the newly elected President Franklin Pierce, with several journalists accompanying them. Lola struck up a conversation with the editor of the *San Francisco Whig and Commercial Advertiser*. Patrick Purdy Hull was a sturdy, good-natured twenty-nine-year-old with whom she immediately hit it off. Though he was not handsome and dressed sloppily, he had a great sense of humor and was a lively conversationalist. The artist was delighted to learn that he was on the list of passengers who would soon, like her, set sail for San Francisco.

After having faced all sorts of dangers in canoes and on muleback, traveling in the majestic Pacific Mail steamship *Northerner* was a pleasure. Though the countess found her cabin insufficient and fought with the captain to get a larger, cooler one, she was polite to the crew. During the two-week voyage, Patrick Hull kept her amused with his tales of bold pioneers and dirty jokes. At last she had found in the Americas a man who made her laugh. He wasn't sophisticated or elegant, but he was witty. Originally from Mansfield, Ohio, Hull had arrived in San Francisco in 1850 to oversee the census in California. The booming city offered many opportunities to get ahead, so he stayed and began working as a journalist. He first started the *Pacific Courier*, which lasted only five months, and later, with colleagues, founded the *San Francisco Whig*, which was more successful.

Lola, in turn, revealed a number of details about her past. She didn't hesitate to tell him about the success she'd enjoyed in Europe or to describe her friendship with the king of Bavaria. She hinted that her first marriage had been a youthful mistake and introduced herself as the widow of Mr. Heald, her last husband, though she had no proof that he was deceased. Fascinated by her seductive beauty and uninhibited nature, Hull encouraged her to do a tour through mining towns such as Sacramento, Grass Valley, Nevada City, and Marysville. The journalist was very familiar with the harsh life of the forty-niners who spent their money on booze and entertainment, their only pleasures. He was convinced that Lola could make a killing in the remote and still wild American West.

At daybreak on May 21, 1853, the *Northerner* steamed through the Golden Gate and dropped anchor in San Francisco Bay. It was a clear morning, and Lola admired the splendid beauty of the wide inlet topped by green hills. When she set foot on dry land, she found herself surrounded by people anxiously awaiting the arrival of the mail the ship was carrying in its holds. It was an unprecedented shipment, consisting of some 275 sacks of priceless letters. Many in the crowd recognized Lola Montez. The artist gave friendly answers to the questions from local reporters. The next day, the *Golden Era* noted, "The world-renowned Lola Montez, Countess of Landsfeldt, arrived in this city on the *Northerner*," and the *San Francisco Whig* announced to its readers, "Among the arrivals by the *Northerner* is Lola Montez, Countess of Landsfeldt. She comes in a quiet unobtrusive manner, and will doubtless succeed in this new field of her enterprise." The adulatory tone of this latter piece was born of the fact that the newspaper's co-owner, Patrick Hull, had fallen in love with her on the journey.

San Francisco surprised Lola; she'd imagined a wilder and more provincial place. Nothing remained of the old town of Yerba Buena, founded in 1769 by a Spanish expedition. When word of gold spread, the tiny village of five hundred had been transformed into a small city where people of every race and creed mingled. Gold seekers all passed through after having traveled halfway around the world in pursuit of fortune. There was no drainage or sewers, and cholera and dysentery thwarted the dreams of many men in their prime. The city that greeted Lola on that radiant spring morning was a lawless, vibrant settlement of fifty thousand.

She quickly secured lodging in the city's best hotel. She had not been able to confirm any engagements in advance, since the boats' schedules were unpredictable, but theater directors immediately started knocking on her door. Within a few days she'd signed an agreement to perform at the American Theatre, considered the finest venue in California, which had been recently renovated to seat up to three thousand spectators. She had to negotiate the contract herself with Lewis Baker, whose troupe performed at the theater, because her agent had quit as soon as they'd arrived. During the voyage, they'd argued about money issues and Lola mostly ignored him, busy as she was wielding her charms on the American newspaperman. Once in San Francisco, Henning had appeared at her door unexpectedly and said, "I'm quitting as your agent. I made a mistake; I'm not cut out for this kind of life, and your mood swings confound me. I'm going back to New Orleans, which I never should have left."

"No, my friend, you're not quitting; I'm firing you. Go back to your boring old job as a telegraphist—I'll show you how much I care about money," she shot back, ripping up a check for $200 in front of him.

"I'd heard a lot about you, Lola, but your behavior is quite unladylike. I wish you luck in California. You're going to need it if you don't get your arrogance and temper under control." And the young man disappeared from her life.

As usual, this incident was reported in the local press and served as publicity before her much-anticipated opening night.

Just five days after her arrival, Lola Montez debuted at the American Theatre in *The School for Scandal*, which the local company knew well and in which the Lady Teazle role was one of her favorites. It was a sensation. Tickets went for five dollars, and scalpers were able to get three times that much, a sum far higher than what the audience had paid in

New York. The reviews were fairly positive. The *Alta California* declared, "Mdlle. Lola evinced all that grace and vitality which might be expected of one who had turned the heads of princes and unmercifully scorned editors and assailants." And the *Golden Era* wrote:

> As all the world and the rest of mankind have either seen or heard tell of this extraordinary woman, we will not speak of her as her notoriety might seem to demand. Suffice it to say that Lola Montez, the artiste, the politician, the noblesse, and the "fair shoulder-striker," is among us and that her name has attracted to the American Theatre the most brilliant and over-flowing audience witnessed in this city, and who have given her talents a most unequivocal endorsement by the cordial manner in which she has been greeted. We can't say that we admire Lola's acting, but we do think her dancing is—"heavenly." Success to the Countess of Landsfeldt. She will appear again at the American tomorrow evening.

Within just two weeks, she was a celebrity. On her opening night alone, the box office took in $4,500, and she was rubbing elbows with the crème de la crème of California society. Thanks to Mr. Hull, who had become her friend and protector, the press had been following her closely since her arrival.

The artist appeared in public frequently and attended opening nights at San Francisco Hall and the Jenny Lind Theatre, which presented Shakespearean dramas, pantomimes, and operas in five languages. She also enjoyed Sundays at the racetracks. Lola was amused to learn that an admirer had named one of his spirited mares after her. The wealthy financier invited her to watch the equine Lola Montez run in a benefit race. Afterward the countess posed smiling next to the winning mare and addressed the public briefly. "Ladies and gentlemen, I am very pleased to know that this beautiful mare christened with my name has won this race. I am glad to have brought luck to these tracks and hereby take the opportunity to call for a women's horse race in San Francisco, in which I would be delighted to participate. I encourage the women in attendance here to support this initiative," she suggested, to everyone's surprise.

The people of San Francisco were eager to see the Countess of Landsfeld onstage, and she did not disappoint. Her "Spider Dance" was a sensation, but the audience's reaction left Lola confused. To her surprise, as she tried to shake the spiders out of her clothing to a frenetic tune, the men shouted, "Search a little farther up, beautiful!" "There, lower down, let's see those gorgeous legs!" Offended, the dancer stopped the show and reprimanded them harshly, but she wasn't able to shut them up; instead, they exchanged barbs with her for a good long while until Lola finally decided to continue her performance. Somebody should have informed her that in California it was common for spectators to participate in shows and that actors carried on unfazed. When Shakespeare's plays were performed on that very stage, the audience always contributed. If they had lines from the play memorized, they would recite them along with the actor; they whistled, clapped, and sang the songs.

Lola's performance received enthusiastic applause, but the reviews were harsh. An editor who had never seen the dance in person wrote that it "cannot be witnessed by a virtuous-minded woman, in the presence of the opposite sex, without the blush of shame and offended modesty upon her cheek." But one who had attended the performance replied that it was "not a whit more indelicate than stage dancing generally. Indeed, it may be said . . . that her skirts are much longer than those of other danseuses we have seen upon the theatrical boards of California."

At the end of May, the American Theatre's company was finalizing its preparations for the opening of *Lola Montez in Bavaria*, advertised as a "unique and extraordinary play based on real events." Lewis Baker had bet heavily on this massive production. Lola had brought with her an orchestra conductor, scores, play scripts, dance programs, and a personal wardrobe, but the supporting actors, sets, stage effects, orchestra, and publicity had to be funded by the theater owner. The countess did not like the attitude of some of the players, who failed to understand the play's historical context. This time her complaints were well founded: there hadn't been enough rehearsals, and some failed to memorize their parts well.

The day after opening night, Lola shut herself in her hotel room and asked not to be disturbed. Incessantly smoking cigarettes, she searched for her name in the entertainment pages. She started with the *San Francisco Daily Herald*, which had always treated her with particular respect. In a lengthy article, it informed its readers of the sold-out show at the American Theatre and noted that, although the supporting cast was not up to snuff, the leads had managed to salvage the performance. But the review in the *Alta California* was not so kind, arguing that the show had not been flattering to its star: "The play represents Lola as a coquettish, wayward, reckless woman, intent on good, it is true; but not the wily diplomatist, the able leader which she is represented in history."

Upset, Lola closed the newspaper, but she had to relent, recognizing that people wanted entertainment and spectacle. "They're right, this play is a farce, an absurd comedy that doesn't reflect the role I played in Bavarian history, nor the influence I exerted on the king," she sighed as her maid, Josephine, helped her dress. She was disappointed, but she still trusted that she would captivate the California public.

Though she had achieved fame and a fair bit of money, her run in San Francisco lasted less than three weeks. *Lola Montez in Bavaria* improved in the subsequent performances, but it drew fewer spectators each night. Nobody wanted to see her perform more than once, and they complained that the actress didn't have a more varied repertoire. Nor did her relationship with Baker help matters. By this point, he was unwilling to continue to put up with the diva, and to his disappointment, he soon discovered that, even if her dances struck some as indecent, others found them dull. One gentleman who attended one night sent a letter to the editor of the *Herald*, in which he called the play "rather prosy" and complained that "Lola takes the lion's share of the dialogue, and gives the Bavarians precious little to say for themselves."

When Baker rescinded the contract on June 8, 1853, he breathed a sigh of relief. Lola could not disguise her disappointment. Unwilling to give up, she started preparing for a long tour through the mining towns of northern California. Outside San Francisco, there were no established local companies, and taking secondary actors with her was too expensive and complicated. So she decided to travel the American West performing her fandangos, boleros, and cachuchas accompanied by a small musical ensemble. Lola selected one of the few friends she'd made during her brief time in the city. Michael Hauser, better known by his stage name, Miska, was an enormously talented Hungarian violinist who had started touring Europe and North America while still quite young. The countess had attended a private recital the musician had given in a San Francisco hotel and later had run into him again at a benefit gala. Thirty-one years old, Miska was a bohemian who loved to travel. In a letter to his brother in Vienna, he described his new friend with poetic admiration. He said that, though she was loud and unpredictable, she was also the most intelligent, courageous, and daring woman he had ever met.

Lola asked Miska to join her troupe. The violinist, entranced by the dancer's beauty and enterprising spirit, happily agreed to accompany her. The tour would begin in Sacramento, but first she had decided to marry Patrick Hull in a small ceremony. The press had spread rumors about the possible union of the celebrated Countess of Landsfeld and the young editor of the *San Francisco Whig*, but nobody knew where or when the happy event would occur.

Early on July 2, 1853, a group of friends and local personalities gathered in front of Mission Dolores's old adobe church in San Francisco. They had all received an unexpected wedding invitation the day before and came together at the appointed hour, six o'clock in the morning. Inside, waiting for the bride and groom to arrive, the attendees settled onto the wooden pews. Some time later, Lola appeared on Mr. Hull's arm, wearing a simple white linen dress decorated with lace. Her hair was pulled back in a bun with pearls. As she moved toward the altar, she turned and signaled for the church doors to be closed to keep out curiosity seekers. The bride was carrying two vases of artificial white roses in her hands, which she gave to Father Fontaine, the officiant, as an offering. After the brief ceremony, the newlyweds headed to the sacristy, where Lola signed the marriage certificate with the name Maria Dolores Eliza Rosanna Landsfeld Heald and claimed to be twenty-seven years old, five years younger than her actual age. They then offered their guests a simple reception with cake, cigars, and cigarettes. A few hours later, the small group returned to Gates House, where they'd reserved a room to rest and change clothes before starting the journey to Sacramento. There was no wedding banquet, and for breakfast Lola and Patrick went to the Tivoli, a popular restaurant, where they had fried eggs and bacon, fresh-baked bread, and coffee.

Lola told a friend that she had married Hull because he was the best storyteller she'd ever met. The real reason was a more practical one. Marrying Patrick allowed her to make a respectable exit from San Francisco's stages, where she had not obtained the success she'd hoped for. The proud bridegroom boasted to his friends about having married the most desirable woman in Europe. He enjoyed the adventure of accompanying Lola on her American tour and writing the occasional article for his newspaper.

When word of the marriage got out, some media outlets expressed doubt about how long it would last and joked about the bride's notoriety. The *Shasta Courier*, always the most disrespectful of Lola, referred to her as "this celebrated artist of unblemished 'virtue.'" After taking their leave of friends, the couple boarded the steamboat *New World*, which was heading up the narrow river to Sacramento. "My dear countess, this is the prelude to the wonderful life of adventures and deprivations that awaits us," Patrick said jokingly as he carried her over the threshold of their cabin.

The next day, they reached the port of Sacramento, which was teeming with boats from all over the world. The Hulls checked in at the Orleans, a newly opened hotel that had a bathtub and heat in every room.

Five years earlier, a fortuitous discovery in these lands had changed the course of California history. The first gold nuggets were found on the vast ranch of John Sutter, a Swiss pioneer who had arrived in California when the region still belonged to Mexico. Though he asked his men to keep the gold a secret, word spread within eight days. Very soon the "Golden Land" was being invaded by waves of people arriving from the east on foot, on horseback, or by wagon. Later they would come by the thousands from Europe, China, Australia, and Latin America.

The rough frontier settlement that had grown up around a fort and a small indigenous village was transformed overnight into the city of Sacramento, with neatly drawn streets, wooden buildings, shops, and a church. Gambling parlors, bars, restaurants, and brothels abounded. Life was not easy, and there were few creature comforts. Men strode down the streets with their pistols at their waists, murders at the hands of bandits were an everyday occurrence, and scores were settled with people's lives. Prices were astronomical, and the merchants who sold supplies and tools to the miners earned a fortune. When they arrived, Patrick took Lola to eat at a restaurant with a menu that consisted of boiled leg of grizzly bear, donkey steak, and jackrabbit. The artist tucked in eagerly, without turning up her nose, though she found the donkey meat as tough as an old boot.

Lola had acquired a new representative, James Adams, who also worked as an agent for the transport company Wells Fargo. The man had arrived a few days earlier to finalize an engagement at Sacramento's Eagle Theatre. The Countess of Landsfeld was offering a wide variety of dances, with several costume changes and musical accompaniment. But the competition was stiff because there were a lot of venues devoted to entertainment and spectacle. One of the most popular artists of 1853 was the famous Norwegian violinist Ole Bull, who brought tears to the miners' eyes with his romantic ballad "Home, Sweet Home" and was considered among the best musicians of all time.

Mr. Adams feared the lady's reaction when she saw the rough venues where she was set to perform. Nevada City's Dramatic Hall had once been a granary, and the only theater in Grass Valley was a room above a bar in which the men often became embroiled in brawls or gunfights.

"Countess, I hope you are feeling at ease. These theaters, if you can call them that, are very old and don't offer many amenities. I must admit that the Sacramento public has a reputation for being harsh, and more than one hallowed actor has been driven off the stage by a hail of eggs and vegetables."

"My dear friend, I have been in rougher places, I assure you," she said. "At this point in my life, I don't think anything could surprise me. I know there will be miners, hunters, and trappers who haven't seen a woman in months. I'm sure that they will respect me, despite their lack of refinement."

"I hope so," Mr. Adams replied dubiously. "I merely advise you not to provoke them or bore them with speeches. They work like dogs all day and are just looking to have a good time."

On opening night Sacramento buzzed with curiosity. The Eagle Theatre was a modest wooden building with a tin roof. Its stage was made of packing crates and lit with kerosene lamps. The seats were long planks propped up on beer barrels. On the tables, candles in bottles provided dim light. Fires were common, and theaters were rebuilt in a matter of weeks. Ladies could enter the Eagle via an external staircase, to avoid going through the bar, where men smoked, drank whiskey, and played cards, surrounded by scantily clad women.

Lola didn't dislike the place, merely remarking that it was the size of the drawing room in her house in Munich. She calculated that, if the tickets sold out, seventy to one hundred people could squeeze in. Luckily, nobody told her about the rats and fleas that infested the place, nor the Californians' habit of spitting on the floor. The artist performed a bolero, a traditional Bavarian dance, and a third dressed as a sailor, then closed the show with her "Spider Dance." The program's impact relied on her violinist, Miska, who amazed the audience with his virtuosity.

Lola received enormous applause and retired to her hotel quite satisfied. But the second night was different. As she was dancing a fandango, a loud laugh was heard from the spectators in the front row. Lola gestured to her conductor to stop the music and strode to the edge of the stage. With anger on her face, she exclaimed, "Ladies and gentlemen, Lola Montez has too much respect for the people of California not to perceive that this stupid laughter comes from a few silly puppies. Come up here! Give me your trousers and take my skirts. You're not fit to be called men! Lola Montez is proud to be what she is, but you don't have the courage to fight with a woman who's not afraid of you, who scorns you. Yes, this woman." The artist wanted to continue her eloquent harangue, but dozens of eggs and rotten apples began flying through the air, and she was forced to take refuge behind the curtain.

The dancer's disappearance left the audience confused and divided. Some hissed, some applauded, and others demanded their money back.

The theater manager, Charles King, announced that Lola Montez would finish her performance shortly. But as the minutes passed, people became impatient. The theater manager asked Miska Hauser to perform again and offered him one hundred dollars if he managed to calm down the audience. The violinist went onstage, and to his surprise, the jeers and shouts subsided. With great enthusiasm, he performed "The Bird on the Tree," one of his own compositions in which his violin imitated a goldfinch's song. The audience liked it so much they called for an encore. When Lola heard the applause the musician was receiving, she went onstage and started dancing with her castanets. But once again they rose up against her, and the hall became a battlefield. Benches and seats were destroyed, windowpanes were shattered, and some shouted, "Scoundrel! We've been robbed!" The manager begged the musician to continue, and Miska played another piece from his small repertoire. Finally, Lola agreed to finish the program with the "Spider Dance," just as they'd planned, which only made everything worse. As she tried to defend herself from the imaginary spiders attacking her, she moved over to a bouquet that an admirer had tossed onstage and stomped on it multiple times. People left the hall in droves.

Lola had to return to her hotel under police protection, but the evening was not over. A few hours later, several dozen people showed up outside the hotel armed with cook pots, skillets, and whistles. The artist went to the window wrapped in a silk robe and, raising her pistol, exclaimed, "You cowards, low blackguards, cringing dogs, and lazy fellows! I would not despise a dirty dog so much as I do you!"

Lola's husband asked her to step away from the window. Patrick, who had witnessed her humiliation in the theater, was very angry. He'd thought he was marrying a great artist, but she was seeming less attractive now; he even felt sorry for her. After the group dispersed, Patrick reproached her.

"That was foolish," he said. "You insulted them, stooping to their level. I told you the people of Sacramento don't take any guff. This isn't

Paris, sweetheart, it's the American West. The men are armed here; don't play with fire."

"I have no intention of getting used to being insulted and mocked," the dancer retorted. "I have never performed for such rude, unrefined people. Did you see the way they threw eggs at me and laughed in my face? How can you be so calm?"

"Lola, forget about what happened. You have to fulfill your contract. The next time you appear, apologize and look repentant; I'm sure their attitude will change, and they will applaud you the way they did on opening night."

That night, Lola had to take laudanum, which she depended on with increasing regularity, to get to sleep. She was anxious and irritated by the idea of performing for those violent, boorish men again. She felt the same anguish she'd experienced the night a frenzied crowd had gathered outside her home on Barerstrasse in Munich. Back then she hadn't been afraid to confront them, but she'd had her faithful Elias and the king himself prepared to lay down their lives for her. She thought about the advice Patrick had given her, to do whatever it took to win over Sacramento's public. She knew how to do it, and it had worked on other occasions. She would present herself as a poor misunderstood woman, frail and persecuted by her enemies, who loved the American people above all else. "They will kiss my hand, admire my talent. They don't know who Lola Montez is," she told herself.

Two days later, a poster announced that she would be performing her Spanish dances again. After the last incident, measures were taken to ensure the artist's safety. Before the performance, the city's police chief went in front of the audience and proclaimed that the first man who displayed the slightest lack of discipline would be arrested. Invitations had gone out to illustrious Sacramento residents to make sure that all went smoothly. Among them was John Sutter himself, who received an enthusiastic welcome.

Just before the curtain rose, with the house packed, the theater director went onstage and begged the audience to be so kind as to allow Lola Montez to address them. The dancer appeared, radiant, and with a serious look on her face, began to speak. "Ladies and gentlemen, there was an occurrence in this theater that I deeply regret. It is a small theater, more like a drawing room. I am very close to you, practically next to you, and the sound is not always clearly understood. I suffer from heart palpitations, and since arriving in Sacramento, I have been very affected by them, which at times makes me feel very bad. As I danced, I stomped my foot on the stage several times, and some laughed, as I supposed to insult me. I have many enemies, who have followed me from Europe and offered me insults, and I supposed that it might be some of them who had come here with that intention. I knew it could be no American, for I have been loved and cherished by Americans wherever I went." She then explained that all had been an absurd misunderstanding and that her stomping was part of her world-renowned "Spider Dance." She added that, absorbed in her role and in the frenzy of the dance, she had unwittingly crushed the bouquet. She closed in a solemn tone: "I will wipe out from my memory what occurred. It was unworthy of me, and I shall speak of it no more. Ladies and gentlemen, if you wish me to go on with my dance, just say the word and I will stay." When she had finished speaking, the audience began to applaud and shouts of "Long live Lola Montez!" and "Bravo, Lola!" rang out. The artist gave a humble bow and left the stage. She then reappeared, looking dazzling, and gave a passionate performance of all the dances on the program, including her "Spider Dance." The show was such a hit that she had to take a bow five times. Those who had accused her of being a thief just a few days earlier were now praising her. The evening was a brilliant success, and the audience, according to reviewers, "made the theater tremble to its deep foundations with the delirium of their applause."

The three remaining performances were well attended, but another incident put her name back in the papers. The *Daily Californian* accused the dancer of having given away tickets to fill up the theater. Lola replied immediately with the following letter:

> To the Responsible Editor of the *Californian*—
>
> The extraordinary article concerning myself which appeared in your paper this morning requires an extraordinary answer. I use this word "extraordinary," for I am astonished that a respectable (?) Editor should *lie* in such a barefaced manner, and be so void of gallantry and courtesy as yourself. I am a woman. I do not advocate women's rights, but at the same time I can *right* myself by inflicting a summary justice upon all jack-an *apes*!!! After such a gross insult, you must don the petticoats. I have brought some with me, which I can lend you for the occasion—you must fight with me. I leave the choice of two kinds of weapons to yourself, for I am very magnanimous. You may choose between *my* duelling pistols, or take your choice of a pill out of a pill-box. One shall be poison and the other not, and the chances are even. I request that this affair may be arranged by your seconds as soon as possible, as my time is quite as valuable as your own.
>
> Marie de Landsfeld Hull
> Lola Montez

The editor ignored her, but the letter, under the title "Pistols or Pizen," was reprinted in other papers and added a new page to the legend of Lola Montez.

After the last performance at the Eagle, which she concluded by declaring that the sun would always shine in her chest when she thought of the noble city of Sacramento, Lola and her husband made a quick trip by steamboat to San Francisco. Patrick had decided to leave his job at the paper and sell his shares of the *San Francisco Whig*. Touring took a lot of time, and his wife was demanding more and more of him. She had signed a contract with the theater in Marysville, a mining town forty miles north of Sacramento. In mid-July, Lola Montez and her entourage boarded the *Comanche*, a small riverboat built to look like the ones that plied the Mississippi, unaware that the news of her scandals in Sacramento preceded her. Her time in the tranquil mining town was even more humiliating than her second performance in Sacramento. The show ran only one weekend, and Lola was in a foul mood. The first night, she fought with the audience, who were applauding listlessly, and called them ignorant men incapable of appreciating Spanish dance. The next day, she fought with Miska, who quit in a huff. He refused to put up with her bad temper and whims any longer. Their relationship was in tatters, and he returned to Sacramento that very night.

The problems also affected her marriage. The police had to intervene in a shouting match she had with her husband in the hotel where they were staying. Lola unleashed all her fury on him, and Patrick told her she was finished as an artist. When she heard that, she lost her temper and shoved him out of the room. She then picked up his suitcases, opened the second-floor window, and hurled them into the street, to the amusement of passersby.

Though the San Francisco and Sacramento papers insinuated that Lola Montez's marriage was over, the couple was spotted a few days later, looking to be as close as ever. Having put the fight behind them, they started preparing for the next stop on her tour, Grass Valley, a picturesque mining town at the foot of the Sierra Nevada. Lola still had Charles Chenal, who had joined them in San Francisco and played the clarinet, the flute, and the piano. There was also her band leader,

Charles Eigenschenk, who served, when the occasion demanded, as a violin soloist. In the rough, remote mining camps where they were now heading, that was all she needed.

Grass Valley was less than forty miles from Marysville, but the trip by stagecoach along winding and rocky dirt roads was long and uncomfortable. The food at the stations was bad, the dust from the road filtered in through the windows, and the constant potholes tried the passengers' nerves. At dusk the stagecoach crossed the verdant valley of Wolf Creek and arrived at Grass Valley. Lola, perspiring and covered in dust, had no inkling that this place would become her home for the next two years. The arrival of any coach was a cause for commotion in town, and people crowded around to check out the new arrivals. That day their eyes were drawn to a lady who descended from the vehicle carrying a poodle in her arms. Immediately they recognized her as the world-famous Lola Montez, the woman with the scandalous past. A young reporter for the *Sacramento Union* approached for an interview. Though she was exhausted from the journey, she patiently answered all his questions.

"Mrs. Montez, what brings you to Grass Valley?"

"After my success in San Francisco, my husband urged me to do a big tour through the mining towns, and I'm sure that the inhabitants here in Grass Valley, honorable and hardworking people, will appreciate my Spanish dances."

"Won't a woman like yourself, a genuine countess who has traveled half the world, get bored in this quiet, remote place?"

"Sir, I am never bored. I am restless by nature and am always making plans. I am eager to ride horseback, explore California's mountains, and see its gold mines. And if the miners wish it, I will perform in Nevada City, Marysville, Weaverville, and wherever they summon me."

"Well then, welcome, Mrs. Montez, and congratulations on your recent marriage. We hope that Grass Valley meets all your expectations."

Grass Valley was a small community of just two thousand, with unpaved streets and rustic one- and two-story wooden buildings, canvas tents, and several sawmills. It bore no resemblance to the idyllic mining town of 1848, when the gold rush kicked off. Back then, all you had to do was pick up a sieve and shake it a little in the waters of the Sacramento River or the American River, and gleaming gold nuggets would appear. That romantic era of solitary adventurers had been left behind, and in its place, the days and nights were filled with the sound of the incessant pounding of machines pulverizing the hard rock in search of veins of the precious metal. The easy surface gold was scarce, and only very occasionally did some lucky miner stumble on a nugget that he could retire on.

The town's first restaurant, a bowling alley, a bookstore, and a brothel had opened the year Lola arrived. The only lodging, the Beatty House, offered no creature comforts. Rows of bunks lined the rooms, and there was hardly any privacy. You could sleep on simple wooden platforms for a dollar, but you had to bring your own bed linens. It wasn't a proper place for a lady, so the Hulls stayed instead in a pretty house on Mill Street, near the center of town. Known as "Gil's Cabin," it belonged to Gilmor Meredith, a bachelor friend of Patrick's who worked in San Francisco for the transport company Pacific Mail Steamship.

Anticipation about seeing Lola Montez perform was running high, and the seats quickly sold out. Miners came from all over the region to see her, happily paid the five-dollar ticket price, and stayed in town to attend the next show a few days later. The countess's first appearance was scheduled for Wednesday, July 20, 1853. Lola offered two performances in Grass Valley, at the small Alta Theater above a bar, and both drew a raucous crowd. She introduced herself only as a dancer and trusted that her sensual movements and striking costumes would captivate the audience, made up primarily of miners eager to see a beautiful woman. The artist performed her Spanish dances in the dim light of kerosene lamps. During wardrobe changes, her two musicians entertained the public with old ballads that the men sang in unison, raising their mugs of beer. But the "Spider Dance" was one of the miners' favorite numbers, and as the artist spun around trying to shake off the spiders, the spectators stomped and clapped in rhythm and shouted, "Go, Lola, you can get them!" and "Take out your whip, honey, and crush them all!"

Her spirits high, Lola and her company headed to Nevada City, another major mining camp a few miles away. This time she performed at Dramatic Hall, a modest venue located above a liquor store. The rabble who filled the room had paid double the usual ticket price, but it was worth it. For an entire week, Lola danced for these coarse, lonely fortune seekers. Many of them were ill and prone to violence and alcohol. And yet they were never disrespectful toward her. On the last night, an admirer wrote a beautiful poem for her on the back of a program, which he left on a wooden bench. It appeared in San Francisco's *Daily Herald*:

> *To Lola Montes*
> *Fair Lola!*
> *I cannot believe, as I gaze on thy face,*
> *And into thy soul-speaking eye,*
> *There rests in thy bosom one lingering trace*
> *Of a spirit the world should decry.*
> *No, Lola, no!*
> *I read in those eyes, and on that clear brow,*
> *A Spirit—a Will—it is true;*
> *I trace there a Soul—kind, loving, e'en now;*
> *But it is not a wanton I view;*
> *No, Lola, no!*
> *I will not believe thee cold, heartless and vain!*
> *Man's victim thou ever hast been!*
> *With thee rests the sorrow, on thee hangs the chain!*

Then on thee should the world cast the sin?
No, Lola, no!

Reading it, Lola could not help getting choked up. She remembered the poems that Ludwig had written to her during their stormy relationship, which initially had pleased her but later came to seem mawkish and sappy. In that moment, demoralized and on the verge of leaving the stage for good, it was flattering to discover that she could still inspire such feelings in a stranger. She had always needed to feel loved to give it her all onstage.

At the beginning of August, Lola and her husband returned to Grass Valley and moved into the cozy cabin belonging to Patrick's friend. Though they'd been trying to keep up appearances, their marriage was in crisis. She wanted to keep performing, but her career was in decline. As had occurred so often before, disappointment came after the anticipation and enthusiasm of the first performance. Most went to see her because of her voluptuous beauty and her reputation as an "immoral woman," but the miners preferred the Shakespeare plays performed by itinerant troupes. They loved the epic tragedies because their own lives were a constant struggle against the elements.

Lola was forced to cancel her next show at the Alta because the room was nearly empty; they had to refund the tickets. Instead, she offered a private performance to a dozen men who were passing through town, titillating them with her "Spider Dance." How much they paid her for this special soiree was never reported, but she apparently made out better than ever.

Patrick kept insisting that her boleros were old-fashioned and too chaste. "Lola, I know these men. Your Spanish dances are boring and always the same. People here are looking for a good time, for performers to brighten their lives and have a drink with them."

"You are speaking to your wife. I'm not just any dancer, I don't have any reason to drink with those men or sing along with their ridiculous songs. I have no intention of stooping any lower."

"Well, sweetheart, I'm afraid you can pack away your beautiful outfits in your trunk, because tonight's show has been canceled too. Not enough tickets sold." A faint smile flickered across his face.

"If that's true, then I've made a decision. It's over. I quit. My career as a dancer in the mining camps is through, are you happy? You can go to the bar with your friends now to celebrate."

Thanks to the ongoing bickering and arguments with her husband, Lola's migraines worsened. Patrick, the happy, carefree young man, was becoming insufferable. She couldn't stand his boastfulness or the way he treated her. But she liked Grass Valley; the landscape was stunning, and the mountain air was good for her health. Sometimes she'd close her eyes and imagine she was in the Bavarian Alps. She even seemed to hear the voice of King Ludwig, whom she missed. Was he still in Munich, or had he escaped to his beautiful Villa Malta in Rome? For the first time, she considered settling down for a good while in this tranquil place. The *Nevada Journal* of August 5, 1853, wrote:

Madam Lola seems to be quite captivated with the charming village of Grass Valley, having for some days been enjoying the hospitality of the Meredith Cottage on Mill Street. It is a cozy scene, these cool, delicious evenings, to see the charming Countess gracefully swinging in a hammock under the piazza, surrounded by the gallant host and a select circle of worshippers at the shrine of Beauty and Genius. In fact, "Gil" is the envy of the whole town; but he deserves his success with the fair; for he possesses a noble heart and "winning ways." A lucky dog he is to have a live Countess at his bachelor box.

And so Lola Montez decided to buy their host's cabin. She had learned from her husband that Mr. Meredith, having gotten rich mining quartz, was thinking about returning to San Francisco. Without question, his cabin was the most beautiful home in the valley, painted white, nestled in the shade of a leafy old oak, and surrounded by a wooden fence. It wasn't very large, but it was quite comfortable and had lovely views of the mountains. On the lower floor was a narrow central hall with rooms opening off it on either side. At the far end, a steep staircase led to the attic, her place of refuge. But the house's best feature was the wide veranda that encircled it. At dusk Lola would sit on the porch swing and peacefully float back and forth. There was an adjoining building where guests and servants could stay, a horse stable, and a shed for storing provisions and tools. A Chinese gardener looked after the garden, which provided superb vegetables to make delicious food for their guests. Lola was determined to leave the stage for a while and have her own home in this mining town ringed by valleys and dense forests.

"Mr. Meredith, I want to thank you for your hospitality and tell you that I haven't felt so at home in a long time. This is without a doubt the best home in the whole valley, and I am certain that with a feminine touch it could be even more charming."

"You are very kind. Your husband is a good friend, and it has been a pleasure to have you here. I'm happy to see that good old Pat has found himself a woman like you. You make a fine couple and can stay in my house as long as you like."

"That's what I hoped to discuss with you. As you know, since our wedding, we have been constantly on the move. We are thinking about settling down for a time in Grass Valley, and I believe that you will soon be leaving. I would like to buy your house. What do you say?"

"I am flattered by your proposal—and, to be honest, surprised. It certainly pains me to sell, but I am sure you would take care of it." Suddenly he seemed to make up his mind. "It's a deal. My cabin belongs to you and Pat. I hope you will be as happy as I have been."

The news that Lola Montez had purchased the house on Mill Street was quickly picked up by the local press. Many did not understand why such a refined woman, a countess, would choose to live in a remote, dusty mining town. But her spirits were renewed. She planned to take horseback trips through the surrounding landscapes, visit the sawmills and the quartz mines that hid veins of gold, and explore a hill north of town that bore her name. It was common to christen mining spots with the names of famous women, and Lola Montez Hill had existed even before she arrived in California.

The dancer acquired Gilmor's cabin, but she was never able to enjoy it with her husband. People soon began whispering that she and Patrick were getting a divorce. They had been in Grass Valley for just two months, and one night when he came home gruff and inebriated, Lola couldn't take it anymore.

"You're just a layabout who wants to live on my dime! You spend your days twiddling your thumbs, drinking whiskey in the bars, and playing pool while I have to earn a living. I am an artist, and I owe my public."

"What public, Lola? Men who devour you with their eyes, use the floor as a spittoon, and are only thinking about sleeping with you? Please, come back to reality, Lola; despite your airs of grandeur, you're nothing but an over-the-hill dancing girl who was never any great shakes."

"I won't let you speak to me like that!" she shouted in a fury. "We're finished! Gather your things and get out! I never want to see you again."

That night, Patrick Hull slept in one of the bunks at the Beatty House, and a few days later, he was seen climbing into the stagecoach headed to San Francisco. For weeks, the newspapers speculated about the reasons for their separation, but Lola said only that she hoped he would "trouble me no more." Those close to the couple explained that the countess had kicked out the newspaperman because it was clear he was trying to live off of her. Her third marriage had been the shortest yet, and Lola had people call her Marie de Landsfeld Heald or Mrs. Heald.

After a few weeks during which she was hardly seen in public, Lola abandoned her tranquil retreat in October. Before the harsh winter came and the roads were cut off by snow, she traveled on the steamboat *Sacramento* to San Francisco to buy some furniture. Among her acquisitions was a large player piano that caused a sensation in Grass Valley. She also took the opportunity to adopt a number of pets, including a grizzly cub. Now that she had a new home, she assembled a sizable collection of animals: in addition to her poodle, Flora, there were four more dogs, a goat, a sheep and a lamb, a horse, three canaries, a bobcat, and a wolf-dog hybrid that followed her everywhere. But the bear, which she named Major, sparked the most curiosity among her neighbors. She kept him chained to a tree in a corner of the yard, and the children always came to see him when they got out of school.

Far from the stage, Lola spent a lot of time working in the backyard, which she turned into another garden. Soon after moving in, she wrote to a friend to ask him to have Sutter send her seeds and cuttings from his celebrated ranch. He complied, and she soon had a small orchard of fruit trees and grapevines, as well as a neatly tended garden of flowers and cacti. When a journalist asked if she was worried she might get bored in such a place, Lola replied, "I doubt it. I will have time to read, write to my friends, cultivate roses, enjoy my dogs' company, and receive visits from interesting people." And indeed, in short order, Lola had established her own court in the heart of Nevada County.

Her house became the center of social life in Grass Valley, and her evening gatherings were renowned even in San Francisco. She was always surrounded by admirers. Every week distinguished gentlemen arrived from all over the United States, looking to invest in Grass Valley's immensely lucrative gold mines. They were sophisticated and highly educated young men, engineers, merchants, and bankers from wealthy American families. On Wednesday afternoons, Donna Lola, as she was known there, would hold lively get-togethers with a motley group of businessmen and artists. As in Paris and Munich, she was the perfect hostess. She knew how to look after her guests and entertain them into the wee hours. She amused them with famous operas, which she would play on her piano. There was always plenty of food, liquor, good cigars, and lively conversation. Sometimes, when Lola was feeling particularly spirited, she would pick up her guitar and sing a Spanish song or perform an improvised dance.

She also loved playing the generous hostess to the performers who came through Grass Valley on tour and, since there was no good hotel in town, would invite them to stay in her cabin. Ole Bull, the Norwegian violinist who had enjoyed tremendous success in Europe, arrived in mid-August. Lola organized an evening in his honor and brought together a small group of friends to meet the talented musician. Mr. Bull was so pleased that he offered those in attendance an impromptu recital in which he displayed his mastery of the violin. Charles Warwick, an actor who arrived in Grass Valley with a letter of introduction for Lola, also appreciated her hospitality. Years later he recalled his first encounter with the Countess of Landsfeld in her rustic home:

> I found the gentle Lola in the back garden, having a little game with a couple of pet bears, with whom she seemed to be on terms of playful and endearing familiarity. She was bareheaded, sunburnt almost to the color of a Mexican, and with her hair hanging in rich profusion over her graceful shoulders. Her dress was of the simplest make and of the coarsest material, a common frock, short in the skirt and sleeves, leaving the shapely arms bare almost to the shoulder . . . I was prepared to find a blasée woman of the world, an artful, speculative adventuress, who, after capturing the heart of the old King of Bavaria, and flitting from one European court to another like an erratic comet, had come among us from sheer ennui.

Mr. Warwick was surprised by Lola's good temper and the way she had so swiftly become one of Grass Valley's most sought-after personalities:

> I can only aver that as I found her she was a generous, chari-
> table, whole-souled woman . . . During my short sojourn in
> Grass Valley, I made the acquaintance of all the principal peo-
> ple in the place, as acquaintance with Lola was a passport to
> the best society in the wild mining town. The Countess was
> a general favorite with all classes, from the rude, uneducated
> miner to the richest and most influential people in the rural El
> Dorado, and was looked upon as a sort of fille du regiment in
> that semi-civilized community.

Among Lola's most fervent admirers was one of the pillars of Grass Valley, John E. Southwick, director and part owner of the Empire Mine. He was an elderly gentleman, polite and with an elegant bearing, the son of an affluent New York merchant. He was smitten by the dancer's charms and offered her financial assistance. Johnny, as she called him in private, bankrolled some of the brilliant parties and salons that Lola organized at her home. If politicians or future investors visited, he would invite them to his friend's house, where they would both act as hosts.

One day he encouraged her to acquire shares of a mine. "My dear Lola," he said, "you know my feelings well, and I would like to help you. As you know, I am one of the initial investors in the Empire Mine, and I admit I am also a very rich man. It is going to be the most productive mine in all of California, and you, my dear, can make a lot of money too."

"Thank you, Johnny, but I'm not really one for business; when I do have money, I fritter it away."

"That's why you have me, to advise you. All you need to do is think about your future and buy shares in Empire. You won't regret it, sweetheart," he insisted in a fatherly tone.

The countess followed Southwick's advice and put $20,000 into his mine, a significant investment that would make her the richest woman in California history.

That first winter in the Sierra Nevada was unlike any Lola had ever experienced. One December day she woke up to find the entire landscape covered by a foot and a half of snow. Grass Valley had been nearly buried after a terrible storm that took down several century-old trees near her cabin. To get into town, she devised an unusual sleigh pulled by a pair of horses, decorating it with several cowbells. The residents of Grass Valley saw her go by "like a meteor through the snowflakes and wanton snowballs." On Christmas Day, the artist set up a large decorated fir tree in her living room and invited the town's few little girls to a lively party. She gave them gifts, played with them, let the player piano run, and prepared a delicious afternoon tea. She had always liked children and had occasionally admitted that she regretted not having been able to be a mother.

Lola rang in the year 1854 in both good spirits and good health. The quiet, carefree life suited her marvelously. For the first time in a long while, she could be herself. She didn't need to pretend or invent a past, because nobody asked about it. Her migraines subsided, as did the attacks of fever that confined her to her bed. She had time to meditate and be by herself. Eventually she started reading a Bible lent to her by a neighbor. She felt that she had matured and wanted to leave behind the frivolous, ambitious woman she'd been in the past.

In February, her name was on everybody's lips once more, though this time her bear was to blame. Major had grown a great deal and was still chained in a corner of the backyard. One day, when the countess gave him some sweets to eat, the animal sunk his teeth into her hand and tried to attack her with his claws. A man who was walking by ran to help and managed to free her hand from the animal's jaws. Though Lola was fond of the bear and it was the first time he had been violent, she decided to sell him, fearing he might hurt a child. Soon an odd advertisement appeared in the *Grass Valley Telegraph* on March 9, 1854:

> Grizzly for Sale: We are authorized to inform the public that any persons or family desirous of obtaining an animal of the above mentioned species for public or family use, they can gratify their desires by applying at the residence of Madame Lola Montez, on Mill Street, Grass Valley. By the way, like his present mistress, Mr. Grizzly is amiably inclined, and was never known to interfere with the rights of others unprovoked. The animal would be a great acquisition to the amusements of families and children, to say nothing about his other good qualities.

This bear incident was the first in a series of mishaps that Lola suffered during those months and that revealed her intrepid spirit. With the arrival of spring, she started exploring the nearby mountains on horseback. One day, while riding along a steep, rugged slope not far from her cabin, she spotted some flowers on the other side of the path. Wanting to pick them, she urged her horse to jump a wide ditch, but the animal slipped and fell backward. Lola was thrown off and landed in a shallow stream. She came through the incident without any broken bones and, within a few days, was once more seen trotting through the valley followed by her dogs. In July, she went on an excursion into the mountains with a group of friends and had to return home early because the man in charge of provisions disappeared with their mules in the middle of the night. When the group finally reached Grass Valley, they hadn't eaten in two days, and Lola was convinced someone was getting revenge on her. Later it was discovered that the missing man had had an accident and had wandered around searching for his animals until he was rescued.

Months passed, and the dancer continued to enjoy her peaceful, bucolic life. Nobody would have recognized the sophisticated and elegant Lola Montez of yesteryear. Since arriving in Grass Valley, she had given up her silk gowns and fine laces, her hats decorated with flowers and feathers, and her delicate kidskin boots. She hardly ever wore makeup, and her hair was almost always loose, hidden beneath a wide-brimmed straw hat. On special occasions she would wrap herself in one of her beautiful cashmere shawls, but she never showed off her jewelry, which she kept safely hidden in her cabin. There weren't many opportunities to dress up in Grass Valley. The town's social life revolved around the churches, the theaters, and clubs such as the Grass Valley Literary Society and the Sewing Circle, where the ladies came together to embroider while catching up on the latest gossip. Lola stayed away from these gatherings; she wasn't on any committees and never went to mass. She told her friends in Sacramento that, for the first time in many years, she was enjoying the small pleasures in life: the company of her poodle, Flora; a dinner with artists passing through town; the letters she wrote to friends in Europe; and the beautiful sunsets from her veranda.

From time to time, the local papers would report that the artist was considering returning to the stage, but it wasn't true. A correspondent from the *Golden Era*, who was passing through town, wrote, "Lola Montez, alias Madame Hull, is still here, rusticating in her rural retreat, seemingly enjoying herself, and can occasionally be seen riding out, puffing her cigar with as much gusto as a Broadway dandy." Then she became involved in yet another of those imbroglios that so delighted the press and briefly brought her back into the limelight.

In November, she got into a dispute with the editor of the *Grass Valley Telegraph*, Henry Shipley. Shipley, who had a reputation for being talkative, arrogant, and a big drinker, had never shown the least bit of liking for Lola Montez. The dancer had confronted him when he'd threatened three musicians, saying that he was thinking about writing a review that would "give these artists fits." Lola insisted that he respect those who made an honest living onstage. Though Shipley promised he wouldn't publish the review, he did not keep his word and wrote a lengthy piece in which, among other criticisms, he suggested that the group of singers had met "for the purpose of inflicting misery upon all who will place themselves within hearing distance." The newspaperman later showed up at her home and attempted to bury the hatchet, but Lola threw him out on his ear, brandishing a pistol after he threatened to unmask her and show the world that she was just a has-been who could no longer even shake spiders off her body.

But what irritated the dancer most was a comment Shipley made in his newspaper about Queen Isabella II of Spain: he compared the Spanish sovereign, renowned for her voracious sexuality and her interminable list of lovers, with Lola Montez. Furthermore, he claimed, they were both experts at interfering in government affairs.

When the countess read it, she stormed out of her cabin with the paper in one hand and her leather whip in the other. She found Shipley sitting at the bar in the Golden Gate on Main Street, calmly drinking a whiskey. With fury on her face, she strode over to him and exclaimed loudly, "I warned you not to provoke me again, you boor. You're nothing but a drunk, a coward who attacks women who can't defend themselves. Well, as you see, I can defend myself!" She shouted this last part while striking him with her whip.

"I see you didn't like my piece," he replied with a sneer as he grabbed her arm. "Be quiet and control yourself. I don't want to hurt you, Mrs. Montez."

"You have no right to tell me what to do, idiot, scoundrel, bighead!" Lola continued, raising her whip in a rage.

The other patrons in the bar were startled. The sight of a woman dressed in black and with a striking feathered hat whipping a blond man with thick sideburns and a tall top hat was an amusing spectacle.

Lola appealed to the miners in the establishment to defend her and even offered to buy them a round of drinks, but it was no use. Instead, she received only a flood of loud laughter and shouts of "Brava, Lola!" and "Get him, beautiful!" Mr. Shipley remained seated, unfazed, smoking his pipe and downing his drink while the countess continued to berate him. Finally he got up, paid his tab, and withdrew triumphantly. Lola left the bar and returned home, very upset. She regretted having been so aggressive in front of the people of Grass Valley, who hadn't seen that side of her before.

In Grass Valley, the incident was swiftly forgotten, but the news that Lola Montez had attacked the editor of an American newspaper with her celebrated whip swept Europe. The dancer had a hard time getting over the ridicule her behavior inspired; for the next several weeks, she shut herself up in her cabin, and her name did not appear in the papers again.

Nevertheless, everybody who knew her during that period had fond memories of her. They emphasized her good temper and her generosity toward those less fortunate. Some remembered her riding many miles to take food and medicine to a poor miner. Or staying up all night at the bedside of a sick boy whose mother could not afford to hire a nurse. One reporter wrote, "She flitted from city to city doing generous things," and noted that she won people's hearts with her kindness.

At the beginning of 1855, Lola traveled to San Francisco to try to hire experienced performers and organize a summer tour. This time her destination was Australia, a country that was experiencing its own gold rush. Lola loved her cabin, but she couldn't imagine ending her days in a place like Grass Valley. In addition, the town was changing and had lost its picturesque, tranquil air. The rustic wooden houses on Main Street had been torn down, and Victorian-style brick mansions owned by the new mining magnates had risen in their places. Every week entire families arrived, ready to settle in this mountain town where lodes offered such abundant ore.

She had always been restless, and though she was wearier now, Lola wanted to keep traveling and earn more money so she could retire to a pretty cottage in the English countryside. She was determined to rebuild her career and, if her health allowed, dreamed of taking her own company to Hong Kong, the Philippines, and India; afterward she would continue on to Turkey and Egypt, and finally return to Europe. She knew it wouldn't be easy; she'd have to rehearse for long hours again, refresh her wardrobe, and, above all, pull together a good cast of players willing to travel to the antipodes with her. She wasn't the energetic young woman of before, but she was still a free spirit and a rebel.

In May, she managed to convince her musical director, Charles Eigenschenk, to join her Australian tour. The little troupe included a tall, dark, and handsome actor for the comic and romantic roles, Augustus Noel Follin. He was twenty-seven years old, had a markedly melodramatic character, and went by the stage name Frank Folland. He had left his wife, from whom he was divorced, and his two children in Cincinnati to seek his fortune in the West. Like many others, he hadn't struck it rich and had been forced to find work shining shoes outside a theater box office and playing minor comedic roles in order to survive. He had met Lola a year earlier at one of her musical gatherings in Grass Valley, and the countess had impressed him with her talent and special magnetism. The actor immediately accepted the proposal, especially when she told him he would also be her agent. She promised to pay him one hundred dollars a week plus a good percentage of the earnings.

A few days before leaving, Frank wrote his family a goodbye letter. He didn't tell them that he'd fallen in love with the celebrated Lola Montez, and he sounded worried:

> I hardly have the heart to write. I have tried to do so twenty times during the past week but could not. Now that the moment has arrived *in desperation* I send a few lines: in three days I will leave California. I am going to Honolulu, Sidney [*sic*],

Australia—China—Calcutta—Bombay—Constantinople and England and so on to Paris and New York. I shall be gone two years or more. I go with the Countess Landsfeld, Lola Montez, as agent—if successful I shall make twenty-five thousand dollars. I have nothing to lose and all to gain: things are and have been very dull in California for months . . . I dare, dare not trust myself to say more. I should die if I did. God bless you. I love you.

    Noel

During that sweltering month of June, Lola closed her Grass Valley cabin and said a sad farewell to her admirers and neighbors. Before boarding the stagecoach to San Francisco, she made a will and gave it to her good friend John Southwick, from the Empire Mine. It was rumored that, thanks to her investments, the dancer had made a lot of money and now owned several tracts of land in Nevada County.

The night before Lola's departure, the actress Laura Keene, recently returned from an Australian tour, and other friends from the theater world gathered in the suite where the artist was staying at the International Hotel.

"To Lola!" they cried. "To Australia, land of opportunities! To a successful tour in Victoria, Sydney, Ballarat, Bendigo! And to your company, which is the best!"

"To all of you, my friends," Lola replied, deeply moved. She raised her glass. "You have given me my joie de vivre and self-confidence again."

On the evening of June 6, 1855, a large group of friends and admirers saw her off at the dock in San Francisco. Ever since she was very young, Lola had had to get used to being separated from her loved ones and starting a new life surrounded by strangers. Now, at thirty-four, she was looking forward to this new challenge, though she'd been tired in recent days and noted a bothersome tingling in her legs. She had loving words for all and promised to return to California. Many of those present had traveled from Grass Valley to be with her until the last moment. At the appointed hour, the captain of the *Fanny Major* gave the order to weigh anchors, and from the deck, Lola heard her friends' cries: "God be with you!" "Come back soon!" As she stood on the deck watching the majestic brigantine leave behind the tranquil waters of the Golden Gate, she took handsome Frank Folland's arm and rested her head on his shoulder. She could not hide that she had hired Frank because she liked him, and though he wasn't a terribly good actor, she thought him a diamond in the rough. He had presence, a deep voice, and a melancholy air that was very seductive. After the disappointment of her last marriage, she hadn't thought she'd ever be attracted to a man again, but maybe now, in this more mature period of life, she had found the companion she needed by her side.

Looking into his eyes and smiling, she murmured, "You won't regret it, darling. You're going to make a lot of money in Australia, and with me you'll never feel alone." He studied her still-beautiful face and kissed her on the lips.

CHAPTER 12

The Curtain Falls

As the *Fanny Major* tied up in Sydney Harbour, an unexpected storm unleashed its fury. Within minutes it was raining buckets, a gale was blowing, and the sky was covered with thick black clouds. To Lola, it seemed a bad omen. The two-month voyage had been difficult and tedious. Though Lola had left in high spirits, a sense of disquiet had settled over her as the weeks passed. She was arriving without an engagement or any letters of introduction, determined to make a space for herself in that land of pioneers. The idea of failing again in such a remote country was distressing. During the long journey, she'd taken advantage of the time to rehearse *Lola Montez in Bavaria* with the members of her new troupe. "Will I still be able to captivate the audience with my wit and beauty?" she wondered. "Will these people know anything about my past, or will I be just a has-been?"

Sydney turned out to be a pleasant surprise. Since its founding, the British colony had been the destination for thousands of prisoners sent from the United Kingdom, where the prisons were overflowing. The convicts who served their sentences in the colony performed hard manual labor building bridges, highways, ports, and prisons. When gold was discovered in New South Wales in 1851, the news spread like wildfire and hordes of adventurers came from all over the world. At first sight, Sydney looked like a replica of London, with its wide, neat avenues with elegant carriages. There were high-end hotels, fashionable shops, Victorian mansions, and public parks with broad lawns.

Lola and Frank Folland got a room at Petty's Hotel, on the lively, centrally located York Street. Surrounded by a large garden full of leafy trees that ensured privacy, the two-story colonial mansion offered forty rooms with bathrooms and the city's best views. All the distinguished visitors who came through Sydney stayed there, and it was a meeting place for impresarios, investors, and wealthy residents of New South Wales, Victoria, and other colonies. Lola soon discovered that she was as well known here as in Europe. Reporters from the biggest papers came to interview her, and within a few days, she'd signed a contract with Sydney's Royal Victoria Theatre, the city's oldest and most famous. Its interior was sumptuously decorated: the seats were upholstered in red velvet, the gold boxes were richly adorned, and hanging from the glass vault of the ceiling were two enormous chandeliers. The dancer immediately resumed rehearsals of *Lola Montez in Bavaria* and hired two experienced local actors to round out the cast.

On Thursday, August 23, 1855, the world-famous Lola Montez's opening drew a large audience—as so often before, mostly male. The hall was packed, and among the local personalities occupying the front rows was the governor of New South Wales. The work was wildly successful, and after her performance, the dancer spoke to the auditorium from the stage, thanking everyone for the warm reception. She also took the opportunity to address the women of Sydney, urging them to come see the play. Though the more conservative papers, such as the *Sydney Morning Herald*, deemed Lola a woman of ill repute, on the whole she received good reviews. Only the Sydney correspondent for Melbourne's *Argus* was tough on her and, after seeing her on the opening night, concluded that her tour would be a failure:

> I am compelled to say that I differ entirely from those
> who think that Lola has any talent for histrionic art
> . . . The piece she played in . . . is about the greatest
> piece of trash and humbug ever introduced before an
> English audience. There is no indecency in the acting,
> but the whole tenor of it, socially, politically, and reli-
> giously, is profligate and immoral in the extreme.

Folland tried to placate her, but Lola was inconsolable. "It's intolerable! I despise Victorian hypocrisy!" she cried, ripping up the review.
"Not even here can I be free of the censure of these narrow minds that
see me only as a sinful creature."

"There, there, Lola, don't get upset," Frank said. "The important
thing right now is your health; we've got a long tour ahead of us."

"It's a vile article, an insult to any woman. If I had the strength, I'd
pick up my whip and put them in their place."

"Darling, you're too good for this garbage. You're Lola Montez,
Countess of Landsfeld, and you shouldn't stoop to their level. The public loves you, and you've been marvelous."

She had been engaged for six performances at the Royal Victoria,
but she was unable to fulfill her commitment. Health problems plagued
her, and she could not disguise her fatigue.

At first she thought her exhaustion was owing to the long trip,
but the terrible headaches and nausea persisted. During one show, she
fainted onstage and had to be seen by a doctor in her dressing room.
Over the next few days, through sheer will and effort, she performed as
scheduled and danced her famous "Spider Dance," which, the publicity
claimed, had been "danced by her upwards of two hundred consecutive
nights in New York." This time the audience filed out disappointed
because, contrary to expectations, the search for the dangerous bug in
her clothing left a great deal to the imagination. On the final night she

was set to perform, a sign hastily went up on the front of the theater: "For health reasons, the artist Lola Montez will not perform today."

On her doctor's recommendation, Lola was confined to her bed, but her admirers didn't forget about her. Every morning her maid brought her bouquets of flowers and visitors' cards with admiring words and good wishes for her speedy recovery. On nights when she had more energy, a small circle of bohemians and outlandish local characters would gather in her suite. The *Sydney Morning Herald*'s theater critic was invited to one of these enjoyable evenings and was astonished by the group the artist had assembled, which included a little Indian boy in a white robe and turban; an artist in a djellaba smoking a large hookah; and the artist's wife, a well-known women's rights activist. Also present were her handsome lover, Folland, who was described as "a recently imported star from North and South American theatres, large-eyed and long-limbed, Lola's 'sheep-dog.'" Next to them were a French dancer, a Russian magician, and the actors and actresses she'd brought with her on tour from California.

Smoking was one of the main activities at these gatherings, and Lola took pleasure in showing her guests "the Spanish mode of enjoying tobacco instead of puffing out its fumes before they were tasted, in the absurd English style." According to one witness, she would take a long puff on the cigarette and then calmly take a sip of water before exhaling a cloud of smoke through her mouth and nose. Though Frank, concerned about her delicate health, asked her to quit, Lola flatly refused. "My dear, it's the only vice that keeps me alive," she replied with a mischievous smile.

The artist had become a huge fan of the Spiritualism then in fashion, and she sometimes encouraged her friends to play spinning tables. Lola would place a round table with a three-footed base in the middle of the room and ask those in attendance to rest their hands on its surface to summon the spirits. The table would shudder, spin, or rise up onto one foot to answer questions. During her convalescence, she devoured the book *The Dark Side of Nature*, a two-volume treatise on the occult, and she considered herself an expert. On one occasion the knocks on the table made such a racket that they woke several guests, and the hotel manager asked Lola to cease such activities.

Lola's health improved, and she added new works to her repertoire. These were light romantic comedies of one or two acts, which she performed with Frank. Every day she was becoming more smitten with the solitary, insecure, and changeable young man who had become her primary pillar of support. Onstage they could not hide their mutual attraction. Though they both tended toward the melodramatic and often argued backstage, Lola knew that she owed some of her success to him. Together they acted in *Antony and Cleopatra*, *The Follies of a Night*, *The Morning Call*, and *Maidens Beware*, pieces that opened during her time in Sydney. Folland took the tour very seriously, rehearsing for many hours and memorizing all of his roles. The effort paid off, and he soon won the favor of critics and the Australian public alike.

In early September, the countess was still enjoying tremendous success onstage. But conflicts between the members of the company were growing. Some actors refused to play the roles they'd been assigned and complained about the favoritism Lola showed Folland. By now Lola understood that she would not be able to perform in China, Hong Kong, India, and other destinations as she'd initially hoped. The more veteran actors from Sydney persuaded her that those plans weren't economically viable. The one-year tour she had envisioned would now be reduced to the major Australian cities. It also didn't make sense to keep paying her troupe when there were professional local actors willing to work for less money. Lola managed to put together a good engagement in Melbourne, and as the date approached, the members of the company grew more restive. Uncertain whether she planned to employ them, they demanded a meeting with her at the Royal Victoria to hash out their differences. Lola didn't show, but her agent arrived to announce that the company had been dissolved and that the artist was going to take only Frank Folland and her musical director and violinist, Mr. Eigenschenk, on the rest of the tour. At this news, the troupe mutinied. They'd all signed a contract, and Lola herself had promised to pay for their return tickets to San Francisco when the tour ended. The actors set out to find lawyers who would defend their rights.

Seeing scandal bearing down on her, Lola started preparing to leave Sydney as soon as possible. The press got wind of the news, and the dancer defended herself. According to her, the Californian actors in her company weren't good professionals: they refused to follow her instructions and charged astronomical rates. Despite how "generous" she'd been with them, they were now turning against her and refusing to perform. While both sides' lawyers hurried to file the lawsuits, Folland bought tickets on the steamship *Waratah*, set to leave for Melbourne on September 8. Early that afternoon, just as the artist was about to board, the sheriff's bailiff, Thomas Brown, made his way through the crowd to deliver an arrest warrant for "Marie de Landsfeld Heald, sued as Lola Montez." She spotted him and managed to escape, scurrying up the gangplank and locking herself in her cabin. When the large wheels of the ship began to turn and the sound of the billowing smokestack announced the departure, the dancer sighed with relief. The ship's captain, an admirer, had refused to hand the countess over to the authorities, and Mr. Brown was forced to watch glumly from the dock as his prey got away. In the end, the actors received compensation from Lola's lawyers. The lawsuits fell apart and the artist suffered no further repercussions.

On the morning of September 11, the *Waratah* steamed into the placid waters of Port Phillip Bay on its way to Melbourne. This settlement was quite different from the clean, puritanical, and very British capital, Sydney. It was a young, wild city on the frontier, still caught up in the gold rush. Though there were a few public buildings made of brick and two-story wooden residences with wide porches, outside the city center was a hodgepodge of tents where gold seekers stayed before heading on to the mining towns of Bendigo and Ballarat.

Men lost their fortunes overnight in Melbourne, and Lola was ready to make a lot of money. When she arrived at the Grand Imperial Hotel on her lover's arm, her only desire was to take a nice hot bath and forget the tension of the past few days. She soon got word that some old friends from Europe were in the city.

One of them was the violinist Miska Hauser, whom she had last seen when they argued and split up in Marysville during her California tour. The musician was afraid that his friend might still be angry with him, but when she learned that Miska was in Melbourne, she wrote him an affectionate note inviting him to visit her at the hotel. In his memoir, Hauser recalled the countess lounging on a sofa while rolling cigarettes and consulting some tarot cards that she'd spread out on the table. The room was full of half-unpacked boxes, hatboxes, suitcases, and trunks. Lola was animated and told jokes and stories all afternoon. Though she looked thinner, she was still a fascinating woman, and he stated that she had improved a lot as a dancer, becoming more refined.

A few days later, she debuted *Lola Montez in Bavaria* at the Theatre Royal, less opulent and elegant than the theater in Sydney but with a capacity of three thousand people. The venue had several bars, and during intermissions the audience would rush out in search of brandy or a shot of whiskey. On that hot September night, the house was packed even though tickets had gone for much higher than their usual price. Folland played the role of the vain and ridiculous Baron von Poppenheim, and the rest of the characters were portrayed by local actors. The play failed to impress critics from the city's major papers, but it was a review published in the *Age* that truly destroyed Lola:

> We do not quarrel with her version of those Bavarian
> events which culminated in the "Affair" of March 1848
> . . . All we complain of is that the drama entitled "Lola

> Montez in Bavaria" is utterly destitute of either plot,
> incident or situation; that the dialogue is made up of
> stilted and clap-trap appeals *ad populum*, stale wit-
> ticisms and exploded jokes. The jokes were indeed
> so bad, that the audience . . . laughed at them con-
> temptuously, the clap-trap was so palpable, that the
> most democratic individual present "sniggered" at it
> derisively.

Worse, it went on to say that Madame Montez's dramatic qualities left much to be desired, that she should consider stepping aside to make room for younger, more talented actresses.

For the first time since leaving California, she seriously considered retiring from the stage again. The *Age*'s critic had wounded her deeply—because he was telling the truth. At thirty-four, she looked older because of her history of hard living and the indifference to her appearance that she'd acquired living in Grass Valley. Even now, she wore long men's frock coats over loose-fitting cotton garments, gloves, and wide-brimmed hats. Onstage she tired easily; she could no longer dance with the energy she had previously or perform the encores requested.

The day after opening night, Lola admitted to Frank that she was worn out. "I think the *Age*'s reviewer was right," she said sadly. "I should retire before it's too late. I'll cancel the tour and we'll go back to my cabin in Grass Valley."

"Don't be silly, Lola. You've invested a lot of money and effort in this tour, and now you're going to throw in the towel? I don't recognize you."

"I'm tired of struggling, tired of performing for lecherous men, of portraying myself onstage. I'm tired of living like this, always on the move, like a nomad."

"Listen to me," Frank said, picking up a newspaper from the table. "Look what the *Herald* is saying about you: 'This capable, beautiful, and fascinating woman captivated the audience with her grace and talent yesterday.' Lola, let's keep going. We have engagements in other cities. We'll fulfill our commitments, and afterward . . ."

"Afterward we'll go our own separate ways, right?"

Frank didn't reply. He needed to continue the tour and save enough money to support his two young children. It had been four months since he'd left the port of San Francisco for Australia, and he missed them keenly, along with his half sister Miriam, to whom he was very close and frequently wrote long letters. One day he showed Lola a photograph of the young woman that he always carried with him, and the countess was struck by the resemblance between herself and Miriam. The girl had pale skin, blue eyes, and long, jet-black hair. Lola thought she was so beautiful that she insisted on keeping the portrait for a few days before returning it. Frank promised to introduce them one day. "When we visit New York, you'll meet her," he said. "You'll get along marvelously."

On her fourth night in Melbourne, Lola appeared onstage playing a duchess in a frivolous work, *The Follies of a Night*, and with Folland performed a comedic rendition of the story of Antony and Cleopatra. This time the *Age* praised her talent for light comedy and noted her innate gift for humor. Even so, fewer people were coming to see her perform, and though her migraines persisted, she added the "Spider Dance" to the bill in the hope of filling the theater once more. When it was announced that, for the first and last time in Melbourne, Lola Montez would be performing the number that had been a sensation on Broadway, tickets quickly sold out. One journalist estimated that some three thousand people attended the performance, and Lola did not disappoint. She danced with her old grace and mischievous humor. At the end, the audience offered her a thundering ovation and the artist, deeply moved, took a graceful bow.

Once again critics were divided; while some praised the elegance of her dancing, the *Argus* lambasted her, claiming that the show was an assault on public morality and not worthy of the Theatre Royal. Critics also dared to suggest that the artist had needed help to come out for her curtain call because she was drunk. Falling back into old habits, Lola responded to the *Argus* with a letter to the editor of the *Sydney Morning Herald*, a competing paper. In it, she defended the art and purity of her dancing, which she had performed in the finest European theaters. Thanks to this publicity, the manager of the Theatre Royal extended her run for three more nights. Again all the tickets sold out, and the hall filled with men eager to see the controversial dance.

Before the curtain lifted, Frank Folland appeared and read a message from Lola in which she explained that the dance was a folk tradition from her native country, Spain, and asked the public to indicate whether they wished to see her perform it. The spectators roared with cheers and applause and shouts of "Spider, spider!" Folland swore on his honor as a gentleman that the accusations levied by the *Argus* were utterly unfounded. He emphasized that Lola never drank and defied anyone to claim to have seen her do so even once. After his speech, he called for a hearty round of applause for the dancer. This time Lola moderated her performance somewhat, and the spider didn't climb so high up her skirts or into her décolletage as on previous occasions.

On September 24, Lola and her company finished up their run in Melbourne and left on a steamboat for the port city of Geelong, where the countess debuted that same night. The city's theater was smaller, with seats for five hundred spectators. This city, too, was eager to see the suggestive dance performed by the beautiful Countess of Landsfeld. To quell rumors about immorality, Lola issued instructions that a text be added to the program: "A young Spanish Girl while amusing herself by dancing is bitten by a Spider or Tarantula . . . and as the poison gradually disperses itself through her frame, she becomes faint and exhausted, falls upon the stage, or reels off distracted." In Geelong, the artist fell ill again, with bronchitis, and stayed in her hotel room for two weeks. Afterward she returned to the stage, and though her health was still frail, she managed to fulfill all her obligations, performing before an enthralled public.

In late November, Lola embarked on the steamship *Havilah*, and three days later, she arrived in Adelaide. The capital of South Australia was less cosmopolitan and had a reputation for being quite puritanical. The owner of the Victoria Theatre announced performances by the "world renowned Artiste Lola Montez, Countess of Landsfeldt, Princess of Bavaria" in two upbeat comedies that delighted the public. On the final day, she performed her "Spider Dance," but in a subdued manner—to avoid offending the authorities and the ladies present.

After enormous success in Adelaide, Lola and her players returned to Sydney. The dancer rang in 1856 at the luxurious Hart's Hotel, in Church Hill, surrounded by admirers and old friends who came to welcome her. Despite all the criticisms, her tour had made a tremendous amount of money. In just two months, she had given more than thirty performances. Now she was to round out her Australian tour in the remote cities of the interior, where female artists were enthusiastically received. Lola had delayed her debut in the mining camps until an appropriate theater had been built. The owners of Ballarat's United States Hotel had complied with her wishes and were rushing to finish erecting a new Victoria Theatre. The imposing auditorium was the largest in the state in terms of size and boasted marvelous acoustics and the latest technical innovations. Its facade was an exact copy of Melbourne's Olympic Theatre, and it could seat up to two thousand people. There were six dressing rooms for the actors, as well as a large private room for Mrs. Montez, decorated in the finest style.

Lola arrived in Ballarat in mid-February, and a welcoming crowd gathered around her hotel, waving flags from a variety of countries, including Bavaria. That night, she debuted at the packed new Victoria. The miners loved her performance so much that some of them tossed gold nuggets onto the stage, shouting "Bravo, Lola!" and "You're so beautiful!" During her stay, the local authorities invited her to visit some of their famous gold mines, and the artist's bravery surprised everyone. The large Victoria Reef Mine was about to open and an elegant leather chair had been provided so she could descend comfortably into the shaft, but Lola indignantly rebuffed this luxury; as a journalist wrote, "thrusting her pretty foot in the noose, she laid hold of the rope with one hand, and with a glass of champagne in the other, descended amidst a wild tumult of delight." Once again the countess had charmed everyone with her audacity and spontaneity.

In Bendigo, Lola survived a dramatic incident. As the troupe was performing *Asmodeus; or, The Little Devil's Share*, a huge storm blew in and a bolt of lightning struck the theater. Lola and Frank, who were onstage at the time, saw a sudden blinding flash followed by a powerful explosion. Instantly the stage curtains caught fire and a strong, gunpowder-like smell filled the venue. Two stagehands were injured by flying debris, and people began screaming. Lola quelled the panic by declaring, "Gentlemen, we had planned lightning and thunder effects throughout the performance, but nobody imagined they would be so realistic. In any case, if another such incident occurs and we cannot continue, I suggest you all go to the bar and have a bit of brandy to forget the mishap." At this, the miners cheered, and Lola instructed her company to continue the show. The curtain lowered and then rose again a few minutes later, whereupon the show went on as normal. The local press praised her cool, especially since the lightning had nearly struck her. "She had to thank Providence for His divine dispensation, no one being injured," a journalist from the *Bendigo Advertiser* wrote, calling it "miraculous."

In spring, the Australian tour came to an end. For nine draining months, Lola and her company had performed in the country's most important theaters. Now she and Frank only wished to return to California. After resting for a few weeks in Sydney and saying goodbye to their friends, the two artists arrived in Newcastle, New South Wales, in late May. There they boarded an elegant three-master headed for San Francisco. Sitting on the deck on that sunny May morning in 1856, Lola watched the Australian coast retreat over the horizon. She was happy to have undertaken the adventure, despite the setbacks and her health problems. She didn't know whether she could continue her artistic career nor whether Folland would stay with her. The actor wanted to meet up with his half sister in New York as soon as possible and then travel to Cincinnati to spend a few days with his children. Maybe he and his wife would reconcile and he and Lola would go their separate ways forever. They had been together almost a year, and Lola was in love with him. The idea of retiring alone to her cabin was not in the least appealing.

On July 7, when the ship was just off Fiji, Frank turned twenty-nine. Lola wanted to celebrate in high style, and they had several bottles of champagne over dinner. There was dancing and laughter, and the festivities went on until dawn. At one point the actor, who had drunk more than usual, left the dining room and went up on deck to get some fresh air and clear his head. Lola stayed behind, chatting with other passengers, but after a while she noticed he hadn't returned. A search for him began, and the next morning, the captain approached Lola.

"Mrs. Montez," he said solemnly, "I am sorry to have to give you bad news. My men have not found Mr. Folland, and we have searched the entire ship. I am afraid he's suffered an accident."

"No! That's not possible! You have to keep looking, I'm begging you!"

"It won't do any good, madam. Your friend has surely drowned. There was a powerful storm last night with high waves."

"Oh, God! Why did you not take me? I want to die!" Lola lamented, letting out a heartrending scream.

With a long voyage still ahead of her, she shut herself in her cabin, lost in her memories. Every day when she woke up, she saw Frank's open suitcases, the bed where he'd slept, and his clothing hanging in the wardrobe. She ordered that nothing be touched, wanting to keep it all just as it had been when he was alive. She was undergoing an intense spiritual crisis. The tragic deaths of the men she'd loved most in life, Henri Dujarier, George Lennox, and now Frank Folland, seemed a punishment for the sins she'd committed. Years later, recalling how much Frank's disappearance had affected her, she wrote:

> Once I lived for and from the world, was carried away to commit all its fearful sins and deceptions. I then loved that world. It was my all. I kissed and worshipped its chains that fettered me. And why was this? Because I lived out of myself depending on it for my happiness, then for my very bread from its vices. Oh, it took me years and years to rise out of its degradations. I loathed myself, loathed sin. I from myself tried to reform, not in outward show, for I never was a hypocrite, but from an inward drawing toward the light which is truth . . . My state was a wretched one, oh fearfully wretched. I began to see what a monster in spirit I was.

By the time the ship sailed through the Golden Gate on July 26 and entered San Francisco Bay, the artist had made an important decision: she would devote herself to taking care of Folland's family and would help them economically as much as she was able. She considered herself responsible for what had happened to the actor, and his death was a watershed moment in her life. Her return to the city did not provoke the same anticipation it had three years earlier, when reporters had been waiting eagerly on the docks. Only the *Golden Era*, which had always supported her, made note of the dolorous period she was going through:

> The admirers of the "divine Lola" will be pained to hear that the death of Folland, her "agent," has nearly unseated her reason. Ever since the event she has mourned and refused to be comforted. She says he

was the first and only man she ever loved—which is quite complimentary to her two husbands—and will henceforth cast aside the foolish vanities of life, and gather jewels which rust not and gold which never perisheth. With this view, she disposed of the major part of her jewelry, and made extensive purchases of spiritual works. Folland was drowned on the anniversary of his birth, which was being celebrated with a supper. He stepped on deck to empty a glass, and being somewhat under the influence of champagne, a sudden lurch of the vessel pitched him overboard. For several days Lola seemed almost distracted, a demonstration of grief which at length gave place to a settled gloom and indifference to everything. One of the best evidences that her anguish is real is that she no longer uses narcotics and stimulants. She has lost her taste for cigarettes and cobblers. May she recover and live to break a thousand hearts.

The dancer rented a small house with a garden, on Telegraph Hill, and settled there with her maid and several pets. She now had a spaniel named Gip as well as other dogs she'd taken in from the street. There were several exotic birds she'd brought from Australia, including a white cockatoo and a lyrebird with a long, showy tail. A visitor described the house as a small zoo full of plants and a great variety of animals. She would stroll through the streets with a magnificent white cockatoo perched on her shoulder and trailed by a pack of dogs, a black veil of mourning covering her face.

Lola wrote to Frank's widow, notifying her of the actor's death and offering aid to her and her two children. She also communicated the sad news to his father, Charles Follin, and his stepmother, Susan Danforth, in addition to his beloved half sister, Miriam. During those sad days,

another piece of news dealt her an additional blow. A California newspaper published an obituary for her second husband, George Trafford
Heald, who died of tuberculosis at only twenty-eight years old. Lola
grieved that he had been lost so soon and, in his memory, decided to
continue using the name Heald on occasion.

Despite her sadness and low spirits, Lola once more attempted
to rebuild her social life. But her former acquaintances and members
of California high society rebuffed her. They considered Lola a lonely
artist long past her prime who bore no resemblance to the bewitching
Countess of Landsfeld of times past. But those who believed she was
finished didn't know her. In Sydney she had seriously considered retiring; now, after furnishing a new house and recovering from a serious
bout of bronchitis, Lola was bored. Returning to the stage would help
her get over her lover's death and allow her to earn more money for
his family. Lola knew that nobody was going to come knocking on
her door, so she went to visit an old acquaintance, Charles Chapman,
manager of the American Theatre. She had performed in this important
auditorium, the most elegant in all of California, three years earlier.
Chapman was surprised by her visit.

"Mrs. Montez, what a pleasure to see you again! You look wonderful, as usual. I knew you had arrived in the city, but obligations have
prevented me from paying you a visit. By the way, I followed your
triumphs in Australia; I know you drove the miners wild . . ."

"Dear Charles, there's no need for flattery—we've known each
other a long time. You should know that I've changed. I've been ill, and
I've traveled such a long distance that I'm completely worn out. But I
need to work. I have suffered an immeasurable loss; my agent drowned
in the Pacific. I want to help his children. I feel that I owe them."

"I understand, and you can count on my support. In fact, in August
actors go out on tour and the theater needs performers to draw crowds.
You're a legend in the States. If we come to an arrangement, we can

schedule some comic works you already know along with some of your
exotic dances. What do you say?"

"I'm sure we can come to an understanding. I can still put a lot of
energy into acting, and I have to admit I miss the applause and affection
of my audience." After shaking his hand, she rose with a grand air and
sailed out of Chapman's office.

On August 7, 1856, Lola Montez, the Countess of Landsfeld,
returned to the stage at the American Theatre with an opening performance of *The Morning Call* and *The Follies of a Night*. These romantic
comedies had been a huge success in Australia when she'd acted opposite
Frank. Now she was paired with another young actor, Junius Booth,
but they didn't have the same chemistry. The countess was well received
during the two-week engagement and brought in a good sum of money.
On some evenings, she included some of her dances, which continued
to draw a considerable male audience. Reviewers, whose opinions she
feared, praised her performances, and all agreed that she had become a
great artist. The *Alta California* wrote: "It is astonishing how this lady
has improved as an actress since she first came to California," and "the
present engagement of LM has been one of the most successful ones
ever made with any artist in this city, as she has had crowded, and
sometimes overflowing houses every night."

After this warm reception in San Francisco, she signed a contract to
perform in Sacramento, but she first auctioned off all her jewelry. For
a while she had been considering parting with the valuable gems that
King Ludwig I of Bavaria had given her, but she had always been afraid
to be without them. For an unmarried woman such as herself, the jewels
would ensure her a good retirement. But now she wanted to bring that
era to a close and leave the vain and profligate Lola Montez behind. She
planned to use all the money earned to pay for the education of Frank
Folland's two young children.

The city's major newspapers announced in huge headlines that the
Countess of Landsfeld's jewelry was to be sold at auction. Valued at

$30,000, it was a magnificent collection that, according to one journalist, was "probably not surpassed by any possessed by a single individual in the United States." The famous auction house Duncan & Company opened its showroom to the public, and over the course of several days, more than five thousand people filed through to gape at the splendid necklaces, brooches, crosses, and earrings made of gold, diamonds, rubies, and emeralds that King Ludwig had given to his lover. But not all of the more than ninety lots that went up for sale found a buyer. San Francisco was a small city, and unlike in New York, there was limited interest in antique jewelry like Lola's. The auction managed to bring in only $10,000. It was a disappointment for the artist, but it meant a sizable inheritance for Frank's family.

In Munich, too, where everything related to Lola Montez continued to be of interest, the papers ran the news of the auction. King Ludwig, who was celebrating his seventieth birthday that August, had managed to tear Lola from his heart some time ago. But when he learned that his lover had sold off his treasures, it was another kick in the gut. In a locked box, he still kept all the letters he'd written to her during their passionate romance, as well as hundreds of poems that his beloved Lolita had inspired, including some tragic and embittered ones that he had never sent. Yes, the old king had recovered from heartbreak, but occasionally he still withdrew to the solitude of his chamber and read the letters that transported him to a happy time.

Lola Montez debuted at Sacramento's Forrest Theater in early September and sold out the venue for all five performances. The first night that she performed her "Spider Dance," many people were stuck outside the venue, unable to fit inside. Back in her hotel room, Lola recalled how, in 1853, she had arrived in this mining town on the arm of Patrick Hull. She hadn't heard from him again. On that occasion she'd performed at the tiny Eagle. She smiled thinking about her second night there, when she'd stood up to the rude miners and been showered with eggs and rotten apples.

From Sacramento, the artist visited Grass Valley, which had suffered a massive fire. Along the main street, the fire had burned churches, shops, and some of the elegant Victorian mansions. Though nobody had died, it had been a devastating blow to the community.

She arrived at dusk, terrified that her cozy cabin had also been destroyed. When she reached the front gate, she was startled to see that everything seemed to be intact. The old oak was still standing, and the rosebushes had survived the wind and snow. The veranda was covered with a thick layer of leaves, and several windowpanes were broken. But the church and other buildings around it had suffered more severe damage. In that period of spirituality and repentance, Lola took this as a sign: "The good Jesus has forgiven my sins, and I will be his best disciple." In short order, the artist sold her wooden cabin, which had once been the envy of the entire valley. She gave the remaining furniture to some of her neighbors who had lost everything. The player piano that had delighted children and enlivened her gatherings went to the Episcopal church. The residents of Grass Valley always remembered her as one of the town's most illustrious figures. One local paper wrote that she was a "creature of generous impulses. She beggared herself by her extravagances and her charity. The wretched and the poor think kindly of her memory. She was frequently found giving consolation to the one and substantial aid to the other . . . We will miss her."

With the arrival of autumn, Lola's health worsened. The damp and the strong wind that blew off San Francisco Bay did not agree with her. The migraines returned, and all her joints ached. After several weeks performing her dances and light comedies at the Metropolitan Theatre, she decided it was time to return to New York. By now she had heard from Folland's family. Frank's widow, Caroline, wanted nothing to do with her, but his stepmother, Susan, seemed willing to accept any economic assistance she could offer. They agreed to see each other in New York; in addition, Lola was eager to meet his half sister, Miriam.

Lola's last performance in California took place on the evening of October 17. She acted in the play *Yelva*, followed by her "Spider Dance," for an enthusiastic audience. The prolonged applause pulled her back onstage several times, and a number of gentlemen threw flowers. Lola addressed some moving words to the attendees and averred that she would never forget the affection of the California public. In light of her imminent departure, the reviews were fairly benign. The *Daily Evening Bulletin* wrote:

> It is very plain, however, to all but herself, that properly "her dancing days are over." Though yet rather graceful in her posturing, she does not display, nor is it to be expected at her age, that degree of elasticity and life which is required to maintain a high position as a danseuse . . . It is vain to endeavor to oppose nature. But in some of her late performances, in such pieces as *The Follies of a Night*, and other light comedies, she has shown that she is one of the most graceful and lively actresses upon the stage, and it is a pity she does not confine herself to such parts.

A month later, Lola Montez boarded the Pacific Mail steamship *Orizaba*. A handful of friends and admirers had gathered to see her off. The artist thanked them for coming, and they all wished her the best. This time she was traveling lighter, accompanied only by her maid and her favorite dog, Gip. The journey, which took more than a month, was going to be particularly difficult for Lola, who was not yet fully recovered from her latest bout of bronchitis. First the ship would head to the town of San Juan del Sur, on Nicaragua's Pacific coast, and from there the passengers would continue by train to Lake Nicaragua. After that they would travel down the San Juan River by boat to the Caribbean, where the steamship *Tennessee* would be waiting to take them to their final destination.

When Lola arrived in New York on December 16, a thick snow was falling and the streets were decorated with garlands and colored lights. Frozen ponds had been turned into improvised ice rinks. Though she had been gone four years, she still had good friends in the city. This time she stayed in a modest hotel in Brooklyn. Before leaving San Francisco, she had put her finances in order and written a new will that superseded the one she'd done in Grass Valley. In the new will, she left all her possessions "to Mrs. Susan Danforth, stepmother of Noel Follin (Frank Folland)," in trust for the actor's children, and asked that they be educated in the Spiritualist faith. With her jewelry sold and all her savings donated to Frank Folland's family, she had only enough money to live for a month in a city like New York.

At the end of December, the dancer met with Mrs. Danforth and her daughter, Miriam, at the hotel where she was staying. When Lola found herself face to face with Susan, she kneeled before her and, sobbing, cried out, "You must forgive me. I have killed your son! It was all my fault!"

"Mrs. Montez, I beg of you to get up," Susan said, gently taking her by the arm. "Do not fret. You are not responsible for my dear Noel's death. Stop tormenting yourself."

"Yes, I am responsible. I organized a birthday party for him and we were drinking, and he then left and I didn't notice at first . . . And a wave snatched him from me. Oh, God! Help me bear this heavy burden!"

Distraught, Lola explained that this terrible event had been traumatic for her, that it had changed her. She didn't care about money and gave Susan a copy of the will she'd drawn up, leaving everything to her. Susan was deeply moved by the artist's grief and generosity. She had heard a lot about Lola Montez and naturally had never dreamed she'd be so remorseful and pious. Calmer now, the dancer turned to Miriam, whose photo had fascinated her. The young woman was even more beautiful in person. She was tastefully dressed and very gentle with Lola. Despite her innocent appearance, Miriam was already familiar with life's heartaches. She had married at seventeen when her mother discovered that she was sleeping with a jeweler twice her age. Mrs. Danforth gave the gentleman a choice between marrying her daughter or going to jail for corrupting a minor. A wedding was hastily arranged, but after the ceremony, Susan forbade her to see the man, whom she considered a libertine. Miriam had the marriage annulled and now, having just turned twenty, was free to marry again.

Besides their physical resemblance, Lola and Miriam had a great deal in common. They were both ambitious, strong, and determined, and they were aware of their powers of seduction. The countess was charmed by the young woman and, soon after meeting her, wrote her an affectionate letter in which she offered her "a true sister's love, pure and devoted." In mid-January 1857, Lola moved to the Follin family residence on Stuyvesant Place. Susan had invited her, unwilling to allow Lola to continue living in a modest hotel when they had a spacious house where she could stay. During that period, the countess realized that Miriam could accompany her on tour, playing the role of her younger sister, "Minnie Montez." The young woman liked the idea, seeing an opportunity to escape her mother's control. Mrs. Danforth, for her part, did not object; indeed, she was happy to see her daughter getting along so well with the celebrated artist.

The tour began on February 2 in Albany's Green Theater. The pair performed in the small venue for a week, and Minnie Montez made her stage debut in *The Cabin Boy*, a two-act melodrama in which she had a small role. The house was packed on opening night, and the audience was delighted by the younger Montez's vivacity and beauty. The tour continued in Providence, where they performed the same play for five nights running at the Forbes Theater. One reviewer wrote, "The younger sister is quite as attractive a personality as she was represented to be, and acquits herself well on the stage, for a novice."

But the artist's idyll with her "little sister" lasted only two months. Lola was eager to continue the tour through different American cities, but Miriam had other plans. That peripatetic lifestyle, constantly on the go, didn't suit her. And the countess soon learned that she wasn't as naive and innocent as she appeared. One night, after their performance, Lola saw Miriam in her dressing room kissing an admirer. When she reproached her for her behavior, Miriam replied harshly, "Lola, you have no business giving me morality lessons. You're not my mother or my sister. I know full well that men are attracted to me, and I'm planning to find a rich husband who'll take care of me."

"My dear, you know how much I love you, but don't be fooled: money won't bring you happiness. They can drape you in jewels, but if you're not truly in love, you will be very unhappy. I'm telling you this from my own experience, Miriam; you've still got time to choose the right path."

"That's ridiculous. You've enjoyed power and wealth, loved many men, even a king and—"

"Yes, that's true," Lola interrupted, "but if I could do it over again, I would change a lot of things. I hurt a lot of people, and neither money nor power has brought me happiness, sweetheart."

Miriam ignored her advice, and after fulfilling their obligations in Providence, they parted ways. A few months later, Lola learned that a New York bank president and former congressman, married and with an impeccable reputation, had purchased an apartment in Miriam's name for their trysts. The young woman ended up leading the same sort of frenetic and dissolute life that Lola had. She cycled through a series of husbands and lovers, made a fortune, lost it, and acquired a noble title.

Lola returned to New York earlier than expected. Her health was failing and she was tired. It was getting harder and harder for her to dance, she had lost flexibility, and rehearsals were grueling. Sooner or later she would have to give up dancing, and although she liked acting in light comedies, there were no good starring roles for older women. The mirror revealed a pale, gaunt face with dark circles under the eyes. She had cut her long, curly hair and now sported a boyish cut that made her features sharper.

As she was trying to figure out how to make a living, a fortuitous encounter opened new possibilities. Lola renewed her friendship with the Reverend Charles Chauncey Burr, a former minister of the Universalist Church and a successful journalist and Democratic speechwriter. At forty years old, he was very handsome, tall, and energetic, with lively eyes and a long beard. He encouraged her to make a major change in her life. One afternoon he visited her at her home, worried by news about her delicate health.

"My dear Lola," he said, "I've heard rumors that you're not well and are leaving the stage for good. I hope that is simply one of your jokes—you're in the prime of life."

"No, Charles, it's not a joke. We artists have to retire before it's too late, and though I'll miss the stage, I know I'm doing the right thing. There is nothing left of the famous Lola Montez you first met. Before, I was just a sinner, until Jesus knocked on the doors of my heart."

"God is love, and He never condemns those who have a good heart like you, Lola. You have started down the right path by renouncing your previous life, but there are still a lot of doors open to you. I've been thinking about it recently, and I think you could have great success as a lecturer. You're good at public speaking, and it wouldn't demand too much effort. I would help you prepare the speeches and improve your diction."

"I don't know, I've never given a lecture. But I have to admit it's an appealing idea. Maybe I could describe my life in Paris, where I met George Sand and Alexandre Dumas—or talk about the false morality of Victorian England or the tyranny of the Jesuits—"

"Of course you can talk about whatever you like," Burr said, "but initially it's best to avoid controversial topics. The audience that attends these talks wants to learn and have a nice time. Lola Montez is still a celebrity, and people will be eager to hear your opinion about universal subjects such as love, success, or beauty."

Lola liked the idea of becoming an orator. Now she'd be able to address the female public and talk to them about fashion, cosmetics, or the art of seduction. If everything went well, she would earn a lot of money and would no longer have to rehearse with an orchestra or travel with a troupe. Everything would be easier and cheaper. Once she'd covered the cost of renting the hall, the rest was all profit to split with her agent.

During the scorching summer of 1857, Lola wasted no time. Every day she and Burr spent several hours giving structure to her first talks. Though the journalist suggested ideas, she wrote the lectures. It was an excellent use for the talent she'd shown in writing hundreds of rebuttals to newspapers around the world.

Lola's debut as an orator took place in Hamilton, Ontario, on the evening of July 29, 1857. For the occasion, she chose a topic she knew well, "Beautiful Women." The hall wasn't very crowded, but she demonstrated her natural gifts as a lecturer. With grace and wit, she began with a discussion of the subjective nature of beauty and then talked about women who have been famous for their beauty, some of whom she'd met in the court of Bavaria. Lola also emphasized that the three essential requirements of feminine beauty were temperance, exercise, and cleanliness. She recommended not drinking alcohol, not abusing strong coffee, and avoiding heavy meals. Tobacco went unmentioned, as she still smoked heavily despite her doctor having warned her against it. As for exercise, she lauded the benefits of long walks in the open air and encouraged attendees to own a dog or two because they were the best antidote to loneliness and melancholy. Two days later, she gave the same lecture to a large crowd at Buffalo's American Hall.

The artist threw herself into her new profession. She and Burr, whom she named her agent, made a strange but tight-knit pair. Together they embarked on a successful tour through New York and the major cities of New England. At each new appearance, her tone, pacing, and presentation improved. She always dressed in a very sober and elegant manner, with her hair pulled back in a bun, without makeup or any jewelry. Her speeches lasted about an hour, and she had dropped all her affectations, including her Spanish accent. Critics were surprised by the clarity and precision of her diction. A correspondent from the *Boston Post* who attended one of her early lectures wrote, "I cannot help thinking that she talks vastly better than she dances, and in my opinion that is her opinion. Her lecture was a decidedly pleasant and profitable entertainment."

When Lola arrived in Boston at the beginning of October, her career as a public speaker was firmly established and she was making good money. One of the city's most feared critics wrote, "She is considerably thinner than represented in the plates we have seen, but the expression on her face and the luster of her eye no artist can do justice to. Her deportment is easy and ladylike, and she delivered the lecture with a grace and beauty of diction we have very seldom heard equaled by the most finished actress." Other journalists were just as enthusiastic, and the artist couldn't believe it when the *Boston Bee* called her "the unquestioned queen of the lecture room." With her usual humor, Lola quipped that, though she had not managed to become the queen of Bavaria, here in America she'd been crowned the queen of oratory.

One month later she arrived in Philadelphia. People were so eager to hear the Countess of Landsfeld speak that the hall turned out to be too small and she had to rent a larger space. It was here that she first gave her speech titled "Gallantry" and where, for the first time, she publicly recalled King Ludwig I of Bavaria. "His Majesty is one of the most refined and high-toned gentlemen of the old school of manners," she said solemnly. "He is also one of the most learned men of genius in all Europe." Since Lola did not take questions at the end of her talks, she avoided having to give explanations about her private life. Initially, many people attended because of her notorious reputation, but upon hearing her, they were surprised by her talent and wit.

When the tour ended in mid-December, Lola returned to New York to rest and recover her voice, which had forced her to cancel an engagement. After having overcome another bout of bronchitis, she was still coughing a lot and slept poorly. Despite her exhaustion, she was happy in her new role and, over the next few weeks, started to write other lectures on topics that interested her. One was titled "Wit and Women of Paris" and another "Heroines of History," in which she surveyed the exceptional lives of women such as Cleopatra and Catherine the Great. Lola had no qualms about including herself in this list of brave and powerful queens, highlighting her role in the fight against the Jesuits in the Bavarian court. She'd found a good way to earn money and held fast to the words of the *New York Herald*: "She promises to be one of the most successful of female lecturers."

But Lola once again found herself in the news for reasons unrelated to her success. A sensationalist tabloid published the following commentary:

> We have to state, with much gratification, that this is the close of Madame Lola Montez's career as a public lecturer. We break no confidence and do not intrude on the secrecy of private life by mentioning that this fair and gifted woman is on the eve of a very brilliant matrimonial alliance. She proposes in ten days from this time to be en route to Paris. Her return to this country may be expected in the spring.

Lola blamed Burr for having leaked this information to the press. Only he knew the secret she'd guarded so carefully. In recent months the artist had been in renewed contact with Ludwig Johann Sulkowski, a forty-three-year-old Austrian nobleman whom she'd first met in Berlin in 1843. In his letters, the prince confessed that he was still deeply in love with her and hoped that maybe now, in this mature stage of life, she would agree to be his wife. He was living in upstate New York and had become a wealthy farmer. Sulkowski persuaded her to meet him in Paris and spend a romantic Christmas together.

Though Lola was hesitant, she accepted the invitation. She hadn't had a break in a long time, and the idea of being wooed in Paris by a gallant, well-educated prince with serious intentions was very appealing. So she packed her bags and, on the chilly morning of December 12, set sail aboard the steamer *Fulton*, headed for the port of Le Havre. When she arrived in Paris, she got a room in her favorite hotel on the Place Vendôme, registering under the name Mrs. Heald. Paris looked like something out of a fairy tale in its Christmas getup, with bustling holiday markets and squares and streets lit up with thousands of lights and hung with banners and garlands. There, in that city full of so many memories, Lola waited eagerly for her admirer to contact her. But she quickly realized that something wasn't right. Through a journalist friend, she learned that Sulkowski not only was not in the city but was a married man. Somebody had wanted to toy with her emotions. When the prince himself was informed, he wrote a letter to the newspapers explaining that there had been a mistake: "I met Mrs. Montez years ago in Berlin, but I have not been in touch with her since. I am a happily married man and the father of five children. I ask that my good name and that of my family be respected."

Lola returned to New York and took to her bed for several days; the headaches were back, and she felt quite dispirited. She had experienced one of the worst humiliations of her life and had no wish to see anyone. "Who hates me so much that they would do something so inhumane to a lonely, defenseless woman?" she wondered. "I have been a fool and lost everything I had." Before leaving for Paris, the dancer had donated many of her belongings to charity and had spent most of her savings on the voyage. To her even greater dismay, when she returned, the American press erroneously reported that she had secretly wed a rich Austrian prince in Paris. With her pride wounded, she made no effort to report the cruel prank to the police or to rebut the claims publicly. Only later did she tell a journalist that "she had broken off the engagement because the prince was traveling about with a celebrated singer as man and wife." Some time later, she would refer to Prince Ludwig Johann Sulkowski in her lectures as an old beau and acknowledged the disappointment she'd experienced, even as she downplayed the events. "Every woman has a right to be a little foolish on the subject of marriage," she said.

When Lola was feeling stronger again, she moved to a small room at 25 Bayard Street, where another acquaintance, Otto von Hoym, lived with his family. When he learned what the artist was going through, this German theater director offered to put her up in his home, located in the heart of Chinatown.

She appeared next at the beginning of February 1858, this time at Hope Chapel with her lecture "Beautiful Women," and once more managed to draw "one of the largest audiences ever to have assembled within the walls of that building." She also made peace with her agent, Mr. Burr, who assured her that he'd never spoken of her trip to Paris and that she could count on his complete discretion. The two needed each other, and Lola decided to sweep what had happened under the rug and focus on her next projects. Burr, who was earning a lot of money from her work and looking to earn still more, had proposed that Lola write a series of lectures recounting her infamous life story. Over the course of long writing sessions, he helped her compile the most relevant events. Though Lola was striving to be a good Christian by correcting the errors of her wayward past, she continued to lie about her childhood and family origin. Lola changed her birth year to 1824, and though she admitted to having been born in Ireland, she claimed that her mother was from the noble Spanish Montalvo family. Only the events from her two years at the Bavarian court were somewhat truer to life. Of course, she presented her relationship with King Ludwig as one of friendship and mutual admiration. The king could breathe easy, since Lola refused to air their private affairs in her lectures, offering only words of praise and admiration for him.

Lola offered her first talks on herself at the Broadway Theatre in late May 1858. She always gave these lectures about her life story in the third person. This allowed her to distance herself from and poke fun at the character. She generally opened with these words:

> Several leading and influential journals have more than once called for a lecture on Lola Montez, and as it is reasonably supposed that I am about as well acquainted with that "eccentric" individual (as the newspapers call her) as any lady in this country, the task of such an undertaking has fallen upon me.
>
> It is not a pleasant duty for me to perform. For, however fearless, or if you please, however impudent, I may be in asserting and maintaining my opinions and my rights, yet I must confess to a great deal of diffidence when I come to speak personally of one so nearly related to me as Lola Montez is.

At the end of her talks, which received enthusiastic applause, she suggested that she would soon be returning to Europe, where she planned to tour the major capitals, if her health allowed.

That spring, a number of New York papers published extracts from the lectures in which Lola Montez described her extraordinary life. It was then that Maria Elizabeth, the wife of prominent Manhattan florist Isaac Buchanan, realized that she'd gone to school in Scotland with the celebrated artist. Mrs. Buchanan remembered her striking, unusual schoolmate quite clearly. She wrote Lola an affectionate letter inviting her to visit her house on Seventeenth Street, just off Broadway, and sent her a floral arrangement with which to decorate the dais at the Broadway Theatre. Lola thanked her for the thoughtful gesture, and a few days later, she went to the Buchanan home for tea. The two women hadn't seen each other in more than twenty-five years; after that reunion, they became close friends, and Maria Buchanan was an important person for Lola in the last years of her life.

Given the success she was enjoying, Lola rented the theater for a second series of lectures that stretched into early June. Only one piece of news briefly darkened that bright moment: through the press, Lola learned that her third husband, the journalist Patrick Hull, had died at thirty-four after a long, painful illness. Though Lola did not have good memories of Patrick, she felt his loss keenly and feared she was cursed: "All of my husbands, save the first, and my young lovers have died tragically and unexpectedly. Sometimes I wonder if Alexandre Dumas was right when he said I brought bad luck to any man who got near me."

The arrival of summer put a halt to all cultural activity in Manhattan, and the artist retired to a little house very far north in the city, in the working-class neighborhood of Yorkville. Her new home, perched on a hilltop and with a small garden, reminded her of her cabin in Grass Valley. There, her career as a writer truly began. Over the previous few months, she had started compiling her lectures, and a modest New York publishing house encouraged her to publish them in book form. Though the critics deemed her speeches very superficial this time, the book sold well and a second edition was soon released. What Lola hadn't expected was that some newspapers would call into question the authorship of the texts. Many believed that the lectures had been written by Chauncey Burr, and even that they were plagiarized. Lola defended herself, writing letters to the major newspapers, such as the *New York Herald*, but the person who helped her most was the editor of the *Cleveland Plain Dealer*, which published an article exonerating the artist:

> Lola Montez is a thoroughly cultivated and remarkably
> gifted woman, whatever her private faults may be; and
> to say that she is incapable of writing the lectures she
> delivers is alike absurd and mean . . . The writer of this
> paragraph will make oath that once upon a time he
> saw the dashing countess take a composing stick, go
> to a case, and with no copy before her set up a sharp
> and racy communication in which a certain editor was
> very handsomely used up. Montez not write? Tell it to
> the marines. She can set type, too.

Lola soon decided to publish a second volume, under the title *The Arts of Beauty; or, Secrets of a Lady's Toilet, by Madame Lola Montez, Countess of Landsfeld.* The author explained in the prologue that she had tried to write a book that was both useful and entertaining. It contained endless practical tips on cleanliness and beauty. She also offered her own wonderful formulas for making face creams and a huge variety of treatments to prevent wrinkles, increase bust size, heal chapped lips, and eliminate freckles. All used natural products, because Lola considered industrial cosmetics pernicious. Fresh air, exercise, scrupulous hygiene, and moderation at meals, she claimed, guaranteed a healthy life and enduring beauty.

The first New York edition of *The Arts of Beauty* was very well received in the United States, where it sold more than seventy thousand copies in just a few months. After this success, the book was translated into a number of languages, but Lola could not prevent it from being republished without her authorization. Some editors brought out as many as three editions simultaneously, with sizes and prices adapted to a range of budgets. Though the author could have earned much more money from those illicit sales, she could not complain. Her speeches and books had rescued her from her financial straits and allowed her to keep renting the house in Yorkville, where she lived surrounded by her pets and a small circle of loyal friends.

Though Lola was trying to become a good Christian, some old habits persisted. In that summer of 1858, she started surrounding herself with picturesque characters who were passing through New York. Indifferent to scandal, Lola welcomed into her home a parade of bohemian artists, fallen noblemen, free thinkers, and members of the Spiritualist sexual liberation movement. Rumors soon spread that the artist was setting up a free-love commune in her home, and several journalists went up to Yorkville to interview her. In reality, Lola's time during these gatherings was spent engaged in her favorite pastime, the art of conversation, of which she was inarguably a master. Her guests were eccentric and unusual because, as she told one reporter, "I love meeting and talking to all kinds of peculiar characters, and normal people rather bore me."

Lola presided over these informal get-togethers seated in a blue silk armchair placed in the center of the parlor and rolled cigarettes for everybody from a bag of tobacco that dangled from her chair. She greeted people enthusiastically as they arrived, offered them a glass of brandy or wine, and suggested a topic to be discussed without any censorship. The interior of her home was richly decorated with flowers and plants, intricately woven Persian rugs on the hardwood floors, and curio cabinets full of objects from all over the world. She enjoyed illuminating the house with candles and creating an intimate atmosphere that would foster relaxed conversation. Lola's wit and talent as a storyteller astonished everybody. One guest wrote, "There was no chance to do anything but listen when Lola talked." Another noted, "There was certainly no topic, within my range, at least, on which she could not converse with some substance of personal experience and reading."

At the beginning of November, she began preparing for a lecture tour through Great Britain. Her health had improved, and Burr encouraged her to visit her native Ireland. A few days later, she embarked on the steamer *Pacific* for Dublin. Lola had hazy memories of her childhood, but she hadn't forgotten the splendid natural landscapes of County Sligo, its inlets with steep cliffs and long sandy beaches. The transatlantic voyage from New York took two weeks and was quite rough. The ship faced churning seas and icy winds. The sight of huge icebergs floating all around kept the crew on high alert.

It had been more than twenty years since Lola had left Ireland for the last time, on her way to India. Back then she'd been a romantic, impulsive schoolgirl married to a handsome officer from the British East India Company. As the *Pacific* drew nearer to the coast, memories of those years crowded her mind. An entire world was resurrected. She thought about her mother, Eliza, whom she hadn't seen again. More than once she had been on the verge of picking up a pen and writing her a letter, but her mother had inspired no tenderness in her at the time. Now older, Lola believed it was too late to overcome their differences. "I was wrong, Mother," Lola thought, "and I hurt you deeply. Running away with Thomas was the greatest mistake of my life. I have paid for it dearly, very dearly. I know you'll never forgive me and that you're ashamed of me. But if you'd given me a little of your love, I might have been a better person."

When the *Pacific* docked at Galway on November 23, a group of admirers was waiting. Lola returned to her homeland a celebrity, and the press was anxious to interview her. She descended the gangway in an elegant black silk dress with flounces, shielding herself from the cold with a fur mantle. She addressed the press with a smile, saying fervently, "I feel great affection for Ireland, land of my birth, which I've always carried in my heart. I am eager to visit my birthplace, which I left when I was only a child."

Throughout her life Lola had never acknowledged her true roots. But she no longer was hiding the fact that she was Irish, even if southern blood supposedly ran in her veins. After answering the reporters' questions, Lola and Burr took the train to Dublin. Though Grange, the town where she'd been born, was 125 miles from the capital, Lola did not wish to visit it. Nor did she travel to Cork, where an aunt lived with her two children. She was afraid of stirring up painful memories and of being rejected by her mother's family.

During the tour Lola spent a lot of time in the company of Burr, who had become her secretary, friend, confidant, and agent. When the actress was feeling inspired, she would write texts in one sitting, and they would revise them together. The two also had long, deep conversations about religious topics. Burr urged her to pray and meditate to achieve inner peace. Lola began keeping a diary in which she explored her deep spiritual preoccupations. On one page, she wrote:

> Oh, I dare not think of the past! What have I not been? I lived only for my own passions . . . What would I not give to have my terrible and fearful experience given as an awful warning to such natures as my own! And yet when people generally, even my mother, turned their backs upon me and knew me not, Jesus knocked at my heart's door. What has the world ever given to me? (And I have known all that the world has to give all!) Nothing but shadows, leaving a wound upon the heart hard to heal—a dark discontent.

On December 8, Lola Montez gave her first lecture in Dublin, a talk titled "America and Its People." Burr had done his job well, and the hall was packed with a sophisticated, attentive audience. When she stood at the lectern, which was upholstered in red silk, Lola received an extended round of applause. Many of those in attendance were surprised by her powerful stage presence, and though her face had aged, her marvelous blue eyes were as striking as ever. With glowing reviews and a rapt public, the artist continued her tour through Scotland, giving three or four different lectures each week. Burr was working hard to promote the tour, and Lola always spoke to overflowing auditoriums.

The only complaint was that the talks were too short to justify the high ticket price. First-row seats often cost more than three shillings, while equivalent places at the lectures given by Charles Dickens went for only two shillings.

In early April 1859, after four exhausting months on the road, Lola arrived in London. She still had good friends in the city, and she stayed with one in a pretty house off Portland Place. Burr rented the elegant St. James's Hall, by Piccadilly Circus, for her first public appearances. The Countess of Landsfeld's lectures did not pique much interest among the English press, but one critic acknowledged her talent: "Within three minutes of its commencement, the Countess had complete possession of her audience." The public listened, spellbound, and left satisfied. Over the next few weeks, despite the persistent rain, Lola managed to sell out every lecture. To her satisfaction, the talks "Comic Aspects of Fashion" and "Heroines of History" drew audiences of mostly women, and in the front rows she recognized a few famous suffragists.

After the final lecture, Burr returned to America, but Lola wished to remain in London a few weeks longer. Some friends encouraged her to rent a furnished mansion in Mayfair. It was a two-story colonial-style home surrounded by gardens, just steps from Hyde Park. Lola couldn't resist, and though she'd started along a path of humility and repentance, she had enough money again to live in high style. She hired several servants, a driver, and a gardener and even refreshed her increasingly worn wardrobe. She had the idea to make money by renting out part of the house to distinguished guests while she enjoyed a pleasant retirement.

But Lola's plans were stymied from the start. She sent visiting cards to old acquaintances and members of British high society, but none were willing to ruin their reputation by lodging in the home of a woman tainted by scandal. To cover the expenses of running her new home, she gave two lectures at St. James's Hall, but few came to hear her. The artist was as bad as ever at budgeting and, within just a few weeks, began to take on debt. She fought with her domestic staff and stopped paying her rent. The property owner promptly sued her, and she fell seriously ill because of the stress. When the suit was decided, all her assets were seized, and she was forcibly evicted. She would have been out on the street if not for the generosity of an elderly couple who had heard about her situation; they invited her to live on a farm in Derbyshire.

In a landscape of hills, gardens, and lakes, Lola soon recovered her health. She was living in a little house with thick stone walls covered with honeysuckle and a steep slate roof. Every day she gave thanks to Providence for having found kind people who had rescued her from penury. She had hit rock bottom again financially, but she hadn't felt so happy and at peace with herself for a long time. The countryside suited her well; she kept busy working in the garden, berry picking, and making excursions. She also spent hours meditating and reading the religious essays of the preacher John Bunyan, whose sermons now guided her life. Every Sunday she went to a Methodist chapel, drawn by the simplicity of the religious service and the kindness of the parishioners. Her only desire now was to serve others, visiting the sick and the poor. Nevertheless, as she noted in her diary, "that will be in the Lord's good time, when He thinks me *fit* for this happiness—that is, when *self* is *burned out of me completely.*"

Lola left her idyllic retreat in the English countryside and returned to New York in November. This time she rented a modest apartment in Brooklyn and moved in with her dogs and exotic birds. Though she was very tired and again suffering from terrible headaches, she could not retire for good because she needed money. All winter, under Burr's supervision, she continued to give lectures in different auditoriums on Broadway and announced that she was preparing to perform in the major cities of the East Coast. Some people began to speak out against Burr, accusing him of exploiting Lola Montez and subjecting her to draining tours for his own financial gain. Though she'd grown extremely thin, only the faint tremor in Lola's right hand and the pallor of her face betrayed that she was ill. From time to time a dry cough obliged her to interrupt her talks, and a cold sweat would break out on her forehead. For many in the audience, it was clear that the Countess of Landsfeld, behind her serene exterior, was trying to mask a serious illness.

Nevertheless, Lola went on with her long lecture tour, speaking in more than twenty cities. From Philadelphia to Cleveland, she continued to fill auditoriums and receive positive press. Her health had not improved during that harsh winter, but she kept going thanks to doses of laudanum and belladonna. In a frank letter to her friend Maria Buchanan, she admitted that she was worn out and dreamed of returning to New York:

> I have to lead a very monotonous life, shut up in my room in the daytime or traveling in cars and lecturing in the evenings to a lot of people that are not interesting to me . . .
>
> I look forward with great pleasure to my return again to N.Y., for it is the only city in America where I prefer living . . .
>
> I have been afflicted for 4 weeks with a most painful neuralgia affection on one side of my face, suffering great pain,— but now we have a perfect spring weather and I am much relieved . . .
>
> The press everywhere is loud in my favor, which is very pleasant, though I don't care in reality much what they do say.

After months of frantic travel, Lola returned to New York at the end of April 1860. She had managed to save a little money and rented an apartment in Greenwich Village, where she lived under the name Mrs. Heald. New York seemed like a better fit, and she felt it was her true home. Her last trip to London had made it clear that a free-thinking, independent woman like herself did not fit into the still rigid, class-bound English society. Here she had good friends and began attending a Methodist church. She felt that she had finally put down roots, and she was heartened by the return of good weather.

By June, the New York heat had become unbearable, often surpass-
ing ninety degrees. One Saturday morning Lola was making breakfast
when she suddenly felt dizzy. She went back to bed, and the room spun
around her. She had a severe headache and could not move the left side
of her body. Her maid, Annie, who came in some days to clean, found
her bathed in sweat and panting. Though the alarmed young woman
tried to revive her, Lola barely heard her and could not speak. Annie
immediately summoned a doctor, who confirmed that Lola had suffered
an embolism; he could only make her more comfortable and wait to see
how her condition developed. Over the next two days, Lola showed no
improvement. She still could not speak, and after the attack, her mouth
had become twisted into a horrible rictus. Early on Tuesday morning,
her eyes were closed and her body cold. She seemed to have gone into a
coma, and the doctor judged that she would be very unlikely to survive
the night.

Though everyone thought her as good as dead, Lola began to
improve slightly a few weeks later. The left side of her body was still
paralyzed and she could not communicate, but the worst of the crisis
had passed. The Buchanans, worried, moved her to their summer home
on Long Island, where Lola continued to cling to life. Everybody was
astonished by the indomitable will she still displayed. By August, the
countess had made some advances, but a journalist who visited was
struck by her deteriorated physical condition:

> Lola was costumed in a half night and half morning
> robe, and she sat in a pretty garden, her hollow cheeks,
> sunken eyes, and cadaverous complexion forming
> a remarkable contrast to the gay flowers. She was
> unable to utter an intelligible word, except spasmodi-
> cally, and after repeated effort. Her mouth was froth-
> ing, like that of one in partial convulsions, and she was
> unconsciously wiping it, as little boys do, by drawing

it across the sleeve of her dress. In fact, she had the
strange wild appearance and behavior of a quiet idiot,
and is evidently lost to all further interest in the world
around her, and its affairs. And so ends her eventful
history! What a study for the brilliant and thoughtless!
What a sermon on human vanity.

One morning in October, three months after Lola had moved into
the Buchanan home, with great difficulty she said to her friend, "I want
to go home. I don't want to be a burden for you all."

"My dear, don't be silly," Maria replied in surprise. "Are you not
happy here?"

"I need to be alone. I can still take care of myself, and I wish to live
humbly to atone for my sins."

"But Lola, winter will be coming soon," Maria said, "and you're not
well yet. Don't rush things. Wait for spring, and then—"

"No," Lola interrupted. "I've made up my mind. I will leave tomorrow morning after breakfast."

Mrs. Buchanan found a room for her in a boarding house a few
blocks from her home in Manhattan. She hired a widowed nurse,
Margaret Hamilton, to take care of Lola and help her with her difficult
rehabilitation. Thanks to her discipline and tenacity, Lola got a little
better each day.

Slowly, she began to recover her speech and was able to walk a few
steps with the aid of a cane. Aware that her illness had no cure and that
she might die at any moment, she asked to draw up a will and left the
little she had to the Church of the Good Shepherd.

In October 1860, Lola received an unexpected visitor. Her mother,
Eliza Craigie, had learned that her daughter was at death's door and
bought a ticket to New York. Now over fifty, she still preserved her
legendary beauty and arrogance. She made the long trip from England
to see about the estate. Lola had no husband or children, and her

mother was her only family. Eliza had followed her through the press: her start as a dancer with an assumed name, her scandalous love affairs across Europe, and her stay in Munich as King Ludwig's lover. She was ashamed of that daughter who appeared onstage scantily dressed and acted like a courtesan. For her, Lola had died a long time ago, but she still hoped to inherit her daughter's fortune. She assumed that, in order to survive, Lola would have disposed of some jewelry, but she was certain the younger woman still had valuable gifts from the king and her other protectors.

When Eliza showed up at the boarding house, she had no idea what she was going to find. Her daughter was in a small room on the second floor that looked onto an interior courtyard. She had only a bed, a nightstand, an old armchair where she rested, and a trunk covered with stickers from hotels and shipping companies, her only souvenir of her trips around the world. Margaret, the nurse, invited Eliza in and withdrew. From some remove, Eliza studied her daughter's fragile figure and her pain-racked face. Lola's beauty was gone; she was a shadow of herself. She exhibited no joy at seeing her mother and said firmly, "You are not welcome, Mother. I've paid for my sins already. The good Jesus has put me to the test, and now I am simply waiting for the moment when I will be reunited with him. Why have you come?"

"I learned through the papers that you were gravely ill, and I wanted to be by your side. It's the least I can do."

"No, Mother, don't lie. You are here for my money; you believe that I'm a wealthy woman, but you could have saved yourself the trip. Your daughter, you see, has gotten rid of everything. I have absolutely nothing. I live off the charity of my friends and the church."

"I see you haven't changed," Eliza replied, looking around the miserable room in horror, "and that your pride prevents you from accepting my help. You are—"

"Mother, I am a poor, humble penitent who prays for forgiveness for her sins every day. Of course I accept the help of the people who love me and care about me, but not yours. And now I ask that you leave me alone. I am tired and want to sleep."

Eliza didn't know how to respond. Mrs. Buchanan had told her that Lola had sold all her jewelry and that the little money she'd possessed had been given to the poor and donated to the church. But Eliza hadn't believed her until now.

She left the room and told the nurse that she would remain in the city a few weeks longer and would visit again. She also said that she'd give Mrs. Buchanan some money to help with the medical expenses. She never returned to the boarding house. Just days later, Mrs. Craigie headed back to England, and though she wrote her daughter several letters, Lola never answered them.

Lola's health continued to improve that fall, and in the evenings she would go out walking on Margaret's arm. She also went to church and, sitting in the last pew, would listen to the minister's voice and ponder his words. She felt weak and vulnerable, but her faith pushed her to be strong and generous. Finally ready to help those most in need, she asked Mrs. Buchanan to let her tag along on one of the older woman's charitable visits to the New York Magdalen Society. The organization aided women who were seeking to get out of prostitution, helping them find dignified work. Lola felt sorry for those marginalized women who were enduring a more dramatic form of the same ostracism she had experienced. In the following days, when her health permitted, she would visit them and give them counsel. She encouraged them to "return to the flock" and give up that world of sin where they would find only unhappiness.

Thanks to a remarkable force of will, Lola managed to walk on her own with only a bit of a limp. In mid-December, her closest friends were convinced that she was going to make it. Christmas Day was cold and windy, but she decided to take a walk down Fifth Avenue. The bustling streets were decorated with thousands of colored lights and fir trees hung with ornaments and garlands. She lingered outside the clothing stores' luxurious window displays and drank hot chocolate in a café near the boarding house. That night, when she returned to her room, she began to feel unwell. She was coughing and had come down with a high fever and chills. She got into bed without undressing and hardly slept. Lola, who had always had weak lungs, had caught pneumonia.

Mrs. Buchanan asked the Reverend Francis Hawks to visit Lola and give her spiritual counseling because her death seemed imminent. The charismatic priest from Calvary Episcopal Church accepted the charge with some skepticism. Though he did not know her personally, he had heard of the famous Lola Montez, an eccentric and seductive artist who'd led an outrageous life. He doubted that such a woman could truly be repentant and feared that, finding herself at the end of her life and driven more by desperation than by faith, she was seeking divine forgiveness.

But on the afternoon that Hawks met Lola, he felt great compassion for her. He found her lying in bed, reading an essay on "the experience of faith" by dim lamplight. The room was full of Bible quotes written in large letters. When the priest asked why, Lola told him, "They are the word of God and they give me the strength to face death, which I think will come for me soon." After spending some time with her and reading the scriptures together, Hawks was convinced that her contrition was genuine: "In the course of a long experience as a Christian minister I do not think I ever saw a deeper penitence and humility, more real contrition of soul, and more bitter self-reproach, than in this poor woman."

Every day, after the morning service, Hawks would appear, smiling, at the door of the bedroom where Lola was impatiently waiting for him. Over the course of these visits, moved by her religious fervor, he spoke to her in simple terms about the love of Christ. Now lacking the strength to go to church, she was grateful for his company. "Who would have guessed that, at the end of my days, I would end up finding consolation in a minister of the church?" she mused.

On Thursday, January 17, 1861, a soft snow was falling over Manhattan and the sky was covered over with thick clouds. Reverend Hawks was about to lead mass when he was summoned urgently to Lola's address. When he arrived, he found Mrs. Buchanan kneeling beside her friend's bed, praying. The ailing woman was lying with her eyes closed.

"Darling, I'm leaving for a while," Mrs. Buchanan told Lola with tears in her eyes. "The priest has arrived."

Hawks sat down beside the dying woman. Taking her hand, he said, "I know you can hear me. I'm here with you. Give me a sign if your soul is at peace and you still feel that Christ can save you."

There was a silence, and then Lola nodded. Hawks started reading a passage from the Bible, and after a few minutes, she opened her eyes as if waking up from a long sleep. Staring at the priest, she whispered, "Luis, are you there? Forgive me, forgive me."

Those were her last words. Lola Montez was not yet forty when she embarked on the final journey for which she had been preparing. Free at last of bonds and suffering, she was now a legend.

Just as she had promised her friend, Mrs. Buchanan wrote a letter to King Ludwig I of Bavaria informing him that Lola Montez had died as a true Christian and that she had never forgotten his generosity. Now seventy-four years old, the king was in Nice, where he led a tranquil life far from the pressures of the court. Queen Therese had died seven years earlier from cholera, and he had never gotten over her loss. Now, upon receiving the unexpected letter from New York, he was overcome by sadness and nostalgia. In spite of everything, Lola had left a deep mark on his heart.

"Oh, my beloved Lolita!" he sighed sorrowfully. "You were my madness and my perdition, but you did not deserve such an ending. I only hope that you find the peace and solace you never had in life."

AUTHOR'S NOTE

The events described in this book are real, as are the letters, eyewitness accounts, and press excerpts that appear in it. I have reimagined only some dialogue to make the narrative more enjoyable. Lola Montez was a great impostor and fooled everyone with her lies and fantasies. It would not have been possible for me to reconstruct her life without the invaluable help of Bruce Seymour, a California lawyer who completed an immensely detailed investigation into one of the most notorious women of the nineteenth century. Bruce published the first serious biography of Lola Montez and generously donated all of his research materials to the Bancroft Library at the University of California, Berkeley. This extensive documentation and the conversations I had with him have been my main sources in writing this book, along with the correspondence between Lola and King Ludwig I of Bavaria, held in the archives of the Bavarian State Library. To recreate some of the settings where she lived, I traveled to Paris, Munich, and San Francisco. In California, I explored the mining cities of Sacramento, Nevada City, and Grass Valley, where she is still recalled with admiration.

Lola Montez is buried in Green-Wood Cemetery in Brooklyn, New York. Only at the end of her life did she acknowledge her true identity. Her tombstone reads:

MRS. ELIZA GILBERT
DIED JAN. 17, 1861

ACKNOWLEDGMENTS

Writing this biography of Lola Montez would have been impossible without the support and assistance of a good many people and institutions. I would first like to offer my thanks to Bruce Seymour for his great generosity in answering all my questions about this fascinating figure who has brought us together for life. Also to the staff of the Bancroft Library at the University of California, Berkeley, especially David Kessler, for helping me with the paperwork to access its funds and the Lola Montez documents held in their collection. On my trip to San Francisco, I cannot forget Ana Lara, who accompanied me not only on my explorations of the places where the "Spanish" dancer performed and lived but also in the arduous task of selecting and translating letters, press clippings, and other documents from Mr. Seymour at the University of California. And to the Harvard Theatre Collection, in Cambridge, for allowing me to use some of the daguerreotypes they hold, taken of Lola Montez during her time in the United States.

In Munich, my gratitude goes to Annemarie Kaindl, of the Department of Manuscripts and Historical Documents at the Bavarian State Library, which granted me access to the correspondence between Lola Montez and King Ludwig I of Bavaria held in their archives; to Anke Palden and Nicole Losch-Maute, at the Bavarian State Painting Collections, for orienting me in my search for remaining portraits of the dancer; and to Dr. Gerhard Immler, director of the Privy Archives, for his willing nature and assistance in the laborious search for historical materials from the period. I would also like to thank Ulrike Barcatta,

director of public relations for the Bayerischer Hof in Munich, and
Marta Maroñas, from the Leading Hotels of the World group, for allowing me to stay at the legendary hotel where the love story between the
king and the dancer played out.

To my editors, David Trías and Cristina Lomba, for their steady
encouragement and enthusiasm. And to Emilia Lope, with whom I
have shared so many wonderful moments, and to Leticia Rodero, from
the publicity department, who has put so much effort and professionalism into promoting my work. Nor could I forget Lola Delgado, for her
work improving my manuscript, and Rebecca Beltrán, for making sure
that my books reach more and more readers through social networks.

My thanks also to Esther González Cano and to KLM/Air France
for their assistance on my research trip to San Francisco.

To the journalist Gemma Nierga and the actor Juana Andueza for
sharing in this literary adventure.

To Belén Junco and Mamen Sánchez for their friendship and support in all of my undertakings.

To Érika Gabaldón, Susana Venegas, and Ana Belén Burguillo, my
"three musketeers," for looking after the author's health.

Additionally, to my friends who have supported me in recent years,
for their constant encouragement, and especially to Pilar González.

Finally, my deepest thanks to my husband, José Diéguez, for his
invaluable help in tracking down and translating documents and for the
suggestions he offered during the long years I spent writing this book.
To my son, Alex, who has been very patient with his mother. And to
my sister, Maite Morató, for always being by my side.

BIBLIOGRAPHY

Aguilar, C. *Max Ophüls*. Directores de cine 28. Madrid: Ediciones JC, 1987.

Allende, Isabel. *Hija de la fortuna*. Barcelona: Plaza & Janés, 1999.

Argenta, Fernando. *Los clásicos también pecan*. Barcelona: DeBolsillo, 2011.

Augustin-Thierry, A. *Lola Montès, favorite royale*. Paris: Bernard Grasset, 1936.

Auriange, Dominique. *Le rêve brisé: Le destin de Lola Montès*. Verviers, Belg.: Gérard, 1967.

Bac, Ferdinand. *Louis Ier de Bavière et Lola Montès*. Paris: Louis Conard, 1928.

Blackburn, Julia. *El desierto de Daisy Bates*. Barcelona: RBA, 2002.

Bloch-Dano, Évelyne. *Flora Tristán, la mujer Mesías*. Translated by Teresa Clavel. Madrid: Ediciones Maeva, 2002.

Brands, H. W. *The Age of Gold: The California Gold Rush and the Birth of Modern America*. New York: Doubleday, 2002.

Bromfield, Louis. *Noche en Bombay.* Translated by Santiago Valdazano. La Coruña, Sp.: Ediciones del Viento, 2007.

Buraya, Luis Carlos. *Los cien mundos de Mata-Hari.* Madrid: Edimat, 2005.

Cannon, M. *Lola Montes.* Melbourne: Heritage, 1973.

Castellanos de Zubiria, Susana. *Mujeres perversas de la historia.* Bogotá: Norma, 2008.

Cendrars, Blaise. *El oro.* Translated by Julio Gómez de la Serna. Rosa de los vientos. Barcelona: Pal-las, 1942.

Certigny, Henry. *Lola Montès: D'un trône à un cirque.* Paris: Gallimard, 1959.

Chalmers, Claudine. *Grass Valley.* Charleston, SC: Arcadia, 2006.

Chartier, JoAnne, and Chris Enss. *Gilded Girls: Women Entertainers of the Old West.* Guilford, CT: Twodot, 2003.

Clappe, Louise Amelia Knapp Smith. *The Shirley Letters: From the California Mines, 1851–1852.* Berkeley: Heyday, 1998.

Colombani, Roger. *Bellas indomables: Mujeres con grandes destinos.* Translated by Merche Comabella. Madrid: Narcea, 2001.

Conte, Egon Caesar Corti. *Ludwig I. von Bayern.* Munich: Knaur, 1979.

Cordingly, David. *Mujeres en el mar: Capitanas, corsarias, esposas y rameras.* Translated by Carmen Font Paz. Barcelona: Edhasa, 2003.

Costello, Conte. *Lola Montes: El rey y la bailarina.* Barcelona: AHR, 1956.

Craveri, Benedetta. *Amantes y reinas: El poder de las mujeres.* Madrid: Siruela, 2006.

―――. *La cultura de la conversación.* Madrid: Siruela, 2003.

de Mirecourt, Eugène. *Les contemporains.* Paris: Gustave Havard, 1857.

[Dyer, Heman]. *The Story of a Penitent: Lola Montez.* New York: Protestant Episcopal Society, 1867.

Eden, Emily. *Up the Country: Letters from India.* London: Virago, 1983.

Foley, Doris. *The Divine Eccentric: Lola Montez and the Newspapers.* Los Angeles: Westernlore, 1969.

Forster, E. M. *Pasaje a la India.* Translated by José Luis López Muñoz. Biblioteca El Mundo 6. Barcelona: El Mundo, 2002.

Ghose, Indira. *Memsahibs Abroad: Writings by Women Travellers in Nineteenth Century India.* Oxford: Oxford University, 1998.

Gilmour, David. *La vida imperial de Rudyard Kipling.* Translated by Diego Valverde. Barcelona: Seix Barral, 2003.

Goldberg, Isaac. *Queen of Hearts: The Passionate Pilgrimage of Lola Montez.* New York: John Day, 1936.

Griffin, Susan. *Las cortesanas.* Translated by Jorge Fondebrider. Barcelona: Ediciones B, 2007.

Hermary-Vieille, Catherine. *Lola Montes*. Translated by Teresa Clavel. Barcelona: Martínez Roca, 1995.

Hodgson, Barbara. *Opium: Histoire d'un paradis infernal*. Translated by André Roche. Paris: Seuil, 1999.

———. *Señoras sin fronteras: Las mujeres y la aventura*. Translated by Jacobo Torres Fraguas. Barcelona: Lumen, 2006.

Hojer, Gerhard. *Die Schönheitsgalerie König Ludwigs I*. Regensburg, Ger.: Schnell & Steiner, 2006.

Holdredge, Helen. *The Woman in Black: The Life of Lola Montez*. New York: Putnam, 1955.

Jourcin, Albert, and Philippe van Tieghem. *Diccionario de las mujeres célebres*. Translated by Vicente de Artadi. Barcelona: Plaza & Janés, 1970.

Keay, Julia. *With Passport and Parasol*. London: BBC, 1989.

Kipling, Rudyard. *Kim*. Translated by José Luis López Muñoz. Madrid: Alianza, 2012.

Lapierre, Dominique, and Larry Collins. *Esta noche, la libertad*. Translated by Adolfo Martín. Barcelona: Plaza & Janés, 1975.

Maillier, Charles. *Trois journalistes drouais: Brisset, Dujarier, Buré*. Paris: Promotion et Édition, 1968.

Mann, Golo. *Ludwig I: König von Bayern*. Schaftlach, Ger.: Oreos, 1989.

Markessinis, Artemis. *Historia de la danza desde sus orígenes*. Madrid: Esteban Sanz, 1995.

Mérimée, Prosper. *Carmen*. Translated by J. Leyva. Madrid: Alba, 1998.

Montez, L. *The Arts of Beauty; or, Secrets of a Lady's Toilet: With Hints to Gentlemen on the Art of Fascinating*. New York: Dick & Fitzgerald, 1858.

————. *Lectures of Lola Montez (Countess of Landsfeld), including her autobiography*. New York: Rudd & Carleton, 1858.

Moro, Javier. *Pasión india*. Barcelona: Seix Barral, 2005.

Morton, James. *Lola Montez: Her Life & Conquests*. London: Portrait, 2007.

Ondaatje, Michael. *El paciente inglés*. Translated by Carlos Manzano. Madrid: El Mundo, 2003.

Papon, Auguste. *Lola Montès: Mémoires accompagnés de lettres intimes de S. M. le Roi de Bavière et de Lola Montès*. Nyon, Switz.: J. Desoche, 1849.

Pasolini, Pier Paolo. *El olor de la India*. Translated by Atilio Pentimalli Melacrino. Barcelona: Península, 1996.

Reichardt, Philip, ed. *Begegnungen, Bayerischer Hof*. Munich: Condé Nast, 2011.

Reiser, Rudolf. *König und Dame: Ludwig I. und seine 30 Mätressen*. Munich: Buchendorfer, 1999.

Robinson, Jane. *Unsuitable for Ladies: An Anthology of Women Travellers.* Oxford: Oxford University Press, 1994.

Roy, Arundhati. *El dios de las pequeñas cosas.* Translated by Txaro Santoro and Cecilia Ceriani. Barcelona: Anagrama, 1998.

Saint-Laurent, Cécil. *Lola Montes.* Translated by Carmen Soler Blanc. Barcelona: Caralt, 1986.

Seagraves, Anne. *Women Who Charmed the West.* Hayden, ID: Wesanne, 1991.

Seymour, Bruce. *Lola Montez: A Life.* New Haven, CT: Yale University Press, 1996.

Shipman, Pat. *Mata Hari: Espía, victima, mito.* Translated by Diego Castillo. Barcelona: Edhasa, 2011.

Stefano, Mario. *Cortesanas célebres.* Translated by Ramón Cortés Más. Barcelona: Zeus, 1961.

Tejera, Pilar. *Viajeras de leyenda: Aventuras asombrosas de trotamundos victorianas.* Oviedo, Sp.: Casiopea, 2011.

Thurman, Judith. *Secretos de la carne: Vida de Colette.* Translated by Olivia de Miguel. Madrid: Siruela, 1999.

Torrellas, A. Albert. *Como las hojas . . . Lola Montes, la amada del Rey-poeta.* Barcelona: Horta, 1944.

Urraca Pastor, María Rosa. *Lola Montes.* Barcelona: MRUPSA, 1940.

Vallejos, Soledad. *George Sand, la escritora indomable*. Buenos Aires: Longseller, 2001.

Varley, James F. *Lola Montez: The California Adventures of Europe's Notorious Courtesan*. Spokane, WA: Arthur H. Clark, 1996.

Walker, Alan. *Franz Liszt*. Vol. 1, *The Virtuoso Years*. New York: Knopf, 1983.

Wilmes, Jacqueline, and Jacques Prézelin. *Lola Montès*. Lausanne, Switz.: Rencontre, 1967.

Wyndham, Horace. *The Magnificent Montez: From Courtesan to Convert*. New York: Hillman-Curl, 1935.

Zauner, Phyllis. *Sacramento*. Sonoma, CA: Zanel, 1994.

Zweig, Stefan. *Momentos estelares de la Humanidad*. Translated by José Fernández Zamora. Barcelona: Juventud, 2014.

APPENDIX

Selections from the Correspondence between
Lola Montez and King Ludwig I of Bavaria

LETTERS FROM FEBRUARY 1848

Letter from Ludwig to Lola dated February 10, 1848, and reply from Lola

Munich, 10 February (9:30 p.m.)

Dearest Lolitta,
I just received a note from Berks informing me of the enormous discontent that reigns in the city. If not for the police holding firm and the assistance of a squadron of cuirassiers, your house would have been attacked. "Tomorrow will be a very dangerous day," he writes, and if you remain there you will not be safe. I am entreating you, if you have ever loved me and still love me, leave the city. The best thing would be for you to leave at first light, without a word to anybody, for Lake Starnberg; I repeat: without a word to anybody. If possible, tell me at what time I can go see you at your home before you leave. You will be able to return the next day. Though it would be better if you left

this very night. I know you are not afraid of anything—
you have already shown that. I fear not for myself but for
you. If blood is spilled in your name, hatred will explode
and your situation will become untenable. We must ensure
that this does not happen. You know that nothing in the
world could drive me away from you. I beg of you to heed
my advice. Lolitta will always love her
    faithful Luis

Munich, night of 10–11 February 1848

My dear Louis,
I beg of you to send from Augsburg two squadrons of the
light cavalry, which is loyal to you. Spraul will deliver this
letter to you. The cuirassiers you have here are worthless. I
beg of you to consider the idea.
    Your very faithful Lolitta

LETTERS FROM APRIL 1848

Letter from Lola to Ludwig dated April 5, 1848, and reply from Ludwig

Geneva, 5 April 1848

My dearest Louis,
Yesterday and the day before yesterday we spent the whole
day searching for a house. After having seen all the ones
available for rent, we found a very small one . . . All the
houses here are very expensive, and this is the cheapest one
we could find . . . and for me the area is very good. The
hotel manager, a relative of Shoemaker's, knows you and is

loyal to you. He had an audience with you because of the Shoemaker matter. Peel, Meller, and he have helped me in the search and are of the opinion that I should rent it until you can come and give your approval. It would be best if you went straight to the house, though you can also stay in a hotel, if you like. So today I will rent it before leaving for Bern. I am leaving in half an hour. Being here, I have gone to the theater once. A couple of Paris's finest artists were performing, but I didn't find it interesting. I forgot to tell you that the sale price goes up to 140,000 Swiss francs, but I hope to be able to acquire it for 130,000, the normal price. That is the cheapest and smallest one here. I hope to see you on the fifteenth. You have no idea how lovely the city and the views from here are . . .

    Your faithful Lolitta

Munich, 10 April 1848

Dearest Lolitta,
Whitbread has just handed me your letter from April 5. I have no objection to your settling in Geneva, but I am not in a position to buy you a house. Your house here is worth approximately 30,000 florins. Selling it will afford you some money. As I've written previously, I cannot offer you more than what you receive each month. Within a week I will be in your arms. What indescribable joy! . . . I don't know how long I can be away from Bavaria . . . I cannot send you money abroad right now, but the security of your investments is very important to me . . .

    Yours until death, Luis

LETTER FROM AUGUST 1848

Letter from Lola to Ludwig dated August 17, 1848

Geneva, 17 August 1848

My ever dear Louis,
In your last letters you expressed many doubts about me,
even though you know that I feel a most ardent and affectionate love for you, the only man in this world to whom
I profess sentiments of love. The others are just traitors
and frauds. I not only love you, but also appreciate and
respect you. There is a big difference between you and the
others . . . The Lord, who knows everything, is witness to
that truth . . . It pleases me when people talk about you,
when they relate the noble ideas and actions of my beloved
Louis. Everybody knows that the people of this place and
foreigners, too, respect you a great deal. That causes me
much happiness, and they say that your renowned name
will go down in history because of your abdication. And
that is a great truth.

My poor horse Abdelkader has died from illness, from
gastritis, which is a shame. Thank God the other, which
has also been very ill, is somewhat better now, but I am
still heartbroken. Mr. Rufenacht is not as open and honorable as people say. It's best if you don't write to him. He
is not worthy of that task. For him, right now, only one
thing exists: money, money, money. He is the one who has
caused me to incur the most debts.

I recently received a visit from a very pleasant man,
Mr. Papon, though he is pro-Jesuit and in the service of
Austria. He came with his mother, the Marchioness of

Sarde, and he told me that Rufenacht informed him that in the next few days I would be traveling to meet you in Malans. The man is a gentleman and would never turn that into any kind of story, but he was appalled that Rufenacht would relay such things to a stranger. Even so, he has given me his word of honor that he will not talk about it without anybody. Rufenacht has also written a most vile letter.

You know that girl Petitpierre was not worthy of being in my home, and they have done all this between the two of them, she and Rufenacht. Her friend was very unpleasant to me. He made me give her more money. It was not fair, since I had paid the girl for six months of work before she entered my service. And she left three months later, so in fact she has my money for three months more. It seems to me, as it does to the whole world, that Mr. Rufenacht's behavior has not been proper.

My dear Louis, I intend to live more simply than I do now. Given that this house is very expensive, I am looking for one that is smaller and cheaper. I also want to do without several servants, which seems much better. Though it will be a big sacrifice to leave this house, your Lolitta is very sensible, and if not for Rufenacht I would have already done so some time ago.

I have asked Mr. Papon to write to you and send you that lovely letter from Mr. Rufenacht. It is hard to believe. My God, people are so artificial; there's nobody in the world but you who is honorable and trustworthy. I think it would be better if you didn't write to Mr. Rufenacht anymore; he has become underhanded and also quite improper. Consider sending me money for the trip; one thousand Swiss francs will be enough. I don't have a penny at home. I don't want to waste any time, my dearest Louis,

till September 2 finally comes; it's almost here. I trust that
fortune will let me see you again. You will see that Lolitta
is always at your disposal and loves you more than ever.
Distance makes love grow when people love each other,
and for me the distance that separates me from you is a
reason for sadness. But I hope that soon everything will
be calmer and more settled, and that you will have more
freedom to act.

I cherish you very much. Goodbye, dear, dearest
Louis. I send you a kiss from my mouth.
[circle indicating where a kiss has been deposited]
Please kiss it—it is the kiss of a tender heart devoted to you.

Your faithful and affectionate Lolitta

LETTER FROM JULY 1849

Letter from Lola to Ludwig dated July 16, 1849

London, 16 July 1849

My dearest Louis,
I am writing to you about a very important matter. Above
all I wish to be guided by your opinion. Some time back,
a young officer from the Life Guards, one of England's
most esteemed regiments, showered me with a great deal
of attention. Even so, given that many people behave that
way with me, I paid it little mind. But three days ago he
came to my house and formally asked me to marry him.
I have spoken about it with Lord Bessborough and Lord
Brougham. Both have offered me the best counsel in my
interest. Since renouncing my own country in favor of

Bavaria, I have lost all right to call myself Spanish. And given that you were also forced to revoke my Bavarian citizenship, I find myself in a very unpleasant and unfortunate situation. I cannot obtain a passport from any country by legal means. If I travel, I am always forced to pass myself off as another person and I must acquire a passport illegally. Furthermore, I need protection. Lord Bessborough says that I should talk frankly to you about all this, about my unfortunate situation in the world, so alone. He thinks the best thing for me would be an honorable marriage with someone from a good family, someone known in London as a respectable man. He is far from being wealthy. His income is eight hundred pounds a year. My heart will always love you with much affection. That is the first thing I told him, before anything else. I love you and will always love you so much that I would be willing to die for you. If I got married, you would continue to send me the money you give me now for the rest of my life, which I do not think will be very long. Otherwise I cannot marry—it is impossible, the family will not allow it. Living without money is horrible. He has promised me that, if we marry, he would not meddle in our relationship. A notary must vouch for that. And that the pension I receive from you is money that is mine alone, that he will not have any rights to that sum and cannot interfere. The proposal he has made me is respectable and good. This gentleman, though he is poor, is known in London as a very honorable young man from a good family. If I married him, he would present me to his family and I would cease to be the pariah I am now. Bessborough says I should get married for my protection. He always tells me it is impossible to live without protection. But first he has made me promise that I would write to you so you can promise me (and your word is as good as gold) that I will receive the same quantity as now until the end of my days. Who knows what will happen. Sometimes a person acts with good or bad results. I want to be able to preserve my independence in case something were to happen. All of my friends gave me the same advice that my loyal friend Bessborough does. You must believe me, I swear before God. I am not in love with that gentleman—it is something completely different. I respect him for his character and he has a good position, and thanks to that I will not be alone and without protection, at the mercy of any who wishes to harm me. Now it depends on you. Dear Louis, if you do not wish me to marry, tell me. I love you enough to renounce this marriage. However favorable it would be for me. The gentleman is known in the best social circles. All of my friends know him as a good-hearted and very honorable man. But if you allow me to marry, our relationship will be the same as ever. I could never change what I am to you. My life belongs only to you and I am yours with all my soul. A husband would not change the love I feel for you, which will remain with me until death. Please do not delay in writing to me; without your permission and your promise guaranteeing my lifetime income, the family of this young gentleman will not consent to the marriage. But Lord Brougham, who knows them, has assured them that you are noble and worthy of being called a king. And I, who know you better than anyone in the world, know that too. Thousands of kisses and the eternal love of

    your Lolitta

LETTERS FROM MARCH–MAY 1850

Letter from Ludwig to Lola dated March 13, 1850, and reply from Lola

Munich, 13 March 1850

I once wrote to you that the world did not have the power to drive me away from you. But your conduct has changed my feelings; that is my response to your letter of March 8, which arrived today. I am enclosing the sums for April, May, and June. Write to me the month before to tell me where I can send another sum in early July. I hope to immediately receive the letters you have offered to return to me.

    Luis

If my letters do not arrive before then, under no circumstances will any sum be sent for July.

Paris, 26 May 1850

It has been eight days since I got out of bed. This is the first time I have been able to write in three months. I had and continue to have the same troubles that I did in Bad Brückenau and Munich, only much worse. And in addition I have suffered from enteritis. My life is miserable, quite miserable. Mr. Heald is worse than a tyrant with me. And ultimately I cannot leave him because I do not have anything to live on. I am penniless. I am in an appalling situation. You have begged me to return your letters to you. But you had sworn and promised to send me those small monthly payments for the rest of my life, and now

you wish to take everything from me. Nobody who had
a heart, not even the very poorest, would be capable of
doing that. If I were independent, God knows I would
not say anything. Still, in the critical situation in which
I find myself, it is very harsh and cruel on your part. I
suffered so very much in your country, and nothing of
what you gave me remains to me. I must tell you this. I
am constantly being insulted as if I were a fallen woman
working the street. The whole time I have been in bed, Mr.
Heald has done nothing to look after me. What's more, he
has spent all his time outside of the house, at the theater
and amusing himself with other people. It has been an
achievement to get him to pay for the medicine for my illness. The problems have been quite serious indeed. Every
day I was taking 28 grams of quinine, and now I take 15
grams daily. I do not have as much to protect me as I did
before. That man spends a lot of time with other people,
and when I ask him to give me something, he tells me he
doesn't have it. Now, Louis, you must see for yourself that
the moment has come for you to keep your word. Many
people (because it is appearing in the papers, I have no
idea how, possibly through Mr. Heald) tell me that you
have withdrawn my pension. Some say I should sell your
letters to be published, but it would be terribly painful to
betray you. I would much rather be able to read your letters myself and recall that time that is now gone forever.
I beg of you not to withdraw my pension. It is the only
thing I have. I cannot be sure of my means of subsistence
from one day to the next. Ultimately my situation is quite
difficult. That is why I beg of you to continue making
those payments you assured me would last the rest of my
life. No other woman in the world suffers more for you

than I, is more persecuted than I. And all because I was with you in Munich. And now, despite all your riches, you do not want to give me even a small pension that would not importune you in the least? In the end I beg of you to continue those payments so I will always have something that is mine. I live in a beautiful house now, but it isn't anything. Mr. Heald has a great deal, seven horses, but nothing for me. Only with enormous difficulty am I able to buy myself a couple of trifles. And what's worse, he refuses to give me even a small sum for my security and independence. Nevertheless, despite everything, my health has improved. I have been much better for several days. They are the same problems that I had in Bad Brückenau and Munich, but worse. My health is very bad and fragile. The doctor, Mr. Duchene, says that I am in a dangerous state and that I must have greater tranquility and many other things to recover my health. I tire easily from writing so much. I hope that you will tell me about your health in detail soon. And also a few more tender words in your letter. I am, as I always was and will be for all my life, the one who loves you so much,

Lolitta

Write to: 3 rue Beaujon, Champs-Élysées, Paris.

ABOUT THE AUTHOR

Photo © 2019 Amaya Aznar

Born in Barcelona in 1961, Cristina Morató is a journalist, reporter, and author dedicated to writing about the lives of great women innovators and explorers that history has overlooked. Her research, tracing the footsteps of these remarkable women, has led her to travel to more than forty countries and has resulted in eight biographies: *Viajeras intrépidas y aventureras* (*Intrepid and Adventurous Women Travelers*); *Las Reinas de África* (*African Queens*); *Las Damas de Oriente* (*Ladies of the East*); *Cautiva en Arabia* (*Arabian Captive*); *Divas rebeldes* (*Rebel Divas*); *Reinas malditas* (*Tragic Queens*); *Diosas de Hollywood* (*Hollywood Goddesses*); and *Divina Lola* (*Divine Lola*), Cristina's first to be translated into English. She is a founding member and the current vice president of the Spanish Geographical Society and belongs to the Royal Geographic Society of London. For more information visit www.cristinamorato .com/home-2.

ABOUT THE TRANSLATOR

Photo © Karla Rosenberg

Andrea Rosenberg is a translator from Spanish and Portuguese. Her full-length translations include novels, graphic narratives, and nonfiction, including works by Manuel Vilas, Tomás González, Inês Pedrosa, Aura Xilonen, Juan Gómez Bárcena, Paco Roca, and Marcelo D'Salete. Two of her translations have won Eisner Awards, and she has been the recipient of awards and grants from the Fulbright Program, the American Literary Translators Association, and the Banff International Literary Translation Centre.